PRESS AND PUBLIC

Who Reads What, When, Where,
and Why in American Newspapers

COMMUNICATION TEXTBOOK SERIES

Jennings Bryant–Editor

Journalism
Maxwell McCombs–Advisor

PRESS AND PUBLIC

Who Reads What, When, Where, and Why in American Newspapers

SECOND EDITION

LEO BOGART

 LAWRENCE ERLBAUM ASSOCIATES, PUBLISHERS
1989   Hillsdale, New Jersey   Hove and London

Lawrence Erlbaum Associates, Inc., Publishers
365 Broadway
Hillsdale, New Jersey 07642

Library of Congress Cataloging-in-Publication Data

Bogart, Leo.
    Press and public : who reads what, when, where, and why in
American newspapers / Leo Bogart. — 2nd ed.
        p.   cm.
    Bibliography: p.
    Includes index.
    ISBN 0-8058-0431-5. — ISBN 0-8058-0432-3 (pbk.)
    1. Readership surveys—United States.   2. American newspapers—
—Circulation.   I. Title.
PN4888.R37B6   1989
071'.3—dc20   89-11728
                                                                                         CIP

Printed in the United States of America
10 9 8 7 6 5 4 3 2 1

CONTENTS

PREFACE TO THE SECOND EDITION

In the eight years since the first edition of this book appeared, the world of newspapers has changed in many ways. Here are just a few.

1. Penetration—the ratio of circulation to the number of people or of households—has continued to go down. Weekday circulation has inched up, but that includes national newspapers (including the national edition of *The New York Times*, the *Christian Science Monitor*, and the *Wall Street Journal*). With the advent of *USA Today*, these have assumed greater importance. The circulation of local daily newspapers has actually been going down in the last ten years.

2. Compared to weekday papers, Sunday shows a comparatively healthy growth in circulation numbers, but penetration is still declining relative to the growth of population and households. The strength of Sunday has been felt in another area as well. Sunday today accounts for 38% of all newspaper advertising volume, compared with 32% ten years ago. This has meant a corresponding growth in the bulk of the Sunday newspaper, including its editorial component.

3. One thing that has made the Sunday paper fatter and sustained the growth of the daily is the steady growth of advertising inserts. Inserts now account for more advertising pages than display on weekdays and almost as many on Sunday. (Most of their pages, however, are tabloid or smaller).

The fact that newspapers now average 55% greater bulk on weekdays than they did 10 years ago and 98% more on Sundays has important implications. There is more physical weight for circulation departments to handle and for carriers to distribute. Because news hole (editorial content) has grown even faster than advertising, there are more pages for editors to fill. There are more pages for readers to contend with. The shift of much retail advertising and a very large proportion of national food advertising from run of paper (ROP) into inserts has also changed the character of the package presented to readers and has weakened traditionally strong food sections.

4. Apart from inserts, newspapers have been changing significantly in appearance and in content. The upgrading of color quality has become a high priority. There has been more emphasis on features relative to news, and more on local as opposed to national and world news. This is a change in balance, not cutting out information, because, as just mentioned, the total news hole has been growing. Both trends run counter to the evidence cited in this book, which shows that most people turn to the newspaper primarily for news rather than for entertainment and are somewhat more interested in what is going on on the national and world scenes than in most local happenings.

What people consider big news is increasingly defined by television. Television news has expanded its time on the air – around the clock on CNN, 5½ hours a day on ABC, if we include *Nightline* and the morning news-variety shows. Local stations typically run between 2 and 3 hours of news a day, and people are watching. The major stories – the dramas they follow and whose protagonists they see in action – are played out in the Middle East, in Central America, in Washington, and in Moscow. People identify these big events with television and see newspapers as the main source on the local news that in the main simply does not engage them to the same degree. Newspapers cannot sacrifice their unique franchise as the local news medium, but they clearly need to strengthen the authority they seem to be losing in the domain of national and world news.

5. There has been a sharp continuation of the drive to package editorial matter in terms of clearly definable and identifiable sections. Although papers have grown tremendously in size, readers are still spending the same amount of time with them as they did in the past. That means that they are reading more selectively than ever. The main news section continues to have universal appeal and may be the only true mass medium left in an era of media audience segmentation. But as newspapers expand in bulk and as individual, physically separate parts become identified with specific subjects, it is inevitable that many busy readers will not venture beyond the first glance and that section audiences will become even more segmented, just as magazine audiences have become. In the long run, this raises some interesting questions about the prospects for spinning these off as separate products, with savings in newsprint and perhaps some increases in circulation reve-

nues. But there are also great risks involved in disassembling the newspaper as we know it.

Newspapers have always built their audiences out of a composite of both generally shared and innumerable minor interests. Editors have never assumed that every reader would read every item, but rather that every reader finds some items that make the whole paper worthwhile. Traditionally, newspaper columns and features aimed at the special interests of pet owners, stamp collectors, and bridge addicts appeared regularly where their fans could find them.

In spite of vastly expanded news holes, there has been a continuing decline in the number of papers who regularly (at least once a week) offer special interest columns and features that appeal to minorities of readers. These are not easily subsumed under a general heading like "Home" or "Lifestyle" or "Entertainment." Of 32 special interest weekday features we have tracked since 1974, all but 2 show a decline. The only one that is up is astrology.

6. There have been great changes in newspaper distribution methods. Computers are now being widely used to manage comprehensive subscriber information systems that permit more efficient solicitation of subscriptions, better customer service, and perhaps more importantly the development of nonsubscriber lists to which free publications can be sent. Centralized control permits office billing and has supported the tendency to use adult rather than juvenile carriers. Newspapers' distribution procedures have become more professional and efficient, but they may have lost some of the sympathetic personal contact that characterized the "little merchant" system at it best.

7. There has been a continuing attrition of choice for the reader. With more and more single ownership combinations abandoning their evening papers and with the death of some major titles, fewer newspapers have to battle a daily competitor for a story, let alone for survival. There is less of the bite and idiosyncracy that once gave every reader the feeling that the paper was something that he had selected personally from among a number of contenders.

8. The regularity of daily reading has continued to weaken. Eighty-five percent of adult Americans are newspaper readers, but fewer regard reading the newspaper as the kind of daily necessity it was just a few years ago.

Newspapers have worked hard to keep their readers. They have raised their price to them at a slower rate than the cost of living and at a much slower rate than advertising increases. They have increased their news holes even more than their advertising volume. Yet it is obvious that they have not yet solved their readership problems. As this book suggests, these do not arise from any one cause, and they do not have any easy solution. But they remain as the greatest challenge that confronts the newspaper business and the many professions that staff and manage it.

In reviewing the original text of this book for the second edition, I have eliminated some documentation that no longer has topical interest. I have brought statistics up to date in every case where it is possible. Where the reader finds me citing studies that seem dated, it is either because nothing more recent is comparable or because they seem to have historical interest in light of the significant changes that I have just outlined.

Leo Bogart

INTRODUCTION: NEWSPAPERS IN TRANSITION

> The basis of our government being the opinion of the people, the very first object should be to keep that right; and were it left to me to decide whether we should have a government without newspapers, or newspapers without a government, I should not hesitate a moment to prefer the latter.
>
> Letter to Colonel Edward Carrington [January 16, 1787]
>
> —Thomas Jefferson[1]

The importance of newspapers for a democratic society is no less than it was two centuries ago. It may be greater. The public's need for information has grown at a steadily accelerating pace as people's lives have become more complex and more interdependent. It is increasingly hard for all of us to cope with the enormous flood of communications that come our way, wanted or not.

Effective citizens must have the feeling that they can cope with events that have shape and definition and that they understand. The very profusion of

---

[1]However, Jefferson also wrote, "I really look with commiseration over the great body of my fellow citizens, who, reading newspapers, live and die in the belief that they have known something of what has been passing in the world in their time."

unconnected bits of information may well create a sense of disorder and chaos, which can lead to civic apathy.

Perhaps the greatest danger to a democratic system is the public's feeling that things are beyond control, that the individual is powerless to affect the march of history. Among the mass media that connect the individual to the world, the newspaper has a unique ability to provoke reflection, to view with alarm what might otherwise be accepted complacently, to create issues for debate and to offer plans for positive action. Thus it offers links between people's own individual and private interests and those they share with the rest of society.

The ability to describe patterns in the meaning of events, to connect facts separated in time and place, to make generalizations—all of these capacities for abstraction reflect unique properties of the printed word. Ideas must always be the newspaper's stock in trade, while broadcasting, which flows in time, must always be specific and concrete, must always deal with individual events here and now.

There is a kind of folk awareness that what appears in the newspaper appears before the whole community. The press records the life of the community and is its traditional voice. But insofar as it records the events of highly specialized interest, whether obituaries, social notices, commodity prices, or basketball scores, it also provides the indispensable means by which individuality is maintained. These are not inconsequential functions.

By any conventional standards of evaluating an institution, the American press at the close of the 1980s is at the acme of power and prosperity. On any weekday, according to the major media research services, newspapers are read by about 110 million American adults, about the same number as those who get any news from television. The political influence of newspapers remains high, and there is evidence that they have more effect than television news on the election of candidates for office.[2]

---

[2]Patterson and McClure found this to be true in their study of the effects of television in the 1972 presidential election (see Thomas E. Patterson & Robert D. McClure, *The Unseeing Eye: The Myth of Television Power in National Politics*, New York: Putnam, 1976). Similarly, analyzing data from the University of Michigan's 1972 election studies, John Robinson found that among Democratic voters, McGovern was the choice of 71% of those who read newspapers that supported McGovern editorially, but of only 46% of those who read pro-Nixon papers. Among Independents, McGovern got 50% of the vote from readers of papers who endorsed him and only 26% from readers of the pro-Nixon press (see John P. Robinson, "The Press as King-Maker: What Surveys from the Last Five Campaigns Show," *Journalism Quarterly*, Winter 1974, pp. 587–594). Patterson's analysis of influences on candidate preference and voting in the 1976 campaign provides further evidence of the greater impact of press over television news, (see Thomas E. Patterson, *The Mass Media Election: How Americans Choose Their President*, New York: Praeger, 1980). Although the 1988 presidential election campaign was widely regarded as a demonstration of television's political power, it was the debates and the advertising that were in the spotlight rather than the newscasts.

Advertisers in 1988 invested $31 billion in newspapers, more than in any other medium. The entire movement of goods to American consumers is based on continuous communication of shopping information through newspaper advertising, retailers' primary promotion medium. With 457,500 employees, newspapers are the seventh largest manufacturing industry. In the stock market, shares in newspaper corporations have generally outperformed the Dow-Jones averages. Newspapers have been sold (when prospective buyers can find a seller) at a price equivalent to as much as $4,650 per unit of daily circulation.[3]

An expanding, maturing, more prosperous population appeared to offer an extraordinary potential for newspapers' growth. Reading skills and proclivities are linked to education, and since the end of World War II, progress in educational attainment has been phenomenal.

At least through the first half of the 1980s, there was also a steady increase in real family income; for more people than ever a newspaper subscription was an affordable expense. Television was firmly established, well past its initial surge of growth. Individual viewing time had remained essentially unchanged for many years, so there was no new threat from that quarter.

Yet for all its prosperity and influence, the newspaper industry has been in ferment. Its technology has been transformed through the rapid adoption of computers and photocomposition. New production techniques reduce the manpower required in printing and distribution, allow editors to handle both substance and format with new speed and flexibility, and carry the potential for creating newspapers that are more attractive to the reader. Newspaper content and appearance are being reexamined and rapidly overhauled. The management structure and sales practices of newspapers are changing. Distribution methods have been radically transformed.

Newspapers weathered the introduction of television far more successfully than any of the other existing mass media, maintaining their growth in circulation and their share of advertising investments. But almost on the heels of TV, another revolution is under way in media technology. Cable provides a constant flow of news and weather information. The coming home communications system will provide computerized access to an even greater array of resources. Beyond that, it will also open up encyclopedic files of background information in the forms of text, photographs, and motion pictures in electronically stored digital form on videodisks. The advent of this new era in technology opens serious questions about the future functions of newspapers and of other traditional print media.

---

[3]The Naples, FL, *Daily News*, with a daily circulation of 34,380, was reportedly sold to Scripps-Howard in 1986 for $160 million. The following year, the Morristown, NJ, *Record* (60,000 circulation) was sold to Ingersoll Newspapers for $155 million. By comparison, cable television systems have been selling at a rate of about $3,000 a subscriber.

Faced with the challenge of telecommunications, many newspapers launched new services that sought to provide electronic means of disseminating their vast stores of information. These ranged from cable channels that simply repeated news headlines (and sometimes classified ad listings) over and over, all the way to sophisticated interactive teletext systems. A number of newspaper organizations launched major experiments in the 1970s and 1980s.

Aimed at the general public, these services were met with a singular lack of enthusiasm and cost their sponsors dearly. However, specialized financial data services found a market very rapidly. Quite obviously, the development of a mass market for home communications systems was going to proceed slowly. Yet with the breakup of AT&T and the scramble of telephone companies for new revenues, it seemed evident that new ways were opening up to disseminate information that newspapers had traditionally considered to be their own preserve as well as information that lay outside it (like pornographic messages—40% of the total on "dial-it" services).

Newspapers would face sharp questions even if new communications systems were not about to emerge. In the 1970s the rate of newspaper circulation growth fell behind the expansion of population and households, and that decline continued in the following decade. According to one influential school of thought, the generation raised in the age of television is accustomed to assimilating information in the form of images and is no longer comfortable with the printed word. Paradoxically, some other observers have contended that in a complex, bureaucratized society people need to read routinely at work and in coping with the requirements of daily life; thus they may be less likely to read for pleasure or for incidental information.

Throughout American history, newspapers have had a uniquely integrative function in defining their communities, but this function has been attenuated by changes in American values and lifestyles. The traditions of a locally owned independent press appear to be challenged by the growth of newspaper chains and of media conglomerates. Where the daily press is still competitive (typically in large cities with deteriorating business centers), major newspapers (particularly afternoon papers) continue to fail or ail.

In the final analysis, the future of newspapers depends on the ability of the people who run them to adapt to the changing requirements of the public. Therefore, the focus of this book is on readers and on the changes in their tastes and habits.

The press has been a popular subject of comment in recent years, with the discussion intensifying when journalists are at odds with public officials, as in the case of the Pentagon Papers and after Watergate. Most of the attention has been placed on the political role of journalists and on the newspaper as an institution; far less has been on the reader. Most studies of readers have dealt with individual newspapers and local situations rather than with the broader national picture. Perhaps this is as it should be, since newspapers show such variability in their character, content, size, and resources that national statistics inevitably blur and distort the many cases that they summarize.

The average reader has a metropolitan paper in his hands, but the average newspaper published is a small hometown product with limited resources and influence. The country's largest local paper, the *New York Daily News*, had a weekday circulation of 1,278,000 in 1987. The smallest daily, the Paxton, Illinois, *Record*, had 1,305. The median position was held by the Bartlesville, Oklahoma, *Examiner-Enterprise*, with a circulation of 12,867.

No generalizations from national studies are immediately applicable to individual newspapers. There are considerable variations in the responses papers get from their readers, just as there are variations in the characteristics of their communities. For example, people in different towns show widely varying degrees of interest in national (as opposed to local) news, show varying attitudes toward the local newspapers, and read them at different levels of regularity. All these variations are obscured when we look at the across-the-board findings of national studies.

Nonetheless, it is the aggregate that must be considered as we examine the changing patterns of newspaper reading throughout this book. Only by considering the overall pattern can we determine the meaning of trends that always assume a different shape in each locality.

Over the years, an enormous amount of information has been accumulated about the reading of newspapers. Much of it has been done to serve the commercial interests, often the competitive advertising sales interests, of individual dailies. Some of this privately done research has been published, some of it is accessible on request, and some remains locked in the files. There is, in addition, a substantial body of scholarly literature produced by students of journalism and communications, sometimes with the cooperation of local newspapers. Of necessity, both the commercial and the academic studies are generally limited to specific situations. Much of the research that is intellectually most rewarding because it deals with the testing of communications theory also turns out to be the most frustrating, because the small samples affordable by university scholars do not yield statistically satisfying conclusions.

This book makes no attempt to present a grand overview and synopsis of the whole literature on newspaper reading. I have limited myself almost entirely to the studies made under my direction since 1960 at the Newspaper Advertising Bureau.[4] Other research references have been included to corroborate or amplify some of our findings.

The studies undertaken at the Bureau have had the primary purpose of

---

[4]Prior to 1973, this was known as the Bureau of Advertising of the American Newspaper Publishers Association.

supporting its mission as the advertising sales promotion arm of the daily newspaper business. This has required accurate, current national information on all aspects of the press and its audience. Most of the studies conducted between 1977 and 1983 were done as part of the Newspaper Readership Project, a special industrywide effort to boost circulation. The most recent big study (1987) was done as part of the Future of Advertising Project, also organized by the Bureau as an industrywide program. Thus, the reader must keep in mind the fact that all the research reported here has been supported by the newspaper business and its Establishment, of which I am a hired hand. However, the interpretations and opinions offered throughout this book are entirely my personal ones. I have been fortunate both in having had the considerable resources of the Bureau to apply to this research effort over the years, and also in the total absence of any constraints on the professional integrity with which this research has been planned and executed.

The individual studies reported in the book are identified on Chart 1. As will readily be seen, most of them are on a national scale, using samples of substantial size. Because of that fact, few measures of statistical significance are included in the text, but all the differences I comment upon, unless otherwise noted, are either unlikely to occur by chance or are corroborated from several sources. The original research reports, which may be consulted in the Bureau's Information Center, provide full technical details.

The individual studies have all been designed and analyzed by my colleagues in the Bureau's Research Department, but valuable help has also been rendered by the research firms whom we have commissioned to do the fieldwork and tabulations. A number of the most ambitious projects (identified as 1961, 1963, 1966, 1972, 1974, 1977, 1979, 1987c and 1988a) have been underwritten by the Newsprint Information Committee.[5]

This book is directed to the thoughtful general reader who knows and respects the importance of the free press, knows also that it has been undergoing strenuous change, and has some concerns about its future. I have tried to make it useful and informative for everyone engaged in the newspaper business who has seen the individual pieces of our research effort and has wanted the whole quilt patched together. Finally, it is addressed to students of journalism in the hope that by becoming better informed about their future readers, they will be all the more inspired to serve them with dedication and enthusiasm.

I begin by reviewing the challenges that face newspapers at the end of the 1980s, after a decade of circulation losses for many dailies and several decades of accelerating social change. Because newspapers have always been the

---

[5]The following companies comprise this committee: Canadian Pacific Forest Products Ltd., Fletcher Challenge Canada Ltd., Kruger Inc., James Maclaren Industries, Inc., MacMillan Bloedel Ltd., Quebec and Ontario Paper Company Ltd., Rothesay Paper Ltd.

voices of particular towns, the changes on the urban scene require special attention in relation to both the civic and the marketing functions of the daily press.

Because these two functions are interdependent, I turn next to the business side of the newspaper business. What readers read, and what newspapers print, can only be understood in relation to the internal economics of circulation and advertising as sources of newspapers' revenues. And these must be considered in relation to the changed competitive environment in which newspapers now operate.

Although nearly every literate adult looks at a newspaper sooner or later, people read with different degrees of regularity. So we must confront the question of who is a reader before we go on to consider all the social and personal factors that account for differences in reading habits.

Though these habits vary among people with different backgrounds, they evolve from childhood on to adolescence and adulthood. The future strength of newspapers depends on their continuing familiarity to the members of future generations, both through their presence in the home and at school.

This brings us to the question of what place newspapers have in the lives of adult Americans, how they are used, and how an individual paper is selected when people have a choice.

The content of newspapers, and how it is changing, is described in the context of a discussion of the nature of news and what makes news memorable.

News is of course the province of editors, and I examine some of their practices and assumptions about their readers, before going on to tackle the crucial question of what content attracts readers. I look at this not only in terms of what people say they read in the paper, and in terms of what they want on general principles, but in terms of how they rate specific items along two key dimensions, interest and importance.

My intention is not to argue on behalf of a predetermined thesis as to how newspapers can continue to prosper, but rather to present the reader with the relevant information, to the degree that it is available. In the final chapter, I pull together my own conclusions and exhortations for editors, publishers, and all other interested parties to consider as they wrestle with the interesting question of whether journalism and marketing are compatible.

Acknowledgments

This book was built on the efforts of a good many people, to all of whom I am very grateful. Both editions of the manuscript were nurtured and typed by Marie Thornton through what must have seemed like interminable convolutions and transformations. In Chart 1, I have listed my colleagues at the Newspaper Advertising Bureau who worked with me on each of the studies on which I have drawn.

CHART 1

Identifying Date	Title of Original Research Report	Newspaper Advertising Bureau Research Analyst	Outside Research Organization	Sample
1961	The Daily Newspaper and Its Reading Public	Frank Orenstein	Audits & Surveys, Inc.	4,368 aged 21 & over / 458 aged 15–20
1962	Where Markets Meet: Intercity	Frank Orenstein	Ilse Zeisel	503
1963	A Study of the Opportunity for Exposure to National Newspaper Advertising	B. Stuart Tolley / Frank Orenstein	Audits & Surveys, Inc.	2,326 plus / 1,406 reinterviews
1963a	The Impact of Blank Space	B. Stuart Tolley	Eric Marder Associates	1,500
1966	When People Want to Know, Where Do They Go To Find Out?	Frank Orenstein	Opinion Research Corp.	1,991 aged 21 & over / 497 aged 12–20
1970	Young People and the Newspaper	Ilse Zeisel	Gilbert Youth Research	1,647 aged 14–25
1971	A Million Miles of Newspapers	Frank Orenstein / B. Stuart Tolley	Audits & Surveys, Inc.	1,714 plus / 1,104 reinterviews
1971a	The Working Woman	Ilse Zeisel / Charles Lehman	Response Analysis Corp.	1,000 women
1971b	News About the News Media	Frank Orenstein	Opinion Research Corp.	2,023
1972	Psychographics: A Study of Personality, Life-style, and Consumption Patterns	Ilse Zeisel	Commercial Analysts Co. / Behavioral Analysis, Inc.	4,136
1973	A Survey of ICMA Members	Charles Lehman		
1974	Shoppers on the Move	Frank Orenstein / B. Stuart Tolley / Charles Lehman	Response Analysis Corp.	5,900 women / 2,700 men
1975	How Readers Get the Papers They Read	Charles Lehman	Opinion Research Corp.	2,075
1975a	Retail Inserts in Daily Newspapers	Charles Lehman	Brehl & Associates	1,413 (four markets)
1975b	Young People's Attitudes Toward Unemployment	Charles Lehman	Gilbert Youth Research	2,250 aged 14–25

1977	How the Public Gets Its News	Frank Orenstein B. Stuart Tolley Charles Lehman Albert Gollin Thelma Anderson Clyde Nunn	Audits & Surveys, Inc.	3,048 adults
1977a	Editors Look at the Daily Newspaper: A Mail Survey	Charles Lehman		667 working editors
1978	Children, Mothers, and Newspapers	Thelma Anderson Albert Gollin	Center for Family Research	1,156 children 6-17; 817 principal childcaring adults (88% mothers)
1978a	Dailies, Shoppers, and Pennysavers	Charles Lehman	Brehl & Associates	800 (four markets)
1978b	One of Our Media is Missing	Charles Lehman		90 (plus 71 reinterviews)
1979	A Study of Newspaper Classifieds	Charles Lehman	Response Analysis Corp.	1,273
1979a	An Inventory of Editorial Content	Charles Lehman		
1979b	Women and Newspapers	Clyde Nunn	Response Analysis Corp.	1,041 women
1979c	A Survey of Circulation Managers	Charles Lehman		
1979d	A Study of "Drop Out Readers"	B. Stuart Tolley	Home Testing Institute	23,000 screening questionnaires, 920 interviews
1979e	The Newspaper in Readers' Minds	Albert Gollin	Brehl & Associates	330 (four markets)
1980	Sunday Newspaper Readership	Charles Lehman	Brehl & Associates	884 (four markets)
1981	Single Copy Buying: A Three-City Study	Thelma Anderson	Henry Senft Associates	1,417 buyers
1981a	Weekday Reading Patterns: A Two-Market Study	Charles Lehman	Brehl & Associates	606 adults
1981b	Assessing the Impact of Newspaper in Education Programs	Thelma Anderson		2,190 children

(continued)

CHART 1 *(continued)*

Identifying Date	Title of Original Research Report	Newspaper Advertising Bureau Research Analyst	Outside Research Organization	Sample
1982	How Does Your Newspaper Rate With Readers?	Albert E. Gollin Charles Lehman Thelma Anderson Nicolas Bloom Joan Lambe Michael Macht	Audits & Surveys, Inc.	1,979 adults
1982a	Changing Lifestyles and Newspaper Reading	Albert E. Gollin Howard Fattell Joan Lambe	National Family Opinion Andrew Beveridge	748 aged 25–44
1983	Newspaper Content Inventory	Charles Lehman		1,310 daily newspapers 572 Sunday papers
1986	Classified: A Study of Prospect Status, Readership, & Interest	Charles Lehman	Response Analysis Corp.	1,174 adults
1986a	An Eye Camera Study of Ads	B. Stuart Tolley Michael Macht	Applied Science Laboratories	12 women
1986b	How Four Readers Go Through Their Daily Newspaper	B. Stuart Tolley		4 men over 35
1987	An Update on Readership	Albert E. Gollin Charles Lehman Nicolas Bloom Carolyn Eldred Dorothy Shea	Response Analysis Corp.	2,049 adults

1987a	Newspaper Content Inventory	Charles Lehman		987 daily newspapers 522 Sunday papers
1987b	ROP Color: Where Readers Want to See It, How It Affects the Newspaper's Image	Charles Lehman Thelma Anderson	R. H. Bruskin Assoc. (Omnitel)	1,006 adults: 480 men 526 women
1987c	The Meaning of Interest; Continuing Ad performance Studies	B. Stuart Tolley Leon Aron	Harte-Hanks Communications	300 adults
1988	The Single-Copy Buyer	Nicolas Bloom	M.O.R.I.	914 single-copy buyers in 5 cities
1988a	Readers of Tomorrow	Charles Lehman Dorothy Shea	SMRB	1,074 aged 12–17

Over most of the nearly three decades covered by this research, Frank E. Orenstein and B. Stuart Tolley have served as research vice presidents of the Bureau. Their contributions are reflected in almost every survey done over this period, especially in the design of our national studies of newspaper audiences and reading habits. Orenstein also analyzed the Intercity study (of which Ilse Zeisel, later a co-worker, was the field director), and with his kind permission I have incorporated sections of a jointly prepared article (cited in Chapter 5) that summarizes the results. In our 1977 study, Tolley was personally responsible for the analysis of "Two Dimensions of News" and of "Frequent and Infrequent Readers" and was co-author of an article on the reading process, which is also cited in Chapter 5.

Albert E. Gollin was project director of the national readership surveys conducted in 1982 and 1987. He studied "The Daily Diet of News" and "Personal Reactions to the News" and has written or provided valuable help on many of the other research reports prepared since he joined the Bureau in 1977, notably the 1978 study of children and adolescents. Charles Lehman, whose other impressive contributions are shown on Chart 1, analyzed data on "The Personal Newspaper" and directed the series of studies of newspapers' editorial content. Thelma Anderson directed parts of the 1977 and 1978 studies and was responsible for our research on the Newspaper in Education. Clyde Z. Nunn wrote the 1977 analyses of youth and Black readership. Nicolas Bloom, Michael Macht, and Joan Lambe assisted with the 1982 national survey; Bloom, Dorothy Shea, and Carolyn Eldred with the 1987 study.

In addition to the analysis of surveys, I have received important assistance in the secondary analysis of other data from my former colleagues, Frederick W. Williams, Jr. and the late Joseph A. Wallis and Richard Martwick. Ann Brady and Susan Hyer opened up the far-ranging resources of the Bureau's Information Center. I have been helped by James Conaghan, Yannis Takos, John Kelley, Robert Isler, the late C. Leigh Dimond, and many others on the Bureau's staff.

Pat Sherred of the Inland Daily Press Association provided current data for the breakdown of newspaper expenses shown in Chapter 2. Andrew Tyndall generously prepared a special tabulation of data from the Tyndall Report for my use in Chapter 7.

Valuable comments and suggestions on a preliminary draft of the first edition of this book were made by William H. Hornby (at the time editor of the Denver *Post* and president of the American Society of Newspaper Editors).

In preparing the manuscript I made use of sections of previously published articles, and I appreciate the publishers' permission to do so. They are:

"Urban Papers Under Pressure," *Columbia Journalism Review*, Vol. XIII, No. 3, September/October 1974, pp. 36–43.

"The Future of the Metropolitan Daily," *Journal of Communication*, Vol. 25:2, Spring 1975, pp. 30–43.

"Editorials Ideals, Editorial Illusions," *Journal of Communication*, Vol. 29:2, Spring 1979, pp. 11–21. This paper has also appeared in a somewhat different form in Anthony Smith (ed.), *Newspapers and Democracy*, Cambridge, MA: M.I.T. Press, 1980.

"Newspapers in the Age of TV," *Daedalus*, Winter 1963, p. 116.

"Mass Media and Community Identity in an Interurban Setting," (with Frank E. Orenstein), *Journalism Quarterly*, Vol. 42, No. 2, Spring 1965, p. 179.

"Changing News Interests and the News Media," *Public Opinion Quarterly*, Vol. 32, No. 4, Winter 1968–69, p. 560.

"Negro and White Media Exposure: New Evidence," *Journalism Quarterly*, Vol. 49, No. 1, Spring 1972, pp. 15–21.

"Television News as Entertainment" in Percy Tannenbaum (ed.), *The Entertainment Functions of Television*, Hillsdale, NJ: Lawrence Erlbaum Associates, 1980.

"The Public's Use and Perception of Newspapers," *Public Opinion Quarterly*, Vol. 48, No. 4, Winter 1984, pp. 709–719.

"How U.S. Newspaper Content is Changing," *Journal of Communication*, Vol. 35, No. 2, Spring 1984, pp. 82–90.

I also wish to thank the University of Chicago Press and Greenwood Press, Inc., for permission to quote the cited passages from Robert Park.

1
THE CHALLENGE TO NEWSPAPERS

Daily newspaper publishers and editors today face tasks and problems that are varied and demanding. They must accommodate to a new era in their own production technology and at the same time anticipate changes in the technology of electronic home communications that will affect newspapers profoundly. They must battle new restrictions to the flow of news, imposed or threatened by foreign governments and domestically by the courts. They must meet the political questions inevitably raised by the growing weight of groups and multimedia conglomerates within their business. But most important, they must consider how their newspapers should change to resume circulation growth at a pace that matches the potential. Such growth is essential for any medium to remain vital and strong. This is especially so for newspapers, whose special attribute among the media has been their nearly universal readership in their respective towns. To understand the situation of newspaper circulation at the start of the 1990s, we must examine what happened to it in the recent past and relate this to the larger forces at play in American society, especially on the urban scene.

THE CHANGES IN CIRCULATION

In 1970, total U.S. daily newspaper circulation fell below the number of households for the first time in recent history, and the gap between circulation and households has continued to widen (see Figure 1.1).

One reason why the public's newspaper reading habits have changed is that they are confronted with different media options than in the past. In the 19th century, the rise of the mass press was made possible by improved machinery for papermaking, setting type, and printing. The press was concentrated in urban centers (389 in 1880) and was highly competitive, with as many as 16 dailies published at a single time (1892) in New York City. Yet in the period of most vigorous competition, newspapers were read by a minority of the population. When readership was far from universal, news-papers had more readers per copy than they do today. Single copies could be exchanged or passed from hand to hand and from family to family.

A rising standard of living brought the newspaper as a daily presence into an increasing proportion of American households, and in many of them more than one paper a day was read. The ratio of circulation to households continued to grow throughout the 20th century and then fell back during the years of the Great Depression. The ratio rose again during World War II and remained high during the first half of the 1960s. Thereafter, it began a decline that reflected the demise of many major city newspapers, some with huge circulations. (The *New York Mirror* was selling nearly a million copies a day when it closed in 1963.)

Challenged by new advertising media, newspapers found it more difficult to maintain their economic base, and the number of markets with competing papers began to diminish. This decline was to some extent offset by the establishment of daily newspapers in new communities previously served only by weeklies or other papers of less than daily frequency. Thus, the

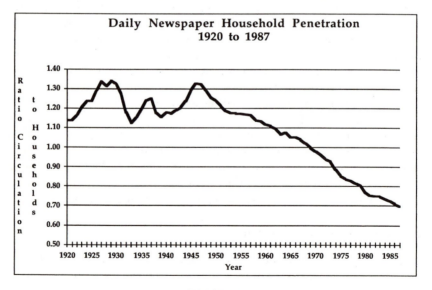

FIGURE 1.1

number of cities and towns in which daily newspapers are published stood in 1987 at 1,536, just below the all-time peak of 1,553 a decade earlier. The number of individual daily newspapers (1,645) was down from what it had been 30 years earlier (1,769) and far less than the 2,226 at the turn of the century.

In the past 35 years, newspaper analyst John Morton points out, 25 second (or, as he calls them, junior) newspapers with a circulation of over 250,000 have failed, many of them taken over before the end by foreign purchasers (Rupert Murdoch, the Toronto *Sun* group) or by American buyers (like Time, Inc. in the case of the Washington *Star*) who "tended not to be sophisticated." Competitive markets like Dallas, Houston, and Denver are young cities without long-established suburbs with their own dailies. In all three markets, a dynamic young publishing entrepreneur, William Dean Singleton, bought the second-ranked papers in 1986 and 1987, though he sold the Dallas *Times-Herald* to a former associate soon afterward.

When papers fold, the survivors do not necessarily get all their advertising, though their prosperity is generally assured. A study among advertisers in the failed Buffalo *Courier Express*, Cleveland *Press*, and Washington *Star* found that budgets formerly allocated to those papers were reallocated to the surviving metropolitan paper 30% to 40% of the time; to suburban papers in 13% to 20% of the cases; to weeklies by 8% to 10%, and to broadcast by 11% to 20%. Between 8% and 16% of the advertisers either cut their budgets or were uncertain how the funds were reallocated.[1]

Unlike dailies, Sunday papers, formerly published only in major cities, have undergone a steady growth in circulation as more towns reach a size that can support a seven-day publication. In 1987, there were 803 Sunday papers published in 776 communities. Their circulation was 58,930,000, 94% of the weekday average of 62,688,000.

Despite the array of choices, fewer people than in the past feel it necessary to read more than a single paper each day. The paper that is most readily dropped is usually the one with less circulation. (In a number of competitive cities, as we shall see, this turns out to be the evening paper.) The paper with less circulation is also apt to carry less advertising, and advertising in itself represents an important attraction. For most readers, a thinner paper probably appears to represent less value. Papers with less advertising also print less news, but to keep up with their more successful competitors they publish a higher proportion of news to advertising.

Many people find it possible to get along without reading a second paper simply because there are more alternate ways for them to spend their time. The total array of media choices continues to grow as more broadcasting

---

[1]Mary Alice Sentman, "When the Newspaper Closes: A Case Study of What Advertisers Do," *Journalism Quarterly*, Vol. 63, No. 4, Winter 1986, pp. 757–762.

stations and more publications start up. And a generally rising standard of living in recent decades has made it possible for many people to take up sporting and other leisure pursuits that they formerly could not afford.

It is common to think of the household or family as the unit of consumption for a newspaper. For every 100 households in 1960, 111 newspapers were sold each day. In 1987, the figure was 71. But that comparison is misleading, because households now include more people living alone and in what might be called unconventional arrangements. And households are smaller, too. In 1960, for every 100 households, there were 212 adults 18 years old and over and 121 children. In 1988, there were 196 adults and only 71 children.

A household can consist of a single individual or of unrelated individuals living together; a family is made up of people related by kinship or marriage. But the size of the average household fell from 3.14 persons in 1970 to 2.67 in 1986. For every 100 families in 1960, 131 newspapers were sold daily. In 1987, 99 were sold. But that comparison is also deceptive, because the composition of families has changed, too, as I emphasize shortly.

We can also consider circulation relative to the potential consumption of individuals. For every 100 people in 1960, there were 33 dailies sold; in 1987, there were 26. But the newspaper reading habit is developed in adolescence, so mature adults must be considered the prime potential readers. In 1960, 36% of the population was under 18. By 1987, that ratio had fallen to 26%.

However, in this period the actual number of youngsters under 18 fell by 2%, while the number of young people 18 to 24, not yet settled down to the stage of rearing a family, grew by 76%. For every 100 young people in that age group in 1960, 365 papers were sold. The ratio in 1987 was 225. For the mature and active adult population between 25 and 64, there were 71 newspapers per hundred in 1960 and 52 per hundred in 1988.

Thus, newspaper circulation has failed to match not so much the growth rate of households, families, and adult population as the demographic explosion in the generation of postwar babies who have entered the ranks of citizens and consumers. One would expect that these people, with their superior level of education, would also be good newspaper readers. Readership correlates highly with education, and between 1960 and 1988, the proportion of the people of 25 and over who had finished high school grew from 41% to 74%.

One out of four Americans lives outside the 281 Metropolitan Statistical Areas. Understandably, daily newspaper readership is lower in areas where no local daily paper is published and where it is hard and costly to arrange same-day delivery of papers from the closest urban centers. Readership on Sunday is even lower in nonmetropolitan areas. Metropolitan Sunday newspapers usually are distributed throughout a broader area than their daily editions.

When more than one paper is published in a particular town, this may be because a single owner produces both a morning and evening paper. In some cases, one may be little more than a remake of the other; in other cases, the two papers are turned out by separate staffs, have a high individuality, maintain independent editorial postures, and are just as competitive editorially as those that are separately owned and competitive for advertising.

In 1961, 91% of the population in metropolitan areas were served by two or more locally published central city newspapers (including those under common ownership), and 30% by four or more. By 1987, the proportions had changed to 32% for two or more and 10% for three or more.

As local newspaper competition was reduced by newspaper failures and mergers, it became harder for readers to find a paper that expressed their own particular tastes, values, and views of the world. Newspapers that tried to cover the interests of the entire community inevitably fell short of elite standards, but they may also have overshot the level of the working class.

Does competition raise the level of readership? A 1979 comparison of the circulation to household ratios of jointly owned morning and evening newspapers found that those with different editorial managements had higher penetration, markedly so (63% vs. 28%) in major markets. This may have reflected the particularities of the individual markets and papers, because by 1987 this was no longer the case. In that year, there were 50 combinations with separate editorial managements for the morning and evening papers and 15 where the same editors produced both papers; for both groups the average circulation-to-household ratio was 61%.[2] It was exactly the same for the 27 markets with competing, separately owned papers and only slightly lower (56%) for the 20 markets with separate ownerships but common publishing operations. Even when the analysis was restricted to 21 major metropolitan markets, the differences were negligible (58% for the competing markets, 54% for those with agencies, and 56% for those with combination papers—all of them with separate editorial managements). In short, there is no longer any evidence to support the commonsense hypothesis that penetration goes up when readers have a choice, except for the obvious fact that it has gone down as the number of choices has diminished.

The number of jointly owned morning/evening papers with combined news staffs rose from 38 of 122 titles in 1980 to 56 in 1987, while 12 papers merged titles or disappeared altogether. In 33 cities, separate competing news staffs were maintained. Even when staffs are merged, the same reporter might be asked to write two separate stories on the same subject.[3] The editors of

---

[2]This analysis was based on the Metropolitan Statistical Area, except in the case of several satellite or suburban cities, where the home county was used.

[3]Clark Newsom, *presstime*, December 1987, pp. 8–9.

papers that had combined their staffs often contended that they were able to do a better job by pooling resources. In some cases, they had expanded the news hole and the total number on staff.

Morning and evening distribution patterns customarily differ. The morning paper is printed and distributed at night, has fewer traffic problems to contend with, and can go out to a broader hinterland. It can get much of its circulation from beyond the city zone (an average of 49% in the top 25 markets), whereas the afternoon paper gets a high proportion of its circulation from the city itself (73% in the same major markets). Thus, comparatively few people in such markets are apt to read both papers. The rate of duplicated readership varies (between 7% and 34%), as shown by a number of local newspaper audience studies (Table 1.1).

In a majority of major American cities, morning papers have been dominant both in circulation and in advertising. But there are large and

TABLE 1.1
Percentage of Total Average Weekday Audience that Reads Both
Morning and Evening Papers, in Selected Metropolitan Areas,
with Two Central-City Dailies[a]

Atlanta, GA	17
Baltimore, MD	22
Birmingham, AL[b]	23
Charleston, WV	34
Fort Lauderdale, FL	9
Greenville, SC	20
Indianapolis, IN	19
Kansas City, MO	55
Lancaster, PA	30
Miami, FL[b]	16
Milwaukee, WI	33
Nashville, TN[b]	23
Norfolk, Va. Beach, Portsmouth, VA	22
Phoenix, AZ	11
Pittsburgh, PA[b]	30
Providence, RI	21
Raleigh,NC	21
Reading, PA	20
Salt Lake City, UT	8
San Diego, CA	11
Seattle, WA[b]	26
Worcester, MA	30

[a]Based on local audience studies conducted by Scarborough Research in 1987.

[b]a.m. and p.m. papers are separately owned though jointly published. Other papers are commonly owned. The Miami *News* ceased publication in December, 1988.

important markets like Milwaukee, Seattle, and Pittsburgh, in which, for historical reasons, the afternoon papers have been dominant. Dailies in smaller, one-paper cities and in suburban communities do not face the logistical problems of metropolitan papers in getting their product to their readers. Hence, they generally publish during the afternoon (permitting more of their staffs to enjoy a conventional workday). This explains why afternoon papers account for two-thirds of the total number published and for 41% of total daily circulation.

The line of demarcation between morning and evening publication changed somewhat as some newspapers went into all-day publication, with both morning and afternoon editions. By 1987, 29 such papers had an aggregate circulation of 5,552,577.

The problems of large metropolitan newspapers have been concentrated in the evening field, in both competitive and noncompetitive markets. The pattern of circulation losses held both in cities where the morning paper was traditionally dominant and in those where the evening paper was dominant. During the 1980s, an increasing number of newspaper owners eliminated their afternoon papers, responding to advertisers' common notion that the duplication of readership represented waste. In most instances, the afternoon papers had lost circulation and were being operated at a loss.[4] Some publishers shifted to all-day publication, with a street-sale afternoon edition of the morning paper. Some applied the staff resources of the discontinued publication to strengthen the morning product.

When the Memphis *Press-Scimitar* ceased publication, 8% of the readers said, "It didn't make much difference to me"; 17% said, "It's too bad, but that's just how business goes sometimes"; 35% called it "a blow to the community"; and 40% said, "It felt like an old acquaintance had passed away." At its demise on October 31, 1983, the *Press-Scimitar* had a circulation of 66,375; the *Commmercial Appeal*, 217,685. On December 31, with a free subscription offer, circulation was up to 244,136. In 1986 it was down to 225,674.[5]

Between 1980 and 1987, there were 49 mergers of jointly owned evening papers, with an aggregate pre-merger daily circulation of 5,495,525. Their circulation after the mergers was 4,833,974, a loss of 12%.[6]

---

[4]The San Jose *Mercury* and *News* put out a combined edition ina test of 4,500 subscribers, with the front page changed to an old English typeface reading *San Jose Mercury News*. When they called 100 a.m. and 100 p.m. subscribers, not one had noticed the change. The papers were then combined into an all-day paper; circulation began to rise 10% in single-copy sales.

[5]Gerald C. Stone, "No Rest-in-Peace for Readers after PM's Demise," *Newspaper Research Journal*, Vol. 8, No. 1, Fall 1986, pp. 13–27.

[6]An independent study of consolidations between 1970 and 1984 indicates that 93% of the total circulation was maintained, or to put it another way, that there was a 7% loss. William B. Blankenburg, "Predicting Newspaper Circulation After Consolidation," *Journalism Quarterly*, Vol. 64, Nos. 2/3, Summer/Autumn, 1987, pp. 585–587.

Changes in the time of publication also took place in many one-newspaper cities. A number of case histories of this process have appeared. Reading habits for the Jonesboro, Arkansas, *Sun* in 1982 did not change significantly when it shifted from evening to morning.[7] When the Eugene, Oregon, *Register-Guard* made a similar shift, perceptions of its news freshness and attitudes toward it did not change.[8] In 1986, the Gannett morning Knoxville *Journal* and the Scripps Howard afternoon *News-Sentinel* switched publication times. A study of 505 subscriber households found that 5% canceled their subscriptions and only 15% switched papers to retain the original delivery time. The morning paper lost fewer subscribers and gained more than the evening paper. The readers' evaluations of the papers' editorial content did not appear to be significantly related to their choice of papers.[9]

The International Circulation Managers Association analyzed circulation changes for 121 U.S. and Canadian newspapers that had switched from evening to morning publication between 1980 and 1986. Sixty-five of them had increased their circulation, but the proportion was higher among papers in every size group above 10,000 circulation than it was for the very smallest papers. Of the 14 large papers with over 100,000 in circulation, 11 showed a gain, and the overall increase was 16%. Of 41 papers under 10,000 in circulation, only 11 increased circulation by switching to morning. In fact, among the smallest papers under 5,000, a net circulation loss was reported after the switch.

A great variety of explanations have been advanced for the comparatively greater vulnerability of metropolitan afternoon papers. One explanation may be considered overriding: the fact that their readership is concentrated in the city itself. Many afternoon papers have traditionally drawn a large chunk of their circulation from street sales. But, they have been hit by declining use of mass transit and thinner pedestrian traffic. Thus, the economic and social problems of the central cities have affected afternoon papers more acutely and directly than the morning press.

In 1987, 87 newspapers with a circulation of 100,000 and over accounted for 68% of morning circulation, and the 413 other morning papers accounted for 32%. This kind of concentration does not exist in the afternoon. Forty-three large evening papers had 28% of evening circulation, and 1,148 other evening papers had the remaining 72%. One hundred twenty-four Sunday papers of over 100,000 accounted for 68% of total Sunday circula-

---

[7]Gilbert Len Fowler, Jr., "An Examination of Readership Changes: Does Altering Publication Time Affect the Reading Habit?" *Newspaper Research Journal*, Vol. 7, No. 1, Fall 1985, pp. 37–44.

[8]Galen R. Rarick & James B. Lemert, "Subscriber Behavior and Attitudes in Response to PM–AM Conversion," *Newspaper Research Journal*, Vol. 7, No. 2, Winter 1985, pp. 11–18.

[9]M. Mark Miller, Shu-Ling Chen, & Stephen E. Everett, "Trading Places: Reader Reactions to the Knoxville Newspaper Switch," Paper presented to the Association for Education in Journalism and Mass Communication (AEJMC), San Antonio, 1987.

tion, and 652 other Sunday papers for the remainder. Altogether, the 147 papers with over 100,000 circulation account for 60% of the U.S. total.

The primary explanation for the overall trend in the circulation statistics is the fact that fewer papers are on sale today in the big competitive markets. Of the 46 papers that stopped publishing between 1980 and 1987, 19 were in metropolitan central cities, and they sold 2,085,000 copies a day. Of this, 1,603,000 came from 14 afternoon papers. We can go back even farther and look at the big-city circulation trends between 1960 and 1987. These included in 1960 a number of dailies that are no longer publishing today. Their total daily circulation when they ceased publication amounts to nine million. These papers went out of business for many complex reasons, but primarily because they could not get enough advertising to meet escalating production costs. They did not go out of business because their readers had stopped buying them.

What if all these papers had generated more advertising, settled their labor difficulties on reasonable terms, and kept publishing? What if they had grown with their markets, at the same rate as the rest of the daily press? In that case, not 26 but 29 would now be sold per hundred population, compared with 33 in 1960.

This little fantasy serves to remind us that newspapers are unique. When they disappear, their successors and competitors never manage to capture more than a fraction of their lost readers. There are two reasons for this: First, each daily newspaper apparently has its own unique and familiar character to which its readers are attuned. They find its disappearance very much like the permanent departure of a friend, who simply cannot be replaced by a substitute. A substantial part of the population with limited reading skills and distinctive cultural interests were readers of the tabloid and popular evening papers that faded during the television era. For many of these people, the community common denominator at which the surviving monopoly papers aim their content may seem slightly out of reach—with too many articles that are difficult to understand, too many elements that seem remote, and not enough that touch their vital interests.

Second, much of the circulation of failed papers has been duplicated circulation. That is, many of their readers, sometimes a majority, were already reading another paper as well. In fact, since advertisers are well familiar with this duplication, and since, as already noted, they are apt to consider it wasteful, this has often been the primary reason for them to withdraw their support. When the paper fails, most readers do not look for a substitute, they make do with the other paper they have already been reading. This helps to explain why the proportion of newspaper readers who read two or more papers on a given day has fallen from 33% in 1970 to 23% in 1987.

In the major markets it has been less the departure of readers than the loss of advertisers that has led to newspaper failure. In fact, the total circulation of the 30 central-city papers that went out of business between 1960 and 1973 —years that saw a wave of mergers and failures—was in the aggregate only 15% below their record high.

Few of the major city newspapers that in recent years failed or merged had been losing circulation at a spectacular rate. In most cases, the declines were gradual and, in percentage terms, comparatively small. These failed papers continued to serve the daily interests of hundreds of thousands of readers. However, when they lost a small part of their circulation, this tended to be followed by comparatively large losses of advertising share, thereby further threatening their economic base.

We can see the effects of newspaper failures and mergers most clearly by examining the case of a traditionally strong newspaper market: Boston. In 1950 (excluding the nationally circulated *Christian Science Monitor*), Boston had seven newspapers, with a combined circulation of 1,552,000. After the death of the *Post*, the 1960 circulation of the survivors was 1,220,000, barely less than the net after the *Post's* circulation is subtracted. The evening *Traveler* was abandoned and merged into the morning *Herald* in 1967. The total circulation stood at 1,077,000 in 1970, with the *Globe* increasing its share. In 1973, after the *Herald Traveler* had been folded into the *Record American* as the *Herald American*, the resulting paper's circulation was less than that of the *Record American* before merger, and the total, along with the morning and *Evening Globe*, was 838,000. In 1979, the *Evening Globe* disappeared. The two remaining papers had a circulation of 857,876 in 1987. To put this in perspective, the Boston metropolitan area grew from 2,422,000 people in 1950 to 4,056,000 in 1987.

It is the death of great metropolitan dailies that arouses comment and concern, although press analyst Ben Bagdikian notes that most failing newspapers are small and that nearly half of them are less than 10 years old. The overall rate of failure among newspapers is less than it is for all forms of businesses in general.[10]

Among the major democracies, the United States ranks at a midpoint in its consumption of daily newspapers. Its circulation of 268 per thousand population in 1984 compares with a high of 562 for Japan and with 550 for East Germany and 414 for the United Kingdom. But it compares well with the 79 in Spain, 82 in Italy, and 212 in France. As we see in Chapter 10, the recent drop in North American circulation penetration was not part of a general worldwide phenomenon.

---

[10]Analyzing the 164 papers that disappeared in the 1960s, Bagdikian found that 26% were published in the central cities of metropolitan areas. However, the largest 15 failed papers represented 82% of the circulation lost. Ben H. Bagdikian, "Report of an Exaggerated Death: Daily Newspapers that Failed, 1961–1970." *Nieman Reports*, Winter 1976/Spring 1977, pp. 19–23.

SOCIAL TRENDS AND NEWSPAPER READERSHIP

During the decade of the 1970s, in which newspaper circulation-to-household ratios fell, a great many changes were taking place in American society that were bound to affect newspaper reading adversely. These include changes in (1) the political climate, (2) where people live, (3) the structure of the population, and (4) the communications environment.

1. The Vietnam war had a profoundly divisive effect. Both the civil dissension and the eventual military outcome brought about a widespread disenchantment with political institutions. In the decade and a half following the Vietnam defeat, a series of other demoralizing occurrences rocked a succession of Washington administrations: Watergate, the Iran hostage crisis, the failure of the space shuttle Challenger, the Iran–Contra affair, the deepening budget and trade deficits, a seemingly interminable stalemate in negotiations to control nuclear arms. In a period in which big news was very often bad news, increasing numbers of people were bound to be disengaged from the news as such. In the American tradition, to be informed on political matters is a precondition for political effectiveness. At a time when an increasing part of the electorate perceived itself as politically impotent, the pursuit of political knowledge may have seemed less meaningful.[11]

2. There was an accelerated movement of population (a) from the Eastern and Central states to the South and West and (b) from the central cities to the suburbs in metropolitan areas. Three-fifths of the metropolitan population now live in the suburbs.

There has been an especially accelerated rate of personal mobility among young people. One third of those in their twenties have moved within a recent one-year period, about half of them into another metropolitan area (Table 1.2).

People who live outside their original communities must go through a transition period before they feel at home with the newspapers of the new locations to which they have moved. And people who have moved out of the central city often no longer feel the need to keep in touch with its problems and civic activities through the central city newspaper. However, they do not necessarily immediately transfer their former loyalties to the new political units in which they now live. The automobile permits people in their daily lives to work, shop, visit, and conduct personal business over a wide range of communities, thereby attenuating the identification with the town in which they have their residence.

---

[11]In their famous study of "The Unemployed of Marienthal," Paul Lazarsfeld, Marie Jahoda, and Hans Zeisel found that during the demoralized days of the Depression in Austria, the newspaper that emphasized political and economic subjects lost 60% of its circulation, even though it lowered its price, while the paper that stressed sports and entertainment lost only 27%, though its price remained constant. *Die Arbeitslosen von Marienthal* (Leipzig: Hirzel, 1933).

TABLE 1.2
Percentage Moving Between 1983 and 1984

Age	In same SMSA[a]	Other moves	Total
5–14	8	8	16
15–29	7	8	16
20–24	16	18	34
25–29	16	14	30
30–34	11	10	21
35–44	7	7	14
45–64	4	4	8
65+	2	3	5
All ages	8	9	17

[a]Standard Metropolitan Statistical Area
Source: U.S. Census Bureau

3. The audience of any medium of communication is made up of individuals, although the consuming or purchasing unit for media is normally the family or household. This is especially true of newspapers for whom home-delivered subscriptions typically account for 85% of paid daily distribution (1987). By comparison, magazines deliver about 24% of their circulation through sales of single copies, each of which represents an individual purchase decision.

Households have grown at a substantially faster rate than either the total population or the adult population, but as already mentioned, households are different than they were, in character and composition.

Marriages come later and produce fewer children; unconventional living arrangements are more popular and socially acceptable; the divorce rate rose from 2.2 per thousand population in 1940 to a high of 5.3 in 1979 and was still 4.8 in 1986. Illegitimate births rose 14% just between 1980 and 1985. In that year, 60% of all Black births were out of wedlock. Nearly 3 out of 10 children, and 3 out of 5 of all Black children, were living in households without their natural father present in 1987. Today, only 4% of all American households conform to the traditional picture-book notion of a working father, a mother who is a full-time homemaker, and two children living at home.

There are more single-person households (24%), more households made up of unrelated people living together (47%). In sum, there has been a substantial weakening of the established strength of the family as an institution. This has a significant bearing on newspapers, since newspaper reading is traditionally an activity that family members share and a source of topics for family conversation.

The steady increase in the proportion of women working (which in 1987 reached 67% of those aged 18–64 and 73% of those aged 25–44) brought about substantial changes in family relationships and routine, putting substantial time pressures not only on those women themselves, but on men assigned to a greater array of domestic chores. The number of weekly hours the average person has available for leisure fell from 26.2 in 1972 to 16.6 in 1987, according to the Harris Poll.

Changes in that most fundamental human institution, the family, adversely affect newspaper reading in at least two respects, and possibly in a third. First, they mean for more and more people a way of life that involves fewer connections with the surrounding community and with society as a whole. They entail greater personal mobility, less time spent at home, more unconventional hours of work and recreation, and attenuation of the traditional ties to neighbors and local institutions—churches, schools, associations. Thus, they represent a diminished attraction to the news of the community, which is the newspaper's stock in trade.

Second, the more adults there are in a household, the more chances that a paper will be bought; the more stable the family structure, the more chances that reading will follow a routine and that a newspaper will be delivered regularly. With more loners and more floaters, the sale of newspaper subscriptions becomes more difficult. A regular subscription is less convenient for individuals who lead an irregular existence. They are harder to contact, to sell to, to collect from. They are likely to have a smaller household income than families with more than one breadwinner. Accordingly, the cost of a subscription is a bigger item in their budgets.

Third, the changes in family structure and the growing number of working mothers may also affect newspapers in another respect. To the degree that parents spend less time with their young children, the early development of reading habits may be receiving less encouragement than it did in past generations. It is an unfortunate human being who cannot recall the happy childhood experience of the bedtime story. Eighty-eight percent of American mothers say they read to their children when they were younger (1978), and as we shall see, mothers want to encourage their children to read independently.

In the absence of benchmark research, we can only speculate that changes in family life, more than changes in educational philosophy, may be partly responsible for the highly publicized declines in scholastic test scores during the 1970s.[12] These declines in turn brought charges of a new illiteracy, supported by public opinion polls that showed a substantial minority of Americans without the ability to apply for a driver's license or to fill out an

---

[12]These declines are difficult to interpret because of changes in the size and character of the school populations tested and changes of emphasis in school curricula. As classes became smaller in the late 1970s, the traditional disciplines were reasserted, and there was some indication of improvement in the indicators of scholastic achievement. In the 1980s, SAT scores edged upward.

income tax form.[13] (Since comparable polls had not been taken 20 or 30 years earlier, their horrifying conclusions could hardly be taken as evidence of a decline in national reading skills.) The continuing rise in educational attainments and the continuing strength of magazines, books, and weekly newspapers both suggest that reading ability is not on the wane. (In fact, average annual per capita purchases of consumer books rose from 11 in 1972 to 14 in 1987, and spending grew 61% in constant dollars, while unit sales of professional books increased by 169% between 1972 and 1984.) But the reading of newspapers, specifically, is surely not independent of the transformations in family style and structure.

Apart from these three great areas of structural change, there have been important changes in the communications environment, both in print and in broadcasting. Television has continued to consolidate its position as an important competitor for total leisure time. Since the typical home now has more than one set, more viewing is done by individual choice, less as a family or group affair. But total viewing hours have remained essentially unchanged. The video cassette recorder (in over half of the homes by 1987) carved out additional time. Cable (in over half the homes) expanded viewing choices and reduced the dominant position of the networks.

Along with the extrinsic forces that were at work during these years , there were also developments unique to the newspaper business that adversely affected circulation. The price of newsprint tripled within a 15-year period of time (1970–1985). Since cost increases were passed along to the reader as well as to the advertiser, the paper became more of an expense than it had been in the past. The demand for newspapers is not inelastic, and price increases are normally followed by a decline in the number of people who buy two papers a day. To save newsprint, some papers cut back on their more costly distribution to outlying areas of less interest to their advertisers.[14]

Urban decay, with all its attendant problems, has reduced the number of distribution points and has made it more difficult to recruit carriers and to collect from customers. In the spreading suburbs there are also new problems of timely and cost-efficient delivery as carrier routes become longer and less manageable.

In major competitive markets, the weaker newspaper has been placed at a substantial disadvantage by changes in advertising strategy. When they have a choice, advertisers tend to concentrate their business in the more successful newspaper rather than to spread it around in proportion to circulation size. As I have noted, the second- or third-ranking paper is especially vulnerable to

---

[13]Often quoted is a poll conducted by Louis Harris and Associates for the National Reading Center in 1971, which showed 15% of the public with serious reading deficiencies.

[14]On balance, this appears to have been offset by expansion of distribution areas by other newspapers.

circulation declines, since these will be reflected disproportionately in advertising losses.

Nearly two-thirds (63%) of weekday circulation is represented by 275 papers published in cities of 100,000 or over. These are the cities in which readership has presented the greatest problems.

THE CHANGING METROPOLIS

The history of newspapers is bound up with the history of cities. It is the big city newspapers whose visibility and newsgathering resources make them a very potent political force. The economic strength of the daily newspaper has been rooted in the city: The city's news is the paper's special province, the citizens have been customers for the paper's advertisers. Yet when people move to the suburbs, they abandon their former civic identity and their interest in city news; also, their patterns of consumption no longer depend primarily on the city.

Because of the vast amount of local information that they print, newspapers perform a unique social function for which broadcasting can provide no real substitute. The newspaper, at its best, continues to be the embodiment of a city's concerns and problems, its affairs, and its official personalities.

Yet, in the big cities, newspapers today face serious problems. The 50 top metropolitan areas have an aggregate population of 111 million, 46% of the country's total and 60% of its metropolitan population.

Although 76% of Americans live in metropolitan areas, 60% of these live in the suburban ring rather than in the central city. Between 1980 and 1987, American cities increased their population by 21%, but their White population grew by only 6%. Even this latter figure is deceptive, since a growing proportion of the White population in such cities as Los Angeles, Chicago, and New York is of Latin American origin and includes many people from whom English is not the primary language. In all central cities, one inhabitant in seven was classed as Hispanic in 1987.

The blighted and impoverished central cities house fewer people who are able to read a newspaper easily, who can afford to buy one, and who want one because they have been raised in households where newspaper reading is commonplace.

Big cities , with their high-rise apartments and more transient populations, have always presented tougher distribution problems. These problems are compounded in decaying cities. Customers are less reliable in paying their bills. Carriers are less reliable in making their rounds, are vulnerable to robbery and assault, and harder to recruit in the first place. Although there are parts of almost any large city where newspapers simply cannot afford to offer home delivery, every metropolitan paper is eager to sell more copies anywhere it can. But newsstands and other small retail establishments endure a precarious existence in inner city slums, and their numbers dwindle each year. Vending racks, vulnerable to vandalism and pilferage, are not an acceptable substitute.

METROPOLITAN DAILIES UNDER PRESSURE

It is no wonder then that newspaper circulation in central cities has declined. The aggregate circulation of morning newspapers published in the top 50 central cities grew by 2% between 1960 and 1987, while the total population of the metropolitan areas grew by 29%. The same cities' afternoon papers lost 80% (47% if one includes all the new all-day papers). In the same period, suburban morning papers gained 20% and suburban afternoon papers, including such giants as *Newsday* of Long Island, grew 63%. Yet these increases hardly compensated for central-city losses.

In general, the worst attrition has taken place among the metropolitan dailies in those markets that have shown the most severe declines of their central-city population, but the relationship between population loss and circulation decline is by no means clear-cut.

Some dailies have been more successful than others in retaining their readers who move to the suburbs by adapting their distribution systems and their editorial contents. Their ability to make this adjustment has in part depended on the strength of their existing suburban competition and the skill and speed with which they have preempted the rise of new competition. (As I describe later, a growing number of metropolitan papers have set up regional or zonal editions to compete with suburban dailies and community weeklies, and some have started new suburban papers of their own.)

The unique problems of the metropolitan press should not be taken to mean that the publishers of smaller and middle-sized papers can sit back and enjoy life while some metropolitan papers suffer. Eighty percent of their revenue comes from advertising, and major advertisers, national and retail, make up their schedules only after they have arrived at a basic decision on the merits of using newspapers instead of other media. A favorable decision rests on the conviction that newspapers, as a medium, are continuing to provide a high level of coverage at a competitive cost efficiency, which advertisers define as the cost per thousand people (or potential customers) reached. As we see in Chapter 2, when big papers lose readers, newspaper cost-per-thousand goes up even when advertising rates stay the same, but little papers are the first to be lopped off the list when newspaper advertising budgets are trimmed. So all newspapers are affected.

To understand what has happened to influence advertisers' judgments and plans, we must examine the relationship between the newspaper and the population whose territory it serves, the relationship between its civic functions in the community and its marketing function for advertisers.

NEWSPAPERS AND THEIR MARKETS

The vast geographic expanse of the United States inhibited the rise of newspapers like those that for a century have blanketed European countries and Japan, distributed by rail overnight from the capital city. The coming of satellite communication expanded the possibilities for national newspapers in the United States. To the *Wall Street Journal* (1987 circulation 1,961,846), the *Christian Science Monitor* (169,925), and the National Edition of *The New York Times* (158,909) was added *USA Today*, published in 34 different locations in the United States and two abroad.

Gannett invested an estimated $700 million in *USA Today*, directly or indirectly, before it turned its first quarter's profit in 1987. This included $210 million for new color equipment installed to print the paper at local Gannett dailies and charged against their own capital budgets.

Although some publishers initially feared that *USA Today* might steal some of their readers, that paper turned out to be additional reading material rather than a substitution for most of its audience. On any given day, only 6% of the readers of this national daily (and 6% of the readers of the *Wall Street Journal*) were not also reading a local paper. In fact, without the 1,324,000 paid circulation of *USA Today* (1,631,000 including bulk sales to airlines and hotels), the total weekday circulation of the American press would have shown a drop between 1981 and 1987 instead of showing a slight increase.

A major national newspaper, whether it is edited in the elite style of the *Guardian* or *Le Monde* or the popular style of the *Sun* or *France-Soir*, typically has a constituency that is based in a social class or political segment. Still, it is a force for national unity, since it provides a common fund of information and intellectual capital for a diverse and geographically scattered population. The "home town" press of the United States is, by contrast, a force for diversity, for the assertion of local interests and local differences.

The localized American press, in distinction to the national press elsewhere, has drawn its strength from a special ability to embody the sense of community identity that gives people roots, that defines for them who they are. Newspapers fix people in space; they say, "This is important to me as a resident and citizen and customer of this town." And historically, they also fixed people in terms of lifestyle and outlook. When readers have contrasting competitive papers to choose among, they can identify more closely with the one they have chosen.

The ties that bind individuals within a given geographic orbit are also crucial to the merchants who are the newspaper's main source of advertising income. People shop within the radius of transportation that is convenient and familiar to them. But what is familiar is inseparable from what is advertised in the local media that define their world.

The polar concepts of "community" and "society" have fascinated sociologists for nearly a century of mankind's movement into an epoch of mass production, mass contact, mass media, and mass mobility. The warm personal relationships that characterize community ties are often contrasted with the tenuous, impersonal, secular relationships that we associate with the Great Society.[15]

If the concept of community involves those human relationships based on spatial propinquity, which are personal, intimate, and based on the primary group, so the concept of the market reflects, in its origins, at least, those relationships based on spatial propinquity which are economic and, therefore, as impersonal as they can be.

To be sure, the relation between seller and buyer, between merchant and customer, can be as intimate and intense as any that human beings can have. Anyone who has struck a bargain in an Oriental bazaar knows that the prevailing code of negotiation places more stress on the game, on the contest of wills and wits, than on the actual economics of the transaction.

But in its historical origins, the emergence of the market suggests the evolution of an impersonal social order. In the classic folk society where neighbors are bound together by kinship and friendship ties that pervade all areas and aspects of life, economic activity is indistinguishable from other cooperative efforts that express the feelings of solidarity and cohesion.

A market must be on neutral ground. It must provide a physical location symbolically separate from personal ties. The bazaar, at the crossroads or at the ford on the river, admirably fills this function. It is a place to which people from different villages may come to exchange their specialized goods and services. In the market one encounters friends in the midst of strangers. Since earliest history, the exchange of gossip and news has been intermingled with the exchange of goods and services. The market is the point at which the horizons of the individual's daily world are extended to encompass the surrounding environment. In the context of the market, the division of labor becomes most meaningful in human terms, as common interests or occupa-

---

[15]See Ferdinand Toennies, *Community and Society* (East Lansing: Michigan State University Press, 1957). Also Robert Redfield, *The Little Community: Viewpoints for the Study of a Human Whole*, the Gottesman Lectures, Uppsala University, 1935 (Almquist & Wiksells Boktrycker, AB Uppsala, 1955). See also Henry Maine, *Village Communities East and West* (New York: Henry Holt & Company, 1889). For a thoughtful discussion of both theory and recent research on this subject, as it applies to newspapers, see Keith R. Stamm, *Newspaper Use and Community Ties: Toward a Dynamic Theory* (Norwood, NJ: Ablex, 1985).

tional roles provide a better basis for rapport than mere residential contiguity.

The weekly bazaar settles down and becomes permanent as tradesmen and vendors establish their habitations where they trade and as still others come to provide them with services. The market as an event in time is replaced by the market as a place where people live as well as visit and (later) as inseparable from the community itself.

In time, the notion of a market as identical with a town broadened into the concept of a trading area from which people are drawn to do their business. The American rural sociologists of the 1920s were fascinated with the radius of influence that a town casts upon its hinterland.[16] They observed that people were subject to the competing influence of different markets and that they would be drawn to one or the other depending on distances, the expense and importance of the purchase, and the size of the market.

In the late 19th century, the invention of the streetcar permitted the expansion of cities by extending the feasible range of commuting to work or shopping.[17] But the invention of the automobile has even more drastically changed the relationship between markets and their hinterlands. Throughout the Western world, but most notably in the United States, the population explosion has created vast built-up areas in which the civic boundaries laid out a hundred years earlier on a surveyor's map no longer set realistic limits on the daily flow of population, the movement of goods, the relationship of residence to work, or schooling or friendship associations.

CITY AND SUBURB

The city began as people gathered behind a protective wall. Cities began as marketplaces, as temple sites, as seats of royal power. However diversified the population, each city unified civic consciousness, economic functions, and political jurisdiction. As the cities of Europe grew, they swallowed their suburbs.

In North America, the palisades that protected pioneer settlements came down within a generation. Until the end of the 19th century, and in some cases beyond, municipal boundary lines were extended to reflect the realities of urban growth. In more recent years, the process of municipal expansion has been generally halted, often by rurally dominated state legislatures.

---

[16]As an illustration, see Augustus Washington Hayes, *Rural Sociology* (New York: Longmans, Green & Company, 1929), pp. 284–298.

[17]Samuel B. Warner, Jr., *Street Car Suburbs* (Cambridge, MA: Harvard University Press, 1962).

There are exceptional cases (Indianapolis, Jacksonville, Houston) where suburbs continue to be absorbed and others (Los Angeles) where boundary lines have from the start been drawn to encompass vast open territories for future expansion. But in most instances, the central city of a metropolitan area can today be defined primarily as a governmental jurisdiction. At its outer edges, the racial and social-class character of the population, the density of its housing, and the lines of its transportation network are likely to be indistinguishable from those of suburban towns, villages, and satellite cities on its borders.

The socioeconomic life of an urban region is indivisible. An infinite series of linkages connects people and institutions of a metropolitan area. They are meshed into a common web of utilities, transportation and communications arteries, financial channels, legal and cultural institutions, specialized skills and services, as well as the traditional networks of trade and work.

The division between suburb and city, originally a distinction between what lay outside the walls and what lay within, has become in popular conception the distinction between middle-class neighborhoods and the built-up business center downtown with its periphery of night life, hotels, and rooming houses, and a surrounding belt of deteriorated working-class and immigrant housing. Beyond, large parts of most American cities consisted of residential neighborhoods that had grass, trees, a certain degree of tranquility and even vestiges of community spirit. Such neighborhoods were until recent years considered by their residents to be suburban in nature, and so they still seem in apposition to the inner city, that euphemism for the downtown slums that have steadily expanded to encompass large sections far from the core.

It is this distinction between inner-city and suburban areas that, despite its increasing imprecision, governs the psychology of those who consider themselves suburbanites. Consider what are generally characterized as urban problems—deterioration of housing, destruction of public facilities, crime, drug abuse, the perpetuation of poverty. These problems are likely to be defined less in terms of social class than race, for by 1980 nearly 27% of the population of the 10 largest cities was Black and another 12% was Hispanic and Oriental. The minority proportion of the public school population was much higher.

The traditional growth pattern of American cities before World War II saw successive waves of immigrants work their way through the slums of the central city and into outlying residential neighborhoods, abandoning at least part of their ethnic identity in the process. But the barriers of discrimination have slowed or blocked this process for Black immigrants from the rural South or for Chicanos and Puerto Ricans. Huge federally aided, low-rent apartment projects have tended to harden the racial composition of downtown residential districts. Even in predominantly White cities like Boston and San Francisco, the suburbanite looking across the municipal borders sees a preoccupation with matters that he[18] regards in racial terms. Welfare recipients, dope pushers, muggers, and rioters are the inhabitants of an alien and hostile world from which he believes he has every reason to insulate himself.

As the city's population changes and shrinks, there is a concomitant change in the function of the central business district. Going out is done by car, and it gravitates toward the shopping centers at the fringes. Downtowns thought to be dangerous after dark lose their attractive power. Parking lots and forbidding glass facades of office buildings replace shops. The connective tissue of streets is destroyed for thruways and traffic circles. While outside of town Holiday Inns and Howard Johnsons multiply on the highway interchanges, many downtown hotels have been boarded up. Department stores close or move to the suburbs. TV has emptied the great movie palaces. Pedestrian traffic is scant and furtive after offices close.

The full extent of this grim picture can best be perceived in contrast to the vitality of urban life in other countries, including many whose material standard of living is far lower than that in the United States but which continue to supply the city dweller with the amenities and the liveliness that make for a sense of place. Much of this contrast reflects the interpersonal stimulation that is possible only when people move about on foot.

THE SPREAD OF INTERURBIA

In his book, *Megalopolis*,[19] the French geographer, Jean Gottmann, has vividly portrayed the development of vast urbanized population belts in the American Northeast, in the North Central Region, and in California. A densely populated connecting network along highways and railroads leads from town to town in a continuous sprawl with occasional focal points.

The homogenization of architecture and highways creates a world without landmarks in which the significant nodal points are smothered in identical row houses, hamburger stands, and gasoline stations.

The inhabitants of this urbanized zone share the common culture and values of the metropolitan society. The traditional definitions of community, city, market are made obsolete. The term *Interurbia* has been used to describe the growing tendency of major metropolitan areas to link up with each other.[20]

The development of interurban sprawl is unthinkable except as the

---

[18]This pronoun is used throughout this book in its traditional generic sense.

[19]Jean Gottmann, *Megalopolis, the Urbanized Northeastern Seabord of the United States* (New York: The Twentieth Century Fund, 1961).

[20]*Interurbia, the Changing Face of America* (J.Walter Thompson Co., no date).

product of a population growth that has taken place most rapidly in suburban areas. This concentrated growth has been one of the features of a mobile society in which one out of six persons moves every year and in which 42% of all people live today in a residence different from the one they occupied five years ago.

The world of Interurbia does not fit the description of suburbia that seemed appropriate a generation ago.[21] In the classical suburbia of the commuter trains (Bronxville, Winnetka, Newton, or Chevy Chase) life has a simple two-way flow from suburb to city and back. Every resident has a certain primary loyalty to the community. This is where one sends children to school, goes to church, has friends, plays, and shops for the main necessities of life.

The central city is the place of employment, the place where one goes for major shopping and entertainment, where special private interests can be pursued. Membership in the local community and membership in the metropolitan area community are compatible and clearly differentiated as to function.

By contrast, the very nature of residence in the interurban society involves multilateral pressures. The outside attraction is not all from one direction. It may come from a number of different places. There is a choice of focal points for work, for voluntary association, for friendship contacts, for the pursuit of avocational interests, and for shopping. People living next door to each other on the same street in an identical row of houses may leave for work in the morning with entirely different destinations. On the weekend, they may head for still different places to go shopping or to a show.

To be sure, they retain residual loyalties to those institutions rooted in their community of residence, to the common schools and churches. They share common interests in the local institutions that minister to the physical space—the police, fire, and sanitation departments, and the like. But these functions may assume relatively less significance in a community that lacks the consensus that arises in suburbia where everyone is oriented toward the same metropolitan center.

Most suburbs have long ago ceased to be mere dormitories as factories and offices have moved out of the city center and into their midst. By the late 1980s, the vast majority of suburban workers were employed outside the central city, either in the same suburban community of in other locations in the area. In households with several family members working, it became increasingly common to find them commuting in different directions.

More diversified patterns of daily transportation also led to more scattered patterns of entertainment, eating out, and shopping.

---

[21]George Lundberg, *Leisure: A Suburban Study* (New York: Columbia University Press, 1934), Ch. II. Also, Harlan Douglass, *The Suburban Trend* (New York: Century, 1925), pp. 3–37.

MARKETS OUTSIDE SPACE

The changing pattern of human activity within a geographical area has weakened the traditional definition of the market as a place where people live and buy. Thus, it has become common to use the term "market" differently than in the past, that is, to define a sector of society distinguished by a common state of mind, a common set of interests, or a common position in the life cycle.

It is now common to speak of the teenage market; the market of junior executives; the market of fashion-minded, upper-income matrons; or the market of young mothers. This way of thinking has its roots in the very realistic observation that people's social relationships and social identities no longer always center on the places where they live. Similarity of occupational or social roles may be much more important in providing them with a common realm of discourse or interest.

This has been reinforced by the emergence of media, particularly magazines, which cater to special interests and which give them a sense of identity both to the members of the particular group to whose interests they are directed and also to advertisers.

Mass media only came into existence when the web of interpersonal contact and gossip grew too complex to serve the needs of a society increasingly segmented in its interests and spread over space. Historically, the mass media have been a force of social cohesion insofar as they provide commonly known symbols and heroes and a sense of vicarious participation in events of common interest.

For more and more people, these symbolic bonds are based on criteria other than geography. And the decline of urban identity has had a profound effect on American newspapers.

THE DECLINE OF CIVIC SPIRIT

Urban problems are commonly discussed in terms of symptoms (crime, poverty) or in terms of population movements. But urban problems can also be traced to a decline of civic identification and pride, which is partly due to a change in the competitive structure of mass media. The arbitrary boundary line between city and suburb has sapped vitality, population, the tax base, and, perhaps most important, civic concern. The sociological notion of an urban power structure assumes that every town has an elite of economically potent individuals with interlocking social connections who make the key decisions. We catch glimpses of these mysterious and patrician presences through the curtained windows of their Victorian drawing rooms in the novels of Edith Wharton and J. P. Marquand. The merchants, manufacturers, and bankers who formed this elite at the turn of the century were themselves residents of the city. Their own personal lives were very much bound up with the fortunes of the city itself. While they no doubt acted to preserve their own interests, they also contributed their talents to the management of civic affairs.

The downtown clubs of America's great cities continue to attract luncheon crowds of businessmen, but their evening emptiness signals the loss of their civic function. Now, not only tycoons, but a very large section of the middle class, have fled to residential neighborhoods outside the municipal boundaries. The economic self-interest of businessmen with offices downtown is now likely to be divorced from their personal interests as citizen-residents.

As businessmen (including newspaper publishers) use the city more and more only as a place to work, new economic pressures are impelling their business interests out of the city, too. The same urban problems that make the city repellent as a place of residence also make it more difficult to do business there.

The very fact that the suburbs are not linked to the central city by a common tax base, a common set of financial responsibilities, a common pool of civic leadership, and a common set of services and institutions has made for a growing disparity in city and suburban lifestyles. The disparity is reflected also in sharp differences between city and suburb in the average person's identification with the area he lives in, his sense of responsibility for its physical appearance, and for the efficiency of its government. All these differences, I must reiterate, go back to the arbitrary political distinction between city and suburb.

The psychological ties between people and their geographic environment evolve partly through the political system and through the periodic ritual of voting for candidates with a specific constituency. In part, they are the creation of the school system. But overwhelmingly, the sense of being part of a city, its scene, and its problems has been the creation of the mass media, especially of the daily press.

THE NEWSPAPER AND THE MARKET

The expansion of the press in both Europe and the United States coincided with the great growth of cities throughout the 19th and early 20th centuries. The growth of mass-circulation newspapers had technological causes; it was also both the cause and effect of a new municipal consciousness.

Newspaper reading increased as cities grew, and the reader's awareness of his city was in turn heightened by the visibility that newspapers gave to municipal personalities and problems. The newspaper provided a common fund of reference points of personality as well as place: people who held office and sought office, objects of adulation or gossip, figures of achievement or scandal. Their names and portraits aroused interest and discussion precisely because they were figures in a local drama in which every newspaper reader could feel himself at least a minor player. The interest was heightened because a highly competitive press constantly presented these common reference points from alternative points of view. Competing newspapers held up different facets of the city's affairs to scrutiny and speculation and often clashed dramatically in their editorial opinions.

Unlike Europe's national and partisan press, U.S. daily newspapers competed predominantly on the municipal level. The circulation range for a daily newspaper was primarily bounded by its distance from other cities and by its time of publication. Streetcars at the end of the 19th century, and motor trucks in the 20th permitted timely delivery of newspapers over larger regions. Different papers competing in the same towns chose to limit or spread out their physical distribution and editorial coverage to different radial distances from the central city. Morning newspapers printed during the night were, of course, able to distribute over a wider range than afternoon papers. By and large, however, the geographical area within which happenings were regularly reported as local news coincided with the area from which the newspaper drew the bulk of its readers.

For the newspaper's editors, it was more efficient and less expensive to provide news coverage of municipal affairs in which *most* of their readers were interested than to attempt comparable reportage for all the towns and villages in the outlying areas where *some* copies were purchased. For a reader in one of these outlying areas, the metropolitan newspaper's occasional stories about his own community might be far too sketchy. Weekly newspapers arose to fill the needs of growing communities outside the central city as well as neighborhoods within the city.

The area in which a daily newspaper found its readers, and in which its editors found news, also tended to be congruent with the area from which its advertisers drew their business. These spheres corresponded closely to the boundary lines of the city itself. Stores that advertised in the paper were downtown stores, and their owners expected people who read the newspaper in outlying residential neighborhoods to travel downtown to do their shopping. In addition, manufacturers who advertised their products in the newspaper had their distributors and warehouses downtown; they bought advertising in many cities' papers to cover the many distribution centers, or "markets."

Even before the government adopted the useful concept of the Standard Metropolitan Statistical Area (based on population density) in 1949, newspapers had invented the "retail trading zone" to describe the wider area, extending beyond municipal borders, in which they had a substantial concentration of readers. This measure provided their advertisers with a bonus of useful circulation outside the city itself.

Some advertisers had more to gain than others from the extensions of a newspaper's coverage. A national advertiser whose product was widely distributed wanted the greatest possible reach. A major department store or a retailer providing highly specialized goods or services might similarly want to attract customers from a very broad region.

Stores attract customers from a wider area for some kinds of merchandise than for others. Marketers have long been familiar with Reilly's Law, which simply says that people are willing to travel further to shop for larger purchases.

For many smaller merchants whose customers were concentrated in town, the newspaper's circulation in the hinterlands represented waste, for which they had to pay as the price of efficiently covering their own primary market. But the purely local merchant's importance to the newspaper also declined.

THE TRANSFORMATION OF RETAILING

Concurrent with the trends that have changed the relationship of city and suburbs has come a transformation in retailing with important implications for the structure of the American press. Its chief characteristics are: (a) concentration of ownership and control and (b) geographic dispersion.

Large chain organizations have won a growing share of the market as small family owned and operated stores go out of business and are not replaced. Chains' share of the grocery business grew from 38% in 1950 to 58% in 1987. In 1987, 28 chain organizations with sales of over a billion dollars each accounted for 44% of all general merchandise sold in the United States.

The chains that have experienced the most dramatic growth are those whose special forte has been the identification of new growth opportunities for suburban store locations. (The K-Mart chain, which increased its volume from $1.7 billion in 1968 to $21.3 billion in 1987, grew from 273 to 2,086 stores in that period—all outside traditional downtowns.)

With this growth, chain organizations have tightened the coordination and control of their merchandising and advertising at the headquarters level to permit operating efficiencies and a higher degree of professionalism; store brands can thus be promoted with identical campaigns from coast to coast. This centralization has changed the nature of the buyer–seller relationship between the individual newspaper and its major retail accounts, which represent the economic underpinnings of its business.

Traditionally, newspaper publishers were bound by personal relationships to the owners of the principal retail stores in town. The managers of the new chain stores are men on the move, each ascending his own organizational ladder and working hard to achieve a transfer to a bigger job in another city. They are less likely to seek or gain admittance into the social network of the local Establishment.

Much of the growth of chain retailing organizations has come about through the construction of new suburban stores, either at shopping centers or at independent sites. In acquiring real estate, retailers attach great weight to the ability of local advertising media to cover efficiently the area from which new customers can be drawn. A new chain outlet is rarely located in isolation. Instead, it is usually located as part of a cluster of stores that can be supported by a single advertising schedule. Central-city locations are almost never sought by the chains. While department stores of the traditional type now do most of their volume through suburban branches, in many cases they have been locked into unprofitable sites downtown by old real estate commitments. Some retailers have abandoned their downtown flagship stores or have gone out of business altogether.

This reorientation took place in the early 1960s, at about the same time as the expansion of the interstate highway system, which cut through and superseded the old network of roads and rails that tied each city to its hinterland. This new system accelerated the movements of warehouses and processing plants to the outer edges of the market and away from downtown locations at the railhead.

Pilferage, vandalism, and other security problems have been greater in downtown store locations. Staffing is more difficult. The customer pool is less affluent. But apart from the specific ailments of the central city itself, central-city circulation has had diminishing value for many advertisers. Over 80% of all retail business in the United States is now conducted outside of the traditional downtown business districts, 54% in shopping centers.

As retailers drew more of their business from the suburban areas, they tended to shift away from traditional advertising outlets. They made greater use of free weekly newspapers ("shoppers") made up entirely or largely of advertising. (I have more to say about them in the next chapter.) Such publications provide pinpointed coverage of every household in the smaller communities from which specific stores or shopping centers draw their customers. The per capita cost of delivering their message is often high, but the total outlay is less than would be necessary to cover the entire metropolitan region through the daily press, which reaches a great many people from whom a particular suburban store is unlikely to draw business.

Other advertisers distributed advertising circulars door-to-door in the particular areas they wanted to cover. Above all, they made greater use of direct mail.

To the degree that these selective forms of advertising are substituted for space in the metropolitan newspaper, that paper becomes less attractive to readers, since, as we note later, advertising represents one of its most useful and informative features.

Paradoxically, as some retailers have chosen to narrow the reach of their advertising, others have moved to broaden it by using television. A television signal can be received in a much wider area than the circulation zone of a typical daily newspaper. A retail chain can promote its store name throughout the reception range of a centrally located television transmitter in what may add up to a number of different daily newspaper markets. When the 30-second commercial became standard in U.S. television in the late 1960s, the number of available advertising units vastly increased. This prompted a heavy selling effort aimed at merchants, the last frontier of potential new business for television, which has been predominantly a national advertising medium. Although the 15-second commercial made its debut on the networks (and represented a third of all network commercials in 1987) it appeared destined to become the standard on spot television as well. In doubling the inventory of positions for sale, it was inevitable that television would redouble its efforts to get local advertising.

Since 1960, retailers' spending in newspapers (which remain their dominant medium) grew sevenfold, but they increased their spending in television by a factor of 25. Local advertisers in 1987 spent four dollars in radio and TV for every five they put into newspapers. The loss of share has been especially serious for the weaker papers in competitive markets.

MARKETS AND MANUFACTURERS

The effects of competition have been even more severe for newspaper national advertising. Television cuts across barriers of distance and geography that have traditionally determined and defined markets. The bulk of its audience watches national network programming. Thus, television tends to subordinate and obscure local market differences. Television's market definitions have facilitated that medium's selling effort.

In more recent years, the definition of viewing areas has been based on annual surveys conducted in all of the nation's 3,138 counties by the two leading broadcast rating services. The American Research Bureau's "Area of Dominant Influence" (ADI) and the A. C. Nielsen "Designated Market Area" (DMA) represent virtually identical aggregates of counties in which most people report that at least half of their viewing focuses on stations located in a particular city. The practice of defining TV markets by this method quickly won popularity among advertising agency planners, because every county in the United States could be automatically assigned to one or another of the 213 ADIs or DMAs. This was simple compared with the problems posed by the 2,162 towns with radio stations and the 1,536 towns with daily newspapers with all kinds of overlapping coverage patterns and (in the case of newspapers) with many rural counties left unassigned to any city.

As television became the dominant medium of national advertising, media planning became more and more a matter of organizing information in television terms. For many large package goods companies, whose advertising and promotion represent a major cost of business, it has become increasingly common to assemble sales data on an ADI basis in order to measure television advertising performance. From this it is only a small step to align sales territories to conform to ADI lines, thus making this the standard unit of sales planning and management, as well as of sales analysis.

The increased acceptance of the ADI definition has substantially affected not only the disposition of advertising investments, but the whole organization of corporate selling activity. It has resulted in a shift of investment strategy among markets. It also has shifted the competitive balance among media, since television will always look better in cost efficiency if measured on a television base, just as newspapers look better when measured on a newspaper base. Moreover, specific newspapers rank higher when arrayed on one basis than on another. Advertisers using comparable yardsticks of efficiency tend to come up with similar solutions to their media selection problems, thereby abetting the tendency to concentrate budgets in the strongest newspaper of each market, out of all proportion to its share of total circulation. The converse occurs to sap the advertising support of the weaker papers in a market, no matter how many faithful readers they have or how excellently they fulfill their editorial functions.

To the new breed of corporate marketers (and to their counterparts in mass merchandising), the realities of flesh and blood, of steel and stone, that used to constitute a market have given way to the data that can be manipulated as computer input: product sales figures, census statistics reflecting sales potential, and cost-per-thousand calculations based on media audience ratings. Mechanistically applied statistical criteria tend to replace qualitative judgments regarding the definition and character of an urban region as well as its desirability as a place to market goods. Inevitably, this standard means a loss of interest in the patterns of human movement and affiliation, the flow of information, the nature of civic identifications and loyalties, and all the other subtle strands that make up the fabric of urban life.

To the degree that advertisers ignore the natural human ecology of the markets in which they distribute and sell goods, they are abetting the process of urban disintegration. For national advertisers, as for retailers, this disregard may be at variance with their long-term advantage.

The changes in marketing and advertising practice are themselves products of the complex transformation of the American scene that has been sketched in this chapter. It is against this swiftly moving background that we must see the place of newspapers in society and in the lives of their readers. Although this book is concerned with the ideas that newspapers communicate, the dissemination of those ideas reflects the organization and operation of newspapers as economic institutions.

2
THE BUSINESS OF
NEWSPAPERS

"Not for love, honor or fame, but for cash." This was the masthead motto of the *Marble Hill* (Indiana) *Era* in 1894. Many publishers today may still consider it a guiding principle, but few would be willing to say so.

The relationship of newspapers to their readers can be understood only when we know something of their economic underpinnings. Freedom of the press is a meaningless concept unless a society can afford one. For readers to read what reporters report and editors edit, publishers must meet their bills, pay their payrolls, and earn the profits that give them the incentive to stay in the newspaper business. This little homily may seem elementary, yet much criticism of newspapers is offered in disregard of its implications. The alternative to an independent, profit-making press is one that is subsidized by the State and responsible to its rulers. And yet to look at newspapers only by the criterion of profit and loss misses their real meaning and value.

American newspapers are a large and profitable business. In 1986, according to Veronis, Suhler, and Associates, newspapers' pretax income totaled $2.5 billion, and their return on $105 billion in assets was 27%. Through the 1980s, newspapers' pretax profits were in the range of 20%, compared with a level higher than 35% for a typical network-affiliated television station. (In the top 10 markets, TV station profits reached 47%.) By comparison, the pretax profit for Standard and Poor's 400 leading industrial companies was 13.5% in 1986. During the 1980s, the average publicly traded newspaper company stock outperformed the New York Stock Exchange Composite Index by more than two to one.

Harry Henry, a leading British market researcher, has argued that newsprint consumption is a far better index of demand for newspapers than the number of copies sold. He suggests that the increased physical bulk of newspapers makes possible an increased flow of information. This tends in the aggregate to reduce the daily demand for newspapers, but it also compensates for the resulting dip in readership. By the same token, Henry argues that the number of individual newspaper titles published "is no indicator whatever of the size of the total newspaper market." He pursues this point to an analogy with package goods, where

> the number of brands in any one product category is no indicator of the category's market size, and indeed growth of the market may well be associated with a diminution of the number of brands . . . just as the size of the market for a grocery commodity is most realistically measured in terms of tonnage, so the size of the newspaper market is most meaningfully assessed in terms of national newsprint consumption.[1]

While this intriguing proposition might be demonstrable in purely economic terms, the press as a political, cultural, and social institution is more than just another business, and the quantities of newsprint it consumes (16% more in 1987 than in 1980, in spite of conservation measures) are not the only indicator of its vitality. The ability of newspapers to consume newsprint depends on their ability to sustain their advertising, which arises from their ability to attract readers.

In Chapter 1, I mentioned that in the American advertising marketplace, newspapers can remain competitive with other media only if they stay in line by the criterion of cost per thousand readers (CPM). If they raise their advertising rates without increasing their audiences, their CPM goes up and their share of advertising is endangered. If they charge readers more, and lose some in the process, their CPM goes up even if their advertising rates stay the same. Newspaper publishers have had to juggle these considerations as they encountered massive rises in newsprint, ink, and energy costs.

THE IMPORTANCE OF ADVERTISING

Advertisers' investment of $31 billion in 1988 was not equivalent to newspaper revenues, since it included commissions paid to advertising agencies and representatives, as well as print, engraving, and other production

---

[1]"The Astonishing Stability of the Newspaper Market," *Ad Map*, April 1976, p. 160.

expenses. The total amount spent by advertisers of all kinds in all media in 1988 was about $118 billion, giving newspapers a 26.4% share. In 1930, long before the advent of television, newspapers' share was 29.8%. Newspapers increased their share (to 39%) through the decade of the Depression, during which total advertising volume underwent a considerable loss. But as national advertising came on strong in the post-World War II economic expansion, newspapers' share of the total dropped while their advertising income grew four and a half times (1940–1960). The major impact of television on the other media came during the 1950s. By 1960, its penetration was almost universal. For the last two decades, advertisers have continued to spend nearly 3 out of 10 dollars on newspapers, which is actually 34% of their spending in consumer media. (See Table 2.1; the *Other* category includes business-to-business advertising and administrative costs.)

However, the mix of newspaper advertising has changed in that period (Table 2.2). Classified ads have gained in importance as a source of income. (In 1988, they accounted for 41% of the revenues, even though they were only 37% of the money advertisers spent—including what they paid printers to produce newspaper inserts.) National advertising represents only about an eighth of newspapers' total and only 11% of all national advertising in consumer media. (Television has over half.) The mainstay of newspaper advertising continues to be local display advertising, mostly placed by retail stores, and as we saw in the last chapter, the competition for these dollars has become more acute and more complex.

American newspapers of colonial times treated advertising as a form of news and interspersed it with other items on the front page, presumably because it was considered interesting to readers. But the readers were the paper's main source of revenues, and until a century ago advertising filled less than half the columns. Today, it has the lion's share of the space on most days in most newspapers, even more in big papers than in small ones. But because

TABLE 2.1
Advertising Investments and Media Share, 1940–87[a]

	1940	1950	1960	1970	1980	1988
Newspapers	39%	36%	31%	29%	28%	26%
Magazines	10	9	8	7	6	5
Radio	10	11	6	7	7	7
Television	–	3	14	18	21	22
Direct mail	16	14	15	14	14	17
Other	25	27	26	25	24	23
	100%	100%	100%	100%	100%	100%
Total $ (in billions)	$2.11	$5.70	$11.96	$19.55	$53.61	$118.69

[a]Source: McCann–Erickson, Inc.

TABLE 2.2
The Changing Mix of Newspaper Advertising, 1940–87

	1940	1950	1960	1970	1980	1988
National	20%	25%	21%	16%	13%	12%
Retail	61	57	57	58	58	51
Classified	19	18	22	27	29	37
	100%	100%	100%	100%	100%	100%
Total $ (in billions)	$.82	$2.07	$3.68	$5.70	$14.79	$31.10

of differences in rate structures between small and large papers, advertising provides four-fifths of the publisher's income, regardless of the paper's size. However, advertising expenditures are highly concentrated. In 1987, 120 papers of over 100,000 circulation generated 70% of all newspaper advertising and 88% of all national advertising.

How much would a daily newspaper cost the reader if it carried no advertising? The best place to begin answering this question is by examining the data from the Inland Daily Press Association's periodic analysis of revenues and expenses, which compiles and averages the figures supplied by hundreds of dailies of all sizes. Table 2.3, adapted from the results of this survey for 1986, compares the breakdown of expenditures for four hypothetical newspapers with circulations respectively of 5,000, 25,000, 75,000, and 200,000. Mechanical costs represent a much larger share of the operating budget of the typical small paper than of the typical large one, whereas newsprint, ink, and handling charges are the largest single cost item for the large paper and less significant to the small one. Circulation and distribution expense goes up as circulation increases (though not in direct proportion), while news, and advertising department costs go down in relation to the

TABLE 2.3
Aproximate Breakdown of Total Expenditures for Newspapers
of Different Circulation Sizes, 1986

	5,000	25,000	75,000	200,000
News and editorial	16%	15%	15%	12%
Advertising department	10	9	9	7
Circulation & distribution	12	13	15	16
Mechanical	18	13	10	11
Newsprint, ink, handling	9	17	20	22
General administration	35	33	31	32
	100%	100%	100%	100%
Total $ (in thousands)	$730	$5,100	$20,600	$61,700

total.[2] According to two security analysts, Eric Philo and Barry Kaplan of Goldman Sachs, labor is 40% of newspaper costs; production labor, 25% to 30%. Half of that is in composing and the mailroom, both of which have been strongly affected by automation.

A paper without advertising could eliminate the cost of its advertising department, of course, and it could reduce its newsprint and ink bill in direct proportion to the amount of space that advertising represents (ranging from 40% for a typical daily of 5,000 to 65% for one of 200,000 circulation). General administrative and overhead costs might be cut by about 15%, but most of the charges that come under this heading are fixed ones. With advertising eliminated, the costs of composition and printing might be cut by about 20%. But news and distribution expenses would remain essentially unchanged, and owners would not be happy with a reduction of return on their investments. The carrier or vendor usually keeps about a third of the amount the reader pays for the paper, and his share normally stays the same when the price goes up.

When all the numbers are put together, it is apparent that a newspaper that currently sells for 30¢ would have to sell for about $1.15 a copy—*and* maintain its present circulation—in order to cover its operating expenses and its present net income.

But, of course, present levels of circulation could not be maintained in the face of such a massive price increase, and every subsequent loss of readership would have to be matched by corresponding price hikes to the remaining readers or by severe reductions of editorial content—a spiral process that could only result in the extinction of the press as it has functioned historically.

All this reasoning, however, fails to take into account a critical consideration in newspaper economics. The advertising that newspapers carry is more than their largest source of income; it also represents one of the most valuable services they offer readers. Shopping is not only an important activity; it is a form of entertainment. And shopping wisely and economically is a skill on which most people pride themselves. So there is an important utility to newspaper ads that keep people in touch with the marketplace and that save them time and steps before they visit the store.

THE UTILITY OF NEWSPAPER ADVERTISING

A variety of surveys have shown that newspaper advertising is especially welcome to readers and that it is perceived as informative and useful, much as editorial content is. In fact, 75% of the men and 84% of the women affirmed

---

[2]For a typical consumer magazine, 28.5% of expenses are circulation sales; 34%, printing and distribution; 9%, ad sales; 9%, editorial; 9.5%, administration; and 10%, profit. (*Media Matters*, September 1987.)

in 1961 that they "like to look at newspaper ads even when I do not plan to buy anything." In 1974, three out of four women (in five cities) agreed that, "When I read the newspaper, I am about equally interested in the advertising and news stories." Our 1967 survey found that the average ad evoked a level of personal interest about three-fifths as great as the average article. And studies of how readers move through the paper make it clear that attention moves readily from ads to editorial matter and back as the reader scans the pages in the continuing search for what is meaningful, relevant, or fun to think about.

Apart from the attitude surveys, however, circulation figures indicate that readers tend to go where the advertising is available, just as advertisers tend to follow the readers. There are exceptions to this rule, when one paper goes after the upper income sector of a market and another goes after the mass. But in general, a fat paper that is full of ads is one that people consider attractive.

Among the advertising media, the newspaper seems to have a uniquely favorable position that reflects its utilitarian character. Among the public, 44% say they look forward to newspaper advertising; 29%, to advertising in magazines; 10%, to radio commercials; and 9%, to advertising on TV (1977). Older people are somewhat more favorable to broadcast advertising, and people of lower education are more likely to say they look forward to ads in all media.

A 1976 Harris study for Sentry Life Insurance Company found that 46% of the public consider all or most TV advertising "seriously misleading." For newspaper and magazine advertising the comparable figure was 28%. Similarly, a survey for the American Association of Advertising Agencies in 1976 found 68% of the public completely or mostly favorable toward advertising in newspapers and 40% favorable to advertising in television. (The corresponding figure for magazine advertising was 58%; for radio, 47%; and for direct mail, 15%.)

In a telephone survey of 1,001 adults, conducted in 1981 by the Opinion Research Corporation, we asked how believable advertising was in each of five media. Sixty-eight percent described newspaper advertising as believable or very believable, compared with 59% for radio, 52% for magazines, 34% for television, and 25% for direct mail. Fifty-three percent described direct mail advertising as unbelievable or very unbelievable; 44% said the same of television; 23%, of magazines; 18%, of radio; and 14%, of newspaper advertising. When asked to select the one most believable advertising medium, 42% named newspapers and 26%, television. Newspapers, as usual, received the most favorable response among the best educated and best off financially.

In answering questions like these, people generally think of advertising for brands or stores. Newspaper classified advertising falls into a class by itself. In the course of a week in 1979, 58% of all adults consulted newspaper classified ads at least once. The average person who did so looked at 2.7 different types of ads, either in the weekday or Sunday paper or both. Thirty percent looked at ads for general merchandise of "things for sale"; 28% checked employment listings; 28%, real estate ads; 24%, car ads; 15%, ads for services; and 14%, ads for recreational or sports equipment. These figures include both weekday and Sunday reading. When we asked about these separately in 1982, 38% of the readers reported having read classified ads in the weekday paper in the course of the past week, and 31% read them on the past Sunday. This was an understated and subjective report, because when confronted with a typical page of classified advertising from yesterday's paper, 39% remembered opening it (1987).

We can move from general attitudes to specifics. As I report in Chapter 8, the average editorial item is rated at least somewhat interesting by 57% of the men and also by 57% of the women (1977). The average local (or retail) ad receives a comparable interest score from 34% of the women and 30% of the men. The average national (brand) ad is interesting to 30% of the women and 27% of the men.

The averages do, of course, combine the scores for both sexes with respect to advertising categories that are primarily directed (as most are) either to men or to women, so these percentages actually represent a very high proportion of either sex. As with editorial matter, however, every kind of subject is of at least some interest to some members of the opposite sex. Both for national and local advertising, food ads generate the most widespread interest.

The averages are identical, incidentally, for frequent and infrequent newspaper readers. This indicates that a heightened interest in advertising does not in itself account for a more regular readership of the newspaper. But it also suggests that newspaper advertising is of interest even to people whose general interest in the paper is low.

These consistent findings indicate that there is a great attraction to many readers in newspaper advertising, quite apart from its part in providing the essential economic support of the American press. A paper with comparatively little advertising seems to be perceived by readers as having less value than one that is crammed with ads.

ADVERTISING AND THE NEWS HOLE

On any given day, the largest metropolitan papers carry seven times as many pages as a typical small town daily (Table 2.4).

Between 1980 and 1986, the average number of pages per issue went up 26% for large morning papers, 28% for evening papers, and 69% for Sunday papers. But the averages conceal great variations, by day of week, for

TABLE 2.4
Average Number of Pages
by Circulation Size, 1982

Circulation size (000s)	Pages
Over 500	100
250–500	81
150–250	65
100–150	51
50–100	43
15–50	38
15–25	27
10–15	21
Under 10	15

example. The number of pages in the paper read "yesterday" in 1982 was smaller on Monday (43 pages) and Tuesday (40) than on Wednesday (60), Thursday (69), or Friday (63). Papers of 250,000 and over averaged 91 pages, those under 25,000 averaged 23. Because the bulk of afternoon papers are published in smaller towns, they were smaller in size (39 pages) than morning papers (67).

The "news hole," in newspaper parlance, represents all the contents of the newspaper other than the advertising. The number of pages a paper can afford to run each day depends more or less on the volume of advertising to which it is committed, as well as on its press capacity. The number of nonadvertising pages has kept pace in recent years with the growth of advertising, increasing from 19.8 pages in the average large city daily in 1970 to 32.3 pages in the identical paper in 1986.[3]

The news hole takes its name from the fact that the paper is made up each day, page by page, with the advertising set in place first, so that editorial matter, and especially the late-breaking news, can be fitted in. (Unexpected events of unusual importance can, of course, require a sacrifice of advertising or the addition of extra pages to make room for news coverage.) The news hole is, however, not filled entirely with news, strictly speaking. It may contain varying amounts of feature or entertainment material, of copy, text, or white space, of staff-written copy, wire service or syndicated material, or mere fillers of space. The character of what goes into the news hole probably has more to do with readers' response to a newspaper than the sheer amount of editorial matter it prints.

Papers carry more editorial content as their advertising pages increase, but in competitive markets the weaker newspaper carries a higher ratio of news to advertising than its more successful competitor. Nonetheless, it carries less

---

[3]This analysis is based on the dailies measured by Media Records, Inc.

editorial content in terms of absolute size, and the advertising represents an added utility for the reader.[4]

Although the size of the news hole (apart from what fills it) reflects the amount of advertising that has been sold, the ability to sell space depends on maintaining circulation, and this in turn depends on the paper's ability to attract readers with good editorial coverage.

To examine this intricate three-way relationship, we analyzed circulation, advertising, and editorial space between 1960 and 1973 in all the big city papers on which data were available. (That means 79 central-city papers published in markets where aggregate daily newspaper circulation was over 100,000.)

The ratio of news to advertising was about the same in morning and evening papers. At both the start and end of the period, it was higher in (the larger) competitive markets than in (the smaller) noncompetitive ones. The news–advertising ratio was lower for papers that gained circulation since 1960 than for papers that lost. However, that is because the total number of pages, news *and* advertising, grew faster in papers that gained circulation than in those that lost. The widest variations were in the bigger competitive cities, where the a.m. papers that had added circulation had 98% more ad pages in 1973 than in 1960, while the p.m. papers that had lost circulation were up only 22% in ad pages.

An advertising executive might say that the papers that showed the largest gains in advertising had the largest increase in editorial pages and in circulation. Editors might prefer to express the relationship this way: Papers that showed the largest increase in news pages showed the largest gains in readership and in advertising. Circulators might put their own function at the starting point. However, circulation, editorial, and advertising specialists would agree that good newspaper management tends to be reflected in all departments, not just one.

The growth of the news hole is itself a function of the growth of newspaper advertising. But papers that gained circulation added both news and advertising pages at a faster rate than those that stood still or retreated. It would be

---

[4]Newspapers cut into their news hole rather than into advertising or circulation during the newsprint shortage of 1973, the Associated Press Managing Editors found from questionnaires returned by 470 papers. Sixty-three percent cut news; 9%, advertising; and only a few, circulation. A sixth of those who reduced news content said they would not restore it even when newsprint became available. In actuality, this did not happen, and news holes continued to grow. Of the papers that had cut news, nearly half said they had reduced international news first, about a fourth cut features and women's news, and one in eight cut national news. (The Minneapolis *Tribune* received 109 calls after it dropped its crossword puzzle and promptly reinstituted it.) The greatest reductions were made by papers of between 25,000 and 100,000 circulation; large papers over 200,000 were least likely to cut news and most likely to cut advertising.

cheerful to conclude (though the case is by no means proven) that those newspapers whose editorial content provides the greatest value to the reader have shown the best ability to prosper in both circulation and advertising.

WEEKLY NEWSPAPERS AND "SHOPPERS"

The growth of free weekly newspapers has presented both dailies and paid community weeklies with important new competition for advertising revenues and for readers' attention. Between 1977 and 1988, the number of paid community weeklies (and semiweeklies) listed in the comprehensive National Newspaper Association Directory fell from 6,518 to 5,451. Total circulation dropped 19%, from 25,655,000 to 20,896,000, with the average paper going from 3,986 to 3,833 copies. At the same time free papers ("shoppers") increased in number from 1,012 to 1,445, with an 89% circulation growth from 11,659,000 to 21,994,000; the average shopper's claimed distribution grew from 11,520 to 16,549.

An earlier analysis in 1978 of 323 nondaily publications in 18 markets indicated that 57% were mainly distributed free. For these shoppers, advertising ranged from 10% to 100% of the total space, with an average of 74%. ("Pennysavers" are free papers that are basically all advertising, though they sometimes include filler material like astrology columns, household hints, or other boilerplate reading matter of a nonlocal character.) For the mainly paid publications, the range was from 16% to 100%, with an average of 56%. Why should anyone pay for a publication that is all advertising? Simply because it is confined to job or real estate listings or offers to swap—a limited functional use. During the 1980s, there was a substantial growth in the number of such local publications, most of them "quarterfold" or magazine size and many with illustrations of cars or homes for sale.

Eighty percent of all adults are exposed to one or more issues of a daily paper in the course of five weekdays (MRI, 1988).[5] In addition, in the course of a week, 39% read a paid weekly and 55% look at a free one (1987).

These national figures obscure the variability in the pattern of weekly newspaper readership, which is shown by a study in four metropolitan areas where free weeklies were distributed (1978a). In one area, free newspapers were read by 72% of those interviewed, and paid weeklies by only 7%. In another area, free papers were read by 32% of the adults and paid weeklies by 35%.

Readership of free papers was substantially higher among young people who have the lowest levels of average weekday readership for daily papers,

---

[5]Mediamark Research, Inc. (MRI) is one of the nationally syndicated media audience research services.

while readership of paid weeklies was at approximately the same level for young and middle-aged people and dropped after age 65 (1977).

People who read either paid or free weeklies are more apt to be frequent readers of daily papers, too. Among women interviewed in 1974 in five cities, 78% of those who read a paid weekly newspaper read a daily regularly, but only 66% of those who were not readers of a weekly. Similarly, in Intercity (1962), a town selected as a case study (see Chapter 5), the presence and substantial readership of the local weekly newspaper did not appear to have any bearing on the daily newspaper's capacity to select its readers from the ranks of those who were oriented toward the town where it was published. Among daily newspaper readers in Intercity, 72% read the local weekly. Among those who did not read a daily, only 46% read the weekly.

The local weekly's detailed listings of real estate transactions and neighborhood social events appear to supplement rather than conflict with the daily local spot news coverage by those daily papers that maintain bureaus or correspondents in Intercity.[6]

Far more people are within reach of shoppers than actually read them. Free weekly papers or shoppers were widely available in 1987, including those published by dailies as supplements to their delivered circulation. Sixty-two percent of the public said one or more were delivered to the home; 60% said they were available in piles or racks at stores or elsewhere. In total, 82% had access to one or more free papers.

Apparently people pay more attention to a publication they have paid for than to one that simply comes their way free. Identical proportions of readers said they read most of the pages in the last issue of the daily paper they had read (72%) and in the last paid weekly they had read (73%). But a substantially smaller percentage had gone through most of the pages of the last pennysaver (54%) or other free weekly (61%) that they had looked at (1978a).

Of those who had read or looked at a shopper in the past seven days, 55% said they had "skimmed through it," 16% had "just glanced" at it, and 29% reported they read it "thoroughly" (1977). The most thorough reading was reported by those with the least education. Similarly, a 1973 study in St. Louis found that when people who had reported reading "most pages" of both a daily and a free weekly were asked which one they had read more thoroughly, 74% picked the daily.

ZONING AND "TOTAL MARKET COVERAGE"

As newspaper penetration declined in the 1970s, advertisers who wanted to saturate sales territories often turned to shoppers or to direct mail. Mail

---

[6]Cf. Morris Janowitz, *The Community Press in an Urban Setting* (Glencoe, Ill.: The Free Press, 1952). Janowitz found that neighborhood urban weeklies and metropolitan dailies served complementary functions.

advertising was stimulated by the reorganization of the U.S. Postal Service, mandated by Congress to be self-supporting, and impelled to seek new sources of revenue. The restructuring of third class postal rates made it possible for mailing houses to combine advertising from several sources into a package that fell within the minimum weight bracket and that could be sent out as presorted, occupant-addressed mail. This was not only economical for the advertiser; it jibed with a common desire to restrict advertising only to those areas from which the best customers were drawn. Thus, the rise of zip-code marketing put newspapers under new pressure to distribute advertising selectively rather than to their entire readership. Advertisers who wanted to "cherry-pick" changed newspapers' economics and thus threatened their mission as the voice of the entire community.

Faced with new competitive pressures, daily newspapers adopted a number of defensive strategies to provide Total Market Coverage (TMC).

In 1987, we were able to identify a total of 478 U.S. newspaper properties, with an aggregate paid daily circulation of about 19 million, that produced publications of their own for distribution to nonsubscribers—roughly a third of those in every circulation size bracket except for the smallest and largest papers (Table 2.5). These TMC products usually carried some nondated feature material taken from the daily paper, along with a certain amount of run-of-paper (ROP) advertising, especially from small businesses that could not afford the full run of circulation. (Many of these nonsubscriber products were put out for specific zones.) Basically, however, they provided an envelope for inserts, and in most cases they were distributed through the mail. Their distribution totaled 22 million, and daily papers had a capacity for an additional six million advertising-only deliveries by mail. This compares to our estimate of about 43 million circulation for all other nondaily papers, paid and free. Three-fifths of the papers of over 50,000 circulation, a third of those of middle size (25,000–50,000), and even a number of the small ones under 25,000 publish sectional or zoned editions once a week or more

TABLE 2.5
Percentage of Newspapers with
Nonsubscriber Publications, 1987

Circulation[a]	
Under 10,000	23
10,000–25,000	35
25,000–50,000	30
50,000–100,000	29
100,000–250,000	45
250,000–500,000	38
Over 500,000	7

[a]Based on daily totals, including combinations.

often, usually with local editorial matter (Table 2.6, 1987a). At one time, the New York *Daily News* offered advertisers 19 different sectional options at least once a week. The sectional editions of some metropolitan papers have been designed to meet competition from suburban dailies as well as from weeklies. However, in some instances they cover such large and heterogeneous territories that it is difficult to match the accompanying editorial matter to the interests of readers in dozens (or even hundreds) of separate villages and towns. Some papers have simply tightened coverage and sacrificed circulation to cut costs and preserve a homogeneous territory.

Daily newspapers had traditionally argued that advertisers gained attention and credibility from the news articles that adjoined their ads, but insert advertisers proceeded on the assumption that their customers were already highly interested in their sales and specials. For them, the paper was merely a vehicle of distribution, to be bought on a commodity basis. Newspapers' TMC products provide admirable efficiency for advertisers, but they undoubtedly encourage the idea that coverage or physical delivery of the message is of equivalent value whether it occurs involuntarily or by choice and in the context of the news. If such a judgment were to prevail, the economics and function of newspapers might change drastically, since their primary function would become one of disseminating advertisements rather than of sifting, publishing, and selling the news.

THE GROWTH OF INSERTS

Retail advertisers' use of shoppers and weeklies stems from their desire to concentrate their advertising on the areas surrounding their stores. The most common way that daily newspapers have accommodated them is by offering to insert and distribute preprinted advertising sections on a zoned basis in

TABLE 2.6
Percentage of Papers that Publish Zoned Editions, by Circulation Size, 1987a

	Editorial and advertising	Advertising only
Over 100,000	69	10
50,000–100,000	56	5
25,000–50,000	33	11
10,000–25,000	9	14
Under 10,000	5	5
Total (by number)	19	11
Total (by circulation)	49	10

particular neighborhoods or districts. In this way, advertisers would pay for only the part of the circulation they needed and not for the full-run distribution they would get with an ad in the body of the paper. National as well as retail advertisers have found this use of newspapers attractive.

Inserts are advertising sections or sheets printed at a central location well in advance and shipped to individual newspaper plants for insertion in the paper. Between 55% and 60% of the total advertising investment goes not to the newspaper, but to the printing firm, which in only a few cases is owned by a newspaper company.

In 1987, newspapers carried 54.8 billion copies of inserts at a cost of $5.5 billion to advertisers. Of the total, 36% represented part-run distribution to selected parts of a paper's market. Retail advertising was 87% of the total, and 55% of the distribution was on Sunday. Inserts accounted for 16% of advertising investments in newspapers. They represented more pages than display (as distinct from classified) advertising on weekdays and for almost as many on Sunday (if tabloid and smaller sizes are counted as pages; inch for inch they were 61% as much as display).

Although national advertisers had used roll-fed inserts[7] for several decades, free-standing inserts only came into widespread use in the 1970s. Their growth stems from the advertiser's desire to take advantage of economies of scale in printing and production and in many cases from the need for color printing of higher quality than is possible on conventional newspaper presses. Inserts permit the advertiser to conduct a coordinated national or regional campaign. They can be used only by those types of retailers whose merchandising plans can be made well in advance—like the major chains and discounters. The reader's attention to inserts appears to stay at about the same level, regardless of how many there are in the same issue of the newspaper, at least up to the number of six (1975a). As for any other element of newspaper content, attention to inserts tends to be selective; customers for a particular store are most likely to look at its advertising.

In 1970, on an average day, a typical major metropolitan newspaper measured by Media Records had 54 pages, of which 21 consisted of editorial matter and 33 of advertising. In 1987, the typical measured[8] newspaper had added 4 advertising pages within the run of the paper and 13 additional pages of editorial matter. However, the paper was now carrying the equivalent of 12 additional advertising pages in the form of preprinted inserts devoted entirely to advertising, bringing its total bulk to 84 pages. The ratio of editorial to total advertising matter had held steady (from 39% to 38%), although within

---

[7]A roll of newsprint preprinted in four-color gravure or offset is fed through the normal production run and overprinted with the paper's regular content on the reverse side (or on additional pages of the roll).

[8]It must be noted that the papers measured in these two years were not identical.

the body of the paper itself it had increased to 48%. It is clear that most of the real growth of newspaper advertising space (as distinct from revenues that reflect rate increases) can be accounted for by inserts. There is no accurate way to estimate how much of this would otherwise have gone into ROP linage and how much would have gone into direct mail, home-delivered circulars, shoppers, or magazines.

As insert advertising became an increasingly significant element of the newspaper, especially on Sunday, the appearance of the run-of-paper product underwent subtle change. Daily and Sunday, newspapers were larger in bulk, and their news holes expanded, keeping pace with the growing number of ROP advertising pages, though not with the additional volume of preprints. Classified advertising pages, usually presented without any inter-larded editorial matter, occupied a greater part of the total.

Thus, the growing importance of inserts has changed the internal economics of newspaper production. It has resulted in newspapers that are somehow different in appearance and structure from the standpoint of both the reader and the editor.

PRICE AND CIRCULATION

"Price elasticity" is the economic term that defines the degree to which consumption demand diminishes as the cost of a product goes up[9]. For some goods, even small price increases result in a loss of customers. For others, demand is virtually inelastic; that is, consumers consider them such a necessity that they give up other things in order to keep on buying them. For a long time, many newspaper publishers would have classified their output in this latter category. Today, few would.

When prices go up, readers drop out. A correlation analysis of circulation trends and single-copy prices for 300 papers between 1965 and 1986 shows that a 10% price increase was associated with a 5.5% decrease in daily circulation. (Subscription price data were not available but generally rise in step with single-copy prices.)

When newspapers gain readers, their advertising rates normally become more attractive in comparison with other competing advertising media. But competitive constraints also make publishers think twice before raising those rates in response to increases in production costs. The problem of main-

---

[9]An examination of pricing changes and market share of national advertising for newspapers and other media found no evidence of cross-elasticities of demand. When other media raised their national rates faster than newspapers, advertisers did not switch to newspapers as a substitute. This indicated that "no other media reside in the same product market as newspapers for national advertising." John C. Busterna, "The Cross-Elasticity of Demand for National Newspaper Advertising," *Journalism Quarterly*, Summer/August, 1987, Vol. 64, Nos. 2, 3, 346–351.

taining readership in the face of price increases is critical to the economic security of the press.

Although advertising represents the major part of the economic support for newspapers, circulation is a not insubstantial cost as well. Americans spent $6 billion for their weekday papers and nearly $1.4 billion for their Sunday newspapers in 1987. This represented 0.30% of all personal consumption expenditures. But in 1960, the comparable expense was 0.49% of the total.

Between 1980 and 1987, the Consumer Price Index rose 37%. In this same period, the average newsstand price of a weekday newspaper went from 20¢ to 27¢, up 35%. By way of comparison, newspapers increased their advertising rates by an average of 90% in the same period. In short, publishers have passed on more of their own increased operating costs to advertisers than to readers.

Would newspapers be better off if they eliminated all the hassle of selling and collecting from readers and simply distributed to everyone at no charge— becoming daily shoppers, as it were? An analysis of confidential data from 13 large papers indicates that two-thirds of their circulation costs are in distribution rather than in sales, promotion, service, and collections. If they were to go to free distribution, the increased cost of delivery to about 40% more homes would considerably outweigh the savings. In fact, considering the extra costs of newsprint, ink, and production, going free would raise a paper's total operating expenses by about one-fifth and at the same time reduce its revenues by the one-fifth now paid by readers. It is difficult to see how advertising could make up the difference.

Inside and outside the newspaper business, a number of observers have argued that readers are getting off far too lightly. In 1988, an 80-page newspaper weighing one pound used 30¢ worth of newsprint.

Newspaper rates, both for advertising and circulation, are generally reviewed each year in a process that begins with estimates of increases in operating expenses and a loosely defined profit objective. Rate changes are drafted to meet these requirements and then modified in anticipation of the probable response of different types of advertisers and of the reading public. A 1987 analysis by Kenneth Longman of Moran & Tucker, Inc., for our Future of Advertising Project, examined how rate decisions are arrived at on a dozen newspapers of various sizes. It indicated that the competitive media whose own rate practices are considered most carefully by newspapers are other print competitors and not the broadcasters who are actually their main rivals.

The rise in the newspaper's price to both readers and advertisers was dictated by increases surpassing the general inflation rate in the newspaper's basic operating costs. Newsprint and ink account for about 25% of the expenses of a newspaper of over 250,000 circulation, 21% for a paper of

50,000, and 13% for a paper of 9,000. Newsprint sold for $187 a ton in July, 1973. By February, 1988, the price had gone up to $660 a ton (Table 2.7). Ink and energy costs also underwent substantial increases. (Not only is energy an important production expense; newspaper circulation van fleets are heavy consumers of motor fuel. And, by the way, it takes 14–22 gallons of oil to produce a ton of newsprint.)

In the Great Depression of the 1930s, daily circulation dipped by 11%, and a paper cost all of 2¢ then. Between 1973 and 1975 (following the Arab oil embargo and sharp rises in energy costs), newspapers raised their price to the reader by 26% and sold two and one-half million fewer copies each day (a 4.5% loss). It seems reasonable to assume that this was in some part a direct response to this added cost.

This is at least the commonly held view of circulation specialists, as reflected in a mail survey of 238 members of the International Circulation Managers Association, with bigger papers and morning papers overrepresented (1974a). Among those whose coverage level had declined since 1967, 3 out of 4 attributed their losses to the increased price of the paper to the reader. The product was blamed by only 2 out of 86. Only a handful blamed their losses on population changes in the inner city. About 1 in 7 blamed competition; 1 in 7 mentioned a decline in the proportion of people who read two papers a day. About the same proportion respectively blamed changes in lifestyle, delivery problems, and production problems. (Papers that had improved their coverage credited effective promotion and improved distribution. One in four circulation managers attributed gains to an improvement in the editorial product itself, but only 2% of those with declining penetration blamed the editorial product.)

TABLE 2.7
Newsprint Prices Per Ton 30-lb. Stock

7/73	$187
11/73	213
3/74	235
1/75	260
4/76	285
12/76	305
4/78	320
10/79	375
8/80	430
1/81	470
9/83	500
10/86	535
2/87	570
7/87	610
2/88	660

Evidence of the price sensitivity of newspaper circulation may be found in the dropoff from March 31, 1974 to March 31, 1975 for several major papers that introduced substantial price increases in that period. The Boston Sunday *Globe* went from 50¢ to 75¢ on December 1, 1974, and its Sunday circulation fell by 8%. The Oakland *Tribune*, which went from a newsstand price of 15¢ in June 1974 to 25¢, raised its Sunday price from 35¢ to 50¢ and its home-delivered subscription price from $3.75 to $4.75. It showed a 12% decline in daily and an 11% decline in Sunday circulation during that period. (Both papers eventually recovered their losses.)

In 1982, at a time of business recession, we asked a national sample of the public about cutbacks or postponement of buying decisions for seven items. Twelve percent said they had cut out or postponed their newspaper subscription, more than the 5% who had put off a new car purchase but far less than the 49% who had cut back on new clothes or the 30% who had cut back on magazines.

Yet, one cannot generalize from such instances. In a period of general price inflation, the public's stoicism has increased. Circulation managers can cite cases in which substantial hikes in both newsstand and subscription prices have resulted in no losses, and sometimes have been followed by gains. Home-subscription rates and single-copy prices tend to go up in tandem, but subscription rates can inch up more gradually because they are not limited by the circulation of coins. Nickels, dimes, and quarters circulate in different quantities, which is why people may find it more convenient to pay 50¢ for a paper than 40¢.

As some of the circulation managers note, the rising cost of the paper to the reader explains at least part of the attrition in two-paper readership, which is reflected in the circulation trends. It also helps explain the decrease in the general frequency of newspaper readership among people of below-average income and those in the age brackets where economic pressures are most acute—among young adults and those over 65.

However, price changes in themselves do not readily explain why individual newspapers gain or lose circulation. Eighty big-city dailies that showed circulation gains between 1960 and 1977 had aggregate gains of 28% and increased their single-copy prices to readers by 152% in that period.[10] Sixty-six comparable big-city papers that failed to gain circulation in the same years lost 16% and increased their newsstand prices by 149%—virtually the same amount. Weekly subscription prices went up by 116% for the papers that gained and 125% for those that did not. For both a.m. and p.m. papers and for competing and noncompeting papers, the pattern holds up: Price

---

[10]This analysis was based on all central-city dailies published in markets with two or more papers where total circulation was at least 100,000 in 1960 and where price data were continuously available.

increases do not in themselves explain the loss of readers. But papers that are losing readers, probably for other reasons, do tend to hold back on single-copy price increases for fear of losing more.

Although the newsstand price of a Sunday paper has increased at a slightly faster rate than that for a daily, Sunday circulation and readership have held up better. Between 1970 and 1986, the price of a typical magazine to the reader has increased even faster (195%) than the price of a newspaper (150%). In that period, adult population grew by 32% and households by 40%. Yet, while daily newspaper circulation in this period increased by less than 1% and Sunday circulation by 20%, magazines went up by 34%. The number of consumer magazines increased by 58% from 1,182 to 1,866. Magazines' growth took place in spite of the demise of the great mass weeklies, the *Post*, *Life*, and *Look*, the first two of which were subsequently revived with only a small fraction of their former circulations. During that same period, the news magazines increased circulation at a slower rate—by 16%—suggesting that news content may have had something to do with newspapers' problems. Paid weekly newspapers fell, but shoppers grew substantially in circulation, as we have just noted. Unit sales of paperback books grew by 80% in the dozen years between 1975 and 1987. In short, in spite of cost increases, other forms of print have prospered during the same time that newspapers have remained virtually static.

If higher pricing is a factor that has inhibited newspapers' growth, it still cannot be the full explanation. The perception of price is inseparable from the sense of value, which brings us back to the psychological connections between the reader and the paper he reads.

BRINGING THE NEWSPAPER TO THE READER

The newspaper's value to its readers depends not only on its content and its pricing, but on its ready and timely availability. Proper distribution is the precondition for success in marketing any product. No matter how good it is, or how great the demand for it, it cannot be sold unless consumers can get it conveniently. In the case of newspapers, as we saw in Chapter 1, the mechanics of distribution have become steadily more difficult. Home delivery, usually through a juvenile carrier, is today the primary means of newspaper distribution in the United States, especially outside of the largest cities. In those cities, the same processes of urban change and deterioration that have adversely affected the market demand for daily papers in big cities have also had a damaging effect on the distribution system itself.

At the same time, home delivery is a steadily more demanding and expensive task. One major metropolitan paper reports that it must sell 25 subscriptions at a cost of $950 to produce one additional unit of circulation by the end of the year. In new suburban developments, the distances between houses are greater and routes become longer, with no greater yield. In the city, it is harder to approach, sell, and deliver newspapers to customers who live in apartment buildings, guarded by doormen and front-door locks. In 1960, only 17% of all new housing starts were for housing units in buildings of three or more units. In 1973, 42% of all new housing units were in this bracket, and in metropolitan areas the proportion was much higher—53%. By 1987, only 27% of the starts were for buildings of this type. There is still a long way to go before the apartment house becomes typical of the American way of life, since only 10% of all dwelling units are in buildings with 10 or more apartments, and by no means are all of these high-rise buildings that pose serious delivery problems.

The spotlight has been put on faulty delivery as the main reason offered by (22% of) subscribers who cancel.[11] But of 450 cancellations checked out in three cities studied by Maxwell E. McCombs, L. E. Mullins, and David H. Weaver, 55% were people who could not be contacted; of those contacted, 29% mentioned moves or vacations as the reason for cancelling their subscriptions. Another analysis of nearly 30,000 nonvacation subscription stops in one city of about 150,000 population found that in 54% of the cases the subscribers were moving. Only 1.5% gave service-related complaints, and the others gave the usual litany of miscellaneous reasons.

There is no way of getting people who are no longer around to keep buying the paper, but historically they have been counterbalanced by new people coming in. The circulation manager must not be concerned just about subscription stops; he must worry about the ones that never start.

To learn more about the dynamics of subscription, Virginia Dodge Fielder and Beverly Barnum interviewed 1,745 new subscribers (or "starts") to nine newspapers at four intervals between January 1986 and January 1987.[12] Their study was sponsored by both editors and circulation executives. After six months, approximately 66% were still subscribers; 56% remained after nine months, and 53% after a year. A third of the new subscriptions were voluntary; two-thirds were sold by the newspaper; within the latter group, 37% were in response to a special offer. Forty-five percent had previously subscribed, mostly within the past year, and half of them at a different address. (These former subscribers were most likely to stay on.)[13]

---

[11]"Why People Subscribe and Cancel: 'Stop–Start' Survey of Three Daily Newspapers," ANPA *News Research Bulletin*, April 5, 1974.

[12]Virginia Dodge Fielder and Beverly A. Barnum, *Love Us and Leave Us: New Subscribers One Year Later*, American Society of Newspapers Editors, 1987.

[13]The retention rate was 67% among people who had subscribed on their own initiative, 49% among those whose subscriptions were initiated by carriers, 41% among those sold over the

Among those who dropped their subscriptions, two out of five gave "no time to read" as an explanation, and another two out of five said that "papers kept piling up before they got read." Over half the people who stopped subscribing and a third of the subscribers agreed that there were "times when you do not read one issue of the paper before the next one is delivered."

About three in ten former subscribers mentioned problems with delivery as an important reason for stopping. Twenty-two percent of those who stopped subscribing did so because they moved. One out of four said they got enough news from TV and radio. Fifteen percent said they preferred another daily newspaper.

People who stayed subscribers and those who stopped were remarkably similar in their responses to a question on the reasons for subscribing. ("To keep up with local happenings" was the answer most often given. "To keep up with national/world happenings" was directly behind.) They also spent exactly the same amount of time reading an average issue of the paper. They gave the paper almost identical ratings for quality. They gave similar answers when asked what medium they would choose if they had to have one source for either local or national and international news.[14] The two groups also gave identical answers to a series of questions about changes in their lives in the past year: in economic circumstances, moves, job, household size, health, and marital status.

The continuing subscribers differed from the dropouts in one very important respect: Those who stopped were less likely to agree that it was important to keep informed on the city and on the world, or that reading a newspaper every day was an important way to keep informed.

If the explanations offered by people who stop getting the paper are sometimes rationalizations for apathy, this in no way mitigates the importance of good service. Seventy percent of weekday subscribers in our 1987 survey described themselves as "very satisifed" with their delivery service and another 23% as "fairly well satisfied." But the 5% who were "dissatisfied" represented some five million readers, a consumer segment that can hardly be treated lightly.

Half of those without home delivery had had it in the past but discontinued it for the usual variety of reasons, including cost, dislike of the paper, and the perennial answer, "no time to read." Half also said they had never been asked to subscribe to a newspaper at their current address. And only a

---

phone, 35% among those solicited by door-to-door crews, and 63% among those solicited by coupons. Retention was actually higher (59%) among those induced to subscribe without a special offer than by those who received one (41%).

[14]In both cases, newspapers were a two-to-one choice for local news and ran roughly neck and neck with television on the national and international news side. The people who stopped their subscription were slightly more likely to prefer TV to newspapers.

minority (22%) recalled seeing or hearing any promotional ads for newspapers in the past month.

WHO BRINGS THE PAPER?

Getting the paper delivered on time to the reader is an increasingly tough proposition. There are continuing problems in recruiting, motivating, and training circulation personnel. In an era of affluence it is harder to persuade adolescents that the earnings from a newspaper route are worth the effort.

On papers of 50,000 circulation and over, the equivalent of an entirely new carrier force must be recruited each year to replace those who leave. On papers between 25,000 and 50,000 circulation 4 out of 5 carriers must be replaced; on smaller papers, 7 out of 10 (1979c).

In 1988, newspapers lost over $100 million a year on "down routes," when carriers failed to make their rounds, according to Roy Newman of the Metropolitan Route Dealers Association. Newspapers have turned increasingly to adult carriers to replace the traditional "little merchants." To meet the decline in the adolescent population, a growing number of newspapers have been reassessing the juvenile carrier system and moving to separate the delivery function from subscription sales and the collection process.

A 1987 survey of circulation managers found that 70% of the carriers employed by a typical morning paper and 90% of those on a typical evening paper were juveniles. (Juveniles serve much smaller routes, so this is not an indication of the number of copies delivered by each system.) The adult system predominated in 41% of the morning papers, but in only 10% of the evening papers. But with the conversion of many evening papers to morning publication, and with the switch of many large papers to independent distributorship systems, the juvenile carriers appeared to be losing ground rapidly.

In our 1987 survey of reading habits, over half of all subscribers (52%) reported that their paper was delivered by an adult, while 33% had a juvenile carrier, and 15% were unable to identify the individual who delivers the paper. Five years earlier, the proportions were reversed, with 36% reporting an adult carrier and 52%, a juvenile. The switch of larger morning papers to adult carrier forces was accompanied by the rise of office billing systems. Half (49%) of subscribers paid by mail, and 66% of these paid in advance.[15] Although the little merchant system, with its human contact between carrier and customer, continued to be the dominant form of distribution on the

---

[15]Most papers give readers a number of options: In 1979, 55% offered monthly billings; 45% let readers pay weekly; 13%, biweekly; 18%, every three months; 12%, every six months; and 11%, annually.

majority of smaller newspapers, it was rapidly being replaced by an impersonal, even invisible commercial relationship.

Computerized subscriber information systems made it possible to bill subscribers directly, relieving the carrier of what was generally considered an unpleasant task. By matching subscriber names against household directories, newspapers could produce mailing lists for their nonsubscriber products and could target their telephone subscription selling more efficiently. Analysis of subscriber records for each carrier or circulation territory made it possible to pinpoint trouble spots in sales or service. Subscriber complaints about delivery or billing could be handled more easily with a retrievable record.

NEWSPAPER SUBSCRIBERS

Forty-nine percent of the adult population are in weekday-newspaper-subscribing households, including 9% who get only weekday delivery (1987). Forty-six percent live in homes where a Sunday paper is delivered, including 6% who get it only on Sunday. But not everyone in a household where a newspaper is regularly delivered necessarily reads every issue. Thirty-seven percent have missed at least one of the last five issues, and 8% have read none of them.

Among readers who missed yesterday's paper, 25% have a subscription, as do 12% of those who say they "never" read a paper. And, to look at the same subject in reverse, among all those who had a paper home-delivered, one out of five (19%) did not read it (1987). Of the people who never read a paper, one in eight (12%) had one delivered to the home; of the "yesterday" nonreaders, one in four (25%) had home delivery. Regular distribution does not guarantee readership every day by every single member of a subscribing household; however, it is certainly a desirable precondition. In 5% of the households where a paper was delivered, it was not read by any adult "yesterday."

The attributes of newspaper subscribers are identical with those of frequent readers. They are people of above-average income, education, and age; people who are married, homeowners, and established in their communities. The proportion of adults with home delivery ranges from 76% for papers under 25,000 circulation to 47% for papers of over 250,000. It is lower in households with one adult (37%) than in those with two adults (55%) or three or more (47%). The subscriber population has aged in recent years. Over half of subscribers have had a newspaper subscription for 10 years or more.

The type of dwelling both determines and reflects the social character of a neighborhood, but it is independently a determinant of the likelihood that subscriptions can be sold and efficiently fulfilled. In 1982, 63% of people living in separate, single-family residences had home delivery, compared to 2% of those in high-rise apartments of six stories or higher (Table 2.8).

TABLE 2.8
Percentage Home Delivery, By Type of Residence, 1982

	Weekday	Sunday
Separate single house	63	59
Two- or three-family house	43	40
Row house	41	47
Mobile home	33	18
Apartment, 5 stories or less	21	26
Apartment, 6 stories or more	2	14

In 1986, 73% of all adults surveyed by the Simmons Market ResearchBureau (SMRB)[16] lived in single-family homes, 6% in duplex units, 8% in buildings of 3 to 9 units, and 8% in apartment buildings with 10 or more units. Another 5% lived in mobile homes. In central cities of over a million residents, a third lived in apartments; in nonmetropolitan areas, 82% lived in single-family homes. Not surprisingly, apartment-house dwellers were younger, more mobile, and more likely to be living alone or with just one other person.

Eighty-nine percent of all subscribers get the paper at home on both weekdays and Sundays (1987). Eleven percent get home delivery on Sunday only. (This proportion has been increasing and in part represents delivery of a large metropolitan Sunday paper to people in smaller towns in its hinterland who get the local paper during the week.) In a study of two cities (1981a), subscribers and nonsubscribers reported reading the same kinds of content, but nonsubscribers were less likely to say the newspaper represented excellent or good value. Two-thirds of them said they would give up the daily paper if they had to choose between it and the Sunday paper; only three out of ten subscribers would.

The importance of home delivery in assuring regular day-in, day-out readership is shown by the fact that 64% of all subscribers had read a paper on all five of the past weekdays, and another 14% of them had read it on four of those days. By contrast, 35% of single-copy purchasers had read a paper on all five of the last five weekdays, and 32% had not read a paper on any of the last five weekdays (1987).

As the circulation figures would indicate, people living in larger cities are more likely to subscribe to morning papers than those in middle-sized and smaller communities, where fewer such papers are published. Conversely, they are less likely to be subscribers to afternoon papers. For papers of under 25,000 circulation, 24% of the home delivery takes place before noon; for papers of over 250,000, the proportion is 84% (1987).

---

[16]The Simmons Market Research Bureau provides an annual syndicated media measurement service based on approximately 15,000 respondents as well as local studies in 51 major markets.

Among "yesterday" readers, the proportion who received a home-delivered paper went from 71% in 1961 to 74% in 1971, 77% in 1977, 71% in 1982, and 72% in 1987. But these figures cannot be interpreted except in relation to the dropping level of average weekday readership itself. The proportion of people who read a copy obtained from a newsstand, store, or vending rack fell from 21% to 18%.

A high proportion of magazine subscriptions are sold at discounted promotional rates, and many newspapers also offer price incentives for new subscribers. But only 9% of current newspaper subscribers said their present subscription was obtained at a cut rate or that they received a gift or premium as an inducement.

THE SINGLE-COPY READER

What about the 51% of the adult public who are not members of a subscribing household? The proportion of frequent readers among them is highest in the biggest cities and in the Northeast, where the traditional urban pattern of public mass transportation and newsstands still prevails to a greater degree than in the rest of the country. The South and West, which have the lowest levels of readership among the regions, also have the lowest proportions of readers among people without daily delivery.

The circulation statements of the largest 100 newspapers, analyzed by Albert Gollin, show that single copies accounted for 19.5% of weekday sales in 1982 and 20.7% in 1986, while on Sundays they went from 22.4% to 25.0%. Historically, single-copy sales have always been more important to papers in larger cities with a more mobile population, a more active street life, more mass transportation and commuter traffic, and more points of sale. Proportionately, single-copy sales are twice as large in large metropolitan areas as in nonmetropolitan areas, where 12% of the home-delivered papers arrive by mail rather than by carrier (1987). In the urban environment, hot news still sells newspapers. When Indira Gandhi was assassinated in October 1984, the Philadelphia *Daily News* sold 6,500 extra copies. The following April the *News* sold 20,000 extra copies after a prize fight.

The newspaper street vendor of the past is fast disappearing from an urban scene with less pedestrian traffic and fewer competing papers to keep him in business. In 1988, New York City had only 296 newsstands, a quarter of the number that existed in the early 1950s.

The growth of chain retailing has also whittled down the number of small independent stationery, candy and grocery stores, of the kind that sold newspapers. Convenience stores do not always find it convenient to carry them. Mass transit ridership in large cities went down as jobs moved to the suburbs. Today's newspaper self-service vending rack hardly offers the reader the appetite appeal of the old-fashioned newsstand or kiosk, with its inviting assortment of fresh publications. Vending racks and the so-called honor boxes are also highly vulnerable to vandalism and to thefts of both newspapers and coins. And they are costly: USA Today reportedly spent over $30 million for its 135,000 vending machines.

In 1987, 25% of the public had bought a single copy on one or more weekdays of the past week, and 35% had bought it on Sunday. Sixteen percent of the public reported buying single copies on both weekdays and Sundays, but fewer (9%) buy only on weekdays than only on Sundays (19%). Of course, people who subscribe to one paper often buy single copies of another, or even of the same paper, when two are needed by different members of the family. Among people who ever buy a single copy, 26% are subscribers. And they are no less attentive to the paper than people with home delivery. Single-copy buyers (those who at least occasionally buy single copies) report spending the same amount of time with the paper as do the subscribers.

Among nonsubscribing weekday readers, three out of five reported buying the paper themselves. Altogether, 8% of yesterday's readers bought their copy from a newsstand, 5% from another type of store, and 5% from a vending rack (1987). Among the remainder, 2% read a paper brought home by another member of the family, and 3% read a copy at work, but 5% acknowledged reading a borrowed paper or one passed along by someone else. Three percent named another source, like reading in a waiting room. Among the Sunday readers, 38% reported buying the copy from a store or rack. In nonmetropolitan areas, single-copy sales are concentrated in various types of stores other than newsstands.

In 1987, 91% of all readers reported that there is a convenient place where they can buy single copies of a newspaper. The percentage was lower among nonreaders, so the lack of access probably resulted in some missed sales. The 18% of "yesterday" readers who bought their own single copies bought them fairly evenly across the week, though sales go up slightly on Wednesday ("Best Food Day") relative to other days (Table 2.9). Single copies are more important on Sunday than they are for the weekday paper.

When people who had bought a single copy of a paper within the past

TABLE 2.9
Single-Copy Buying, 1984[a]

Monday	97
Tuesday	89
Wednesday	117
Thursday	94
Friday	98

[a]100 = Buy any weekday

week were interviewed in five cities (1988), 34% said they liked to buy the
paper when they wanted it and 23% said it was convenient for them to pick
up a copy while they were out buying other things. While three out of five
made some reference to the positive aspect of buying their papers this way,
one out of three offered a complaint about delivery service, and one in five
said they had no time to read the paper every day. When questioned directly
as to why they did not subscribe, 41% mentioned a positive aspect of
single-copy buying, 36% complained about the quality of home delivery, and
28% brought up the "no time to read" argument. The answers did not vary
substantially from city to city.

In an earlier study of single-copy purchasers, 1,417 interviews were
conducted at coin boxes, newsstands, and stores in three cities, alternately
with people who had just bought a paper and with nonbuyers who said they
were subscribers. The same evening, about half of them were interviewed
again by telephone (1981).[17]

When asked whether there was anything in particular about that day's
issue that encouraged them to buy it, 29% said there was, with about half
referring to a specific section or feature. (These proportions did not change
significantly on the Best Food Day.) Nine out of ten said they always bought
the same paper, and three out of ten said they also subscribed to a paper—in
most but not all cases, a different one. Among these people, two out of five
said they bought a paper every day; of the purchasers who were not also
subscribers, two out of three did.

In their news preferences and habits, single-copy buyers closely resembled
the matched group of subscribers, though they read both daily and Sunday
papers with somewhat less frequency. The small proportion in both groups
who did not read the paper every day were asked whether they read it on
certain days mainly because of something in the paper or something about
those days. Only 11% said it was the day itself that was important, and those
who referred to content mentioned advertising, news, and features in equal
proportions.

---

[17]The three cities all had both morning and evening papers, with different ownerships in one
case. The papers ranged between 17,000 and 270,000 in circulation, and single copies accounted
for between 8% and 27% of their total sales. About half the purchases were from a vending
machine or rack, about half were made before 11:00 a.m., and three out of four were made by
men.

When asked why they only buy single copies, 41% of the purchasers gave reasons connected
with the service problems of home delivery, 13% mentioned the convenience of purchase, and
28% said they read too infrequently to subscribe. A third of them said they might turn to home
delivery in the future. Only half of them had ever been asked to subscribe while at their present
address. (This figure went up to three out of four in the one competitive market.)

Nine out of ten were satisfied with the number of places where a paper could be bought near
them, and two out of three always bought it at the same location. In three out of four cases, more
than one paper was available at that location.

While 92% of the subscribers read their paper at home, only 63% of the single-copy buyers did; many of them were on the way to work. But 80% brought their papers home. Thirty-eight percent (compared with 13% of those who got the paper home-delivered) said they were the only adult readers of that copy.

Two out of three buyers said they would go elsewhere to buy their favorite paper if their usual outlet was sold out. Purchasers at a particular kind of outlet tended to prefer it, whether it was a vending rack or a store. The vending rack was considered a time-saver, but sometimes described as beset by mechanical problems. Stores offered the chance to buy other items, some human contact, and no worries about the exact change. In three out of five instances, other items could be bought at the same location as the newspaper. This was a positive attraction for only one-fourth of the buyers, but nearly half bought other things half the time or more often when they bought the paper.

Since single-copy purchases are less likely to be read at home; they may be more likely to be passed along to people outside the family, including people who do not buy a paper at all that day. And since single-copy sales concentrate in big cities, this could explain why the papers in the 40 top markets measured by SMRB in 1987 had 2.49 readers per copy, compared to 2.12 for the country as a whole. (In the same markets, Scarborough showed 2.58.)[18]

The single-copy sales picture varies greatly from paper to paper. Among circulation managers whose papers' coverage (or circulation-to-household ratio) levels fell in the mid-1970s, nearly half reported an actual drop in circulation, and all but two of these reported greater losses among subscribers than in single-copy sales (1973). Of those that gained circulation despite a drop in coverage, two out of three got their biggest gains in subscriptions, and one out of three got them in single copies.

Among those who had an increase in the proportion of subscriptions, the principal explanations advanced were better delivery, good promotion, and increases in the single-copy price that made the subscription a better buy. But paradoxically, price increases were mentioned just as often by those who were gaining most in single-copy sales; they also attributed this to more vending machines, to apartment living, mobility, and other changes in lifestyle that discourage regular delivery.

The deaths of major urban newspapers, with their large street sales, reduced the national ratio of single copies to subscriptions. Yet for surviving dailies, single-copy sales became more significant as the frequency of news-

---

[18]This is partly an artifact of methodology. In an experiment conducted by the *Los Angeles Times*, telephone interviews like those conducted in the local market surveys produced a 21% higher level of claimed weekday reading than personal interviews like the national SMRB and MRI studies, and a 25% higher level for Sunday.

paper reading dropped. People on the run might drop home delivery and instead choose to pick up a paper on occasional days.

Regular everyday readership diminishes when people must make the effort of purchasing a copy each day instead of finding it at the door. The problem can be dealt with only by returning the single-copy distribution system to the level of efficiency it had a generation ago or by increasing the presently static level of home subscriptions.

The shifting proportion of single-copy and subscription sales, the more tortuous logistics of distribution, the drop in multiple-newspaper reading, the uneasy balance of pricing to the reader and the advertiser, the mounting pressure of production costs and competition—all these economic factors must be kept in mind as we move to consider the actual process of newspaper reading.

3
THE AUDIENCE FOR NEWSPAPERS

Who reads newspapers, how often? To find out, it is essential to observe readers and to question them. The changing reading habits shown in the statistics on circulation are also reflected in the evidence from surveys of the reading (and nonreading) public, which are the source of most of the evidence presented in this book. Establishing and measuring readership is itself a fairly recent development in the long history of newspapers.

THE CONCEPT OF THE "AUDIENCE"

Newspaper readership can be defined and measured in a variety of ways. If a reader is described as anyone who ever looks at a newspaper, then practically everyone who can read fits that description. Newspapers are so widely disseminated that no one who has the capacity to read them can be said to be completely beyond their reach. More commonly, readership is defined in terms of the number of people who read a paper on a given day or over the course of a particular week (generally modified to mean five consecutive weekdays because of the distinctive circulation patterns of Saturday and Sunday papers.)

Newspapers have measured their audiences primarily in order to satisfy the demands of advertisers who compare media in terms of the number and kinds of people who can be reached with a particular budget.

Until comparatively recently, the measure of any publication was the publisher's claim as to how many copies were printed and sold. Since 1916, these claims have been verified by an independent audit conducted by the Audit Bureau of Circulations, an organization that represents not only the print media, but advertisers and advertising agencies as well. Paid circulation represents the actual distribution of copies of a publication. But a periodical in a doctor's waiting room or barbershop may be looked at by dozens of people, while one delivered to the door of a vacationing family may never find any readers at all. Anthony Trollope in *The Warden* (1855) distinguished circulation from readership, as Charles Lehman points out:

> They say that forty thousand copies of the *Jupiter* are daily sold and that each copy is read by five persons at the least. Two hundred thousand readers then would hear this accusation against him; two hundred thousand hearts would swell with indignation.

With the advent of commercial broadcasting, it became necessary to find an equivalent to the audience figures produced for radio and later for television. These ratings represented the number of people listening to a program and were in no way equivalent to the circulation figures represented by copies of periodicals. The competition for advertising put magazines under pressure to switch their yardsticks of size from circulation to audience. Unlike daily newspapers, monthly and even weekly magazines can typically accumulate a large number of readers per copy between the date of one issue and the next. Since newspapers are published every day, and since much of their content is ephemeral, a single copy has a shorter lifespan and can accumulate fewer pass-along readers.

Audience surveys transformed American magazines by changing advertisers' perceptions and uses of them and thus changing the way their publishers and editors designed them. American newspapers have also conducted audience research since the mid-1930s.

Audience studies focus attention on the number and characteristics of readers, as opposed to the number of copies sold. Such studies have naturally been more important in the larger, more competitive newspaper markets where papers must convince advertisers of their unique advantages by showing the characteristics of people who read them as well as their mere numbers.

Surveys made for advertising reasons can be helpful to editors by providing information that enables them to differentiate their readers from the population as a whole. But these surveys generally differ in design, scope, and methodology from the research most commonly done specifically for the guidance of editors. This kind of research typically takes readers through the different parts of the paper to determine what they remember having seen or enjoyed. Such studies are usually not conducted with the same kind of sampling scope or precisionrequired to win a hearing from advertisers. They are therefore not very useful when it comes to examining overall trends in newspaper readership.

DEFINING NEWSPAPER AUDIENCES

On a national scale, surveys of newspaper reading have been conducted since before World War II by a variety of research organizations. Standard polling questions have been asked in rather general terms. ("Do you read a newspaper regularly, sometimes, or not at all?") Such questions are likely to be defined differently by different people. Therefore, the replies do not have the same validity as a sequence of questions which the respondent must answer by volunteering the names of the papers he reads at least occasionally and further volunteering the information that (before "today") a particular paper was last read "yesterday."

Reading "yesterday" (or on the last weekday) sets a criterion that guarantees greater specificity of response than a question that asks about the frequency of readership in general terms. This procedure was used in our 1961 study, the first national survey of its kind to undergo technical review by the Advertising Research Foundation. It therefore represents the first benchmark against which subsequent national surveys can be compared. Since that time, audience surveys made for individual newspapers have also for the most part followed variants of the same basic questioning technique.

Trends in readership can be tracked by considering survey data over time. However, it is commonplace to find variations in the results of surveys that measure the identical phenomena. These can be accounted for by the statistical tolerances that go with sampling and also by the human factors associated with fieldwork. There are also differences in the exact methods employed by different survey organizations in constructing questionnaires and instructing interviewers. Even when we compare surveys made by the same organization and with identical questioning procedures, we often find inexplicable changes, differences, or incongruities that cannot be attributed simply to the random variations that occur as a result of statistical probability. (The theoretical range of these variations depends on sample size and on whether the responses are evenly balanced or lopsided.)

It must be regarded as a fortuitous coincidence when surveys made by two different research organizations produce identical statistics. The problems of comparability are even greater when we examine survey data accumulated by different organizations at different points in time. Even though the objectives of the questions may be the same, differences in phrasing will produce different results. And then even with the same questions, the way the fieldwork is carried out is likely to be different. Important nuances may be introduced by differences in the position of the question in the interview. And even a minor change in the construction of the interview schedule introduces variations that can make the resulting figures look puzzling.

The perplexities of such comparisons are compounded when we examine survey results for particular subgroups of the population. Definitions are likely to be less consistent and the statistical tolerances swing wider as the subsamples get smaller. For this reason, in interpreting survey results it is always desirable to have several corroborations of a trend rather than to base it on the figures from just two studies.

THE EXTENT OF NEWSPAPER READING

Nearly every literate American (85%) looks at a newspaper at least occasionally (1987). Since not every adult member of every family is at home every day, or manages to look at a newspaper, the level of individual readership is less than the proportion of households in which the paper is present. In 1982, a newspaper was read "yesterday" by someone in 75% of all households. (A special study was made of 152 cases where the primary respondent's report could be checked with other individuals in the household; this matched in 83% of the cases, overstated reading in 7%, and understated it in 10%.) One out of ten adult newspaper readers in 1987 had acquired a paper through pass-along—that is, in some other way than through a home subscription or single-copy purchase made either by themselves or by some other member of the family.

Differences in the demographic profiles of morning and afternoon newspaper readers simply reflect differences in the character of the communities where morning and evening papers are published. As we saw in Chapter 1, morning papers are most often published in cities. Smaller towns and rural areas tend to have a somewhat larger proportion of people at lower levels of education and income. (Household income is highest in the largest metropolitan areas and lowest in nonmetropolitan areas.)

Throughout the 1960s, studies made by a number of commercial research organizations for advertising planning purposes showed the level of average weekday newspaper readership to fluctuate between 76% and 80% and of Sunday readership at around 65%. Between 1970 and 1979, the proportion of adults over 18 who read a newspaper over the course of five weekdays remained at the level of nearly 9 out of 10 but there was a decline from 78% to 70% in the proportion who were readers on any given weekday, and from 72% to 69% in the proportion of adults who read a Sunday newspaper. In the period 1980–87, the five-day total slipped to 80%, average weekday readership (according to SMRB) went from 69% to 65%, and Sunday's from 67% to

63%.[1] In our 1961 survey, 73% of all adults said they read a paper every single day. The National Opinion Research Center's General Social Survey found that the proportion of the public saying they read the paper "every day" fell from 73% in 1967 to 54% in 1982, but it was at about that same level in 1987. The total of those reading a paper at least once a week was 91% in 1967, 88% in 1982, and still 88% in 1987.

Readership of the Sunday paper was 19% less than average weekday readership in 1961 and 18% less in 1971, but it has since risen to about the same level. Sunday circulation in 1987 stood at 95% of the average Monday to Friday level, and the average issue audience was 66% compared with 65% on the average weekday. Sunday newspapers evidently accumulated more readers per copy. More members of a household are at home on that day, with more time for reading. As a weekly publication, the Sunday paper has a longer life than the daily. It is apt to be kept in the house longer, and therefore there are more occasions to look at it. The Sunday paper is more costly, and therefore more likely to be exchanged or passed on to others outside the household.

In part, these reasons also explain why Sunday newspapers retained their penetration levels during a time when daily audience percentages dipped. There were other reasons as well. More Sunday editions were started by papers that formerly had none. (Between 1970 and 1987, the total number of Sunday papers increased by 217, from 586 to 803.) As a day of leisure, Sunday retained relative immunity to the time pressures of the work week. Many people who had reduced their frequency of reading the weekday paper put the Sunday paper into a different category of necessity, almost like a separate medium. And finally, the Sunday paper, with its heavy emphasis on entertainment and utilitarian features, was less objectionable to those who found the news oppressive or disturbing.

The Sunday paper has a slightly more youthful readership than the daily paper, since it attracts somewhat more occasional weekday readers. But the difference is slight indeed. The median age of the Sunday reader is 41.6 years (according to the 1988 MRI report); for the weekday readers, it is 43.1; and for the total adult population, it is 40.1.

Most newspapers do not release separate circulation figures for their Saturday editions, but surveys show that readership of the Saturday newspaper is also less than on Monday through Friday. It was 8% less in the 1961 study, 25% less in 1971, and 9% less in 1987. Some small papers do not publish a Saturday edition, and a number of Saturday afternoon papers

---

[1]MRI showed weekday reading at 60%, using virtually the identical question sequence as SMRB and also with a large national probability sample of personal interviews. MRI used a single interview, SMRB an average of two, demonstrating my earlier point about the mysterious variations in audience measurement.

ceased publication in the 1970s and 1980s or switched to morning editions. In 1972, there were 793 Saturday afternoon papers. By 1987, the number had fallen to 331. Since most Americans do not go to work on Saturday, newsstand and vending rack sales are less on that day. The strength of the ever-bulkier Sunday paper may also have deterred Saturday reading.

Readership on Mondays and Tuesdays is consistently lower by a few percentage points than on the other days, reflecting the fact that many papers carry less advertising on those days. Also, the prolonged presence of the fat Sunday paper may provide some minor distraction from the daily paper at the start of the week.

The total audience for a particular newspaper is essentially the same on any two weekdays (whether these are consecutive or separated by a time interval of a week or a month). But some of the people who read the paper on the first day will not be readers on the other, and vice versa. Studies made in 50 top markets by Scarborough Research and SMRB in 1987 show an average turnover rate of 26% to 27% for both morning and evening newspapers. But individual rates ranged between 9% for the Buffalo *News* (with high market penetration and a high proportion of subscriptions) and 50% for the Phila-delphia *Daily News* (with a lower penetration of the television-defined market and a high proportion of single copy sales).

Since the number of people who *never* read a weekday newspaper has remained approximately constant, the data indicate a decline in the fre-quency of reading among newspaper readers. Of the people who read the newspaper on any given weekday, 73% have read it on all five of the last five weekdays. (Nine percent read it on four days, 4% on three, 7% on two, and 8% on one.) This is a smaller proportion than it used to be (it was 82% in 1971). It is the regularity of reading, rather than the incidence of reading, which has shown a change.

Naturally, the people who read the paper every day are more intensive readers by other yardsticks as well. In 1961, they were twice as likely to be "yesterday" readers of more than one paper; they were 21% more likely to say they read the paper "thoroughly" rather than just scanned it, and they were 27% more likely to have spent at least a half hour with the paper they last read.

Not everybody, of course, has the same chance of being a faithful newspaper reader. As common sense tells us, newspapers have their greatest following among people of higher educationand social status, who are most at home with the printed word. Moreover, newspaper reading is an acquired habit that is strongest among people of maturity who are rooted by material self-interest and emotional attachments to the community that the news-paper represents. I shall be presenting the evidence on this subject in some depth. But we are concerned at this moment with the trends and we shall be looking closely at the variations in readership levels among different segments of the population.

In the 20 years between 1967 and 1987, SMRB surveys showed a decline from 76% to 65% in total "yesterday" readership. The rate of decline (that is, the proportion of change from the 1967 level) was much less for college graduates (10%) than for those who had not graduated from high school (23%). And it ranged from 20% in the 18–24 age group to 7% among those over 65. But as Table 3.1 shows, there is a sharp discontinuity between the 45–54-year-olds (who were over 25 in 1967) and the next younger group, 35–44, who were in their teens and early 20s during the period of massive upheaval in values and mores. The age cohort who were 35–44 in 1967 had the highest level of readership then, and they still have the highest level of readership 20 years later. But succeeding age groups have shown progressively greater attrition in their regularity of reading.

The drop in average weekday readership was somewhat more pronounced in the central cities of smaller metropolitan areas and in suburban areas than it was in the largest metropolitan central cities. It was greatest in nonmetropolitan areas. It was greater among women than among men and equally great among full-time housewives and among women who work outside the home. It was considerably less among people in professional and managerial jobs than among blue collar workers. It was greater among Whites than among Blacks. But in no identifiable subgroup of the population did average weekday readership stay the same, let alone show an increase, during this 20-year period.

MULTIPAPER READING

As the number of directly competitive metropolitan newspapers has been reduced, there has been a drop in the number of people who read two or more

TABLE 3.1
"Yesterday" Readership, by Age, 1967–1987, and
Rate of Change (SMRB)

	1967	1987	Rate of change
18–24	71%	57%	–20%
25–34	73	60	–18
35–44	81	67	–17
45–54	79	71	–10
55–64	78	72	– 8
65 +	72	67	– 7

different papers on an average weekday. In 1961, it was 34% of those who had read any paper on that day. It was 32% in 1970, and 23% in 1987. Expressed in another way, between 1970 and 1987, two-paper-a-day readership dropped from 28% to 15% of the total population. The drop was especially marked, as Table 3.2 shows, in the metropolitan central cities and suburbs.

Readership of more than one paper a day is closely linked to the very same variables that make for regular readership in the first place: age, education, income, and in the case of women, working status (Table 3.3).

People who read more than one paper a day are often getting the news from several geographic origins. They may read a suburban paper and a metropolitan paper, a hometown paper and one from another city, the *Wall Street Journal* or *USA Today* and the local press. (In 1961, 71% of readership was accounted for by papers published in the same county as the reader, another 10% by papers published in another county in the same metropolitan area, and 19% by papers coming from a different area.)

In 1987, the percentage of total metropolitan newspaper audience that represented duplicated readership ranged from 8% in Salt Lake City to 55% in Kansas City, according to Scarborough local market surveys. (The SMRB results show similar variations.) The average level of duplication in two-paper markets was not very different in single-ownership combination markets (16% according to Scarborough and 22% according to SMRB) than in markets with fully competitive papers (20% in Scarborough and 17% in SMRB) and those with combined business operations but separate editorial ownerships (23% in Scarborough and 19% in SMRB). In the competitive markets, duplication was no different in those cases where two morning papers went head to head than in those where readers had choices in the morning and afternoon. The duplication between the two metropolitan papers is only part of the story of newspaper competition, since our analysis does not take into account the people who read both a metropolitan and a suburban daily or those who read both a Fort Lauderdale paper and one from Miami or Hollywood or West Palm Beach.

People who read more than one daily newspaper apparently find that these papers perform different functions for them. The person who reads more than one newspaper a day might be considered equivalent to the one

TABLE 3.2
Percentage of Adults Who Read Two or More
Papers a Day, 1970 and 1987 (SMRB)

	1970	1987
Central cities	28	15
Suburbs	30	11
Nonmetropolitan	18	6

TABLE 3.3
Percentage Reading One or More Newspapers "Yesterday"
by Age, Education, and Income (SMRB, 1987)

	Read Any	Read 2 +
Total	65	15
Age		
18–24	57	11
25–34	60	12
35–44	67	18
45–54	71	19
55–64	72	18
65 +	67	12
Education		
Graduated college	78	25
Attended college	70	18
Graduated high school	66	14
Attended high school	56	9
Did not attend high school	45	5
Household income		
$60,000 and over	78	27
$50,000–59,999	76	25
$40,000–49,999	72	19
$30,000–39,999	70	17
$20,000–29,999	64	13
$10,000–19,999	59	10
Under $10,000	48	6
Men	67	17
Employed women	64	15
Nonemployed women	61	10

who reads both *Time* and the *New Yorker*. One is not a substitute for the other.

When more than one newspaper comes into a given household, different individuals may gravitate toward one or the other or may be the purchasers in the first place. Or sometimes one paper may be the family's primary choice and the other one read only for particular features or for an update on the news. Among people who had read two or more papers "yesterday," exactly half said in 1961 that one was their main paper, and half said they were equally important. Two out of three said the papers covered the news diffferently, especially the news of direct interest to them.

Why do people read more than one paper? Those who do so primarily referred to the newspapers' news function, rather than to the special features that are often credited with winning readers. In 1961, 19% of those who read more than one paper "yesterday" explained that this gave them better general coverage of the news: 20% referred specifically to more complete coverage of local news, and 6% each mentioned national and international news. Another 17% observed that they get different opinions by reading several papers, but only 3% singled out columnists and editorials. When asked what made the two papers they read different in their news, the same subjects were mentioned in approximately the same order of importance. But when these readers were asked what they would miss if they could only read one paper, 33% mentioned local news; 11%, national; and 9%, international news; while 10% said they would miss having different opinions, and 15% referred to columnists and editorials. The emphasis on missing local news suggests that for many of these two-paper readers, a metropolitan paper might be retained as a first choice and a local community daily sacrificed.

FREQUENT AND INFREQUENT READERS

About two-thirds of the people who did not read a paper "yesterday" read one at least occasionally, and a third might be classified as true nonreaders (1987). On the other hand, among "yesterday's" readers, some are actually infrequent readers for whom "yesterday" just happened to be "the" day. Four out of five people (79%) say their yesterday was routine, and they are more likely to have read a newspaper than those whose yesterday was unusual (1982).

Why do some people read the paper on certain days and not on others? To investigate this, 539 newspaper readers were interviewed by phone on two different evenings about a month apart, and 505 of them also completed questionnaires (1981a). The study was done in "Northeast Metro," a declining major industrial center with two competing dailies and fast-growing "Southwest City," with two papers under common ownership.

More than 9 out of 10 who had not read and did not expect to read a paper on a particular day said it was because of something to do with the day itself, usually because they were too busy. Only a handful said they already had the news from other sources or were uninterested in the news of that day. Those who missed the paper on any given day were looking at books and magazines to the same degree as the newspaper readers, indicating that other forms of reading matter were not a substitute. Moreover, they watched somewhat less television.

So another approach to the analysis of readership is to compare people who read with high frequency (five or four weekdays out of five) and those who read less often, differentiating both these groups from the true *nonreaders*, who practically *never* look at a newspaper. Subscribers, understandably, are most likely to be regular readers. Among those who read a paper "yesterday," 75% of frequent readers have home delivery compared with 33% of infrequent readers. Frequent readers report spending 47 minutes a day with the newspapers; infrequent readers, 29 minutes (1987).

Readership patterns for men and women have been closely parallel, even though on the average, women still have slightly less education than men do, and readership increases with education. (This has been the historic pattern, but younger women are better educated than young men.) Average weekday readership is just a bit lower among women (63%) than among men (67%).[2]

When we compare nonreaders with frequent and infrequent readers, we find considerable differences that go beyond the conventional indicators of age or social position. These seem to reflect differences in personality, in the use of other media, in attitudes toward media, and in the kinds of functions or satisfactions sought from them.[3]

Such essentially psychological or attitudinal differences, in themselves, might be considered to represent the causes of differences in reading habits. Or they may be thought of as merely the concomitants or secondary effects of demographic differences, since those who live differently also think differently. Frequent readers in 1987 were more likely to be married (69%) or widowed (7%) than the infrequent readers (58% and 4%), but because they were older as a group, fewer of them (38% compared to 50%) reported that there were children in the household.

It comes as no surprise that, in contrast to nonreaders and infrequent readers, frequent readers of the daily paper are also more likely to be frequent readers of the Sunday paper and of news magazines. They are more often found among those who are currently reading a fiction book (78%) than among all other newspaper readers (69%) (1982). They are comparatively more oriented to the news and information aspect of the newspaper than they are to its entertainment value.

They are more likely to talk about current events in their everyday conversation. They talk more about politics and have a greater confidence in their own ability to influence local government. They are more involved in their communities (1977). Of the frequent readers, 75% said they had voted in the 1984 election; among the infrequent readers, the proportion was 55%; however, the party allegiances were virtually the same for the two groups. Frequent readers were more likely to belong to voluntary associations and to be active in them. The frequent readers were considerably more likely to

---

[2]These data are from SMRB, 1987. Other studies show a narrower gap between the sexes, but a slight difference is always apparent.

[3]However, frequent and infrequent readers responded very similarly to a series of questions asked in our two-city study (1982) in an effort to classify people in terms of their optimism or pessimism.

claim they were registered to vote (78%) in 1987 than the infrequent readers (64%).

All these attributes might be said to be mere reflections of higher social status. (There is ample evidence that higher social status carries with it a greater sense of well-being, more social participation, a greater facility in personal communication.) Frequent readers were older and had higher incomes, but their educational achievement closely resembled that of the infrequent readers. (The explanation is that younger people, with lower incomes, are better educated than older ones, but also less likely to be regular readers.)

In our 1982 survey, we questioned people about their leisure activities, which we classified as *recreational* (sports, exercise, movies, shows), *social* (visiting, entertaining, meetings), *individual* (shopping, hobbies, reading), and *engaged* (working at home or at odd jobs, hunting, fishing). In every case, frequent readership of newspapers was most often found among the most active.

This finding was reinforced in our 1987 study. Three out of five people said they do not have enough time to do all the things they want to do, but the proportion goes up with education and income. People who say they don't have enough time are less likely to be frequent newspaper readers (56%) than those who say that time is not a problem (63%). But the ones who complain about time are not really the most active. Except for the youthful activity of moviegoing, frequent readers are more likely to have engaged in leisure activities within the past month (Table 3.4).

A third of the infrequent readers (compared to one in eight among the frequent readers) say they only read the parts of the paper that interest them. While frequent readers say they want mostly news (58%) rather than features (14%) in their paper, the margin of difference is less dramatic (40%–28%) for infrequent readers. However, they show similar leanings when asked for their main source of news on different topics.

Infrequent readers show far less dependence on the paper in forming opinions, staying in touch with the world, deciding how to vote, and

TABLE 3.4
Percentage of Frequent and Infrequent Readers
Engaged in Activities Within Past Month, 1987

	All readers	Frequent readers	Infrequent readers
Go to a movie	27	26	30
Hobby	46	52	43
Exercise/active sport	43	49	41
Attend meeting	34	39	31
Attend sports event	23	25	24
None	7	6	6

planning their time. They show less appreciation of the paper's entertainment value and even of its coverage of accidents and crimes. But they are more likely to say they use the paper to follow up on news they have found out about elsewhere and that the paper helps them in conversation. Frequent and infrequent readers give equal weight to the paper as a source for information about shopping and celebrities and as a way of passing the time.

Frequent and infrequent readers give rather similar ratings to their newspapers, with the frequent readers slightly more favorable. The infrequent readers are also less able to express opinions on the paper's fairness and editorial practices.

What accounts for variations in newspaper reading frequency? The geographic region in which people live makes more of a difference than anything else. There are proportionately fewer frequent readers in the South and West than in the eastern and central states (Table 3.5). The South and West are the least urbanized parts of the country and have somewhat lower average levels of educational attainment. Also, these regions have had the greatest population growth in recent years. They therefore have a relatively large percentage of mobile people, many of them young, who have only recently arrived in their communities. However, regional differences in newspaper readership are not simply a by-product of their differences in income levels. In every bracket of household income, more people in the Northeast read newspapers than those in the South or West.

The newspaper reading habit becomes fixed when people strike independent roots—when they get married, start families, and begin to accumulate property and civic involvements. However, an anomalous fact is that people who have small or grade-school-aged children living at home read the newspaper less frequently than others of comparable age (1977). The explanation may well be that child care uses both time and money, as does newspaper reading. As a direct consequence, at least some young couples raising a family on a shoestring may get along without a newspaper.

The infrequent readers and nonreaders cannot be lumped together. In fact, neither group is itself homogeneous. The nonreaders are strikingly different from the other two groups. Frequent readers (in 1987) include a

TABLE 3.5
Percentage Who Read a Newspaper "Yesterday"
by Census Region (SMRB, 1987)

Total adults	65
Northeast	72
Midwest	66
South	61
West	63

higher percentage of college graduates (23%) than infrequent readers (15%) and a smaller proportion of people who are not high school graduates (18% compared with 22%). However, among nonreaders, only 8% are college graduates, and 38% did not complete high school.

The age differences among the three groups are more notable, as Table 3.6 indicates. The infrequent readers have a decidedly youthful profile; the frequent and nonreaders, an older one. The minority of nonreaders among the elderly obviously are concentrated at a different social level and at a higher age level than the frequent readers.

The older nonreaders include a high proportion of people with low incomes, poor education, and narrowing interests. Without children at home, they seem to have withdrawn from the wider world. Younger nonreaders also seem to be individuals who are disinterested in their broader surroundings and have withdrawn into their immediate personal relationships (1977).

As for the infrequent readers, those under 35 appear to include the most transient, unsettled, alienated element of their age group. Although they respond to entertainment, many of them seem to be turned off by the news itself, including the news of their local community. By contrast, the infrequent readers over 35 are characterized by their blue-collar, working-class background. They are people with a highly localistic orientation and a general apathy toward the wider aspects of the news.

Older people are, of course, more apt to be widowed and living alone, and newspaper readership is lower in families with fewer adults. Quite apart from the increasing number of the elderly, about 50 million adults under 65 were in one- or two-person households in 1987. Among those under 65, according to SMRB, average weekday readership in 1986 was 58% for those who lived alone and 53% for those in two-person households. In those two-person households, readership was higher for married couples (72%) than for those individuals who lived with children or other adults (63%).

Those who look at a newspaper infrequently cannot be characterized as

TABLE 3.6
Frequent, Infrequent, and Nonreaders, by Age, 1987[a]

	Frequent	Infrequent	Nonreaders
18–24	8%	22%	12%
25–34	18	31	27
35–44	22	20	18
45–54	16	10	13
55–64	15	9	11
65–74	14	5	10
75+	8	2	9

[a]N (unweighted) 987, 730, 332, respectively.

people who simply don't read at all. Three-fourths of them read magazines, and one out of six regularly reads a news magazine. But somehow or other the daily newspaper represents lesser value and lower priority than other forms of reading matter.

Perhaps the greatest distinction between frequent and infrequent readers is in their comparative preference for newspapers and television. Forty-three percent of the frequent readers say newspapers are more important to them as citizens and voters, and 26% name television (1987). Among the infrequent readers, television is named by 50%; newspapers, by 19%. But while the infrequent readers watch more TV in general, they watched considerably less of the news (Table 3.7). (The nonreaders who caught the news spent the most time watching it, but that is a by-product of their greater addiction to TV generally.)

Among people in subscribing households, frequent readership is at the same high level regardless of sex, city size, education, income, occupation, or employment status. But even when the paper is delivered every day, frequent readership is lower among younger people than among older ones. It is slightly lower among mobile people and lower for Blacks than for Whites— even in families that have the paper at home. The explanation may simply be in the matter of a more mobile lifestyle, but it suggests greater weakness in the reading habit, even when the paper is available.

THE RATIONALE FOR NOT READING

Those individuals who neither subscribed to a daily newspaper nor had read one "yesterday" were asked in the 1971 study why they did not subscribe to a paper. Four percent said their subscription had not been solicited, 12% complained of delivery problems, and 9% insisted that they usually did pick it up at a newsstand or read someone else's copy. Only 7% made specific statements about the product, with 4% saying the news was too depressing to read and 3% saying they disliked the paper's editorial policy; 12% said they got all the news they needed from TV or radio, and 2% said they were away

TABLE 3.7
TV News Viewing, by Newspaper Reading Frequency, 1987

	Watched TV news yesterday	Minutes spent with TV news (by those viewing)
Frequent readers	71%	60.4
Infrequent readers	63	51.0
Nonreaders	57	62.8

from home too much of the time to subscribe. Ten percent said the paper cost too much, 22% said they didn't have enough time to read it, and 30% said they were just not interested.

Younger, more mobile people with lower incomes were more likely to say they were "just not interested." Older more settled people most often complained about delivery problems.

Housewives under 30 who had not been subscribing to the newspaper were asked why in 1973. Some were already readers: 7% said that they did not subscribe to the newspaper because they bought it from the rack or newsstand; 2% said they got the paper free, perhaps at work or from a trial subscription. Thirty percent said they were "just not interested" in it, 22% said they had "no time to read," and 10% said it "cost too much." Twelve percent complained of poor delivery, and 12% said they got the news from television and radio. Only a handful—3%—complained about editorial policy and 4% about "bad news."

The strength of the reading habit for any individual does not, of course, remain constant throughout a lifetime. Can we identify the reasons why particular readers change? One paper that carefully followed up to find out when subscribers had stopped found that one in three had simply switched to a competing daily, and one in four had moved; 8% had complaints about the service, and another 8% had objections to the editorial content.

A special study was undertaken to examine the reasons why people reduce their newspaper reading (1979c). As a first step, self-administered questionnaires were returned by a nationwide consumer panel of 24,000 people. Thirteen percent said they had increased their reading frequency, and 12% said they had cut back on their reading in recent years. Eight hundred readers were then selected for personal interviewing; 200 each who were stable in their reading patterns, either frequent or infrequent (as defined earlier), and 200 each who had either increased or cut back.

Those who had cut back generally resembled the stable group of occasional readers, although they were somewhat younger and had lower income. Had these dropout readers encountered changes in the overall quality of their newspapers that might have made them unhappy or disaffected? Only 21% were aware of any such changes, about half the proportion among people with stable reading patterns. In other words, the dropout readers seemed to be less sensitive to or aware of the newspaper's content. But among those who were aware of changes, 81% felt that they had made the paper worse. Among those whose reading habits were unchanged, but who were aware of editorial changes or innovations, only half were critical.

Was it the poor quality of delivery service that made these readers drop out? Apparently not to any significant degree, because only 15% described their delivery service as unacceptable. Among the stable readers, both frequent and infrequent, the equivalent figure was 12%. (It was 6% among those who said they were reading more than formerly.)

A variety of studies have found that when people who seldom read the paper or who have stopped their subscriptions are asked why, "No time to read" is a commonly given answer. In this instance, 57% of the dropouts claimed to have less time than they used to have. Among the infrequent readers, 47% said this; among the frequent readers, and those who had stepped up their reading, the figure was 33%. But in reality, there is no basis for the dropouts' claim that they were too busy to read the paper, if this means having more responsibilities. Fewer of them had children than those who were reading *more* often. They were no more likely to have recently started classes or courses that could eat into their free time. Somewhat fewer of them were new home owners with additional chores and preoccupations. And they were just about as likely as the others to have recently started a new job or a more demanding job that could take more of their time.

What most seemed to characterize the dropouts was an exceptional apathy about what was going on in the world around them. When asked whether their interest in news had increased or decreased, 12% said their interest in international and national news was greater than it used to be—only a third as many as gave this response in the other three groups. They also showed substantially less interest in state and local news and also in news of the schools and neighborhood. By contrast, the people who had increased their reading showed substantially more interest in local and neighborhood news than those with unchanged patterns, including the frequent readers.

LIFE CHANGES AND READING PATTERNS

To investigate how and why individuals' reading habits change in the wake of significant life events, we questioned a national sample of 748 adults between the ages of 25 and 44 by phone on three occasions over an 18-month period in 1981 and 1982. An analysis by Andrew Beveridge (1982a) found that 86% of those identified as frequent readers on the first interview were also frequent readers on the second and third interviews. The same stability was found for 79% of newspaper subscribers and for 76% of "yesterday" readers. But our interest was in the exceptions, like the 12% of subscribers who dropped their subscriptions and the 22% of nonsubscribers who became subscribers. Of all those interviewed three times, 60% were consistently frequent readers and 20% consistently infrequent ones, and their respective characteristics jibed with what was well known from previous research.

What accounted for the changes among the remaining 20%? The answer cannot be found in the degree of general interest in the news, which was unrelated to changes in newspaper habits. Use of the newspaper as a main news source did, however, have a positive effect, as can be seen in Table 3.8.

Price changes and satisfaction with the paper and its delivery service, surprisingly, were unrelated to changes in reading or subscribing, but those who changed were more likely to report that their reading habits had been altered in the year before they were first interviewed. They may simply have reverted to former patterns during the period covered by the study.

A check of substantive interest in different types of newspaper content supported the common-sense observation that strong news interests would sustain or foster regular readership. So does a sense of the newspaper's importance. Those who said they spend the right amount of time with the newspaper were more likely to stick with it then those who said they spend too little time with it.

And attitudes toward the paper itself—its fairness, accuracy, and "bad news" content—also were unrelated to changes in reading pattern. Frequent viewing of TV news seemed to have small though detectable effects that were ambiguous in nature; it seemed to weaken readership among frequent readers and encourage it among infrequent readers. But changes in the amount of TV news watching, or of TV watching in general, were not related to changes in newspaper habits. Heavy use of other media appeared to go with increased use of newspapers.

People who moved in this period and those whose marital status changed were most likely to change their reading frequency. If they were subscribers, they showed a greater tendency to stop; if nonsubscribers, to start.

Those who increased their involvement in community organizations during this period also increased their reading frequency. There was no indication that people with the greatest life responsibilities and time pressures or with increased responsibilities and pressures were adversely affected in their newspaper readership.

Contrary to our initial hunch, job changes turned out to be unrelated to

TABLE 3.8
Main News Source and Subscribership, 1982[a]

	World news		Local news	
	Newspaper	*Other*	*Newspaper*	*Other*
Nonsubscribers, both interviews	69%	80%	71%	82%
Converted to subscribers	31	20	29	18
N	(54)	(193)	(101)	(149)
Subscribers, both interviews	91%	86%	91%	82%
Stopped subscribing	9	14	9	18
N	(171)	(323)	(328)	(166)

changes in reading patterns. However, people who described themselves as confident in their outlook on society were more likely to increase their reading; the less confident were more likely to read less. Better-educated and older people tended to increase their reading, and poorly educated and younger people to reduce theirs during the 18 months they were followed. In short, the usual demographic differences in propensity to read newspapers were accentuated with the passage of time.

HOW PERSONAL MOBILITY AFFECTS READERSHIP

The first task in assuring that people will read newspapers is, as I suggested in Chapter 2, getting newspapers to them. In 1977, a majority (62%) of readers said they hardly ever missed seeing the paper. The main explanation is that the paper was at the door every day. People who are often on the move don't want newspapers piling up outside when they're not at home, because it is both a waste of money and an invitation to trouble.

Circulation managers who attribute readership losses to changes in lifestyle are likely, when asked to explain this, to refer to the increased mobility of the population (1973). It is true that more of the American public is in motion than every before in history. Two out of three families take vacation trips in the course of a year, only 40% of them in the summer; frequent, short trips are replacing the traditional two-week vacation. Mobility in the United States has increased along with more vacation days. And people have the means to take off whenever they wish. Eighty-six percent of all working Americans drive to their jobs.

Three-fifths of the 86% of households that own cars own more than one, which makes the proportion even higher in households with more than one adult member. This means that, increasingly, the car is a personal rather than a family possession. Rather than a force for cohesion as it was in generations past, it is a means by which individuals can detach themselves from the rest of the family group.

But apart from this casual itinerant movement, the population is shifting residence as well. Contrary to what is often said, people are actually making fewer permanent moves than they did in the recent past. According to the U.S. Census figures, between 1960 and 1961, 20% of the population moved to a different house, and 6.3% moved to a different country. Between 1983 and 1984, the percentage who moved dropped to 16.8%; half (8.3%) moved within the same metropolitan area.

Over a period of time, a minority of the total population accounts for a high proportion of all the moves that are made. This minority is especially difficult for newspapers to reach, both for the simple physical reason that they are elusive customers for the circulation department and also for the psychological reason that they lack the community roots that editors nurture.

Some people who move outside their original metropolitan area go into an outlying exurban community and remain within the circulation orbit of the same daily newspapers. Conversely, some people who move within the same metropolitan area go from one suburban community with its own daily to another suburb with a different paper; they must shift their newspaper reading orientation dramatically.

Mobility confronts the newspaper circulation department with an unprecedented subscription sales and servicing problem. Most newspapers consider every subscription start and stop as a fresh transaction, even when it involves something as simple as an extended weekend vacation. By this method of reckoning, some papers find it necessary to sell as many new subscriptions each year as their total subscription circulation at any point in time. To compensate for the attrition of existing subscribers, newspaper circulation departments must sell about 25 million new starts each year, many of them to people who have subscribed before. The cost of doing this (at some $12 per order) can be estimated at $300 million a year.

There is a widespread assumption that after retirement, people normally pack up and leave for the Sunbelt. Actually, only 5% of those over 65 moved outside their home area in a recent one-year period; 2% changed residence in the same area (Table 1.2). The people who are most likely to move are those under 30. Young people have always left home to strike out on their own. This mobility helps explain why the daily reading levels of young adults are not higher than they are. It takes a fairly long process of adjustment and familiarization before one feels really at home with a new community and its newspaper. Among frequent readers, 24% have lived at their present address for less than two years (1987). Among infrequent readers, the proportion is 41%; among nonreaders, it is 36%.

This disparity in reading habits between people who have moved and people who have stayed in the same town is comparable, regardless of their age levels. And people who don't feel permanently rooted in the community (those who *expect* to be moving within the next three years) are also less likely to be frequent newspaper readers.

NEWSPAPER READING AND SOCIAL STATUS

At any age level, people of higher income and education are most likely to be heavy users and seekers of information and regular newspaper readers. In fact, this differentiation begins in childhood, as Table 3.9 shows. Thus, the media environment created by the family's means, way of life, and social status is carried over from one generation to the next.

TABLE 3.9
Percentage of Children Who Read Newspaper "Yesterday",
by Age and Mother's Education, 1978

	Mother's education		
Child's age	At least some college	High school graduate	Less
6–8[a]	3	6	10
9–11	26	25	11
12–14	48	46	32
15–17	61	49	29

[a]The inconsistent response within this age group probably reflects the unreliability of response from children who are so young.

Over a five-day period, the cumulative newspaper exposure of people at different income and educational levels reveals only small differences. But on any given weekday, newspapers are read far more often by people at the upper end of the social scale (Table 3.3). This pattern is similar to that for magazine reading and the reverse of television viewing, which gets the most time from people of lowest income and education, who tend to have the most time on their hands (Table 3.10).

TABLE 3.10
Magazine Reading and TV Viewing, by Education and
Household Income (SMRB, 1986)

	Magazine reading[a]	Television viewing[a]
At least some college		
$30,000+	154	53
$20,000–$29,999	127	73
Under $20,000	108	88
High school graduate		
$30,000+	123	80
$20,000–$29,999	88	100
Under $20,000	75	115
Not high school graduate		
$30,000+	92	100
$20,000–$29,999	53	147
Under $20,000	40	167

[a]Index of 100 is average number of magazines read and hours spent watching TV.

A long series of studies, academic and commercial, has demonstrated the tendency of better-educated persons to be oriented more strongly to print than to the broadcast media, and for the reverse to be true at lower levels of education and social status. In 1961, among the college educated, 45% reported that they "would feel quite lost" if they had to get along "for quite some time" without newspapers, but at the same time they said that they could get used to the absence of TV; only 7% gave the reverse answer. However, that proportion who would "feel lost" without TV and could get along without newspapers rose to 12% among those with no more than a grade-school education, while the proportion who would "feel lost" without newspapers and could get along without television went down to 28%. Apparently, although less-educated people relied less on newspapers, at least at that date, they did not rely correspondingly more on television. They just felt less strongly about the mass media as such.

Social differences are most dramatic when we consider the reader's active behavior in relation to the newspaper as an institution. The more unusual or selective the activity, the greater the contrast between persons at different educational levels. Thus, the proportion of the public who reported having written a letter to the editor at some time or another ranged from 2% (among those readers with a grade-school education) to 29% (among those with college degrees, 1982).

This suggests that as one ascends the social scale there is a greater sense of ease, intimacy, and personal relationship between the reader and his paper. It seems as though the better-educated reader is more likely to view the hometown paper as an institution made up of people doing a job, subject to personal influences, and capable of rendering a service. For those lower on the educational scale, the newspaper as a major institutionof power appears more remote and impersonal.

There is a complex relationship between an individual's educational level and the regularity of his newspaper reading, as well as the number of papers read, the thoroughness with which they are read, and the amount of time spent reading each paper. As education goes up, so does the proportion of readers who read more than one paper, the regularity of reading (expressed in terms of the number of days of the week on which a paper is read), and the thoroughness of reading (as reported by the respondent). But the person with a college education spends less time with the average paper than does the person who has never gone beyond grade school. Since the college-educated individual reads more papers each day, he spends more time with newspapers altogether, even though his reading speed takes him more quickly through each one.

Since people who earn more money are better educated, they are more efficient readers. Persons in upper-income households (over $40,000) spent 38 minutes per day with each paper read in 1987 compared to 45 minutes in households under $10,000. But 28% of the readers in the top income group read two or more papers per day compared to 13% of those in the lowest income bracket.

Since reading habits are related both to age and education, it is important to remember that these attributes are also independently linked. Young people stay in school longer than in the past, as I noted in Chapter 1. In 1950, 14% of the population over 25 had attended some college; by 1982, that had increased to 36.5% for Whites and 26.5% for Blacks (whose rate improved even more dramatically). The proportion of high school graduates rose from 41% in 1960 to 77% in 1988.

Given the close connection between education and readership, a higher educational attainment among young people would seem to promise a substantial increase in the level of newspaper reading. Actually this has not taken place. In 1987 a smaller proportion of adults under 30 were reading the paper on a typical weekday than in the recent past.

To be sure, trends in educational attainment can only be measured in terms of the number of years of completed schooling. This measure does not reflect changes in the quality of education, in the degree of emphasis on traditional reading and writing skills, in classroom discipline, or in grade-to-grade promotion practices.

Social position is generally reflected in a greater than average sense of personal potency, in a broader range of interests and activities, and in more participation in voluntary groups. It is not surprising, therefore, that people who are active in civic affairs and organizations should rank above average in newspaper readership. (The National Opinion Research Center found "every day" newspaper reading reported in 1977 by 75% of the adults who belong to three or more voluntary associations, but by only 49% of those who have no memberships at all.) Even when these civically more active people are compared with others within the same income levels, it is clear that they tend to be more regular newspaper readers. Our 1961 study found that a critical difference occurs at the lowest income level, where activists are far more apt to be regular readers.

Demographic differences are characteristically associated with personality differences. Even though people at any given social or age level show tremendous psychological variability, differences in personality, outlook, or living habits that can be found in large populations are more easily explained by social differences than the other way around. This explains the inconclusive results of an attempt to link newspaper reading to differences in personality type, defined by responses to a battery of 500 self-rating questions (1972). Eight prototypical male and eight female personality clusters were evolved through the statistical technique of factor analysis. The very small variations in the percentage of "yesterday" newspaper readers found in each group could be attributed simply to the age and social class differences among them.

A dozen years later, a currently fashionable way of classifying people in

TABLE 3.11
Newspaper Reading by Personality Type* (SMRB, 1984)

Achievers (21%)	77%
Socially conscious (12%)	74
Belongers (39%)	69
Experimental (6%)	67
"I am me" (3%)	66
Emulators (8%)	61
Survivors (4%)	48
Sustainers (7%)	46

*The proportion of the public in each personality type group is shown in parentheses.

terms of "Values and Life Styles" (VALS)[4] was applied by SMRB to its national sample, with the aid of a small selection of statements by which respondents rated themselves. The results, shown in Table 3.11, indicate that newspaper reading was highest among the upwardly mobile "achievers" and "socially conscious" (not surprisingly, since they are the best educated) and dropped off among the "survivors" and "sustainers" at the bottom of the social heap.

THE WORKING WOMAN

The great changes in household income and living patterns and in family structure are inseparable from the changed participation of women in the economy. The new feminism that emerged in the 1970s was based on a fundamental transformation of women's traditional roles. A growing proportion of women of working age are in the work force. (In 1987, it was 67% of those between the ages of 18 and 64, up from 50% in 1970 and from 37% in 1950. This included, in 1987, 65% of all mothers of children under 18.) Of these working women, 77% had full-time jobs.

The number of working women who say they have worked continually grew from 33% in 1971a to 42% in 1979b. Moreover, an increasing proportion expected to be working two years later—84% of all those holding jobs in 1979. There was also a dramatic increase in the proportion of nonworking women who said they *might be* working in the future, from one third in 1971 to nearly half in 1979. Work had evidently become the norm.

This is reflected in a vitally important attitudinal change that took place in the 1970s. In 1979, but *not* in 1971, working women were regarded more positively than full-time housewives, both by themselves and by the house-

[4]See Arnold Mitchell, *The Nine American Lifestyles: Who We Are and Where We Are Going* (New York: Macmillan, 1983).

wives not working. At the earlier date, a typical working woman was described as someone who "has a full life" by 71% of working women, but by only 57% of housewives; while the housewife received this description from 52% of working women and from 64% of housewives. Each group tended to see itself more favorably relative to the other. By 1979, working women continued to have a favorable self-image, up to 76% from 1971, and 62% of the housewives also agreed. But the attitudes of housewives toward themselves and the attitudes of working women toward the full-time housewife role showed a striking decline in esteem.

The increase in the proportion of women who work outside the home has directly paralleled the trend for women to complete more years of education. In fact, much of the improvement in general educational levels is accounted for by the narrowing of the traditional gap between men and women. Women accounted for 38% of the bachelor's degrees granted in 1960–61. In 1984–85 they accounted for 51%. As this trend can be expected to continue, it should raise the level of women's participation in the work force and incidentally of their newspaper readership.

Surveys have consistently shown that women who work outside the home are somewhat more likely to be newspaper readers, both weekday and Sunday (SMRB in 1987 showed 64% of working women read "yesterday," 61% of other women did). But this is because employed women add to their families' earnings and fewer of them are in the lowest household income bracket, where readership is lowest. Within each income group, employed women are actually slightly less likely to be readers. Working mothers are more likely to be frequent newspaper readers than are their counterparts in the home, and their children at any age are also more likely to be readers (Table 3.12).

Although women who work outside the home have more demands on their time than traditional housewives do, they have more money to spend and participate more actively in the world around them. They have broader information needs and recreational interests. Far more of them than of full-time housewives report visiting friends, eating meals out, going to the movies or the theater, engaging in participant sports, going to sports events as

TABLE 3.12
Children of Employed and Nonemployed Mothers
Who "Ever Read" a Newspaper, 1978

Child's age	Employed mothers	Nonemployed mothers
6–8	43%	27%
9–11	73	55
12–14	78	74
15–17	83	77

a spectator, attending club meetings, or taking vacations away from home (Table 3.13). All this is reflected in their newspaper reading.

As we see in Chapter 6, newspapers publish much more special interest material directed at men than at women readers. But asked whether there was more in the paper for men or for women, 76% of both employed and nonemployed said "about the same amount" (1979b).

However, working women were more likely to say that there is more in the paper for "women like themselves." (Incidentally, the straight information approach of newspapers attracts less feminist criticism than television's fictional portrayals. A majority of both employed and nonemployed women believe that newspaper articles present women as they should be presented but that television shows do not.)

Our analysis of reader interests (discussed in Chapter 9) shows that in general working women have more interest in a much greater variety of newspaper subject matter. They show particularly greater interest in serious news items: military and political subjects, the environment, social problems, items dealing with racial and minority issues, and energy. They are also better than average readers of letters and advice columns. They are less parochial in outlook; 25% say they are "much more interested in news of my own city or town" than in national or world news. Among the housewives, 33% are much more interested in the local news.

There are some newspaper subjects in which employed and nonemployed women have equal interest. They show equivalent interest in crime, in dramatic stories of hijackings and hostage takings, in stories of accidents and disasters, and also in the traditional women's subjects: food and home and garden (1977).

But this apparent similarity masks some real social differences (Table 3.14). For example, college graduates show much more interest in traditional women's news if they are full-time housewives. A working college graduate is likely to have career interests that make domesticity less absorbing. High

TABLE 3.13
Activities of Employed and Nonemployed Women, 1979b

In Past Month	Employed	Nonemployed
Visit friends	81%	78%
Eat meals out	78	62
Go to movies or theater	40	22
Engage in participant sports	31	13
Attend sports event	18	10
Attend club meeting	37	33
Vacation away from home[a]	66	57
N	(736)	(305)

[a]Within past year

TABLE 3.14
Percentage Showing at Least Some Interest
in Average Item of "Women's" News, 1977

Education	Employed women	Nonemployed women
College graduate	54	77
High school graduate or some college	70	70
Some high school or less	73	61

school graduates or those with some college show exactly equivalent interest in such items. But among those less well educated, it is the working women who show the greatest interest in homemaking, food preparation, and the like. The very fact that they work suggests a drive toward self-improvement that is also expressed in their domestic life.

THE MINORITY READER

A major force affecting circulation and audience trends is the changing racial composition of the big central cities, with great increases in the proportion of Blacks and (in certain regions) of Latin Americans and people of Asian origin. In 1988, minorities (as lately redefined) accounted for one-fifth of the total population; Blacks were 11.5%; non-Black Hispanics, 6.3%; and Asians, 1.5%.

For over 100 years, American cities have experienced waves of immigration in which newcomers from very different cultural environments have been gradually absorbed. They have acquired new language skills and the habits of urban living, and their children have been educated and have taken on the newspaper-reading habit. (Newspapers published in their own languages have helped in their orientation; 39 dailies had a circulation of 1,105,000 in 1988, of which 43% was in Spanish.)

In spite of the special barriers imposed by physical appearance and racist traditions, there might be reason to expect that the new residents of the cities will be acculturated as their predecessors were and that as they are brought closer to the mainstream levels of income and education, they will become regular newspaper readers. This expectation might be especially strong in the case of the millions of Black Americans who are newcomers to the urban scene.

Newspapers represent a unique force for social cohesion. There is no other medium of communication that has the same socially integrative function. By providing a common pool of information, newspapers bind together people who live in a particular geographic area and share interests that come from the same environment, the same problems, and common politics. Thus, newspapers exert a force that tends to reduce social distance—the mutual sense of apartness between different groups—and thus works to eliminate social differences.

People whom the Census Bureau classifies as *Hispanics* are the fastest-growing identifiable minority in the United States, but they encompass a great variety of national origins, differences in appearance, cultural heritages, and positions in American society. Chicanos in San Antonio, Texas, Cubans in Miami, Florida, Puerto Ricans in New Haven, Connecticut, Dominicans in Paterson, New Jersey, and Colombians in Queens, New York, may carry a common designation in newsrooms, but they all have distinctive identities. Fifty-two percent of SMRB's Spanish-speaking respondents read a daily newspaper "yesterday" in 1987, but this aggregates 10th-generation New Mexicans of Castilian lineage and Ecuadorean "illegals," so the number must be used with caution.

In 1982, six percent of those interviewed said that Spanish was the language most often spoken at home, and nine percent said it was another foreign language. Even among the Spanish-speakers, 53% were frequent newspaper readers. Among those who mainly used another foreign language, the proportion of frequent readers (71%) was the same as among the English-speaking majority (70%).[5]

The nine Spanish-language daily newspapers published in the continental United States had a circulation of 473,000 in 1988, a fraction of the estimated

---

[5]In a 1980 telephone survey study of 820 Mexican Americans and 765 Anglos in seven Southwestern cities with Gannett newspapers, only 16% of the Hispanic respondents said they read Spanish only, and another 11% said they read mostly Spanish. Thirty percent of them were nonreaders of newspapers, compared with 12% of the Anglos, although 45% had read a paper on at least five of the last seven days. (For Anglos, the proportion was 68%.) Mexican Americans rated their satisfaction with newspapers and other media higher than did Anglos. (Texas Hispanics surveyed by Stephen Reese were also more likely than White Anglos or Blacks to agree that "media coverage of people like me is basically fair and unbiased.")

Only 12% said they would prefer to have the entire newspaper in Spanish, but 54% said they would prefer to have part of it in Spanish. One in four said there was at least one person in the household who did not read the paper because it was in English.

The content interests of Hispanics were not very different from those of Anglos. They showed somewhat greater interest in news of crime, accidents and disasters, and entertainment features; somewhat less interest in national politics and editorials.

In five of the cities, questionnaires were administered to 5th- and 10th-grade school children. The difference in newspaper use between Hispanics and Anglos were not as sharp as those among adults. They appeared to reflect social class rather than language orientation. (Among Anglos, 73% had home delivery; among Hispanics, 50%.) For both groups, newspapers were read primarily "to know what's going on," but Hispanic children were more apt than Anglos to refer to the paper's entertainment aspects; to say that it cheers them up and helps them forget their problems. (Bradley S. Greenberg, Michael Burgoon, Judee K. Burgoon, and Felipe Korzenny, *Mexican Americans and the Mass Media*, Norwood, NJ: Ablex, 1983.)

3,500,000 for Spanish magazines, weeklies, and other publications. Newspapers in cities with large Spanish-speaking populations have tried hard to woo them as readers, recognizing that the same family often includes grandparents who speak no English at all, parents who can read it with some discomfort, and children who are completely bilingual in speech but who may have far better reading skills in English than in Spanish. In Hoboken, New Jersey, the Hudson *Dispatch* experimented with a Spanish-language page, which simply seemed to alienate its non-Hispanic working-class readers. The Miami *Herald*, published in a city where Cubans have become the predominant ethnic group, produced a daily section *("El Herald"* curiously, rather than *El Heraldo)* for distribution in Cuban neighborhoods. This was substantially expanded into *El Nuevo Herald* (with 90,000 distribution) in 1987, in an all-out effort to bolster declining penetration levels within a city in which the competing *Diario de las Americas* had attained a circulation of 64,000. In 27 metropolitan Sunday papers, with a combined circulation of 1.2 million, *Vista*, an English-language supplement aimed at Hispanic readers, was being distributed in selected neighborhoods, aimed at the new generation of U.S.-educated young people whom editors were anxious to attract.

The problem of increasing Hispanic readership concerns a number of metropolitan newspapers; the problem of increasing Black readership concerns nearly all of them. If Black readership of newspapers lags behind that of Whites, this is clearly interdependent with how and what newspapers cover in the news (not only news of Blacks, but subjects that interest Blacks). It also relates to the question of Black participation in the staffing and management of the newspaper business itself.

Historically, Blacks have been ignored or underrepresented in news coverage and almost absent from the professional ranks of American journalism. "Minority" employees made up 6.6% of the 54,700 newsroom employees of daily newspapers in 1987, according to an American Society of Newspaper Editors (ASNE) employment survey. (By contrast, Blacks held 8.7% of all professional positions on commercial TV stations and 7.8% of all professional positions on commercial radio stations.)

When we compare the newspaper-reading patterns of Blacks with those of the White majority, it is apparent that they reflect the more general social disadvantage of Blacks in American society. It is not surprising that daily newspaper readership is lower among Blacks than among Whites. What may be considered surprising, rather, is that readership is as strong as it is. Among Whites, 66% read a newspaper "yesterday" and 67% Sunday in 1987; among Blacks, the levels were 61% and 58% (SMRB).[6] Black women showed a

---

[6]Black readers spent 35 minutes reading the paper on a typical day in 1987; White readers, 42 minutes.

somewhat lower level of average weekday readership (59%) than Black men (63%), as did the White women (64%) compared to White (non-Spanish-speaking) men (68%).[7]

Present readership patterns are derived from past experiences. Only 66% of Blacks say they had a newspaper at home as a child, compared with 82% of the Whites. But proportionately as many Blacks as Whites report that the teacher used the newspaper in school when they were children.

One reason why Black adults read fewer newspapers is that more of them are in the youthful age bracket, in which readership is generally lower among Whites as well. Forty-six percent of the Black population in 1987 was under the age of 25. The corresponding figure for Whites was 37%. The remarkable difference in the age distribution of the two groups makes the subjects of Black readership, recruitment, and proper representation in content all the more vital for newspapers as they contemplate the next generation of readers.

Another demographic fact that supports the same point is that there is now a considerable difference in the urban concentration of Whites and Blacks. Before World War II, the typical American Black lived in the rural South. A remarkable transformation has taken place, with 82% of the Black population living in metropolitan areas by 1987 and 60% in the central cities (where only 27% of the Whites live).

Yesterday's statistics on the Black population are rapidly outdated. The proportion of Black high school graduates rose between 1970 to 1987 from 13% to 60%. The proportion of the Black population over 25 that had been to high school went from 26% to 79%. That kind of dramatic revolutionary change carries with it a great many consequences, among them a greater familiarity with the printed word.

Data on Black reading, listening, and viewing habits have changed very rapidly as a reflection of the changes just described. They are also remarkably volatile for another reason. In dealing with a population that is as highly mobile, as inherently suspicious of many of the enterprises of the White society, as skeptical about the explanations that researchers use, and as fearful of the possible consequences of answering questions, the interview procedure from which all our data in the final analysis derive is much more vulnerable to criticism and the numbers much more erratic from one survey organization to another, from one interviewing period to the next. The rate of Black cooperation in surveys is low, even with Black interviewers.[8] (Even

---

[7]It is not improbable that the Black men who are accessible to interviewing underrepresent the "underclass," with its low incidence of readers, whereas female samples are more representative.

[8]Black interviewers were used in the 1977 study, which oversampled the Black population in order to get 679 completed interviews.

the U. S. Bureau of the Census, with its vast resources and professional skills, has encountered severe criticism of its ability to count accurately the size of the Black adult male population.)

Reflecting these sampling uncertainties, the available sources disagree in the specific statistics on reading trends among Blacks, but they lead consistently to the conclusion that their overall weekday reading levels have been relatively stable, compared to the drop we have noted among Whites in the 1970s. (SMRB shows "yesterday" levels down from 80% to 66% for Whites between 1970 and 1987 and from 61% to 58% for Blacks.) It is not unreasonable that Black readership should have held up better, given the rapidity of change in residence, education, and income.

RACE DIFFERENCES AND SOCIAL DIFFERENCES

In comparing the media habits of Blacks with those of Whites, we are dealing with a great many factors that have nothing to do with the subject of race per se. Blacks and Whites live in different kinds of areas and in different neighborhoods in the same area. They have different average age levels and tremendous differences in average income and education. These distinctions make it an especially complex job to tease out truly racial differences in media exposure. Simply to compare overall levels of television viewing or reading for Blacks and Whites without acknowledging their respective levels of age, income, education, or urbanization would be silly. In particular, we have to address ourselves first to those differences that reflect social class and only afterwards to the added dimension of race that makes a difference in what people do with their time.

When Blacks are compared with Whites at the same given level of education or income, the racial differences in reading frequency diminish, but they do not entirely disappear.

Among Blacks as among Whites, newspaper readership is greatest among people living in larger metropolitan areas and among those of higher income and education. Even when we try to compare Blacks and Whites at comparable social levels, race does make a difference. There are a number of explanations for this:

1. Within any given educational or income bracket, the average level of Blacks is generally below that for Whites, so that the two groups are never strictly identical.

2. If newspaper readership among Blacks is less than among Whites, that reflects in part a sense of disengagement or alienation from the society that

the newspaper reports on and from the civic entity that the newspaper represents. The difference might be accounted for by a feeling of hostility, or at least of apathy, toward the newspaper as an institution. It can readily be seen as the White man's paper, as establishmentarian, as a reflection of a different world and a different set of values.

In the Kerner Commission report,[9] "one interviewer" was quoted as an authority in the following terms: "The average black person couldn't give less of a damn about what the media say. The intelligent black person is resentful at what he considers to be a totally false portrayal of what goes on in the ghetto. Most black people see the newspapers as mouthpieces of the 'power structure.' " And then the report went on to say: "Distrust and dislike of the media among ghetto Negroes encompass all the media, though in general the newspapers are distrusted more than the television." No evidence is presented to support this, nor do I know of any that would. But even if this theory accurately applied to only a minority of the Black population (and who would doubt that it does?), it would provide a partial explanation of the difference in reading habits.

3. Within any given income or social class level, differences in readership between Blacks and Whites might also reflect differences in response to the contents of the paper itself. There might be the sense on the part of the Black reader that the paper underreports news that is of direct relevance and interest, the events that affect his life, the people that he knows, thinks about, and to whom he relates.

4. There might also be the simple explanation of vocabulary. The language that newspapers use is not the language that some Black people feel comfortable with. It does not represent the cadences of their own speech.

5. There is another very important reason, already discussed, why there is such a large difference between Black and White newspaper readership: the disintegration of the delivery system in the inner cities.

BLACK MEDIA AND BROADCAST NEWS

The problems of distributing newspapers in the ghetto represent the one qualifier to a statement that could otherwise be made: In the United States today, there are no racial differences in the physical accessibility of media. (There are, of course, differences in the *economic* accessibility of publications

---

[9]Report of the National Advisory Commission on Civil Disorders (New York: Bantam Books, 1968), pp. 362–389.

because of their cost.) Almost everybody, Black or White, has a radio and a television set. And everyone has access to a great variety of publications. In Black areas, these publications overwhelmingly reflect the society as a whole. All Black publications (daily and weekly newspapers and magazines) have an aggregate, per-issue circulation that amounts to less than one copy per Black household. By comparison, the per capita circulation of all general newspapers and magazines is equivalent to five copies per U. S. household (including Blacks).

The Black community press had an aggregate claimed[10] circulation per issue of 3.6 million in 1987, which is only 4% of the circulation of the general press (daily and weekly). But frequency of publication vastly increases the relative opportunity for readership of the general press. In 1987, there were only three Black-owned newspapers appearing four or five days a week, as well as 185 Black weeklies and semiweeklies. Thus, with the exception of two major magazines, *Ebony* (1,771,000 circulation) and *Jet* (806,000 circulation), the periodicals to which Blacks have access are primarily those that serve the community at large.

Between 1960 and 1987, the claimed circulation of Black newspapers doubled, whereas the adult Black population grew by 55%. Still, only 33% of Blacks (compared to 41% of Whites) reported (1987) that they read a paid weekly newspaper. Thus, the surveys jibe with the circulation data to demonstrate that the Black press has a very tiny penetration of the Black population compared to the impact, day in and day out, of the general press among Blacks.

A significant number of radio stations (225, or 3% of the national total of 8,943 commercial stations) cater for at least a few hours a week to the special interest of Black audiences, with Black announcers and disk jockeys, musical selections appealing to Black tastes, and Black gossip and news. Do these stations create any greater degree of loyalty on the part of their listeners than other stations do? All persons who listened to the radio on the previous day were asked: "Did you leave your dial set mostly to one station yesterday or did you listen to two or more different stations?" (1967). The proportion of listeners who said they stayed with a single station was remarkably high, reflecting the high degree of individual personality that radio stations have achieved in an era of transistorized private listening. But the proportion turns out to be identical (73%) for Blacks and for Whites. The Black who stays with a predictable source of "soul music" is no different than the White teenager who keeps tuned to a particular rock and roll station, the White college professor who keeps his hi-fi set at the classical music outlet, or the White

---

[10]Most of these newspapers have not had their circulation figures verified by the Audit Bureau of Circulations, which checks the publishers' statements of most dailies.

farmer who tunes his set consistently to the local station whose weather and crop reports speak directly to his interests.

Whether or not they listen to Black-oriented stations, Blacks spend less time in total listening to radio, because a smaller proportion of Blacks own cars and drive to and from work. They are far less likely to listen to daytime radio than are Whites. In the evening hours, the difference disappears. However, with television the figures are reversed. In total, Blacks watch TV about 39% more than Whites do (as a reflection of their lower social status and of more hours of daytime viewing), and their program preferences are somewhat different.

As I emphasize later, exposure to radio and television news comes about as a by-product of exposure to broadcasting itself. (Much of news listening and viewing comes about because people have tuned to a station in anticipation of entertainment programs or because they already have the set tuned to a station when the news comes on.) This explains why the percentage of Blacks and Whites watching any television news on an average day was virtually identical in 1987, but Blacks spent a sixth more time watching. (A higher proportion of Whites [48%] than of Blacks [34%] had heard a radio newscast.)

Although actual exposure to TV news is comparable for Blacks and Whites, it looms larger for Blacks relative to newspapers. This is reflected in their attitudes toward the two media. Over the years, the Roper research organization has periodically asked a national sample, "From which [medium] do you get most of your news?" Television has had an edge over newspapers among the White population. (Both are well ahead of radio and magazines.) The edge became overwhelming, more than two to one, when the same question was asked by Lee Slurzberg Research of a Black urban sample in 1977.

Social class differences may provide most of the explanation, but it must also be recalled that a higher proportion of the more youthful Black population has grown up in the age of television.

MUST "WHITE FLIGHT" MEAN NEWSPAPER LOSSES?

Does a shift in the racial balance of the central city automatically mean a circulation loss? In the 1960s, 12 of the 15 major newspapers that failed were published in cities with a declining White population and a rising number of Blacks. In cities with those characteristics, and with a competitive press, 11 other newspapers lost circulation in the city zones, but 25 showed gains. In the noncompetitive cities where the same racial change was occurring, though not as dramatically, the ratio of success to failure was much the same: 11 up and 13 down. Many newspapers have continued to show circulation gains in spite of substantial shifts of racial balance within the central city.

What of the growth markets, in which total population Black *and* White, continued to grow in the central city? In the competitive newspaper situations, 3 papers disappeared, 4 failed to gain circulation, and 12 went up. In the single-ownership cities, 20 papers gained circulation and four did not. It is clear that overall growth in a market does not guarantee gains and that the substitution of Blacks for Whites in the central city does not guarantee losses either.[11] Canada, 96% White, has had the same readership problems as the United States.[12] So, this is not a simple Black and White matter. It is rather a matter of how relevant the metropolitan newspaper can be to people who are in increasing numbers disengaged from the principal local events and personalities on which it reports.

Findings like these are not in keeping with the conventional wisdom. Overall, however, there are few surprises in the look we have taken at the newspaper audience in this chapter. The orientation to print is manifest among people of above-average education and social status. The use of newspapers is linked to the strength of the ties between the individual and the community.

---

[11]In competitive markets, the correlation is +.05 between the change in newspaper circulation in the city zone (1960 to 1970) and the change in the Black proportion of this population. In noncompetitive markets, the correlation is −.20. The correlations are +.47 and +.05, respectively, between circulation and the change in the White proportion of the population (but this relationship masks a third element—the change in the overall size of the population).

[12]It should be noted, however, that recent immigration has brought an influx of non-English-speaking "New Canadians" into Toronto and other major cities, raising the population base without correspondingly increasing readership.

4
THE EVOLUTION
OF READING HABITS

Regardless of their social attributes or origins, all human beings change their living patterns—and their uses of information—as they go through the life cycle that runs from birth to death.

Newspaper reading cannot begin until a child has achieved the ability to read and the motivation to pursue reading as a voluntary activity that is independently satisfying. In old age, the deterioration of visual and mental faculties can result in the attrition of a lifelong readership habit. Between these extremes, newspaper reading may be defined as an activity of maturity. It is concentrated in those years in which people exercise the greatest responsibilities, have the largest income and the heaviest interest in consumption, the most intense involvement in civic affairs, and the most complex needs for information in their daily lives as citizens and as consumers.

THE READING CYCLE: AN OVERVIEW

In over half (53%) of the households with children between 6 and 17, parents describe their children as newspaper readers, but in only 30% of those households does an adult tell us that a paper was read by a child "yesterday" (1987). When parents are regular readers, the children are naturally more

TABLE 4.1
Newspaper Reading, by Age

Age	Weekday paper	Sunday paper	
	Read yesterday	Read last Sunday	Read on all past 4 Sundays
6–8	6%		18%
9–11	21		30
12–13	33	46%	
14–15	43	45	
16–17	47	53	
18–24	57	61	
25–34	60	66	
35–44	67	69	
45–54	71	68	
55–64	72	70	
65+	67	62	

Source: Data for children 6–11 are from 1978 study; teenage data from SMRB Teenage Survey, 1988; adult data are from SMRB 1987.

likely to read, too. In households with frequent readers, the rate of reading "yesterday" for children 6 to 17 (46%) is more than three times the rate for children of infrequent readers (15%) and more than six times the rate for children of nonreaders (7%).

Table 4.1 shows how newspaper reading, daily and Sunday, changes with age. In early primary school grades, when children are learning to read, at ages 6 to 8, a third at least occasionally look at a daily newspaper, and over half look at a Sunday paper. Even very young children are accustomed to the daily presence of the newspaper in the home as a familiar object of interest to their parents, but they themselves have only occasional reason to look at it. Only a handful look at an average weekday paper, and typically for only a few minutes. Two out of three who say they "ever" read or look at a paper can name it.

By the time children move into the next age bracket (9–11), a majority think of themselves as at least occasional readers. And of this group, 89% can actually name the newspaper they read. Still, only 21% read the paper on an average day, and only 30% on all four of the last four Sundays. By the ages of 12 and 13, the proportion of "yesterday" readers has grown by over one-half; it plateaus among the 14- to 17-year-olds.[1] (At a later point, we consider how

---

[1]These figures were lower than those reported by SMRB in a 1981 national survey of teenagers. They found that 52% of youngsters between 12 and 14 were newspaper readers on an average day. Among those 15–17, the proportion rose to 67%, and it was 68% among those 18 and 19. While boys and girls showed about the same reading level among the younger teenagers,

the child's newspaper reading habits develop in relation to other changes in the use of the mass media for information and entertainment.)

The age of 18 marks the beginning of legal adulthood and, conventionally, of graduation from high school. The subsequent age bracket most commonly used in surveys, 18 to 24, covers a period in which living patterns become much more complex and differentiated. Some young people leave their hometowns for college or work; others enter the labor market or attend college while living with parents. Many set up new independent living arrangements. Marriage and parenthood assume different forms for women who enter careers and for those who become housewives. Each of these various paths has its own consequences for newspaper reading.

The central distinction is between those young people who stay at home and continue to find the family newspaper available and those who do not. Among those who do, use of the newspaper increases, continuing the generally upward course established in childhood and adolescence. But those who go off on their own, either to establish an independent household or to go to an out-of-town college, must learn the new habit of buying the newspaper at an age when income is typically low. It is no wonder that daily newspapers lose readers among that group.

Levels of weekday newspaper readership continue to go up until people reach their mid-30s. Then it levels off and begins to decline after the age of 65. Chronology in itself is not the only explanation of why newspaper reading changes at different age levels. Young people and old people are more likely to be living alone than people in their 40s. The presence of other people in the household adds to the likelihood that a newspaper will be read, simply because it adds to the chances that someone else may have brought one into the house.

GROWING UP WITH NEWSPAPERS

The children now attending school are being reared by the first generation of parents who have themselves grown up with television. To learn what part newspapers play in their upbringing, we must look at the whole pattern of media exposure as it evolves in childhood and adolescence.[2]

---

male readership rose relative to females after the age of 15 (75%–61%). Since newspaper penetration fell between 1978 and 1981, the differences in reading levels apparently reflect differences in the survey methods.

[2]The data reported in this section are based on personal interviews conducted in 1978 with a national probability sampling of 1,156 children between the ages of 6 and 17 and also with the principal child-caring adult in their families—817 in all. (Since 88% of them were mothers, rather than fathers, aunts, grandmothers, etc., they are referred to as *mothers* in the text. The specially trained interviewers came from the Center for Family Research.)

Two simple, but basic generalizations should be made at the outset.

1. Adult social class differences in outlook, in childrearing methods, and in media habits are transmitted to children in highly visible ways.

2. Changes in media habits parallel changes in the child's own development. And the media are themselves an important influence on that development. By the ages of 6 to 8, 61% of the children in 1978 could correctly identify President Jimmy Carter, but even more, 70%, could identify TV personalities Donny and Marie Osmond. Within the 9- to 11-year age group, 83% knew who Jimmy Carter was, and 8% could identify Egyptian President Anwar Sadat. By mid-adolescence, 15 to 17, Sadat was known to one in four. Nearly two-fifths at that happy age did not know what inflation was. Only 12% knew what the SALT Talks were. But 84% could identify Donny and Marie (Table 4.2).

HOW CHILDREN SPEND THEIR TIME

American children grow up in a mass media environment. Most pervasive of all the media is television. In 26% of the households, mothers told us the set was on for at least nine hours a day (although only half of the mothers said they themselves watched three hours or more) (1978). Thirty-five percent of the children have their own sets as—of 1978. The proportion ranges from 16% of the 6- to 8-year-olds to 45% of those 15 to 17. TV is the most popular daily activity for children (Table 4.3). About 9 out of 10 watch it every day or almost every day. It's an even more popular activity than getting together with friends or talking with friends on the phone. Listening to the radio is a daily activity for nearly all teenagers. But radio is less important than reading books or stories for smaller children.

TABLE 4.2
Percentage Correctly Identifying Public Figures and Issues by Age, 1978

	6–8	9–11	12–14	15–17
Jimmy Carter	61	83	90	92
Donny & Marie Osmond	70	78	87	84
Inflation	2	14	46	63
Martin Luther King, Jr.	4	22	36	46
Equal Rights Amendment	–	8	24	38
Anwar Sadat	1	8	16	26
SALT Talks	–	–	5	12
N	(345)	(283)	(275)	(253)

TABLE 4.3
How Long Television Set is on During Average Weekday
(Mother's Report), 1978

Less than 1 hour	1%
1–3 hours	16
4–8 hours	56
9 or more hours	26
No answer	1

How else do children spend their free time? Sports rank close to the top for boys between 9 and 14. Arts and crafts and shopping with mother are everyday activities for substantial minorities of younger children. Clubs and after-school lessons are not common daily activities at any age. The media keep coming up strongly. Comic books are an activity of early childhood, 6 to 8, but they are an everyday presence for only a fourth of these younger children. Music and records shoot up as a daily feature of teenage life after the age of 12, and moviegoing increases sharply after 14. About a third read books or stories for fun almost daily up to the age of 14, when magazines and newspapers become more important.

Most children's media activities take place in the family environment. At any hour of the day, most of children's television viewing is done along with other people (Table 4.4). In spite of the fact that so many children have their own sets, watching television seems to be more fun when it's done with brothers and sisters or parents around. One reason is that a tremendous amount of viewing occurs while something else is going on at the same time — eating, conversation, playing, reading, even homework (Tables 4.5 and 4.6).

The reading matter that children have available is in good measure determined by what is in the house. In about two out of three households with children, the newspaper is a daily presence. Magazines are present in about 7 out of 10 families. One-quarter of the children have their own

TABLE 4.4
"Yesterday's" TV Viewing by Children, 1978[a]

	Morning	Afternoon	Evening
Alone	29%	24%	12%
With brother/sister	55	56	61
With parents	19	20	50
With friend	6	12	10
Other	5	5	4
No answer	–	1	1

[a]Columns add to more than 100% because of multiple combinations of joint viewing.

TABLE 4.5
Children's Activities While Watching TV "Yesterday," 1978[a]

	Morning	Afternoon	Evening
Eating/drinking	42%	37%	35%
Talking	11	17	21
Playing games	8	8	6
Dressing/undressing	14	2	5
Reading/writing	2	4	3
Homework/studying	—	3	3
Household chores	1	1	1
Other	2	2	2
Nothing else	32	38	38

[a]Columns add to more than 100% because of multiple activities.

subscription to one or more magazines, but whether or not they do, 55% read magazines that are subscribed to or brought home by other family members or that they find somewhere else (Table 4.7).

One-third of the mothers hardly ever get to read a book themselves, and another third are infrequent readers. But four out of five say that their children read books, even when they don't have to for school, and their children agree: About two out of three have read some book, not for school, within the past month. One-third have used a library book not required for schoolwork. And a majority of parents have bought one or more books for their children in the past year. So mothers care about what their children read (Table 4.8).

And they overwhelmingly approve of their children's reading, viewing, and listening habits. About 1 in 7 is indifferent; 1 in 7 disapproves of comic books, and 1 in 10, of TV. Almost none disapproves of newspaper, magazine, or book reading or of radio listening (Table 4.9).

One reason parents approve of their children's media habits is that they feel that they are guiding them. Even among mothers of children 6 to 8, 61% say they talk to their child about things in the newspaper; that proportion rises to 78% with 15- to 17-year-olds (Table 4.10).

While parents turn to the newspaper to establish conversational links with their children as they mature, the reverse is true of TV. Mothers offer fewer suggestions on TV shows as their children get older. (More of these, however, relate to educational and public affairs programming.) Most mothers of younger children also set rules to control reading as well as TV and moviegoing. By mid-teenage, a majority of youngsters are no longer bound by media rules (Table 4.11).

So far, we have seen that American children are being raised in an environment saturated with media experience. This experience arises out of the context the family offers and is subject to the influences and controls it

TABLE 4.6
Children's Free-Time Activity, 1978

	"A lot"	"Everyday or most days"		
	6–8	9–11	12–14	15–17
Watch TV				
boys	84%	92%	91%	82%
girls	86	90	94	85
Get together with friends				
boys	79	79	84	85
girls	77	78	72	82
Participate in sports				
boys	63	79	84	73
girls	47	72	68	52
Listen to radio				
boys	29	55	70	87
girls	34	57	82	92
Talk on the telephone				
boys	27	44	60	60
girls	45	60	81	75
Listen to records				
boys	27	31	53	56
girls	37	35	66	64
Read newspapers (not counting schoolwork)				
boys	13	32	47	61
girls	8	27	40	60
Read magazines				
boys	26	28	32	32
girls	23	35	39	46
Do arts or crafts				
boys	37	30	25	11
girls	46	40	30	18
Read books, stories (not counting schoolwork)				
boys	30	27	19	11
girls	46	36	31	26
Go shopping, window shopping				
boys	29	12	14	10
girls	33	21	23	28
Read comic books				
boys	29	15	18	3
girls	16	16	8	4
Go to club or team meeting				
boys	12	12	18	16
girls	16	8	10	9
Take lessons after school				
boys	8	8	5	4
girls	12	10	7	7
Go to movies (at least once a week)[a]				
boys	6	13	6	14
girls	13	6	13	20

[a]Different frequency used for movie going.

TABLE 4.7
Magazine Reading Among Children, 1978

Have own subscriptions		26%
and read other magazines		
(home or elsewhere)	16%	
don't read others	10	
Don't have own subscriptions		74
read other magazines		
(home or elsewhere)	39	
don't read others	35	
Total reading other magazines		55

TABLE 4.8
Children's Book Reading by Age, 1978

	6–8	9–11	12–14	15–17
Have read a nonschoolbook in past month	67%	75%	69%	55%
Have taken out a library book (not for school) in past month	29	37	37	25

TABLE 4.9
How Mothers Feel About Children Using the Media, 1978

	Strongly approve	Approve	Disapprove, disapprove strongly	Doesn't matter to me
Books	57%	36%	– %	7%
Magazines	28	59	1	12
Newspapers	33	52	2	13
Radio	14	66	2	18
TV	8	69	10	13
Comic books	7	50	15	28

exercises as long as the child is under its roof. Where do newspapers fit in this scheme of things?

Compared with other media habits, regular newspaper reading develops rather late with children. At any rate, newspaper reading ranks low in terms of what children say they like, while watching TV ranks very high. However, attitudes toward TV (and toward books) become less favorable with age, whereas attitudes toward newspapers (and radio) become more favorable (Table 4.12). Moreover, as children get older they rate newspapers increasingly higher for telling them things they want to know about. By the time they are 15 to 17, newspapers are rated close to TV in this respect (Table 4.13).

TABLE 4.10
Mothers' Discussion of Media, 1978

	6–8	9–11	12–14	15–17
Discuss newspaper stories with child	61%	70%	74%	78%
Suggest TV programs to child	66	60	54	42

TABLE 4.11
Children Who Say Parents Set Rules, 1978

| | Boys | | | | Girls | | | |
About:	6–8	9–11	12–14	15–17	6–8	9–11	12–14	15–17
Amount of TV watching	46%	42%	33%	10%	49%	35%	25%	14%
Kind of TV programs to watch	61	60	50	13	56	65	46	21
How often they can go to the movies	58	53	39	12	52	50	35	16
Kind of movies to see	71	77	69	35	64	74	69	44
Kind of books or magazines to read	50	64	61	36	50	61	59	30

TABLE 4.12
How Much Do Children Like the Media? 1978

	6–8	9–11	12–14	15–17
Watching TV	4.57	4.51	4.31	4.04
Reading newspapers	1.86	2.43	2.73	3.13
Reading comic books	3.17	3.39	2.77	2.14
Listening to radio	3.16	3.71	4.20	4.46
Going to movies	3.91	4.07	4.08	4.06
Reading books	3.47	3.35	3.17	2.95
Reading magazines	2.65	3.09	3.33	3.33

Average score on scale of 1–5; higher score = like more

Reading the newspaper on anything like a regular basis does not happen until teenage.[3] Up to the age of 14, boys consistently show more exposure to newspapers than girls do, but in the 15- to 17-year age group, girls pull up to the same level. SMRB data (1971) show more readership among boys in the 12- to 14-year group (when sports interests are high) but actually show more among girls aged 15 to 17.

[3]This is also borne out by the retrospecitve accounts of young people aged 14–25 (1971a). About half (47%) report that they started reading the paper when they were 11 or older, perhaps in response to school assignments. A third (33%) started between the ages of 8 and 10 and 20% at the age of 7 or younger.

TABLE 4.13
How Much Do the Media Tell Children What They Want to Know? 1978

	6–8	9–11	12–14	15–17
Watching TV	4.13	4.12	3.96	4.01
Reading newspapers	2.82	3.36	3.86	3.94
Reading comic books	2.62	2.52	1.93	1.64
Listening to radio	2.93	3.59	3.68	3.76
Going to movies	3.27	3.37	3.09	3.23
Reading books	3.56	3.62	3.69	3.64
Reading magazines	2.74	3.25	3.54	3.60

Average score on scale of 1–5; higher score = like more

Daily reading time goes from 9 minutes for the 6- to 8-year-old child who looked at a paper yesterday to 19 minutes for the mid-teenage readers. (Among adult readers, the corresponding figure is 32 minutes.)

Compared with the weekday paper, reading of the Sunday paper starts earlier and continues stronger. Half of the 6- to 8-year-olds read it at least sometimes, and 18% say they have done so on every one of the last four Sundays. Among teenagers, four out of five are Sunday readers, and 45% read every Sunday.

What gives the Sunday paper its strength? Certainly the relaxed communal pattern of family reading and the varied features. But far and away of greatest importance is one of those features—the *comics*. Even among the younger children, three out of five are comics readers, and the proportion rises to three-fourths of those between 9 and 17. More young children report reading the Sunday comics than say they read the Sunday newspaper itself (Table 4.14). Evidently some of them think of the comics section as something separate from the newspaper.

Apart from the comics, half of all U.S. newspapers regularly run weekday feature material aimed at children. Of these, 90% use syndicated material, but half of this number also run locally prepared children's features, and the remaining 10% rely exclusively on locally written material (1979a).

When we ask young children (6–8) what is in a newspaper and what people look for in it, comics are far and away the one thing they mention first. Their

TABLE 4.14
Sunday and Sunday Comics Reading, by Age, 1978

Age	Ever read Sunday paper	Read Sunday comics
6–8	52%	61%
9–11	71	74
12–14	78	78
15–17	81	75

TABLE 4.15
Familiarity with Newspaper Content, 1978
"What kinds of things are there in a regular newspaper?"
(Probe) "What kind of things do people look for in a newspaper?"

	6–8	9–11	12–14	15–17
Total who can name some content of the newspaper	60%	81%	90%	90%
Subjects mentioned				
Comics	39	47	45	37
Sports	17	44	58	52
General news	21	26	25	35
Ads (general)	12	18	19	18
Classified ads	6	12	18	26
Weather reports	6	18	18	17
Accidents, disasters, etc.	15	16	14	13
Social news	6	11	18	19
Local news	3	11	18	22
Movie ads	4	12	16	10
U.S. news	4	7	16	11
TV & radio listings	5	14	9	9
Foreign news	1	6	13	11
Front page	2	7	8	14
Personal advice	1	6	11	12
Horoscopes	1	4	7	14
Puzzles, games, etc.	6	5	4	4
Editorials	—	3	6	8

answers to this question change as they get older; they mention sports, generally news, and classified ads as they enter teenage. But comics continue to be important through the teen years (Table 4.15).

Even though young children have only fleeting contact with the paper, three-fifths of the 6- to 8-year-olds (and almost all the older children) can give at least some description of what's in it. A minority of children, but only a minority, have some contact with the newspaper as an institution. By mid-teenage, one in three say they have visited a newspaper plant. Even fewer have seen a film or television show on how a paper is put together, and 15% have read an article or a book on the subject (Table 4.16).

Is the newspaper comprehensible? Apparently so, at least for children over 8. A majority of the younger ones say they have a lot of trouble reading the paper, but in the next age bracket, 9 to 11, only 12% say that the paper is hard to read, and by the mid-teens, the proportion is down to 4%. Maybe children do not really understand it all, but in the familiar family setting the newspaper does not seem strange or forbidding (Table 4.17).

TABLE 4.16
Contact with Newspapers as Institutions, 1978

	6–8	9–11	12–14	15–17
Have seen movie or TV show about newspapers	25%	31%	33%	30%
Have visited newspaper plant	3	18	29	34
Have read an article or book on newspapers	5	12	16	15

TABLE 4.17
Ease of Reading Newspapers, 1978

	6–8	9–11	12–14	15–17
Have no trouble	9%	33%	57%	78%
Have a little trouble	34	55	37	18
Have a lot of trouble	57	12	6	4
	100%	100%	100%	100%

TABLE 4.18
Exposure to the News, by Age, 1978

	6–8	9–11	12–14	15–17
Pay attention to front page	24%	56%	74%	83%
Listened to radio news yesterday	13	26	44	55
Watch TV news everyday or most days	13	23	41	40

At the age of 6 to 8, only one in four children pays attention to the front page most of the time. By the time they are 15 to 17, five out of six are doing so (Table 4.18).

As children grow up, exposure to the news increases through all media. Among the 6 to 8's, 13% say they heard news on the radio "yesterday." Among those 15 to 17, it is 55% (not surprisingly, since this age group listens to radio music which newscasts interrupt at regular intervals). Similarly, regular viewing of television news goes from 13% to 40%.

The favorite newscasters are local, not the network personalities (Table 4.19). And what children say they watch on the TV news are the incidentals to which they can relate. Girls mention the weather and boys mention sports far more than general news. However, no newscasts are mentioned when children are asked to name their favorite television programs. In the happy world of childhood, the news and cares of the wider world are intruders that only gradually receive a welcome (Table 4.20).

THE DEVELOPMENT OF NEWS INTERESTS

The ability of newspapers to capture the attention of readers depends on their coverage of the subjects that readers find meaningful. As a child grows older,

TABLE 4.19
"Which people who tell the news on TV do you like?
What are their names?"[a]

	6–8	9–11	12–14	15–17
Name network newscasters	15%	19%	20%	26%
Name local newscasters	83	84	83	80

[a]Asked of TV news-viewers.

TABLE 4.20
"What parts of TV news programs do you like to watch?" (1978)[a]

	Boys	Girls
Name sports	58%	29%
Name weather	37	53
Name general news	10	11

[a]Asked of TV news-viewers.

more and more of the preoccupations of the adult world (and more of the newspaper's content) become relevant.

Whether they are children or adults, people's needs and interests relate to what they talk about. We asked mothers how often various subjects were discussed in the family's conversation and compared the results with what children said they were personally very interested in (Table 4.21).

For all kinds of families, far and away the number one topic of frequent conversation, mothers told us in 1978, was the rising cost of living. Smaller children were insulated from this problem. Only 16% were very interested in

TABLE 4.21
News Topics—What Families Talk About and What Children Are Interested In, 1978

	Mothers reporting frequent discussion	Children "very interested"			
		6–8	9–11	12–14	15–17
The rising cost of living	81%	16%	29%	42%	54%
What's happening in schools	68	36	44	49	54
Things that happen in your neighborhood	53	39	48	62	59
Young people using drugs	48	16	34	49	51
Crime and robberies	45	24	42	44	50
What your local government is doing	28	13	15	23	25
Problem of losing or not being able to find a job	26	17	29	39	61
What President Carter is doing	23	17	15	12	19
Pollution problems	20	19	30	35	39
What's going on in other countries	18	12	12	12	16

it. By the time they were in their mid-teens, the proportion had grown to 54%, and job hunting had become the number one subject of concern. At that age, what was going on in the neighborhood was of similar interest, and it was by far the most interesting subject, of those on our list, to children at every other age level. These local happenings deal with people and places children know and to which they can relate.

One subject of relatively much greater interest to children, particularly to teenagers, than to their parents, was environmental pollution — not something that most adults spend a lot of time talking about, but very real, very threatening, and very arousing to a good many teenagers.

What was going on in the schools was of even greater interest to children at every age level, and their interest grew as they got older. But news of what the President was doing, news of what local government was doing, and foreign news all ranked comparatively low both as subjects of family discussion and as subjects of concern to children, compared with the matters that seemed closer to hand.

The changes in children's general interests are mirrored in the changes of their newspaper interests. Not surprisingly, children respond to different things in the paper than their mothers do. Comics, sports, and puzzles and games arouse roughly twice as much interest from children as from mothers.[4] Entertainment-related features get roughly parallel interest. For all other types of material, children's interest levels are very substantially lower, though as they get older, they come closer to the adult level (Table 4.22). At every age, children who read the newspaper more frequently are more responsive to its actual news content, though no less interested in its entertainment material, than children who read less frequently.

Comics are a favorite newspaper feature at every age, although among teenage boys sports are an even stronger favorite. Girls develop a strong interest in clothes and fashions by the time they are 12 to 14, but they do not build up a corresponding interest in the food pages. Personal advice columns begin to attract girls in their mid-teens. So do horoscopes and stories on show-business personalities. But girls at this age are still not very interested in engagements, weddings, and births (the social news).

Entertainment is, needless to say, a strong teenage interest. Even by the time children are 9 to 11, about a third are using the television logs and the movie listings. Interest in popular music and records builds somewhat earlier in girls than among boys. Hobbies do not have strong general appeal, but as youngsters reach mid-teenage and begin to think about jobs and cars, they

---

[4]Questions were worded somewhat differently in the mothers' and childrens' questionnaires to facilitate interviewing. Naturally, what people (adults or children) report they read "most of the time" represents an orientation rather than a literal statement of fact.

TABLE 4.22
Parts of the Newspaper Read "Most of the Time," 1978[a]

	Mothers	Boys				Girls			
		6–8	9–11	12–14	15–17	6–8	9–11	12–14	15–17
Asked of both mothers & children:									
Local news	73%	7%	20%	36%	42%	7%	8%	30%	50%
U.S. news	55	6	12	32	33	3	7	14	20
Personal advice	49	3	4	9	15	1	14	32	48
Foreign news	42	2	8	14	23	1	3	9	14
Editorials	35	2	1	10	8	–	1	6	7
Celebrities, movie stars	33	4	13	19	18	7	13	40	40
Classified ads	29	2	5	20	28	1	5	11	26
Comics, jokes	27	49	64	54	54	59	61	69	62
Social news	24	1	3	7	4	5	9	19	23
Hobbies	23	6	11	11	4	4	8	10	13
Sports	17	18	43	67	62	9	13	20	26
Puzzles, games	11	21	14	14	6	28	22	31	21
Business news	10	3	4	3	3	1	1	1	4
Asked differently for mothers & children									
Women's pages about fashion, food, recipes	47								
News or ads about clothes and styles		5	6	9	6	5	15	43	54
Food and recipes		4	6	5	2	9	11	10	12
Movies, TV, other entertainment reviews or listings	36								
Movies listings		16	35	50	45	16	26	64	61
TV, radio listing, news		15	29	34	41	12	24	41	45
Music ads, news		4	14	27	33	10	12	46	32
Front page		10	34	57	62	8	28	52	60
Horoscopes		3	10	25	18	5	20	46	67
Teenage news		3	2	7	10	3	4	32	38
Ads other than classified	39								
Obituaries	38								
Political columnists	18								
Book reviews	16								

[a]Among those who read a newspaper.

develop an interest in the classified ads.[5] Special columns or features for teenagers are read "most of the time" by only 10% of the teenage boys and by 38% of the teenage girls (not all papers carry such features).

Taken together, the responses suggest a scattered and diversified pattern of readership with rather low emotional involvement. This is also suggested by the fact that, at every age, about 7 children in 10 can't think of anything in the paper they would like to see more of. And at any age, only one in seven can think of anything not now in their paper that they'd like to have. The things they mention, by the way, are things that newspapers already print. There appears to be a real absence of focus in the child's view of the newspaper; there is also a minimal acknowledgment of straight news as an element of newspaper content.

Are children accurate reporters of their own reading habits? Their reports do agree with what adults tell us when we ask them to think back to their childhood years.[6] Comics are by far the part of the paper that they most universally remember reading when they were children (1977). They are mentioned by 87%. Sports news is mentioned by 49% of the men and by 8% of the women. Women's pages are mentioned by 12% of the women and 3% of the men. Women also are more likely to recall puzzles and games (17%, compared with 10% of the men) and the magazine section (9% compared with 5% for men). Movie ads are recalled by similar proportions (17%). But the front page headlines are mentioned by only 20% of the men and 22% of the women. It is clear that news, as opposed to entertainment, represents a comparatively minor part of the childhood newspaper reading experience, as adults recall it.

NEWSPAPERS IN THE SCHOOL

I have commented on the evolution of newspaper reading in relation to the place of the newspaper in the child's home. The classroom is another

---

[5]In an earlier survey of young people 14–25, the proportion who have placed a classified ad themselves ranges from 16% of the high school students to 33% of those who are out of school (1971a).

[6]Eighty percent of adults reported (1977) that there was generally a newspaper at home when they were 11 or 12 years old. (The proportion was 82% among Whites and 66% among Blacks; it ranged from 92% of those who have been to college down to 62% of those who did not finish high school.)

Younger adults were much more likely to report childhood exposure to the newspaper. The figure drops from 95% of those 18 to 24 down to 70% of those 55 and over. This reflects (a) the more immediate recollections of those for whom childhood is a more recent experience; (b) changing educational practices, with increasing use of the newspaper by teachers in recent years; and (c) the higher educational attainments of younger people, with a greater probability of exposure to the newspaper in the course of a more extended educational experience. Nonetheless, the decline in regularity of reading would undoubtedly have lowered the levels reported here had the question been repeated 10 years later.

TABLE 4.23
Mother's and Children's Aspirations, 1978

To be remembered as:	Mother's wish for child	Child's wish
Good student	80%	48%
Star athlete	4	21
School leader	13	8
Most popular	2	19
No answer	1	4
	100%	100%

important place where children are under adult guidance and where the newspaper enters the scene. The interaction between parent and teacher is traditional in American school experience. In 1978, 85% of the mothers interviewed had gone to talk to the teacher within the current school year. And educational achievement continues to be at the heart of mothers' hopes for their children: 80% would most like their child to be remembered in school as a really good student rather than as a leader, a star athlete, or as most popular. Their children have accepted these values—and being a good student is also the main goal for the largest number (Table 4.23).

Eighty-four percent of the mothers would like their child to go beyond high school, 58% to get a college degree, and 13% beyond that. And 65% of the children themselves say they definitely or probably will go to college. Only 8% say they definitely won't. (This strong interest in self-improvement suggests that the steady rise in educational attainment will continue in the future.)

The newspaper is widely used in school, whether at the teacher's own initiative or as part of a formal Newspaper in Education program. Among the 6- to 8-year-olds, 22% report that a teacher has used the newspaper in the classroom or for assignments, and this proportion grows as the child's school experience lengthens (1978, Table 4.24). It is 94% among those 15 to 17. Two-thirds have had it within the current school year. Newspapers are used mainly for reading and language skills in the early grades and more heavily in social studies from the age of 9 (Table 4.25).

Does this have the parents' approval? Eighty percent of the parents approve of using the newspaper in school—primarily as a guide to current events.

TABLE 4.24
Use of Newspapers in School or for Assignments, 1978

	6–8	9–11	12–14	15–17
Have ever used newspaper in school or for assignment	22%	52%	85%	94%
(Used in current year)[a]	(75)	(79)	(67)	(59)

[a]% based on those who "ever" used for school.

TABLE 4.25
"What school subjects was newspaper last used for?" (1978)[a]

	6–8	9–11	12–14	15–17
Social studies	18%	41%	53%	52%
Reading or English or language arts	25	33	25	33
Science	10	10	11	8
Math	8	6	2	1
Art	12	6	2	–
Health, nutrition	3	2	2	4
Other	9	3	6	5
No answer	18	5	4	2

[a]Columns add to more than 100% because newspaper may have been used in more than one subject.

And how do the children react to it? Two-thirds who express an opinion "love" it or "like" it, and the proportion goes up as they get older. In fact, most children of every age like school itself very much; only a minority acknowledge (to an adult interviewer, to be sure) that they feel negative about it (Table 4.26).

Adults confirm what children tell us about the use of the newspaper in school. Forty-three percent of adults recall that any of their teachers used a paper regularly as part of classroom work or assignments (1977). This figure naturally represents the accumulated educational experience rather than a particular school year's exposure, and it includes informal efforts on the part of individual teachers, as well as organized Newspaper in Education programs.

As with exposure to the newspaper at home, recollection of school use of the paper is much higher among younger and better-educated people. However, it is at approximately the same level for Blacks (46%) as for Whites (42%).

There are some indications that school use of newspapers varies with the quality of the school system; in the Northeast it is higher in the suburbs; in the South it is higher in metropolitan areas.

Most of those who recall using the newspaper in school had it in high school (22% had it only in high school, 13% in both high and primary school, and 7% in grade school only).

TABLE 4.26
Children's Attitudes Toward School, 1978

	6–8	9–11	12–14	15–17
"Love" or "like" idea of using newspaper for schoolwork[a]	60%	65%	67%	75%
"Love" or "like" school	70	67	73	67

[a]Based on all children who have an opinion, whether or not they have used a newspaper.

"NEWSPAPER IN EDUCATION" PROGRAMS

A 1987 survey conducted for the ANPA Foundation by the Media General Research Department identified 573 papers with Newspaper in Education (NIE) programs. These included all papers of over 100,000 circulation, 85% of those between 50,000 and 100,000, 48% of those 15,000–50,000, and 11% of the smaller ones. Altogether, these papers accounted for about 76% of all newspaper circulation. However, only 14 of them employed more than three full-time people on their NIE staffs. In three out of five cases, a single coordinator carried the full load. Most programs offered the newspaper at half price, with government funding paying the way, and one in eight gave all the papers away. But apart from the cost of the newspapers (which 4 out of 10 papers offered at least to part of the pupils), newspapers invested money in staff training and supplementary materials, which 9 out of 10 provided.

In the 1979 school year, NIE programs reached approximately three million pupils (about 1 in 10 of the national total) in 16,000 schools (about 1 in 5), and 90,000 teachers (or 1 in 20). Some 45 million copies of daily newspapers were distributed in the course of a school year to pupils. Nearly two-fifths of the papers provided subscriptions for a semester or school year, but many of the programs were of short duration, with a two-week order the most typical kind (1979a).

There is great variability in the way programs are carried out, the kinds of training offered to teachers, the grade levels at which the newspaper is used, the kinds of classroom subjects to which it is related. In the early primary grades, the newspaper is used mainly to teach fundamental reading skills; in junior high school and high school it is an adjunct to teaching current events and civics. But the newspaper has been used also to motivate children to learn arithmetic and fundamental economics, home economics, career planning, history, government, and a great variety of other school subjects.

Altogether, only about one hundred persons in 1979 could be identified as full-time newspaper staff specialists in education, but for every one of these there were three others who devoted some of their time to this purpose in newspaper circulation, promotion, or public relations departments. In two-thirds of the programs, some teacher training was offered, usually through workshops. Many of these carried college credit, usually at a graduate level. But apart from the organized effort to make newspapers a part of the school curriculum, thousands of teachers make use of newspapers on their own, both to stimulate interest in reading and to illuminate the subjects they teach.

Confirmation of the value of NIE programs came from an experimental study carried out among 5th grade inner-city pupils in Richmond, Virginia, and among 11th and 12th graders in San Francisco (1981b). In each city, children were divided into three matched groups, one a control group without an NIE program and two with different levels of NIE exposure. Tests were run before and afterward to get background information, check newspaper reading habits and attitudes, and measure political and social information, interest, and awareness. In both cities and at both age levels, the children with the most intense exposure showed the most positive change; those with no exposure, the least.

CHILDHOOD EXPOSURE AND ADULT READERSHIP

People who have had more schooling are more likely to report childhood exposure to newspapers both at home and at school.[7] It is therefore not surprising to find that childhood exposure is also linked to adult newspaper reading habits. Of those who had the paper at home as children, 70% are currently frequent readers, and 67% are subscribers (1977). Of those who did not have the paper at home, 56% are regular readers and 49%, subscribers. Today's frequent readers are also more likely to mention more sections that they looked at as children (2.1, compared with 1.8 for infrequent readers), especially adult-oriented material like sports and women's features and the Sunday magazine.

Adults who used the newspaper in school as children are slightly more likely to be frequent readers now, and they are slightly more likely to be subscribers. Although the differences are small, they are consistent at every age level. The figures are complicated by the intervening influence of education, which, as we have seen, varies among the various groups. Children who had the newspaper at home as a daily presence would probably be more likely to grow up to be newspaper readers, whether or not they had the paper in school.

Among the small minority of Whites who did not have the newspaper at home but who did have it in school, the present proportion of current subscribers is 58%; it is 52% for those who had it neither at school nor at home. Among Blacks, the effect of the newspaper in school is even more marked when it was lacking at home. Of those who had it in school, 41% are now subscribers, but only 26% of those who had it neither at school nor at home. (The effect is less marked for frequent readership—56% and 54%.) And among Blacks who had the newspaper at home (although with less regularity than among Whites), the proportion of current subscribers (61%) and of frequent readers (68%) is also considerably higher than among those who did not. (Only 41% of this group are now subscribers and 55%, frequent readers.)

The reading of the newspaper has other important consequences. Among

---

[7]Table 3.9 documents the relationship between social class origins (as reflected in the mother's educational attainment) and childhood exposure to the newspaper.

TABLE 4.27
Support for Political Rights, 1978[a]

Age	Readers	Nonreaders
6–8	69	46
9–11	97	70
12–14	136	96
15–17	169	123

[a]All children = 100.

15- to 17-year-olds, a composite index of familiarity with public figures and issues was developed from the array of questions asked on this subject. We can take the level of familiarity among 15- to 17-year-olds who had no exposure to the newspaper as a benchmark. Those who had the paper only in school scored 16% higher. Those with the paper only at home were 41% higher. And those exposed to the newspaper in both places had a knowledge level that was 53% higher than where there was no exposure at all.

This higher awareness was also translated, among the newspaper readers at every age level, into a greater understanding and support of the basic rights that are part of the American political heritage (as measured by a series of questions taken from the National Assessment of Educational Progress, Table 4.27).

It is apparent that the use of the newspaper in the schoolroom will be even more important to the preservation of reading habits if an increasing proportion of young families continue to get along without the newspaper in the home on a daily basis.

CHILDHOOD, ADOLESCENCE, ADULTHOOD

Readership surveys, like most market and opinion research, usually sample the population of legal adults, 18 and over. This means that the age of 18 generally represents the bottom limit of "youth," when people of different age levels are compared. Since this is, of course, an arbitrary break point in the evolution of reading habits, we can take a fresh approach to the subject by considering what happens to young people between the ages of 14 and 25, a 12-year age span that covers the gamut from childhood to maturity (1970).[8] In

---

[8]I have already cautioned the reader about the difficulty of making direct comparisons among the statistics yielded by different research organizations through surveys conducted at different points in time. This study found that 73% of the individuals sampled reported reading a newspaper "yesterday," a considerably higher percentage than other studies conducted more recently. The difference partly reflects a real decline in the level of newspaper reading among young people, but it also in part may reflect the vicissitudes of survey technique. To avoid

this age group, as with the general population, there is a faint (2%) difference in newspaper reading between the sexes, with males having the edge.

We have already seen that the progression in reading with age reflects the expansion of interests that accompanies maturation, as well as the opportunities presented by the family environment. Among high school students, who generally have the newspaper available at home, daily readership increases by 13% between the freshman/sophomore years and the junior/ senior levels, and the proportion who read two papers a day doubles. (But only 6% of the high school students had bought a paper themselves "yesterday.")

Among college students who continue living in their hometowns (and generally still with their parents), readership continues at about the same level in college as in high school. Academic, social, and work pressures probably account for a 5% drop from the level attained in the last two years of high school.

Young people who go to college, and especially those who go to an out-of-town college, represent a selective segment of the high school population, with an above-average family environment that should facilitate newspaper reading.[9] Still, those who leave home and go away to college must acquire the habit of buying a newspaper for the first time. Their daily readership is 23% less than it averages through the high school years, and it is also 23% less than it is among those college students who live with their parents. But among other young people who are no longer living with their parents, readership is 31% greater. This apparent discrepancy can in part be accounted for by the likelihood that these groups differ in average age, social status, and state of independence. The ones living with their parents are apt to be younger, still dependent, and from lower socioeconomic strata, where the initial family level of reading is lower.

When asked how they became regular readers, 37% mention a growing interest in current events as a result of external happenings that appeared significant ("during the riots and the assassinations and the Vietnam War," as one high school girl explained). One in four refer to the required use of the

---

confusion, the significant findings of this study are expressed in comparative terms rather than with absolute percentages.

[9]A 1975 study by Belden Associates among students at 10 major universities found that only 39% had read a daily newspaper on the previous day. This included 28% of the freshmen and sophomores (recently removed from the familiar home reading situation), 39% of the juniors and seniors, and 59% of the graduate students. Reading of news magazines was, in the aggregate, at an even higher level. Somewhat over one-third in every grade group were readers of *Time* and nearly a third said they read *Newsweek*. Over a third of the undergraduates were readers of *Playboy*, and among both undergraduates and graduate students, nearly 3 out of 10 were readers of the *Reader's Digest* and of the *National Lampoon*.

newspaper in high school classes. Others mention specific needs or interests that the newspaper satisfied. "I fell in love with the Milwaukee Braves." "When I started to look for a job when I turned 16." "I began dating and looking at movie schedules." "When I got married I wasn't rushing with my job to go out on a date and I wasn't sitting home at night studying—I had more time to read." "When I came to Knoxville. I was going to business college and I kept up with the local news here. I wanted to know what was going on in Knoxville." "I got married and my life changed in many ways. I looked for bargains in the paper, for groceries, clothing, etc."

As several of the preceding comments suggest, a key determinant of newspaper reading among young people is their marital status. Among the married, reading is considerably higher both among those still in college (27% more than among single students) and those not in school (34% greater than among the unmarried).

Similarly, young people with jobs are more likely to be readers, if they are out of high school. Among those still in high school, there is no difference between those who have outside jobs and those who don't, but employed college students are 18% more likely to be readers, and those who are out of school and have jobs are readers 17% more often than those who don't.

Apparently not many of the college students keep up with the news of their home communities. Only 20% of those who read a newspaper "yesterday" read one from out of town. This proportion is higher among those attending an out-of-town college.

Student newspapers were published in all the colleges attended by the students interviewed, and in almost all the high schools. And these papers appear to command almost universal interest. Eighty-five percent of the high school students and 77% of those in college reported reading the latest issue of the school paper.

Young people who are not attending school represent a heterogeneous mix, ranging from high school dropouts to college graduates. What they have in common is that they are on their own. Their overall rate of regular readership is identical with that of the high school population. Even though a good many of them continue to live with their parents, many have established households of their own, and like those who have gone off to college, they must acquire the habit of buying a newspaper themselves before they can become regular readers. Not surprisingly, those who have had at least some college are 21% more likely to have read a paper "yesterday" than are the ones who have not gone beyond high school.

The selective process that perpetuates social class differences in later life is already at work in high school. Students in academic programs are 26% more apt to be newspaper readers than those taking a vocational or commercial course. Those who expect to go on to college read 39% more often than those who do not. And those college students who are planning to do graduate work are 17% more likely to be newspaper readers than those who will stop with their undergraduate degrees.

For the entire 14 to 25 age group, newspaper readership is (14%) higher among those who are active in clubs or organizations, as is true of the general adult population.

The variations in readership of the Sunday paper parallel those reported for weekday readership. (In fact, among young people who read the paper "yesterday," 77% also had read all four of the past four Sunday papers.) Among readers of the weekday paper, both boys and girls report picking an average copy up 2.4 times, and 62% say they go through the paper page by page. There is little variation from this average at any age level. (This is less than the 70% of adult readers who gave the equivalent answer in 1961.) And their reading interests are more narrowly focused. Forty-eight percent, compared with 35% of the general public, say they generally turn to a specific feature before going routinely through the paper.

Among newspaper readers, high school students are more likely to read just a single paper (68%) than college students (43%) or those out of school (42%). Those who were familiar with more than one paper were asked if they had a preference (which most of them did), and why. Four out of 10 (41%) said the paper they liked had better news coverage, and 1 in 7 (14%) specifically mentioned that it had more local news. One in 4 mentioned the paper's editorial policies as a positive factor. One in 6 mentioned the technical qualities of the printing or layout, which they preferred to the other paper's. One in 10 mentioned the amount or character of the advertising. Others talked about specific features, writers, sections, or news coverage.

It should come as no surprise to find that the very same reasons that are given to explain why one paper is preferred are the ones given to explain why the other paper is rejected. Thirty percent say it has less news coverage, and 10% specifically say it has less local news. Twenty-seven percent object to the editorial policy, and the proportion is higher – 39% – among the more politically conscious college students. Fourteen percent complain about the quality of the printing or the appearance of the paper. Small proportions object to the writing or to specific sections or features. But only 6% are unable or unwilling to articulate any reason why a particular paper is not preferred, and a mere 2% don't explain their positive preference. Similarly, when asked, "What would make you more interested in newspapers?" 12% give no answer, 24% say that everything is fine as it is, and the positive suggestions are spread out over a great variety of subjects. The largest cluster of responses centers around the demand for more sports coverage, especially from the high school students.

What is most striking about all of these responses is that they seem to reflect the acceptance of a conventional adult definition of what a newspaper is: a vehicle of information. How this develops can be seen when we consider how often young people look at 28 different types of editorial content.[10] As Table 4.28 shows, their reading interests include a good many entertainment features but also encompass a considerable number of special interests. Though half are regular readers of horoscopes, half also claim to be regular readers of editorials, and nearly a third of the boys and young men say they are readers of the business news. Advertising gets substantial readership, though the mix of what gets regular attention is different than that of the general adult population. Movie and theater ads are especially well read, and there is strong readership of classified advertising for jobs and cars.

Three out of 5 high school girls report that they regularly read teenage news. This is a high proportion because most larger and middle-sized newspapers do not run such features. Somewhat surprisingly, about a third of the girls who are in college or out of school still report that they regularly follow teenage news. Gossip columns are followed by half of those in high school and college, but by only 1 in 7 of those out of school. Conversely, food and society news are regularly followed by only 3 out of 10 girls in school or college, but by almost half of those who are out of school.

Among both sexes, interest in comics, puzzles, and games goes down after high school, while interest in more serious news content grows.

THE YOUNG ADULT READER

Among young adults 21 to 25, 90% reported reading a newspaper at least once a week, 45% said they read one daily, and only 2% said they never read one, according to a 1985 survey of 3,600 conducted by the National Assessment of Educational Progress.[11] The percentage of daily readers was 49% among men and 41% among women; it ranged from 24% for those who never went beyond grade school to 50% of those with a college degree.

Newspaper reading, as we have been describing its evolution, becomes a firm habit as mature adults establish the connections and responsibilities that expand their information needs. This happens when they take jobs, start families, and become active consumers, taxpayers, and citizens with a multiplicity of links to their communities. It has therefore always been true that people in the early years of adulthood read newspapers with less regularity

---

[10]The answers were obtained with this question: "Now, here are some cards . . . On each you will see sections or features you may find in any regular daily newspaper. Take these cards and first sort out those items you just about never or hardly ever look at. Now, take the remaining cards and sort them into . . . those you generally look at almost daily, those you look at a few times a week, those which you look at only once a week and the remainder you look at less often than once a week."

[11]Irwin S. Kirsch, Ann Jungeblut, & Donald A. Rock, "Reading Newspapers: The Practices of America's Young Adults," Paper delivered before the American Society of Newspaper Editors, Washington, D.C., May, 1988.

TABLE 4.28
Regular Readership of Editorial Features by Young People, 14–25, by Sex, 1970
(Percentage Reading A Few Times A Week or More Often)[a]

	Total	Male	Female
News	81%	81%	81%
Comics	66	65	68
TV, radio listings	63	61	66
Sports	57	77	36
Horoscope	49	33	66
Editorial page	49	50	47
Movie reviews	47	40	54
TV, radio reviews	44	38	51
Fashion	39	11	69
Political columnists	38	43	32
Advice and etiquette	36	19	54
Teenage column or news	34	26	42
Weddings and engagements	29	13	45
Food	26	14	39
Puzzles and games	26	23	29
Society–social events	25	12	38
Music reviews	24	21	27
Business, finance	23	31	15
Gossip columnists	21	10	32
Recording reviews	18	17	20
Theater, ballet reviews	18	16	21
Obituaries	16	11	20
Art reviews	13	9	17
Book reviews	13	10	16
Sewing	11	1	21
Hobbies	8	10	9
Gardening	6	3	9
Bridge	3	4	3
None of these	3	7	2
Average Number of Features Read:	8.9	7.6	10.3

[a]Totals are more than 100% because of multiple mentions.

than those in their 30s and 40s. However, the discrepancy in reading frequency between younger and older adults grew during the 1970s.[12]

What this may have reflected most of all was the coming of age of the extraordinary generation that emerged from the baby boom that followed

---

[12]This is shown by studies tracking the same individuals over time as well as by the trend data already reported from our own research. In a national study by M. Kent Jennings and Richard G.Niema, 1,119 high school seniors were interviewed in 1965 and reinterviewed in 1973. Their parents, also interviewed, showed a modest decline in readership in this eight-year interval. But the level of readership of the young people remained about the same. They were only 25 years

World War II. In the peak year of the boom, 1952, there were 31% more babies born than there had been 10 years earlier, and even 18% more than were born in 1978. As it grew up, this generation overcrowded schools and other institutions, including the job market. The Vietnam war and the draft created a central political issue for its members and gave rise to the neo-radical movement of 1968 and the years that followed.

The spirit of rebellion that was manifested in the Chicago convention riots and the aftermath of the Kent State massacre gave way to the trauma of Watergate and the subsequent period of political and economic inertia. Opinion surveys traced a decline in altruism and idealism among this age group during the 1970s and a growing narcissistic preoccupation with its own self-interest. This tendency was even more marked among the new crop of teenagers that followed their more activist predecessors.

Political changes represented only one aspect of the unique experience of this generation. They were the first to grow up in a society unburdened by legally sanctioned racial segregation. They were the first to be reared with television since infancy, the first to grow up with the Pill, with uncensored films, and with a dramatic change in the sexual mores. The rising use of drugs, the increased rates of juvenile crime, mental illness, and suicide are merely indicators of deep-seated transformations in mood and deportment. This was a generation that emerged into adulthood with a high degree of skepticism toward the institutions that their parents took for granted. And as they moved into the years of family formation, their values and their media habits were being inculcated in yet another generation.

Still, it must be remembered that among young people, as among older adults, shifts in values can occur rapidly. When the 1970 survey of 14 to 25 year olds was repeated in 1975, a sharp drop occurred in the percentages who

---

old, on the average, when they were reinterviewed, and therefore still in an age group that had not advanced to typical adult reading levels. Nonetheless, their reading frequency had not increased, as might have been expected from their growing maturity (see "Continuity and Change in Political Orientations: A Longitudinal Study of Two Generations," *The American Political Science Review*, December 1975, pp. 1316–35).

An analysis (by Clyde Z. Nunn of The Newspaper Advertising Bureau) of surveys made in 1972 and 1977 by The National Opinion Research Center makes it possible to follow everyday newspaper readership trends among people in two age cohorts (or groups). Readership declined from 45% to 40% among those who were between 18 and 23 in 1972 (and between 23 and 28 in the second interview). But among those who were between 24 and 29 in 1972 (and 29 to 34 in 1977) readership increased from 48% to 52%. This suggests that the major upward shift in newspaper reading occurs after the age of 30, after an interval during the mobile and readjusting years of the mid-20s. However, another explanation of the data is that they may simply reflect the different experience of two generations subjected to distinctive historical experiences (the older group was less involved in the rebellious era of 1968–70). But inexplicably—except through the vagaries of statistical error—the greatest decline in readership in this sampling occurred among people who were in their 30s in 1972. People who were 54 or over in 1972 were reading more by 1977.

said that working for peace or for a better society were extremely important life goals, and a rise in the proportion who emphasized "understanding myself" and "getting a secure steady job." But the findings also showed striking differences between people at the low and high ends of the age range studied, even though in the eyes of their elders they might easily have been lumped together as members of the same "young generation." Surveys of college freshmen by the American Council on Education have found that the number one life goal in 1967, "developing a meaningful philosophy of life," was named by only half as many 20 years later, while "being very well off financially" doubled its adherents and was being cited by three out of four in 1987.

It has already been noted that young people move around more than any other part of the population. Their greater restlessness is also seen in their future plans. Of those 18 to 24, 36% expected to move to another town or city within the next three years (1977). The corresponding figure was 29% for those 25 to 29. It was only 14% of those 30 and over.

This very high mobility makes it all the harder to capture their interest and their loyalty for the local newspaper, or even to pin them down long enough to sell them a subscription. More of them are apartment dwellers; far fewer are homeowners. More of the women work outside the home or are looking for work. Two of every three unemployed adults are under 35.

Yet the young adults of the 1980s are the best educated in history and perhaps more cosmopolitan than any earlier generation. Their interests are specialized and segmented. While they are not reading daily newspapers as frequently as their parents did, they are reading. Individuals aged 18 to 34 account for 40% of the adult population but for 45% of all magazine reading. They are 45% of all readers of *Time* and 47% of the *National Enquirer* (MRI, 1987). Are they resistant to the newspaper habit because they have grown up in the presence of television? The fact is that they watch considerably less TV news than the average adult.

Since so much of the current preoccupation of newspaper executives is with young adults (and properly so), two rather obvious truths should be kept in mind. The first is that a very substantial majority of them continue to go through the traditional cycle of finishing school, getting a job, a spouse, a residence, and a newspaper subscription. The nonreaders who concern and perplex many publishers are a minority. The second point is that young people, just like any other age group, are not cut from one mold. They show exactly the same patterns of variability in newspaper reading by social class, education, race, and type of residence.

Their comparatively tenuous relationship to the community of residence relates directly to newspaper reading. Among those 18 to 24 in our 1977 study who had lived in the same community for less than three years, a full 33% had not read a newspaper on any day of the last five weekdays. Only 41% had read a paper on four or five of those last five days. By contrast, among people over 30 who had lived in the same community for three years or more, 73%

were frequent readers and only 14% were nonreaders.

Among people 30 and over, 15% read no newspapers in the course of five weekdays. Among those 18 to 29, the comparable figure was very similar— 18%. Yet, the average reading frequency was lower for those under 30 than for those older. A similar pattern applied for Sunday readership. The difference in readership between younger and older people is, therefore, primarily a difference in reading frequency. But this difference is reflected in attitude as well. The proportion of women who in 1974 agreed, "I really feel lost when I don't have the paper every day," was only half as large among women 18 to 29 as among those 65 and older.

A newspaper is most likely to be read when it is consistently available, but availability does not guarantee readership by all the members of a family. And home delivery in 1977 was at rather similar levels among younger and older people when frequent and infrequent readers, and nonreaders, are compared.

Young people participate less in the political process than older ones, as a massive research literature documents. This is understandable, since awareness of news and politics evolves through adolescence, as we have seen. Among people 18 and over, 57% said they registered and voted in the 1988 presidential election, according to the Census Bureau. (The actual turnout was 50% of those eligible). Of those under 25, 36% reported registering and voting.

People who voted are more likely to be frequent readers than people who did not, as I have already noted. Among those under 30, the difference between voters and nonvoters is especially dramatic. This might be explained as a matter of interacting cause and effect. Active citizens sustain their political interest through the news media, but newspaper readers are also impelled by the information they absorb toward more active political participation. Needless to say, both political consciousness and newspaper reading go along with greater education.

It is to be expected that the frequency of newspaper reading is greater among the politically potent—people who feel that their opinions have an influence on local government. This was true in 1977 among people 30 and over; it was especially true among those 25 to 29. However, it turns out that among those 18 to 24, there was no difference. This reinforces our earlier observation that among this group the real distinction is between those who live with their parents and those who do not.

We have seen children first come to the media for fun and become acquainted with the comics long before they become aware of anything else in the paper. Since the use of information and news comes later, it is not surprising that even young adults are comparatively more oriented to the newspapers' entertainment aspects than older people are, as we see in Chapter 9.

By the onset of adolescence, interests are already sharply defined by gender, as Table 4.29 shows. Among boys 12–17, 51% say (1988a) that they

TABLE 4.29
Teenage (12–17) Interests, by Gender (1988a)

Very interested in information about:	Boys	Girls
Jobs, careers	51%	58%
Clothes, style	34	62
Rock, concerts, tapes	40	42
Local H. S. news	34	47
Local H. S. sports	38	34
Professional sports	50	19
Science and space	37	22
Movies	28	29
Cars, motorcycles	45	11
Other countries	23	32
Computers, PCs	29	24
Show business, TV	16	25
Horoscopes	8	18
Personal advice (Dear Abby)	5	14
	(535)	(539)

are very interested in information about jobs and careers; 50% name professional sports; 45% cars and motorcycles. Among girls, 62% are very interested in news about clothes and style, 58% in jobs and careers, and 47% in local high school news. Only 23% of the boys and 32% of the girls are very interested in news from other countries.

Among the boys who are Sunday readers, 56% say they regularly read the sports pages, 49% the comics, 31% the entertainment section, and only 30% the main news section. Among the girls, 47% read the comics, 31% the entertainment section, and 30% the main news section. In spite of the attraction of softer feature material, 52% of the teenagers say they would stay with the weekday paper and give up the Sunday paper if they had to choose, and 44% would prefer Sunday because of its variety of news and features.

In examining how newspaper reading evolves and changes with age, we face again the same complexities that we observed when we used the other conventional and convenient ways of classifying the public. The use of newspapers and of other media of information and entertainment cannot be separated from the process of maturation. These are bound up with the changing context of family and work life, of aspirations and economic constraints. In an evolving historical environment, in which the media are themselves agents of change, the experience of each generation is bound to be somewhat unique, and the social setting somewhat different from what it was at the same age of life only a few years earlier. At any age, perhaps we can best understand the absence of motivation to read the newspaper by taking a closer look at the motivation itself.

5
LIVING WITH NEWSPAPERS

Why do people read newspapers? The question is deceptively simple and the commonsense answers that first come to mind do not necessarily penetrate the deeper complexity of tangled motives, conscious and unconscious, that find an outlet in such widespread behavior. Newspapers have for so long been such a deeply embedded institution in Western urban culture that the practice of reading them has a momentum of its own, independent of the psychological needs that brought it about in the first place. Like the practice of instilling literacy among the young, acquiring useful current information is generally accepted as essential in a civilization in which creature comforts and material progress depend upon the mastery of information. Marcel Proust wrote of

> that abominable, voluptuous act called "reading the paper," whereby all the misfortunes and cataclysms suffered by the universe in the last twenty-four hours—battles which have cost the lives of fifty thousand men, murders, strikes, bankruptcies, fires, poisonings, suicides, divorces, the cruel emotions of statesman and actor, transmuted into a morning feast for our personal entertainment, make an excellent and particularly bracing accompaniment to a few mouthfuls of *café au lait*.[1]

---

[1] Marcel Proust, *Pastiches et Mélanges*, Paris: Gallimard, 1970. (Cited by Pierre Bourdieu, *Distinction: A Social Critique of the Judgment of Taste*, Cambridge, Mass.: Harvard University Press, 1984.)

141

Knowing the news ultimately relates to the fundamental psychological need for survival—being aware of one's surroundings, of potential threats or advantages to one's self-interest. But keeping up with the news (however broadly defined) does not merely have a utilitarian function; it also establishes and reinforces the connections between the individual and the social environment, defined narrowly as the hometown or community or defined more broadly as the country or the world. Newspapers, among the mass media, uniquely express this social bond, because of the sheer volume of information they carry from which every reader can select what is relevant. The uses of the newspaper in conversation, or in establishing social contacts or social status through conversation, may really be seen as derivatives of this other larger function. And the newspaper's uses as entertainment or diversion seem much like those of the other media.

But because newspapers do embody the social links that establish individuals in their communities, their visible presence has been a constant reminder to people that they "belong." Thus, the real strength of the habit of newspaper reading has been nothing less than the daily reaffirmation of the individual's bond to those around him. When reading is perceived as discretionary, as less than universal, the habit may quickly lose its hold.

All mass media provide their audiences with diversion and with orientation. They do so in different proportions, at different occasions and with different sectors of the public. In recent years, a considerable body of scholarly effort has been applied to identify and classify the psychological roots of media experience, which now occupies such a very large percentage of waking hours.

Elihu Katz, Michael Gurevitch, and Hadassah Haas searched the academic literature on mass communication and identified 35 different psychological needs that the media have been said to satisfy.[2] They classified these into five groups:

1. Cognitive needs, related to knowledge and information.
2. Affective needs, "related to strengthening aesthetic, pleasurable, and emotional experience."
3. Integrative needs, involving confidence, stability and status.
4. Another set of integrative needs, "related to strengthening contact with family, friends, and the world."
5. Escapist or tension-reducing needs.

Different media fulfill these needs in varying degrees, and therefore complement each other.

But many or all these needs are present in the media exposure of a given

---

[2]Elihu Katz, Michael Gurevitch, and Hadassah Haas, "On the Use of the Mass Media for Important Things," *American Sociological Review*, Vol. 38, No. 2, April 1973, pp. 164–181.

individual, much of which reflects what is conveniently accessible, and the patterns of family life to which its members accommodate.

People come to the media for many reasons: They seek inspiration, amusement, instruction, and a sense of participation in the great events of the time. But above all else, the media experience is a pastime, an activity that people engage in at certain hours of the day when they have nothing of overriding importance to do and when they simply want to relax from chores or evade boredom.

When people are confronted with a choice of mass media content, they will generally take the easier way. They prefer to get communications through minimum effort. They prefer simpler to more complex and demanding content. They will normally prefer entertainment to information.

What is informative for one person may be merely entertaining for another, and vice versa. Nor is the boundary between information and entertainment a matter of what is timely. The fundamental difference is that information exists largely outside of time. There is also an aesthetic element involved in acquiring information, but information is mainly an end in itself rather than a tool for the pleasure of learning. Entertainment and cultural pursuits must be savored within the time dimension; they are, in effect, ways of agreeably passing time. This represents a crucial distinction between communication through broadcasting and through print. The advent of broadcasting not only changed the mixture of entertainment and information in newspapers' columns; it also changed the nature of its utility to its public.

In this chapter, I consider the uses to which people put newspapers in daily life, the patterns of news consumption from all sources in the course of the day, and the manner in which different kinds of readers approach the paper and move through its pages, daily and Sunday. But since people read specific newspapers, rather than newspapers in general, we must also think about how they come to choose the papers they read, when they have a choice, and about how the character of those papers affects the size of the local audience.

REASONS FOR READING

How important is the pastime function of reading? "Just relaxing and passing time" as a reason for reading that day's paper was mentioned in our two-city study (1981a) about as often as keeping up with local or world news. Still, when pinned down to the main reason, four times as many readers referred to the information in articles or ads as to the pastime aspect.[3]

---

[3]Similarly, the research firm of Clark, Martire, and Bartolemeo, in 1,202 interviews with a national sample in 1983–84, found that 73% said that "keeping up with the news" was what they liked best about newspapers as opposed to "interesting stories about people, places, and things to do."

When asked "the single most important reason" for reading a daily newspaper, 72% of the readers surveyed in our four-city study (1979e) said it was to keep up with current events and to keep informed, but advertising was referred to next most often, by 26%. Others referred to specific types of news: sports (22%), local news (19%), world news (14%), state (13%), and national news (13%). Ten percent referred to features, like the comics or crossword puzzles, and 7% mentioned the entertainment guides, but a total of 38% mentioned other elements of content: business news, opinion or advice columns. In contrast to these extensive mentions of the newspaper's actual content, only 22% referred to habit or to the social or psychological gratifications of reading.

The information provided by the newspaper may be considered in relation to the roles that people play in different aspects of their lives. We asked how relevant the paper was to readers as "a husband or wife, parent or family member," as a citizen or voter, in their main work, as a consumer, and in leisure-time activities. About 9 out of 10 women said they considered the paper relevant to all these roles except work, where the proportion dropped to 2 out of 3 women over 35, some of whom held no jobs. Among men, 9 out of 10 rated the newspaper as relevant for their voting and consumer roles and in their leisure pursuits, 4 out of 10 for their family roles, and only 2 out of 3 in their occupational roles. (This seems to suggest that newspapers might do a better job of translating business news into terms that people find useful or pertinent on the job.)

In this study, respondents were presented with a list of 11 reasons for reading the paper, derived from the "uses and gratifications" uncovered in previous research. As Table 5.1 shows, the greatest importance was ascribed to the most socially acceptable reasons, those that referred to the newspaper's information content. Reasons that articulated the social or psychological motivations for reading (aid to conversation, habit, practical utility) ranked closely behind. Acknowledgments of newspapers' function as a pastime or an escape mechanism were low on the list. Readers who preferred the news to other parts of the paper were inclined to mention more reasons as very important, but they were especially more likely to refer to their reading as a habit and to say they feel "out of touch" without a paper. Readers who preferred features to news were more likely to mention the utility function ("helps me to plan my day").

As in our national studies, the preference for news over other elements in the paper was greater among men than among women, and among older rather than younger people. But there were also great differences among the four cities: for instance, in Los Angeles, only 28% of the women said the news stories were most "meaningful or valuable" to them, while in Kansas City, 64% gave this answer. Curiously, readers who preferred news and those who preferred other parts were almost equally likely to say that reading helps them

TABLE 5.1
Uses and Gratifications of Newspaper Reading, 1979e

	Proportion saying reason is "very important"		
Reason (use or gratification):	Total	Prefer news	Prefer other part of paper
Newspapers help me to follow up on news I heard about elsewhere	59%	63%	50%
Reading a newspaper helps me to form opinions about social and political issues	59	65	51
Reading is worthwhile for its own sake, whether it's a newspaper, a book, or magazine	59	60	56
Reading the paper helps me to keep up conversations with other people about what's happening	53	55	50
When I don't have a paper to read I feel out of touch and isolated	51	60	34
Newspaper reading is a habit with me— I feel like something is missing if I can't read the paper when I usually do	51	59	38
Things I read in the paper often help me to plan my day or decide about things to do or buy	35	30	42
People need to be able to read news about accidents, crimes, and human tragedies	27	29	22
The paper tells me about celebrities and interesting people I like to know about	24	25	22
When I read the newspaper it takes my mind off other things and helps me to relax	24	27	18
Reading the newspaper helps to pass time and gives me something to occupy myself with	15	18	10
N	(330)	(197)	(125)

to keep up conversations "about what's happening," but the news-oriented were much more likely to say that reading the paper is a habit and that they feel out of touch without it.

Of those who preferred news, 72% replied (not illogically) on a different question that they would prefer a paper that is mostly news to one that is mostly features. But among those who preferred other parts of the paper, the answers were not clearcut: 38% wanted a paper that is mostly news, 32%

wanted one that is mostly features, and 30% volunteered the reply that they wanted a balance.

When asked why they preferred the news, people expressed a general interest in staying informed, interest in specific kinds of news, or a feeling that news affected their lives. Those who preferred other parts of the paper usually mentioned special interests or the utilitarian aspects of features or ads; one in five actually expressed disinterest or dislike of the news. (The changing balance of preference for news and features is discussed again in Chapter 9.)

The motives for newspaper reading were also examined in our 1987 national survey, with the aid of 11 reasons, 8 of which were repeated from the earlier study. Readers were asked to indicate all those that applied to themselves "strongly," "somewhat," or "not at all." As Table 5.2 indicates, about half gave as a strong motive the ability to follow up on news they have encountered elsewhere, their enjoyment of the variety of news and features, and (somewhat surprising for its candor) the reports of accidents, crimes, and tragedies. Only a handful said that they are strongly motivated by the utilitarian help the newspaper gives them in deciding what to do or how to plan their time, and only one in five stressed the idea that the paper gives them something to do to pass the time.

Infrequent readers are far more likely to attribute importance to every one of these reasons, apart from the use of the paper as a shopping guide. As important motivations for reading, women mention the paper's pastime value more often than men do. Men are more likely than women to say that the paper helps provide subjects for conversation and helps them form opinions on important issues and less likely to say it tells them about celebrities and

TABLE 5.2
Motives for Reading Among Frequent and Infrequent Readers, 1987

% *Say it applies "strongly"*	*All readers*	*Frequent readers*	*Infrequent readers*
Follow up on news gotten elsewhere	50%	58%	38%
Variety of news and features	48	59	33
Accidents, crimes, tragedies	46	51	39
Help in forming opinions	41	49	29
Conversational topics	38	48	23
Where to shop	35	35	36
How to vote	26	31	19
Feel out of touch if don't read	25	37	8
Celebrities, interesting people	24	28	18
Something to do to pass the time	21	24	16
Decide what to do, plan day	6	6	4
N	(866)	(511)	(355)

guides them in shopping. Older people and those with the most education are most apt to say the paper helps them to talk with others. Older people are also more inclined to stress the opinion-forming aspect of the newspaper, its help to them as voters, its value as a shopping guide and as a pastime, and the fact that without it they feel out of touch. Young people give relatively low weight to newspapers' help to them in forming opinions, to the entertainment value of the variety of news and features, and to help in deciding how to vote; hardly any of them agree that they feel isolated and out of touch when they don't have a paper to read. They are more apt to cite the value of the paper in shopping and as a pastime.

For those with the least education, accidents and crimes, celebrity news, and shopping guidance are important, as well as the newspaper's role as a pastime. People with more education are less likely to give weight to celebrity news, shopping guidance, crime and disaster news, or the paper's pastime value and more likely to say that reading the paper helps them in conversation. Compared with Whites, Blacks give more importance to the newspaper as a reporter of human drama—accidents and crimes and celebrity news. They also give greater weight to the newspaper's utility in shopping and to its pastime aspect.

LIVING WITHOUT NEWSPAPERS

One way of determining the newspaper's function for its readers is to see what happens when the paper is not available, in a protracted strike. Three New York newspaper strikes have served as occasions for such research. The first occurred just before the start of the age of television, the second toward the end of TV's primary growth period, and the third well after its maturity.

In 1945, Bernard Berelson found strikebound readers missing the newspaper as a "tool for daily living." He also identified six nonrational gratifications: respite or relaxation, social prestige, social contact, security, reading for its own sake, and ritual or habit.[4] In a similar study in 1958, Penn Kimball identified two other functions: "occupation" (keeping busy or passing time) and "stimulation" (from sex or violence).[5]

During the 1978 newspaper strike in New York City, we interviewed 90 readers to learn what they missed most, and reinterviewed 71 of them after

---

[4]Bernard Berelson, "What Missing the Newspaper Means," in Paul Lazarsfeld & Frank Stanton, editors, *Communications Research, 1948–49* (New York: Harper, 1949), pp. 111–129.

[5]Penn Kimball, "People Without Papers," *The Public Opinion Quarterly*, Volume 25 (Fall 1959), pp. 389–398; and Penn Kimball, "New York Readers in a Newspaper Shutdown," *Columbia Journalism Review* (Fall 1963), pp. 47–56.

the strike ended (1978b). Eleven percent most missed the front-page news, and an additional 21% mentioned the other general news pages; 23% mentioned sports, 12%, the editorials; 8%, the financial news. These accounted for over half the total mentions (aside from those who missed "everything" or "nothing"). Another 13% mentioned the retail ads and 7%, the classified ads. Nine percent missed columnists, and 7% missed their favorite comics. Another 7% mentioned the women's pages. No other feature was mentioned by more than a few. It appeared that what the readers missed most was in the traditional areas of news coverage rather than in the realm of fun and games.

"I don't know what's going on," "I don't know what's happening locally" were among the reactions. Others mentioned "the advertising and the selling, what's on sale and the buys and stuff. The want ads, jobs and things." Apart from these utilitarian aspects of the newspaper, the nonrational gratifications identified by Berelson and Kimball were also in evidence, with "reading for its own sake," ritual, and social contact occurring most often, but few responses reflecting nostalgia for crime news (the "stimulation" category).

About 1 reader in 4 appeared to be indifferent throughout the strike to the absence of the three metropolitan dailies, in a number of cases because substitute and suburban papers were still available to them. By contrast, about 3 out of 10 felt a continuing loss or concern throughout the strike. whether because of their hunger for news or because of their dependence on the newspaper as a defense against boredom. "It's just like a smoker who couldn't get any cigarettes. You go in the morning and you don't have the newspaper, and you're used to browsing through it. The TV just gives you a flash; it doesn't give you much of the news." "It just felt like something was missing during the day." "Well, I thought 'maybe tomorrow and maybe tomorrow.' It's been terrible. As time went on I kept feeling worse." "Well, it's pure hell. My husband is used to having his papers with his breakfast, and he's not fit to live with at breakfast. It's really quite dreadful."

An additional one in five shared these sentiments, but only after an initial period of indifference based on the expectation that the strike would be of brief duration:

I get most of my news from the paper. [The first day] it didn't bother me . . . I didn't think it would last long . . . after that it really affected me. You really missed it. You're so used to reading it every day. It bothers me now. I'm trying to get all kinds of papers, magazines, everything.

I think I'm a little less informed than I like to be. [The first day] it didn't really bother me, to tell you the truth. The first two weeks it didn't bother me . . . then I began to get a little bothered by it. There are certain enjoyments that I felt I was deprived of, that a paper had come to be a form of relaxation coming home from work to read, and it wasn't there for me, so I felt a little deprived and didn't really enjoy the strike too much after a while.

And another one in five, after being concerned at first, managed to adapt to the absence of their regular papers, accepting the strike substitutes or TV as their sources of news, as the following quotations suggest:

> I didn't feel anything until Sunday, and on Sunday I felt annoyed because of habit. Habit is such that one feels annoyed when you don't have what you're used to. I quickly adjusted, being a flexible, well-adjusted adult. I substituted the *Time* magazine. I still would like to have my Sunday *Times*, but if I don't it's no tragedy.

> It's a little more difficult to get to know about the news but I listen to the television and I read other papers that give you the information, and I find that I'm able to live without it. [The first day] I was very much disturbed that such a thing could happen, that a newspaper could go on strike like that and that the world could be turned upside down because of it . . . I adjusted to it, like people have to adjust to everything in life. I adjusted to no newspapers.

> I don't miss them too much. I have the local newspaper, the Gannett *Press* and the Daily *Argus*, which I enjoy reading very much. Some of the sales, it kind of puts a crimp on things, but that's about it. [The first day I felt] shocked. Well, the first day—well, you look for your morning paper—the *News* is a morning paper, you know—the paper I get now which I'm relying on is an afternoon paper. A morning paper, you know, is what you look for. You look for the scores for the sports the night before, you look for the sales for the day, but the afternoon paper now, after you get used to it, it makes up for it. You get used to it, that's all. I had a subscription. I think I'll drop the subscription now.

This last comment suggests that there is a distinction in the psychological function of morning and evening papers, just as there is between weekday and weekend papers. Newspaper researcher Kristin McGrath describes the morning paper as a "bracer" that sets the reader up to face the day's tasks, and the evening paper as a "reward" to come home to after the tasks have been accomplished. But this intriguing distinction does not account for the fact that many people are simply reading the paper most conveniently available to them at whatever time of day they can.

NEWS EXPOSURE THROUGH THE DAY

In contemporary America, there is almost universal contact with the three major media. In the course of an average weekday, nearly 9 out of 10 (87%) of the adult public watch some television (in 1987), while two out of three listen to the radio, and about the same proportion reads a newspaper. Only 3% of the public fails to have contact with any of the three. But the audience profiles of the three media differ substantially. Radio, like newspapers, draws people of above-average income and education. The television viewing pattern is different; people at the highest income and educational levels are least likely to watch television in the course of a given day (Table 3.10). More young people than older ones are radio listeners and fewer are newspaper readers or heavy television viewers. Blacks listen to radio less often than Whites (though or because they watch more TV).

Naturally, the audience for news represents only a part of the total audience for radio and television. Still, on a typical weekday, 67% of Americans watch some television news and 45% hear some news on the radio (1987).

Exposure to news occurs on a somewhat different timetable for each of the three media. Figure 5.1 shows hour by hour the times when a newspaper is read throughout the course of the day, and Figure 5.2 shows the timing of exposure to television news (1982). By comparison with the broadcast pattern, newspaper reading is rather evenly distributed across the hours of the day.

In a detailed examination of our 1977 national survey, we found that before the end of lunch, 63% of the public got news from one or more sources; between lunch and dinner, it was 75%; and after dinner, 46%.

Fifty-nine percent got their first exposure to the news before they were through with lunch, another 19% had their first contact between lunch and dinner time, and 4% saw or heard no news until after dinner. Radio was the initial source for 43% of the public, the newspapers for 35%, and television for 22%. TV news was more significant as the first news source for people of lower education and income.

Only 3% of the public read a newspaper morning, afternoon, and evening, but a majority looked at it in *two* different parts of the day. Of those who read one or more newspapers on a given day, 52% picked up a paper on more than one occasion, 30% on two occasions, and 22% on three or more occasions. (This, of course, includes those who read two or more papers a day.)

In 1987, 59% of those who read a paper on a given day read it before the end of lunch, 34% between the end of lunch and the end of dinner, and 34% after dinner.

Although as might be expected, most morning papers are read in the morning and most evening papers in the evening, the time when a paper is published offers no necessary guarantee of when it will be read. Eighty percent of the reading of morning papers is done at home and 16% at work (with some readers doing both). For evening papers, 94% of the reading is at home. The very fact that a newspaper is typically picked up on several

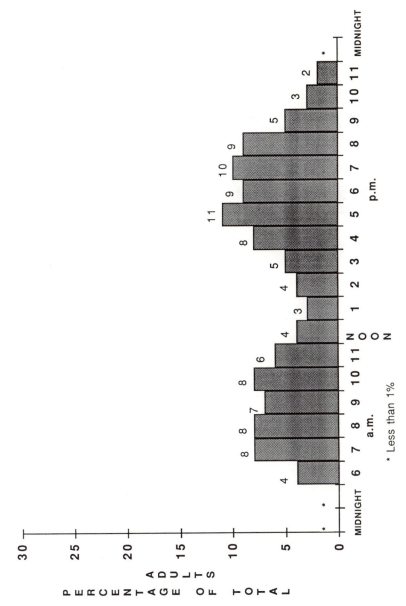

FIGURE 5.1 Hour-by-hour readership of newspapers, 1982 (base: total adults).

* Less than 1%

151

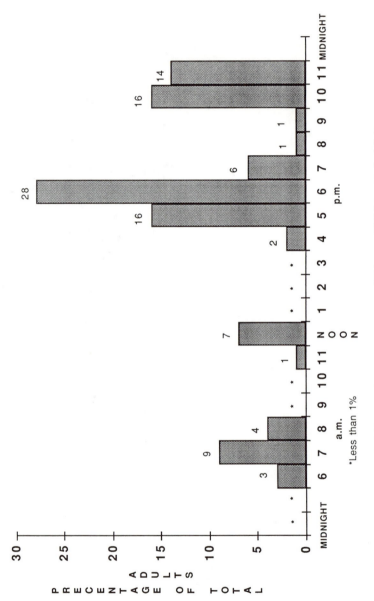

FIGURE 5.2 Hour-by-hour viewing of TV news, 1982 (base: total adults).

different occasions means that reading takes place over an extended period of time after the paper is received or purchased.

Of course, the fluctuations in readership reflect the hours of publication and distribution for morning and evening newspapers. But both types of papers are being read around the clock. For morning papers (still citing our 1977 study), 53% of the reading occasions occurred before lunch time, 33% between lunch and dinner, and 15% afterward. For afternoon papers, 62% of the readings occurred between lunch and dinner time, 26% in the evening after dinner, and 12% in the morning. Some of this represented reading of the preceding day's paper, and some represented reading of afternoon papers whose first editions appear early in the day. (Some morning papers with afternoon editions have become all-day publications and a few retain the old bulldog edition that appears at night; similarly, as noted, some evening papers now publish morning editions.) Altogether, though, 97% of "yesterday's" readers read yesterday's paper (1987).

People who read morning newspapers are generally exposed to news in the morning, while this is less true of those who read only afternoon papers. Exclusive readers of morning papers are slightly less likely to get news from any source in the evening after dinner.

At different periods of the day, each of the broadcast media has a large exclusive audience for its news. In the morning, 37% of the public were exposed only to radio news in 1977; in the evening, 42% were exposed to no other news source than TV. Sixty percent of all radio newscasts were heard at home; 21% in the car, primarily during the journey to or from work. Six percent were listened to at work; 13% in a variety of miscellaneous places.

The proportion listening to radio news drops off among people in their 50s and 60s who simply listen to radio less than younger people. Radio news exposure is also lower among less educated, lower income people who are more likely to let a day go by without turning on the radio, simply because they watch so much TV. Thus, it is understandable why infrequent newspaper readers, with their lower education and income, are also less likely to turn on the radio or to hear a radio newscast on an average day. The average adult listens to 1.75 radio newscasts a day. This figure is higher among people over 25 and generally rises with education and income (1977).

Although increasing age means that more time is spent with television, it means even more dramatic increases in news viewing. To illustrate, the percentage watching television news in the peak early evening viewing period ranged in 1977 from 29% of those 18 to 24 to 82% of those 65 and over.

Because of its scheduling, television news viewing is much more sharply concentrated in time than exposure to news on radio or in newspapers (Figure 5.2). Of all adults, 27% watch at least some television news in the morning, 26% watch it in the afternoon and early evening period from lunch through dinner time, and 49% after dinner (1987). Of course, the pattern of

TABLE 5.3
Reading Style, 1987

	Weekday		Sunday
	Total	18–24	Total
Start with front page, go right through	45%	19%	32%
Turn first to other section, go through the rest	18	21	24
Read some sections, skim the rest	14	21	16
Only read certain parts, skip the rest	20	39	25

TV news viewing reflects the present program timing practices of the broadcasters. The introduction of round-the-clock news programming on cable television has already changed audience habits and expanded the aggregate amount of TV news viewing time.

THE READING PATTERN

How do readers approach the newspaper? Three-fourths of them (73%) say that they like to set aside certain specific times of the day for their newspaper reading, with 40% mentioning a time after the evening meal (1971). (Leading less patterned lives, only 61% of single individuals say they generally set aside certain times to read the paper, compared to 76% both of the married and of the divorced and widowed.)

The typical reader, as can be seen in Table 5.3, starts with the front page of the paper and methodically works through the rest of it, while about one reader in five turns immediately to a particular feature or section of special interest and then returns for a methodical reading of the rest (1987).[6] One reader in seven skims the parts not read, and one in five skips them altogether. There are no differences in the pattern between morning and evening papers or (somewhat surprisingly) among papers of different circulation size (and hence differences in physical bulk).

---

[6]In 1982, two out of three readers said they went through the paper page by page on their last reading, reading whatever was interesting, whereas the remaining third said they only looked at certain pages or sections. In 1971, the majority of readers (53%) started their reading with the front page and went on through the paper; 8% preferred to start off their reading somewhere inside the paper. Another sizable group (37%) turned first to specific items and then went through the rest of the paper. The reader's path through the newspaper was also studied in Boston, Kansas City, Los Angeles, and Atlanta (1981a). Generally comparable patterns prevailed, although there were some variations from city to city. Of the 330 people interviewed, 90% read the paper at home, almost all at certain times: 34% after dinner, 25% before or during breakfast, 21% after breakfast, and 24% in the afternoon. Half the readers said they moved through the paper from the front to the back, and half turned directly to specific pages of interest. In either case, most read the interesting things and scanned the rest, but 10% said they read most of the items in the paper carefully.

It might be inferred that for many who skip the parts they don't read, the newspaper's principal attraction is an entertainment feature or some specialized area of the news, like sports, business, or the TV page. However, for the majority, the general news—as the editors assess and display it—would appear to be of most value. Younger readers are much more likely to skim or skip altogether rather than to go through the paper systematically.

Charles Dickens (in *Dombey and Son*), at a time when papers were much smaller, could say of a reader, "He has his newspaper and would be quite contented for the next two hours." The average amount of time a reader reported with a paper on a typical weekday was 45 minutes in 1987. One-paper readers spent 38 minutes; and two-paper readers, 71, suggesting that they spent slightly less time with each paper they read. College graduates, who are also more likely to read more than one paper a day, spent less time (44 minutes) than those readers with less than grade school education (50 minutes)—a reflection of their greater reading speed and efficiency. Readers of 65 and older spent 60 minutes a day on the average, nearly double the time (32 minutes) reported by those 18 to 24.

In metropolitan areas of over a million, where papers averaged 81 pages in size, the average reader spent 52 minutes. In smaller metropolitan areas, where papers averaged 43 pages, reading time was 40 minutes. And in nonmetropolitan areas, with 31 pages, the time was 37 minutes. Readers spend more time with papers that offer them more.

Reading time, logically, depends not only on the size of the particular paper, but on the number of papers read in a given day. A one-paper reader spent 31 minutes yesterday with a daily of under 25,000 circulation, but 52 minutes with one of over 250,000. However, someone who read two papers typically spent 51 minutes altogether if the principal paper was a small one and 68 minutes if it was over 250,000.

A substantial part of newspaper readers are able to devour the whole package at one gulp. Fifty-five percent read the paper at one sitting, 37% pick it up at several different times, and 5% report no set pattern (1987).

Nine out of 10 readers (87%) say the items that interest them are easy to find in the paper they usually read. Most readers say they make use of the index, 28% regularly and 49% occasionally.

The proportion who finish the paper at one sitting is higher among young people 18–24, who are most on the move, and also among people of 65 and over, with more time on their hands and fewer active interests that lead them immediately to some specific item inside the paper (1971). The average reader picks up a given issue on about two different occasions (1.9 times in 1977).

The smaller the paper, the better able the reader is to get it all down at once. Among readers of papers of 24 pages or less, 49% immediately read almost everything they want. This drops to 39% of the readers of fat papers of 70 or more pages; 28% of these say that they read only part of what they wanted, but this answer is given by only 19% of the people who read thin papers.

The fact that a fourth of the readers feel that they never get to read everything of interest in the paper has led to the theory that more prosperous and ample newspapers are frustrating their readers, leaving some with a sense of wasteful guilt that can only be assuaged by giving up the reading habit altogether. If this were so it would especially apply to better-educated people who should be more inclined to have this feeling as befits their more widely ranging interests. However, as we have seen, the decline in readership since the early 1970s was at the other end of the social scale.

It is precisely the physical bulk and variety of the large metropolitan paper that attracts a great many readers. In a study in 1973 for the *Louisville Courier-Journal* and the *Louisville Times*, the comment was made to readers that these newspapers "usually have more pages toward the end of the week than early in the week." They were asked, "In general, would you say you prefer the bigger papers or the smaller papers?" Forty-four percent preferred bigger papers and 25% smaller ones. The reason most often given, both by those who wanted bigger papers and those who wanted smaller ones, related to the larger amount of advertising in the bigger papers. Forty percent of the people said they spent more time with ads in the bigger papers that carried more ads, 10% said they spent less time, and 45% said they spent about the same time. Smaller proportions also said they spent more time with the nonadvertising matter. In short, a fatter paper does get greater readership, at least as the readers perceive it.[7]

Nearly three out of four readers (73%) say their ideal daily newspaper would be of about the same thickness as the one they now read most often (1982). This proportion is not significantly different among readers of small papers of 24 pages or less (73%) than among readers of thick papers of 81 pages or more (70%). However, of the minority who prefer a different size, readers of thin papers overwhelmingly want them thicker and readers of fat papers overwhelmingly want them skinnier.

The readers of thicker papers (who are, of course, likely to be in the largest metropolitan areas) are somewhat more likely than readers of smaller papers to express satisfaction with the paper as an information resource. Among the 15% who want a thicker paper, four out of five say they would like more news coverage. Of the 12% who prefer a thinner paper, three out of five would like less advertising.

The proportion of people who read the paper thoroughly is somewhat greater for people over 50 than for those under 50. But otherwise there are no

---

[7]*Highlights from the Results: The Louisville Continuing Market Study, March 1972–May 1973,* prepared for the *Courier-Journal* and the *Louisville Times,* Belden Associates.

startling differences in the reading patterns reported by sex, race, income, or education. Older people and Blacks look at their papers slightly more often than the average.

The eagerness with which the newspaper is read appears to depend on the reader more than on the paper. Large papers of 70 pages or over are just as likely to have their readers report they read them thoroughly as smaller papers are. Understandably, papers with fewer than 24 pages are slightly more likely to be picked up only once by a reader.

As already mentioned, newspaper reading is overwhelmingly an activity that takes place inside the home: 89% of all readership occurs there. Although in the nation's media capital, New York, newspaper reading is often mistakenly identified with the commuter train, only 2% of the nation's readers looked at "yesterday's" paper on the way to or from work in 1977. Women are substantially more likely than men to read at home, while men are more likely to read at work or on the way there. However, even men do most of their newspaper reading at home.

SMRB asks newspaper readers whether they "usually look at every page of the entire newspaper, or . . . tend to read or look at only some pages or sections." Sixty-three percent of the readers say they usually read every page, and those who read only certain pages are asked to identify the ones they usually read, with the help of some title cards. The results, shown in Table 5.4, support the notion that most pass by the typical page, regardless of its content. Even the food and home pages are reported looked at by 71% of the men readers and sports by 72% of the women. However, readers aged 18–24 are less likely to say they usually read every page (51%) and especially less likely to say they look at pages devoted to business, editorials, food, and home furnishings. College graduates are slightly more likely to say they look

TABLE 5.4
Types of Daily Newspaper Pages or Sections Usually Read, (SMRB 1986)

	Adults	Men	Women
Usually read every page	63%	63%	62%
Read certain pages or sections	37	37	38
Business, finance	76	78	74
Classified	76	76	76
Comics	76	76	77
Editorial page	78	77	79
Entertainment	80	77	84
Food, cooking	77	71	82
General news	92	92	93
Home furnishings, gardening	74	71	78
Sports	80	88	72
TV, radio listings	76	75	78

TABLE 5.5
Page Opening by Education, 1987

College graduates	64%
Some college	67
High school graduates	69
Some high school or less	70

at the editorial pages, but otherwise there are no real differences among different educational or income groups.

Sixty-seven percent of the public report that they go through the paper page by page, reading whatever interests them; 25% report that they scan the paper quickly; 4% say that they only read some specific items (1971).

The fact that most people say they go through the paper page by page suggests that they are looking for their money's worth and that they are trying to make certain, in effect, that they are not missing anything that might turn out to be important. This generalized description that people make of their own reading habits jibes with the answers they give when they are asked what pages or spreads of a newspaper they have actually opened and looked at.

OPENING TO THE PAGE

As a measurement concept, page opening has been validated in magazine studies conducted at a considerably longer interval after the original readings than in newspaper studies done on the very next day after the paper appears. In copies of the magazines placed with readers who were later to be interviewed, the pages were lightly glued together at the edge. The copies were later collected to verify whether or not the seal was broken for pages the readers claimed to have opened and unbroken for pages they did not remember opening. The reader's reports turned out to be true over 90% of the time.[8]

It must be realized that opening is reported not only through recollection of what is on the page measured, but also because of what is on the facing page, which may have a different character altogether. (The last page of the newspaper's entertainment section may face the first page of the sports section, for example, but if the spread is opened, both must be counted even though only one may get a particular reader's attention.)

---

[8]*Exposure of Advertising, An Experimental Study Conducted for Life Magazine by Audits & Surveys Co., Inc.*, Time, Inc., 1959, New York, and *A Study of Advertising Penetration in Look Households, A National Survey Conducted by Audits & Surveys Co., Inc. for Look Magazine*, Cowles Magazines, Inc. 1959, New York.

The perennial problem in readership studies is that it is tedious to take someone through a thick publication. The longer an interview, the greater the attrition in responses due to fatigue. To avoid this problem, detailed questioning was done only on a fraction of the pages in each paper covered in our 1963, 1971, 1982, and 1987 surveys.[9] (Because spreads consisting only of classified advertising present a special measurement problem, they were excluded from the sample of papers in the surveys before 1987. They are reported separately for 1987 but are not included in the totals.)

In the 1987 study, page-opening levels averaged higher for White readers (69%) than for Blacks (56%); they were higher for people of 55 and over (74%) than for those 35 to 54 (67%) and lowest for those 18 to 34 (60%). This suggests that those kinds of people who are least likely to read newspapers also read them more selectively when they do read them. But this is not true when we examine page opening by educational attainment. Table 5.5 shows that the best-educated readers fall somewhat below average in page opening, in all likelihood because they are apt to be younger as well and because they are also more likely to be reading several papers a day.

Essentially, the time spent reading a weekday paper has not changed very much, even though the size of the paper has enormously increased, as we saw in Chapter 1. This suggests that readers are reading more selectively, particularly since special interest sections are more easily identified. Page-opening levels bear this out. The average page (excluding spreads consisting of solid classified advertising) was opened by 82% of the readers in 1963 and by 84% in 1971. In 1982, the level had dipped to 77% and in 1987 it was 67% — not too unexpected a change when we remember that the number of pages had grown by 55% in that five-year period. (Reflecting the circumstances under which newspapers are read by people who obtain them in different ways, page opening was 70% among subscribers, 66% among purchasers of single copies, and 52% among the more casual pass-along readers).

The trend did not mean a decline in the absolute number of pages opened (since there were so many more in the paper to begin with) but rather an

---

[9]In 1963, interviews were limited to six spreads randomly selected from those on which at least one national ad appeared. The sampling excluded the first and last pages of the paper and spreads consisting only of classified advertising. (This was to fulfill the study's primary objective of measuring national advertising. In practice, this eliminated spreads that carried only editorial matter, only retail ads, or a combination of the two.) In all, 25,858 pages were measured. In 1971, a random sample of six spreads (12 pages) was drawn from all the pages in each measured paper, eliminating those that only carried classified advertising. Front and back pages were included this time as well as spreads that carried editorial matter or retail ads in addition to the ones with national ads. Although this study represented a complete sampling of daily newspaper pages, the results were almost identical with those for the earlier partial sampling. The sampling procedure used to select spreads was again slightly different in 1982 and 1987. (Front pages were oversampled in 1982 but given only their appropriate weight when the final averages were computed. In 1987, all spreads and pages were included in the universe, and six spreads were measured.)

TABLE 5.6
Page Opening, by Number of Pages in Daily Newspaper, 1987

	Average no. of pages	Percentage opened	Estimated no. of pages opened
10–32 page newspaper	21	78	16
33–48 page newspaper	40	68	27
49–80 page newspaper	56	69	39
81–204 page newspaper	120	63	76

TABLE 5.7
Percentage of Editorial Items Read on Opened Pages, by Number of Pages in Newspaper, 1982

	Number of pages			
	24 or less	25–40	41–60	61+
Average, all items	29%	34%	38%	41%
International news	36	40	42	41
National news	29	37	35	42
State & local news	29	30	33	33
Editorial page items	32	26	31	34
Sports	20	27	35	46
Amusements	30	34	39	42
Other general interest	32	38	37	41

increasingly more focused pattern of reading, especially among young people. Readers spending the same time with more pages to contend with had to distribute their attention differently. Actually, the level of page opening, as Table 5.6 shows, does not go down in proportion to the number of pages in a particular paper. Even with papers of very large bulk (between 81 and 204 pages), nearly two out of three readers looked at the typical spread.

But the larger the paper, the greater the number of items reported read on every opened page (1982). For the smaller papers, 29% of the items on opened pages were reported read; for the bigger papers the figure was 41% (Table 5.7). In short, a larger paper, with more specialized sections, is read somewhat more selectively, but also more completely.[10]

Bulky papers are, of course, most likely to be the ones with the largest

---

[10]As the number of pages has grown, a decline in readership of specialized sections has been observed in studies of individual newspapers. A New England Sunday paper measured by Market Opinion Research of Michigan in 1983 and again in 1986 found declines of between 3 and 20 percentage points (equivalent to drops between 6% and 38%) in the percentage of readers who said they read individual sections "without fail."

TABLE 5.8
Page Opening, by Circulation of Daily Newspaper, 1987

	Percentage of pages opened		
	Adults	Men	Women
Under 25,000	75	71	78
25,000–50,000	78	79	77
50,000–100,000	69	65	72
100,000–250,000	65	64	65
250,000 +	63	63	63

circulation, and, as in past studies, page opening (1987) showed a strong correlation with circulation (Table 5.8). The average page was opened by 77% of the readers of papers under 50,000 circulation and by 63% of those over 250,000. Since, as already noted, smaller papers are more likely to be published in the afternoon, opening averaged 70% among p.m. papers, 66% in the morning.

Pages located far forward in the paper were opened by a higher proportion of readers than those toward the back (Table 5.9). Attrition in page-opening levels from the front to the back is best explained not by the theory that the reader's attention wanes as he moves through the paper, but by the simple fact that sections oriented primarily to one sex or the other (sports, business, food, society news) are almost inevitably found toward the back of the paper.

TABLE 5.9
Page Opening, by Location of Page in Newspaper, 1987[a]

	Adults	Men	Women
Front page of paper	97%	97%	96%
Average interior spread	68	67	68
First interior spread[b]	77	74	81
Second interior spread	71	70	73
Third interior spread	64	65	64
Fourth interior spread	66	66	66
Fifth interior spread	56	57	54
Sixth interior spread	53	59	44
Front page of section	66	62	71
Back page of section	60	57	63
Back page of paper	61	58	63

[a]This excludes spreads of classified advertising only.

[b]This is the randomly selected spread nearest the front, not the first one randomly selected for each interview.

To examine the relationship between content and page opening, we examined both the labeled designation of the section in which the page was located (Table 5.10) and also the dominant subject matter of the particular page, which may or may not coincide with that of the section in which it was located—for example, comics located in an entertainment or second news section (Table 5.11).

Four out of five readers open the typical spread of general news, which includes opinion pages. At least three out of four open pages dominated by lifestyle or society features, events calendars, fashion, health, science and technology, or comics. Nearly three men in four open the typical sports page, three in five the average business page (including pages of financial tables). But about half the women readers also open those pages, just as a majority of men open the typical fashion or lifestyle page (but not the average food page).

Sections devoted entirely to classified ads have their average page opened by two out of five readers (39%), but as Table 5.12 shows, pages made up entirely of display advertising get virtually the same opening as pages made up entirely of editorial matter. When we incorporate the classified-only pages into the average for all advertising, this lowers the score somewhat, but it is apparent that the presence of advertising on a page does not reduce the likelihood that readers will turn to it. (Table 5.12 also tells us that pages made up exclusively of advertising account for only a slightly greater proportion of the total than those with no advertising at all.) Moreover, the level of page

TABLE 5.10
Daily Newspaper Page Opening, by Type of Section, 1987

| | Percentage opening page | | |
	Adults	Men	Women
Average page, excluding all-classified[a]	67%	66%	69%
Main news section	80	77	82
Other news (area, region, local)	75	71	79
Editorial, op-ed, letters, columns	80	81	80
Business, finance	56	59	52
Sports	59	71	47
Lifestyle, women, home	68	61	78
Food	53	30	69
Entertainment, TV, movies	60	57	63
Classified section	39	40	37
Other features: fashion, science, travel	72	66	78

[a]Spreads consisting entirely of classified advertising were excluded from the average for consistency with earlier page-opening research that did not include measures for such spreads.

TABLE 5.11
Page Opening by Dominant Content, 1987

	Adult readers	Men	Women
Editorial opinion/Op-Ed	83%	83%	83%
National/International news	80	80	81
Advice columns	79	81	77
Local/State/Regional news	74	70	78
Comics pages	74	68	80
Health/Science/Technology	73	73	73
Lifestyle/Society[a]	78	67	88
Fashion[a]	75	55	94
Calendar of Events[a]	75	64	85
Movies[a]	69	62	77
Entertainment	61	61	60
Sports	60	72	46
Business	57	61	52
Food	56	37	71
TV/Radio	55	46	64

[a]Statistical bases are very small.

TABLE 5.12
Daily Newspaper Page Opening, by Type of Advertising on Page, 1987

	Adults	Men	Women
Display advertising only	67%	66%	69%
Classified advertising only	39	41	38
Both display and classified	53	57	49
No advertising on page	69	68	69

opening remains constant regardless of whether advertising or editorial matter is the dominant element (Table 5.13).

Pages devoted solely to classified advertising grouped under different headings get a varied response. Pages devoted to automotive (28%) and employment (29%) classified get somewhat lower opening levels than those given over to real estate (35%). The highest level (45%) is achieved by general or miscellaneous types of classified ads, which include general merchandise, personal announcements, and others that may carry more human interest for a reader not specifically in the market.

The proportion of those who open a page who say that they read one or more articles or ads on it was 51% for right-hand and 50% for left-hand pages in 1963. When it comes to pages of primary interest to one of the sexes,

TABLE 5.13
Page Opening, by Ratio of Editorial to Ads, 1987

Pages with	%	% pages opened
All advertising[a]	28	59%
More ads than editorial	23	67
Same amount	10	68
More editorial than ads	15	69
All editorial	24	69

[a]Includes all-classified pages.

selectivity showed itself even more at the level of reported readership than at the original point of page opening (Table 5.14).

The greater the number of news items or ads on a page that is opened by the reader, the greater the likelihood that something will attract attention. When there was only one item (typically an ad) filling an entire page, 33% of the readers remembered seeing it in 1963. When one or two other items were added, there was more incentive to stop, and 53% of the readers remembered at least one of them. When there were six or more items, 65% of the readers remembered at least one of them, and 40% remembered two or more.

SUNDAY

Three out of five Sunday newspaper readers regard the Sunday and daily papers as "alike", while two out of five regard them as "different" (1980).

TABLE 5.14
Page Opening, and Reported Readership, by Sex, 1963

Type of content	Percentage of readers who open average page		Percentage of those who open page who read one or more items	
	Men	Women	Men	Women
General news	82	88	64	63
Amusements	84	90	62	52
Radio, TV	83	80	68	65
Miscellaneous	80	85	52	60
Sports	85	69	60	38
Business and finance	77	68	54	42
Food, fashion	73	88	42	70
Society	81	94	43	68

Interestingly, the nature of the difference most often cited is the volume and character of the news, while the presence of a magazine is next often mentioned. Only small numbers of people refer to the greater number of sections in the Sunday paper or to the color comics.

Half (48%) of all adults who ever read a paper would give it up on Sundays if forced to choose between that option and the weekday editions, whereas 35% would choose weekdays (1987). But the proportions are reversed (33%–51%) among young people 18 to 24 and 32%–58% among those with the lowest family incomes (under $10,000) who are least likely to be readers in the first place.

Why do people read the Sunday paper? When a variety of possible answers are brought up, virtually everyone (98%) mentions keeping up with the news, either local (87%) or national and international (91%) or the weekly summary (69%). Seventy-nine percent say they read the Sunday paper for the advertising; 72% for information about movies, TV, and other entertainment; 65% for regular features on hobbies and interests; and 44% for the comics. Eighty-one percent say that "just relaxing and passing time" is one of their reasons for reading (1980).

Faced with the logistical problems of distributing a Sunday package of increasingly unwieldy bulk, a number of papers in the mid-1980s began the practice of delivering some advance sections on Saturday to their seven-day subscribers. *The New York Times* reported that readers who got advance sections of the Sunday paper on Saturday were well satisfied with the arrangement and that it gave them more time to get the heavy paper read.

In 34% of the homes where newspaper readers were interviewed in 1987, there were still parts of the previous Sunday's paper around later in the week, with the TV booklet most often mentioned. (Frequent readers were more likely [39%] than infrequent readers [28%] to say that parts of last Sunday's paper were still around.) There is abundant evidence that Sunday reading takes place in a more relaxed mood than on weekdays and in a setting of familial sociability. Two-thirds of the Sunday readers share their paper with others, and half say they always share it. The larger Sunday paper is read more selectively than the daily, with a third of the readers saying they go right through from the beginning to the end, one in four starting with a favorite section (or perhaps after the main news has been preempted by another family member) and another one in four reading some parts and skipping others (Table 5.3).

The typical Sunday paper is published in six sections, but when circulation is taken into account, the average Sunday reader has a paper of nine sections, and some large papers carry as many as 22. What readers look at in these individual sections naturally depends on which ones are available to them. In general, the types of subjects that are most commonly offered as sections also turn out to have the highest level of reported readership among people who have the section available (1979).

While it would be prohibitively expensive to attempt to get page-opening information for the thick Sunday paper in the way we have done for weekdays, our 1987 survey did ask readers what sections they read "regularly," "now and then," and "never." Since the questions were not asked only of people who read a specific issue of a specific paper, and since not every Sunday paper carries every type of section, the answers shown in Table 5.15 should be taken to reflect relative levels of interest rather than literal measurements of actual readership.

With the exception of Real Estate, a majority reported reading each of the 15 individual sections on which they were questioned either regularly or "now and then." As might be expected, the main and local news sections get the largest regular readership, and other sections get different levels of attentiveness for each sex. Business and financial news sections were reported read "regularly" by 41% of the men and 18% of the women, fashion sections by 46% of the women and 11% of the men. Sports sections were read "regularly" by 64% of the men and 22% of the women, whereas food, home, and entertainment sections had more women than men readers. For other sections, the gender differences are small. Advertising inserts show considerable strength. Frequent readers are more likely to say they regularly read more different sections of the Sunday paper. (There is no difference for

TABLE 5.15
Reading of Sections in Sunday Paper, 1987

	Read regularly	Look at now and then	Put aside	Not available
Main news	75%	17%	4%	—
Regional, metro news	49	28	18	—
Local	71	20	4	1%
Business, financial	29	27	39	—
Comics	40	21	33	1
Editorials, opinion	33	32	30	—
Entertainment, arts	34	34	26	—
Fashion, lifestyles	25	29	39	1
Food	36	25	33	1
Home, garden	27	30	37	1
Magazine	49	24	22	1
Real estate	15	24	55	—
Sports	42	18	34	—
TV booklet	49	20	24	2
Travel	23	32	40	—
Ad inserts	46	26	24	—

advertising inserts, and only a small difference on the TV listings. The disparity runs two to one, however, for the business sections, the editorial and opinion section, and the travel section; infrequent readers have a narrower view of the world.)

Although substantial numbers of Sunday readers do not read something in every section, they in effect apply the same kind of screening process that takes place with the weekday paper. The person who does not want to be bothered with the travel section or the book review must look at it before passing it on to another family member who may want it. And if something on the front page of that section catches his eye, he may very well be pulled inside. The very variety of content that maximizes the appeal of the Sunday paper makes it unlikely that every reader will read everything. Three-fifths of those who share their paper say the other readers read sections that they themselves do not look at (1980).

USING THE ADS

As we noted in Chapter 2, advertising represents an important informational component of the newspaper and a strong attraction to readers. Most readers (54%) say their ideal newspaper would contain the same amount of advertising as the one they now read, 30% prefer less, and 6% actually say they want more (1987). For the Sunday paper, in spite of the much greater volume of advertising it carries, the answers are virtually the same: 50% same, 31% less, and 9% more.

Newspaper advertising covers an enormous gamut of products and services. Of 16,605 different display ads (five column inches or bigger) examined in our 1982 study, the largest number in any one category (9%) were for movies and other entertainment, but this reflected the multiplicity of small ads for individual theaters and represented a much smaller percentage of the advertising space. Altogether, 45% of the display advertising space was taken up by ads of a half page or larger, which represented only 14% of the total number, while a third of the space was accounted for by the 70% of the ads that were less than a quarter page in size.

Classified ads are read not only by people who are actively in the market for a house, a car, a boat, or a job, but by others who browse periodically to assess the worth of their own property or skills or simply to keep current on important aspects of what takes place in the community. For example, 47% of the men and 22% of the women say they generally try to keep up with what's available in cars, apart from any immediate interest they have in buying, and of these, 59% mention classified ads as their main source of information. (By way of comparison, 18% mention television and 17% friends or co-workers.) (1986). Similarly, 43% of men and 38% of women try to keep up with real estate trends, and of these, 63% say classified ads are their main source, whereas 28% mention friends. And among the 40% of men and 35% of women who try to keep up with the job market, 59% say classified ads are their main source, and 35% mention friends.

Personals, legal notices, and other types of classified ads often carry considerable entertainment value. People generally look at specific categories of classified advertising rather than at classifieds generically. Nationwide, on any given weekday, nearly two out of five newspaper readers (38%) in 1986 looked at classified ads in the three major categories of real estate, employment, and automotive. Twenty-four percent read ads in one category only, 11% looked at two, and only 3% at all three. As might be expected, the people who consulted the ads under any of these headings included a high proportion of those whom the particular advertisers wanted to reach. For example, only 5% of the population had an active interest in buying a car, but 43% of this small key group had read automotive classified ads within the past week, and 9% had followed up on the ads. However, even among those who expressed no interest in buying a car, 10% had looked at the ads.

Naturally, the characteristics of people who read different types of ads reflects the nature of the markets themselves; for instance, people under 35 read employment ads much more than more mature people settled in their jobs. And people use classified as sellers, not just as buyers. Half (50%) have placed a classified ad (1982).

EVERYDAY USES OF THE NEWSPAPER

Classifieds are not the only form of newspaper advertising that engages readers actively. Over half (56%) clipped a coupon from the paper within the past three months. In addition, 45% of the men and 67% of the women in 1971 had clipped one or more editorial items within the past three months.[11] Men clipped news reports, broadcast schedules, sports and financial articles, editorials, and hobby items. Women mentioned social news, birth and obituary items, and recipes. Half of those who clipped an item still had it at home at the time of the interview. A third had passed a clipping on to someone (66% had done so within the past month).

Apart from their reading, people have a variety of other forms of contact with newspapers as institutions. In 1982, 13% reported having written a letter

---

[11]These proportions were even higher in 1971 than in 1961, when 53% of the readers had clipped one or more editorial items from the paper and 28% had clipped one or more ads within the preceding three months.

TABLE 5.16
What People Most Often Talk About, 1977

Personal subjects		54%
Children, grandchildren	15%	
Other family matters	17	
Jobs, careers	19	
Acquaintances, interests	18	
Current events		47
Economic situation	20	
Religion	11	
Other news	23	
Politics		20
Sports, education, amusement, arts		40
Sports	19	
Movies, TV, reading	13	
School	11	
Miscellaneous		28

to the editor at some time in the past. In 1961, 43% had visited a newspaper office or plant; 23% had written or phoned the paper to get information.

Far more people (65%) say the newspaper is more important to them than TV (15%) in their role as shoppers (1987). Nearly twice as many (42% vs. 23%) say it is more important in planning leisure time. But in helping them as citizens and voters, slightly more (36%) name TV than newspapers (33%).

Perhaps the most important social function of newspapers is to be a catalyst for conversation and human contact.[12] The news is an integral part of daily life. Since conversation is the glue that binds society together, people were asked in 1977 what they most often talked about with friends, relatives, and acquaintances. Most of them mentioned a number of subjects (so the percentages in Table 5.16 add up to more than 100%). A total of 54% talked mostly about one or more personal subjects. But, in all, 47% talked mostly about current events, and another 20% talked politics. Forty percent mentioned sports, schooling, entertainment, amusement, and the arts—all subjects in the news.

Men and women tend to talk about different matters; men more about work, politics, sports, and entertainment; women more about family matters and acquaintances. But apart from that, men and women have about the same high degree of conversational interest in news and current events.

---

[12]For case histories of how newspapers provide material for conversation, see Leo Bogart, "Adult Talk About Newspaper Comics," *American Journal of Sociology*, Vol. 612 no. 1, July 1955, p. 26; and L. Erwin Atwood, Ardyth B. Sohn, & Harold Sohn, "Daily Newspaper Contributions to Community Discussion," *Journalism Quarterly*, Vol. 55, No. 3, Autumn 1978, p. 570.

Young people of 18 to 24 talk much more than their elders about entertainment and sports and about jobs or school and show a much smaller interest in politics and in current events generally. As we see in Chapter 9, this is reflected in their reading habits.

Among the newspaper readers questioned in our four-city survey (1979e), nine out of ten said inflation was a subject that often came up in conversation, while unemployment was mentioned by only 17%. Drugs and crime were each mentioned by 40%. The newspaper read most often was rated as a very good way of keeping informed on such subjects as inflation, sports, crimes, and political news, but not on "things that happen in the neighborhood."

Similar findings cropped up in the 1982 and 1987 national surveys, which found that the respondents' most-often-read newspapers got the highest ratings for keeping them informed on sports and crime and the lowest for neighborhood happenings (not surprisingly!), pollution problems, and minority news (Table 5.17).

Older people gave higher ratings than younger ones on every subject, with the greatest disparity on the topics of national and local government news, crime, environment, and minority news. Although not every subject was rated in both surveys, national government news got a higher rating in 1987, and sports and crime got lower ones.

In another study (1981a), "keeping up with current events" led the list when newspaper readers in two cities were asked how often 14 subjects were on their minds "these days." Other than that, the subjects of greatest concern seemed to be highly personal ones. Politics ranked low. Table 5.18 shows

TABLE 5.17
Percentage Rating Newspaper as Doing a Very Good Job, 1982 and 1987

	1982	1987		
	total	Total	18–24	65+
What President and Congress are doing	26	32	18	38
Things that happen in neighborhood	18	21	25	31
What's going on in other countries	31	28	23	29
What local government is doing	30	28	20	36
Sports events, news	49	37	34	39
Crimes, robberies	45	35	23	46
Youth using drugs	25	–	–	–
AIDS epidemic	–	31	18	34
Health topics	19	–	–	–
Minority groups	–	17	11	24
Environmental pollution	15	19	10	25
Unemployment	36	–	–	–

TABLE 5.18
Central Life Concerns:
% Who Often Have Topic on Mind, by Age, 1981a

	18–34	35–44	45–64	65+
Keeping up with current events	48	51	76	75
Finding enough time to do everything	54	73	57	33
Getting together with friends	62	39	47	44
Making more money	62	56	44	27
Cutting expenses	41	46	54	48
Developing my personal abilities	55	49	36	27
Getting more exercise	43	58	40	33
Watching my diet	31	47	49	32
Sports	44	25	31	35
Taking pleasure trips	30	18	24	27
Politics	13	20	30	47
Furnishing my home	15	41	20	14
Finding ways to pass time	21	6	13	31
Planning for retirement	3	9	35	14
N	(218)	(84)	(146)	(56)

substantial differences between younger and older persons.

Presumably what is on people's minds is what they most talk about. People of above average education talk more about politics, as one might expect, but conversation about other kinds of news events is about equally common at every educational and income level. News is grist for nearly every conversational mill. Of course, what people talk about depends on what is going on in the world as well as in their personal lives, and this is where the news media come into play.

THE PERSONAL LINK

The public seems to have an instinctive awareness that news in the paper is spread out for everybody to see and to talk about. An indication of this may be found in the answers to two related questions asked in 1961: "Suppose you had a teenage child who won a good citizenship award at school. Where would you most like to have it reported?" Sixty-five percent chose the newspaper; 17%, TV; and 6%, radio. But if the teenager were in trouble, 43% would find a newspaper account of this most disturbing, 29% would be most disturbed if it were on TV news, and 5% by a report on the radio.

In 1961, people felt closer to the newspaper they read most often (40%) than to the television channel they watched most often (33%) or the radio station they listened to most often (14%). In 1982, television had 40%; newspapers, 33%; and radio, 15%. What accounts for this change? The channels watched most often by most people are network affiliates, with only a modest amount of locally originated programming. It is the local news shows that help give a television channel its identity. Thus, the answers to this question show how powerfully TV newscasters—show business personalities who enter the home day after day—affect overall ratings of media performance.

Can newspapers compete with television news in this area by building public recognition of their own by-lined writers and columnists? Forty-one percent of the readers said in 1982 that they regularly follow a particular columnist or reporter. (In two-thirds of the cases, a syndicated columnist was named.)

Of those who follow a by-lined writer, 72% feel they know what he or she is like as a person, and 76% say they would like that writer as a friend.[13] Some newspaper managements encourage reporters and editors to become public personalities through platform and television appearances. Others discourage the development of such stars on the grounds that it leads to salary demands, inflated egos, and defections to other employers. But the evidence seems to indicate that readers' sense of the character of those who write what they read strengthens their attachment to a paper.

Of the 41% who regularly read a columnist or writer in their own paper, 65% mentioned syndicated columnists—especially the two sisters, Abigail Van Buren ("Dear Abby") and Ann Landers.[14]

HOW READERS RATE THEIR PAPERS

Most people have a very favorable attitude toward their local newspapers. Within the five cities covered in the 1974 study, 75% (on average) mostly agreed that "the newspaper gives me important news stories and details that I can't get from radio or TV"; 65% mostly disagreed that "these days, subscribing to a newspaper costs more than it's worth"; 73% agreed that "when I read the newspaper I am about equally interested in the advertising

---

[13]In 1961, about half the public (47%) reported that they regularly followed a newspaper writer, reporter, or columnist. Among these loyal readers, 79% said they would like to have this individual as a friend, 63% said they had a feeling for what he or she was like as a person, and 44% said that if that column were dropped from the paper, they would feel they had lost a personal friend.

[14]A 1988 Harris Poll found that 63% of American women and 43% of the men say they follow at least one advice columnist, with Dear Abby and Ann Landers tied for first place.

and news stories"; 83% agreed that "I like to get my news from the paper because I can pick it up or put it down whenever I want"; 81% disagreed that "the news in the paper is stale; by the time I get it I already know just about everything I'm interested in." Similarly, 76% disagreed that "you can't count on getting your paper at the time you want it"; 81% disagreed that the paper takes too long to read; 79% agreed that "I like the paper because it is well organized; I can easily find out what I want to know about."

On all the above issues, attitudes varied only very slightly from city to city. However, on a number of other key propositions there were significant local variations, as Table 5.19 shows, that reflect differences in newspapers' performance.

When readers are asked to select between pairs of statements about the newspaper, their responses lean heavily in a favorable direction (1982). For example, 69% agree that "on most days, there are things in the paper that are very important to me" (as opposed to, "on most days, hardly anything in the paper makes much difference to me"). Similarly, 77% chose "the daily newspaper gives me most of the information I want about the things that really matter to me" over "I have to go elsewhere to get the information I want."

Men are more likely than women (73% compared to 65%) to agree that "on most days there are things in the paper that are very important to me." Blacks give this answer more often than Whites, even though it is also more likely to be given by those of the highest income and education. People in nonmetropolitan areas are less likely to agree with this statement.

Reading is generally regarded in a positive light, whereas watching TV arouses ambivalent attitudes. As shown in Table 5.20 from our two-city study (1981a), most people consider watching TV dull and "mostly a waste of time," but think it is better than reading to "help you unwind after a hard day." By

TABLE 5.19
How Attitudes Toward Newspapers Vary Locally, 1974

		Five-city average	Least favorable	Most favorable
Disagree:	"The newspaper pushes its own political views more than TV newscasts do."	50%	58%	43%
Agree:	"One of the main things I like about the newspaper is that it has items about people and events around here."	77	68	84
Agree:	"I really feel lost when I don't have the paper every day."[a]	71	60	77

[a]This is the only statement on which attitudes showed a significant difference by age.

TABLE 5.20
Statements Matched With Reading and Watching TV, 1981a

	Total[a]	Men	Women
Positive statements			
Helps you unwind after a hard day			
Watching TV	55%	62%	49%
Reading	39	33	46
Gives a lot of useful information			
Watching TV	28	22	34
Reading	65	73	57
Gives you things to talk about			
Watching TV	40	34	46
Reading	50	55	45
Gives you ideas for things to do			
Watching TV	22	22	22
Reading	66	68	65
Helps you understand current events			
Watching TV	43	38	47
Reading	49	54	43
Keeps your mind active			
Watching TV	17	15	20
Reading	75	78	72
A good escape from everyday routine			
Watching TV	46	55	38
Reading	46	37	54
Negative statements			
Mostly a waste of time			
Watching TV	77	80	73
Reading	6	8	5
Dull			
Watching TV	58	58	58
Reading	20	26	15
Hard on the eyes			
Watching TV	32	35	29
Reading	49	51	48
N	(505)	(160)	(345)

[a]Pairs do not total 100% because "equal," "both," and "no answer" have been omitted.

contrast, reading "keeps your mind active," provides "useful information" and "ideas for things to do."

Yet the public's involvement with television has become progressively greater in recent decades, while its dependence on newspapers has diminished. In 1961, when daily readership was at a high point, half the public said they would feel "quite lost" if they "could not buy any newspapers around here for quite some time," far more than gave the corresponding response for television (Table 5.21). By 1982, the answers were identical for newspapers and for television *news*.

However, the reactions were predictably different by age and income. For newspapers, the proportion that would feel lost ranged from a mere 15% of those 18 to 24 to 53% of the over-65s; for television, the range was from 33% to 47%. The percentage who would feel lost without newspapers did not vary much by income level, but for TV it ranged between 24% of the highest income group to 55% of the lowest.

The individuals who say they could "easily do without" the newspaper or without television news are to a large extent the ones who are not exposed to that medium on an average day. But of the remainder, nearly half think that while they might miss newspapers or television news, they could get along without it. This suggests a casual or ambivalent attitude toward the news itself that, among other things, erodes the regularity of newspaper reading.

An extensive list of criteria was used in 1987 to get readers' evaluations of the paper they most often read, on a scale ranging from a low score of 1 to a high of 9. On all these measures, ratings tended to cluster in the upper-middle end of the scale, with a high of 7.6 for readability of the type and a low of 6.0 for impartiality. Table 5.22 shows the percentages of those who gave the highest ratings (7, 8, or 9) to each criterion. The paper typically gets the highest score for its mechanical aspects (organization and legibility) and its lowest rating on fairness and the separation of facts from opinions. Smaller papers are rated higher than bigger ones on coverage of local stories. The biggest papers get the highest ratings from their readers on value, interest, professionalism, and readability; the lowest ones, on genuine interest in the community.

Compared with less frequent readers, frequent readers give consistently higher ratings to the most-often read paper. Frequent readers, in particular, give it higher marks for its organization, graphics, interest level, readability, and liveliness (if that is the opposite of "boring"), as well as for its investigative

TABLE 5.21
Changes in Media Attachment, 1961 & 1982

	If . . . became unavailable			
	Daily newspaper		*TV*	*TV news*
	1961	*1982*	*1961*	*1982*
Would feel quite lost without it	49%	33%	28	34
Would miss it but could get used to it	30	44	36	45
Could easily do without it	21	23	36	21

TABLE 5.22
Percentages of Readers Giving Their Newspaper a High Rating, 1987[a]

	All readers	Frequent readers	Infrequent readers	Circulation	
				Under 25,000	Over 250,000
Easy-to-read print size	79	81	76	85	79
Organized to find what you want	77	82	69	79	78
Readable, understandable	75	79	69	64	82
How good it looks	68	72	62	70	65
Value for the money	68	70	66	59	74
Quality of its people[b]	67	68	65	59	66
Brings to light what public ought to know	65	68	62	60	65
Covering local news not on TV	63	64	60	70	59
Accuracy	62	64	59	53	61
Interestingly written	61	65	56	51	63
Genuinely interested edin this community	58	61	52	56	45
Not boring to read	58	61	54	49	67
Photos, maps make news understandable	58	61	53	49	61
Separating facts from opinions	45	47	43	44	49
Fair, impartial to all sides	43	46	38	41	42

[a]Score of 7 or more on a scale of 1–9, among those rating each point.

[b]Two out of five respondents were unable to rate their paper on this point; on other aspects of the paper, nonresponse was very low.

flair. But frequent and less frequent readers differ very little in their appraisal of the job the paper does in covering various news subjects.

Only 46% of the readers reported in 1982 that they had previously read another paper; 27%, in the past five years. When the past paper was compared with the present one, the comparison was generally favorable: 41% called the present one better, 21% felt it was worse, and 38% said it was about the same. Among the readers who had always read the same paper, 41% said it was better than it had been five years earlier; 4%, worse; and 55%, about the same.

DO EDITORIALS REFLECT PUBLIC OPINION?

The American press is, on the whole, conservative, a business run by businessmen. In most national elections, a substantial majority of newspapers generally support the Republican candidate in their editorials, although in 1964 Lyndon Johnson was favored by more than Barry Goldwater. When circulation is taken into account, the conservative orientation of the numerous small-town dailies no longer carries the same weight, and liberal metropolitan voices ring out more strongly. In contrast to their publishers, reporters tend to lean toward the Democrats. A survey of 85 editorial page editors showed that in 1984, although 56% of their papers endorsed Reagan, only 36% voted for him themselves.[15]

"Liberal bias" was charged in a well-publicized study of 238 journalists on the staffs of the three networks, PBS, the three news magazines, *The New York Times*, the *Washington Post*, and the *Wall Street Journal*.[16] But the characteristics of this national media elite are by no means identical with those of a cross-section of news reporters and editors in the full spectrum of the nation's press. Such a study, made in 1983, showed that 58% described their politics as middle of the road, and similar proportions put themselves left (22%) and right (18%) of center.[17]

Surprisingly, the political leanings of news executives were not significantly different from those of ordinary staffers. Journalists were slightly more likely than the general population to describe themselves as independents, and they were a little more Democratic and less Republican than the public's 45–25 split at the time of the survey.

A few years later, in 1987, 37% of the public described its political orientation as Democratic, compared to 24% Republican, though an increasing proportion of voters (24%) like to think of themselves as independents. How, if at all, is the discrepancy in outlook between publishers and their public reflected in readers' attitudes toward their newspapers?

It must be remembered that the traditional separation of editorial opinion from news reporting softens the sense of dissonance. Moreover, the polarization of party allegiances that occurs in national elections and in statewide contests is considerably more intense than the rivalries that occur in local races, where newspapers' editorial support is far less predictable. And beyond the question of electoral endorsements is the indisputable fact that for most of the year, editorial commentary concerns issues to which party loyalties are irrelevant.

Readers do, in fact, pay attention to newspapers' editorial opinions. The typical editorial gets exactly the same level of reported readership (25%) as the typical newspaper article (1971). It actually gets above average readership

---

[15]Byron St. Dizier, "Editorial Page Editors and Endorsements: Chain-Owned vs. Independent Newspapers." *Journal of Newspaper Research*, Vo. 8, No. 1, Fall 1986, pp. 63–68.

[16]S. Robert Lichter, Stanley Rothman, & Linda S. Lichter, *The Media Elite: America's New Powerbrokers*, Bethesda, Md: Adler and Adler, 1986.

[17]David H. Weaver & G. Cleveland Wilhoit, *The American Journalist: A Portrait of U.S. News People and Their Work*, Bloomington: Indiana University Press, 1986.

among men (30%), though it is below average (21%) for women. As could be predicted, editorials are better read by people who have been to college (31%) than by those who did not complete high school (20%), which explains why they are read more by Whites (26%) than by Blacks (15%). In spite of the superior education of young people, their low interest in politics is reflected in lower editorial readership (19%) than among people of 50 and over (29%).

Smaller papers are more likely to run canned editorials than larger ones and also tend to run fewer of them. Whether because of this difference in what they print or because of the differences in their characteristics and the outlook of their readers, the average editorial in papers of less than 50,000 is not as well read (23%) as the average one in papers of 250,000 and over (30%).

Thirty-five percent of the readers say they try to read editorials "on a regular basis," while 43% say they "sometimes glance at them," and 22% say they never look at them (1982). As might be expected, regular readership goes up with income and education, and it is higher among those over 45 than among those younger. Those who read editorials regularly are more inclined to agree with the paper's editorial viewpoint than are those who only glance at them sometimes. (Half of those who never look at them cannot answer the question.)

Two-thirds (67%) of the readers in 1982 said that the "regular columns and other signed articles on or close to the editorial page" "represent a wide range of opinions," wheras 25% said they "mostly reflect just one viewpoint."

In 1987, 20% of the readers believed that their paper's editorial opinions affect the way it reports the news; 47% felt that news and opinions are kept separate. Since another 10% had mixed views on the subject, it is clear that there was a significant minority who were ready to suspect bias, just as other studies have shown.

Our findings are also consistent with those studies in what they show of the public's opinion of the paper's political leanings. The largest number (43%) saw it in 1987 as middle of the road; somewhat more (22%) saw it as mostly conservative rather than as mostly liberal (14%).[18] And while equal proportions (16%) said they mostly agree and mostly disagree with the newspaper's editorial positions, most (46%) said, not unintelligently, that they sometimes agree and sometimes don't. A substantial proportion of

---

[18]In 1982, 40% rated it "middle of the road"; 22%, conservative; and 14%, liberal. (Television was perceived as slightly to the left of center, with 34% describing the news program they watch most as "middle of the road," 26% as liberal, and 19% as conservative.) Readers were inclined to agree with their paper's editorial viewpoint, with 15% saying they "generally agree" and 47% saying they "sometimes agree." By contrast, 3% said they "almost always disagree," 12% said they frequently disagree, and 9% volunteering the comment that they agree and disagree equally. These figures indicate a shift from the 1971 responses: 27% said that "summing everything up," they generally agreed with the editorial positions; 47% said they sometimes agreed; 16% frequently disagreed, and 4% almost always disagreed.

TABLE 5.23
Percentage of Papers that Publish Op Ed Opinion Pages, by Circulation Size, 1979a

	Carry at least once a week	Carry daily
Over 100,000	86	74
50,000–100,000	63	42
25,000–50,000	47	29
10,000–25,000	34	18
Under 10,000	19	9
Total (by number)	39	22
Total (by circulation)	69	53

readers do not have a choice if they want to read their hometown paper, so the degree of agreement might be considered impressive. On the other hand, it should give publishers no comfort to know that a sixth of their readers rarely or never feel that the paper's opinions echo their own.

The more remote the issue on which the paper takes a stand, the more likely readers are to accept its opinions. On local politics, opinions divided almost evenly in 1971, with 55% supporting the newspaper's position.[19] On national issues, 62% agreed with its views; on world events, 67% agreed.

The best-educated people actually more often disagree than agree with the newspaper's position on local politics, and though they tend on balance to support its views on national and world events, they are less accepting of them than people with less education. Except on the subject of world events, disagreement is greater among Blacks than among Whites. Disagreement is also higher among the people with most income and among young people. But the extent of this disagreement should not be overstated. Even among those 18 to 24, only 8% said in 1971 that they almost always disagreed, and 20% disagreed frequently with the newspaper's general point of view. In fact, a substantial majority said they generally agreed with the paper's positions on local politics, national issues, and world events.

Papers representing 53% of total weekday circulation offer a variety of viewpoints on an op-ed (opposite editorial) page on a daily basis, and papers with an additional 16% of the circulation run such a page in their weekday editions at least once a week (1979a, Table 5.23).

While 43% of the readers say that news and editorial opinions are kept

---

[19]The relatively high degree of disagreement on local issues is at variance with the assumption that newspapers always support, never threaten, community values: "The blandness and timidity of much of the American press, I think, comes partly from the fact that the local daily is seen (by itself as well as by others) as a Civic Leader as well as a newspaper—responsible for boosting the town as well as for keeping an eye on it." Calvin Trillin, "On Using Newspapers," *More*, December, 1973, p. 24.

separate in the paper they usually read, 5% believe that opinion influences news "all of the time" and 27% feel it happens at least on occasion (1982). The regular readers of editorials are not only more likely to express views on this point, they are also more likely to charge bias.

When asked to describe the most-often-read local newspaper's editorial position on "important issues," 24% of its readers brought up its political leanings, 18% its objectivity, 13% its agreement with their own views. As in the earlier national survey, readers were more inclined to agree with the paper's editorial stance on remote national or international issues than on matters of local politics.

However, readers' descriptions of "today's paper" were virtually identical in two very different markets (1981a).[20] Three out of five said it had mostly bad news, three out of four said it was interesting rather than dull, almost all said it was easy to read, and nearly three out of five said it had mostly new information. The remaining two in five thought it had mostly "old" information. Curiously, two-thirds of this group still described the paper as interesting.

How much influence do people attribute to the press? In the same study, local daily newspapers were ranked far behind other institutions in their power to affect the public's well-being. But the people running newspapers elicited more confidence than those running any of the nine institutions on which respondents were questioned. (However, these respondents were all regular newspaper readers.) And when we asked a national cross-section of the public in 1982 to rate the same nine major institutions, they were realistic in saying that the federal role of government had a "great deal" of power to affect the well-being of people in their community. Local newspapers were named by 21%, TV stations by 18% as having a great deal of power, half as many as those who named major corporations, organized labor, or banks.

In 1971, the Harris Poll showed that the level of public expression of "a great deal of confidence" in the press was at 60% of the level for other nongovernmental institutions (major companies, organized labor, medicine, religion, colleges) and at 85% of the level of confidence given to the federal government. In 1986, a similar poll found lower confidence in most institutions, but confidence in newspapers was now 73% of the average of nongovernment institutions and slightly higher than confidence in the federal government. It was evident, in short, that the public's respect for newspapers

---

[20]Readers in the two cities also gave similar answers when asked what items in that day's paper were of particular interest to them. Only 1 in 6 thought of nothing in particular. Three in 10 mentioned crimes, accidents, or other local or state news. One in 4 mentioned national news, and similar proportions mentioned international news, sports, and miscellaneous features. One in six named advertising.

and their managements held up very well at a time when readership levels were dropping.

SELECTING A NEWSPAPER: THE INTERCITY STUDY

If newspapers give people a sense of identity with others who share common interests, how can they serve this function in an interurban setting where the individual not only has ties to the local neighborhood but contacts that may range over a number of surrounding cities and towns? In an era of great mobility and blurred civic boundaries, there can be, among residents of the same interurban community, a wide variety of orientations. The choice of a newspaper should reflect the same type of selectivity that is reflected in living, visiting, traveling, shopping, and working behavior.

A town of about 25,000 ("Intercity") was selected for study in 1962 because it lay under cross-pressure from a number of different surrounding towns. Apart from a weekly newspaper, it has no mass media of its own, but it is served by mass media emanating from five big cities and two smaller cities no more than 40 miles away. There are a number of other smaller towns and villages within a 25-by-40-mile area around Intercity. Intercity has a relatively long history, an established core or center, and a surrounding suburban sprawl of new development.

Like any interurban area, Intercity is characterized by a high degree of personal mobility: 18% of the respondents had lived there for less than 2 years; less than half had been in the town for over 10 years.

In spite of its interurban location, it is an independent community rather than an appendage or suburb of any big town nearby. This is shown by the high proportion of its principal wage earners who work in Intercity itself— 37% — and also by the fact that the remainder are spread among a great many of the surrounding communities. Nearly everyone interviewed (97%) had been out of Intercity for some purpose within the previous four weeks, and 89% had been outside the previous week.

As with work patterns, travel outside Intercity covers a broad array of communities. There is no single, main line of travel. Within the past week, two cities had each drawn over a third of the Intercitizens, three other towns had each drawn about a fourth, and eight other communities had been visited by between 2% and 14% each.

People travel out of Intercity for a considerable variety of reasons, and there are remarkably small differences between men and women. In the past seven days, over half have gone shopping in other towns; nearly half of those interviewed have visited out-of-town friends or relatives; over a fourth have gone elsewhere for a snack, drink, or meal; 1 in 10 has gone to a movie or show; 1 in 10 to a religious service; 1 in 8 has gone to a meeting of some out-of-town group or club. In addition, 31% of men and 39% of women had sought medical treatment out of town in the last six months. Each of the surrounding towns has a variety of attractions for Intercitizens and yet each town balances these attractions in a way which is uniquely its own.

"Yesterday," 89% of those interviewed read one or more papers, an average of 1.8 per reader, mostly home delivered. Intercity is one of those towns where a visitor can drive down a typical street of identical houses and find the different colored mailboxes of papers that originate in different nearby cities.

In general, those people who read *only* a paper published in one of the larger, more distant cities of the group show a more cosmopolitan outlook than do those who read a paper from one of the smaller, more nearby cities (regardless of whether they also read a paper from the more distant metropolis).

Intercitizens report themselves to be more interested in national and international news than in local news. However, individual dailies show substantial variation in the extent of their appeal to people who have a national or a local news orientation. One of the "Central City" papers appeals strongly to readers with a cosmopolitan orientation and one does not. Conversely, one of the "Elm City" papers appeals strongly to readers with a parochial orientation and one does not. In short, the character of the individual newspaper seems to shape its audience regardless of where that newspaper originates.

Why do some readers choose to read a daily newspaper that is published in one city while their neighbors pick a paper from another? A number of factors turn out to be highly predictive. Persons who formerly have lived in a nearby town, or who say they might move to another community in the next five years, are present readers of that town's newspaper in 7 cases out of 10.

If someone in the family works in a town outside Intercity, this increases the likelihood that members of the family will read a paper published in that town. To take just two illustrations, 6% of the Intercitizens read the Plant City paper "yesterday," but in families where a breadwinner commutes to Plant City, the proportion is 44%. In families with a commuter to Naborcity, 62% read the Naborcity daily; the over-all readership is 18%.

Those who go to a particular town are more likely to read that town's newspapers than those who do not. Moreover, the more frequently they visit, the greater the likelihood that they will read the local paper (Table 5.24).

The relationship between visiting and newspaper reading remains the same regardless of the reasons that bring people to visit a town. Whether people went to a nearby community to visit friends, see the doctor, go to a show, restaurant, or club meeting, between 40% and 50% had read that town's newspaper "yesterday."

TABLE 5.24
Visits to a Town and "Yesterday" Readership of its Newspapers in "Intercity," 1962

	Percentage who read newspaper originating in each town among those who:			
	Visited 5 times in last week	Visited in last week	Visited in last 4 weeks	Did not visit
Elm City	74	53	47	18
Naborcity	79	37	32	4
Plant City	62	28	19	2
Central City	83	70	67	43
River City	25	35	28	11
Metal Town	18	3	3	—

Altogether, 41% of the Intercitizens had gone shopping in the past week in a town where a daily newspaper is published. Others, of course, had shopped only in Intercity (which has a complete variety of stores in its business district) or in nearby hamlets, villages, or shopping centers where there is no daily newspaper. Of those who had shopped in a newspaper town, 60% had read that town's newspaper "yesterday."

Looking at the data from another point of view, the proportion of readers of a paper who visit the town of publication, the same sort of relationship is revealed: The readers of a town's papers are much more likely to visit that town than are other people. For instance, in the course of the last week, 57% of the readers of an Elm City paper went to Elm City, while the same is true of only 11% of those who were not among this reader group.

Since there is such a strong relation between shopping and visiting a nearby town and reading its daily newspaper, it is reasonable to ask whether television viewing shows the same relationship. Intercity is within viewing range of channels originating in four nearby cities, one of which yielded only 1% of "yesterday" viewers. But between 30% and 50% had watched a channel from one of the other three cities "yesterday." Unlike the daily newspaper data, there is no significant difference between the viewers and nonviewers in the proportion who have in the past week or month visited each of the towns whose TV station they watched yesterday. Moreover, there is no difference in visiting between those who watch a town's station most and those who watch channels originating in other communities.

Of those in Intercity who went shopping within the past week in a television town, 31% watched that town's TV channel yesterday. Of those who had gone shopping within the past week in a newspaper town, 60% read one of that town's newspapers yesterday.

The percentage who have been in each town for any reason within the last seven days shows no particular difference between "yesterday" viewers and nonviewers. As an example, 33% of those who watched a Naborcity channel "yesterday" have been in Naborcity within the past seven days. So have 35% of all the other people. But of those who "yesterday" read the Naborcity newspaper, 72% have gone to that town in the last week, compared to 27% of the nonreaders. The results are similar for the other markets.

In a period of growing complexity in living and work patterns, each daily newspaper sorts out its readers from the surrounding population. Its audience selectively concentrates on those who look to that community as the place to visit and shop.

The relation between the newspaper and its market appears to be a two-way affair. People go from Intercity to Plant City, River City, or Central City because they are attracted by news of local activities or by the ads in the papers describing the specials of the day. But they are drawn to read those papers because they are the voice of the very towns where they are accustomed to going. And the day-after-day, month-after-month exposure to the news minutiae of a particular nearby town inevitably creates a sense of identity with its people and institutions.

DISTINGUISHING AMONG NEWSPAPERS

In the past, intense competition in large cities made for newspapers with sharply distinctive political viewpoints, cultural orientations, and social class appeals. Today, except in a handful of cases, the press generally aims to cover the spectrum of interests, viewpoints, and taste levels in the entire community. It tries to offer something for everyone and to avoid alienating any significant category of the public. Yet the evidence indicates that individual newspapers differ substantially in the characteristics of their reading publics and in the degree to which they penetrate their communities.

To some degree, these variations merely reflect the substantial heterogeneity of American regions and cities. Differences in size, in the local economies, in the ethnic and racial composition of the population, in history, traditions, and propinquity to other populated areas cause individual cities to have differing educational and income levels and differences in their characteristic age and household composition. But all the differences, imposing as they are, do not totally explain the sharp variability of newspaper reader profiles from place to place.

This variability exists both in metropolitan areas where the central-city papers compete and in those where they are under a single ownership. The range of variation is quite comparable both for morning and afternoon newspapers. (It is also true of those single-ownership situations, where audience figures are available only for the combined readership of both papers.) The data are derived from local market audience studies conducted according to comparable methods. With only a few exceptions, the papers represented are large ones, with circulations of over 100,000.

Scarborough's 1987 report on the top 50 markets found average readership among adults to be 68% on weekdays and 74% on Sundays. But this aggregate concealed great differences. Readership of any daily in individual metropolitan areas ranged from just under 60% in Louisville, Atlanta, and Cincinnati to 81% in Boston, Buffalo, and Nassau/Suffolk. Readers-per-copy averaged 2.7 daily and 2.6 Sunday. But the number of readers-per-copy ranged from less than 2 in Louisville to 3.6 for the New York *Daily News*. Similarly, the SMRB survey of the top 50 markets in 1987 found that average-day readership of all papers ranged from 57% in Nashville to 81% in Monmouth County (Asbury Park), New Jersey. The readership of individual central-city papers ranged from 15% for the San Bernadino *Sun* to 73% for the Buffalo *News*. Where the coverage figures are low, they reflect the presence of strong competition from nearby cities or from suburban dailies in the same market. Moreover, a few elite papers, notably *The New York Times* and the *Los Angeles Times*, have flourished by appealing primarily to an upper-income minority constituency within a large geographic region.

Charles Lehman examined the characteristics of people in the individual markets covered by Scarborough's 1987 local surveys in relation to the variations in the proportion of people in each market who read a newspaper "yesterday." As expected, there were modest positive correlations between newspaper readership and household income (+ .13) and the percentage of two-income households (+ .10). (A perfect relationship would be + 1.0; a perfectly inverse one − 1.0.) The absolute size of the market was only faintly related to the level of reading (+ .08). That level was negatively associated (slightly) with the proportion of low income households (− .09), the percentage of Blacks (− .12), and the percentage of people who had not finished high school (− .15). There were much stronger positive correlations with median age (+ .32), the percentage never married (+ .38), and the proportion with cable TV (+ .35), and negative correlations with the percentage married (− .19), the percentage divorced or separated (− .54), and the proportion who had lived in their present home for two years or less (− .45). Further evidence of how mobility discourages regular reading was found in a negative correlation (− .40) with the percentage owning two or more cars or other vehicles and with the average March temperature (− .43). The Sunbelt's "lotus eaters," Lehman suggests, are less likely to be avid readers.

Of all Americans aged 18 and over, 40% are under 35. This proportion is higher in areas of growing population and lower in declining regions. However, the variations are nowhere as great as those represented in the characteristics of individual newspaper audiences. The proportion of readers who are under 35 ranges from 20% to 45%, demonstrating that some papers are far more successful than others in attracting the youthful readers that most editors want.

Similarly, the regional variations in educational facilities and attainment can account for only a limited part of the striking variability shown by individual papers. Seventy-five percent of the population over 25 are high school graduates or better. But one paper has only 59% of its readers in this bracket, whereas another has 89%. It must be concluded that the character and content of individual papers continues to determine the size and nature of their audiences to an appreciable degree, within the limits of their market potential.

This conclusion is supported by an analysis (made at the Newspaper Advertising Bureau in 1974 by Frederick W. Williams) of newspapers in 12 metropolitan areas that had a high ratio of circulation to households (or "coverage") and 12 matched metropolitan areas of approximately equal size that had low ratios of circulation to households. The successful markets sold at least 100 (the average is 107) copies for every 100 households; the less successful markets sold 79 or fewer (the average is 69) copies for every 100 households.

The high-circulation markets fell into this category because among other reasons) more daily newspapers were being published there (a total of 36, compared with 28 in the low-circulation group). Competition makes for greater readership, and competitive markets, for historical reasons, are different from the other kind.

A comparison of these two sets of markets showed that the ones with high readership were more stable. Between 1960 and 1970, their households grew by 19%, compared with a 31% growth in the low readership group. So one explanation for the lower circulation levels was the more rapid growth of these markets and the inability of the newspapers to convert as many of the newcomers to regular readership. As further evidence of their stability, the high-readership markets had smaller families, more single-person households, a lower birth rate, and an older population. They had higher levels of education and voting and a higher proportion of home ownership. They appeared to have a different economic base, with much more of the government revenue coming from taxes and a much higher percentage of the population employed in manufacturing. They had a higher ratio of retail sales to spendable income. All of the high markets had colleges; 5 out of the 12 low markets did not. The high markets were also more apt to be on the main airline routes. Needless to say, such differences are beyond a publisher's control.

As we have just seen, there are things about a market which make it more or less likely to enjoy strong newspaper circulation. But the papers in these markets also revealed some interesting differences when their content was analyzed. The papers in the high group were more likely to have political party affiliations than those in the low group. They published fewer editorials

TABLE 5.25
Percentage of "Usual" Readers of Each Paper Who Rate Each Type of News Coverage
as "Excellent," 1974

Women	Paper A	Paper B
Food	30	21
Society	28	20
Fashion	25	15
Home	23	15
Men		
Own local community news	15	15
Downtown news	23	16
Metropolitan area	27	11
National	41	13
World	35	13
Sports	45	17
Business	22	10
Editorial	46	16

per issue, and a smaller proportion of those were on local topics; fewer of their editorials ended up telling the reader what should or must be done. They carried more advertising and editorial coverage addressed to women. They were more likely to accept ads for X-rated movies. They listed more circulation executives among their managements, and when they were asked for copies of their papers, 86% responded, compared with 53% of the less successful group.

THE MARKET OR THE PAPER

Studies of readers' attitudes reinforce the conclusion that different newspapers arouse a very different kind of response. Consider how people in two different cities (among the five studied in 1974) rated various types of news coverage in the papers they "usually" read (Table 5.25). These variations in reader ratings were translated into striking differences in daily readership. In the market where the more successful newspaper was located, daily readership (of any paper) was a third higher than it was in the other market. Readership among adults 18 to 29 was 70% higher.

Differences like these may partially reflect differences in the characteristics of markets and their populations rather than the content or style of the papers.[21] The variation in tastes is also reflected in magazine circulation-to-household ratios. For instance, in one market, *TV Guide*'s penetration is

---

[21]Other studies have found a relationship between media usage and the structure of the local community. See, for example, an analysis of 19 Minnesota towns by C. N. Olien, G. A.

half the national average; in another it is 25% above the national average. Similarly, in the first market, penetration of the news magazines is 12% less than the national average; in yet another market it is 9% greater. In part, this variability may also represent a response to the deficiencies and strengths of the available newspapers. That is, to some degree, people must turn to magazines and other publications when their local newspapers inadequately cover their interets.

But magazine reading may be complementary to that of newspapers and reflect cultural and social attributes linked to interest in the news itself. Like newspapers, the news magazines show a considerable variation in their penetration from city to city. For example, *Time* magazine's circulation is equivalent to 5.2% of U.S. households, but it is equivalent to 4.2% of households in Memphis and 9% of households in Boston, one of the country's most intense newspaper-reading markets.

The differentiation of reader attitudes toward individual newspapers is also apparent within a particular market, even where the papers are published by the same company. A study in one single-ownership city by Belden Associates found that among people who read the morning paper, 50% described TV and radio as their main sources of news, and a similar proportion (46%) named newspapers. Among those who read only the afternoon paper, 72% named TV and radio and a mere 22%, newspapers. But among those who read both papers, only 40% named TV and radio, and a majority (58%) named newspapers. (The implication of this last finding is that two-paper-a-day readers are much more apt to be dependent on them.)

To what degree can the variations in market penetration among individual newspapers, or in their history of circulation success, be accounted for by editorial distinction? Only a handful of cities (like New York City and Los Angeles) still sustain sharply distinguished elite and popular papers, and *The New York Times* is not the circulation leader in its market, but the *Los Angeles Times* is. Still, both their circulation records have been more positive than those of their mass-oriented competitors, and their economically upscale audiences have been extremely attractive to advertisers. Moreover, the loyalty and intensity of readership is not measured in the size of the audience. To illustrate: *The New York Times* polled its market in 1972 using the same question repeatedly asked by Roper Associates as to which medium people would choose to keep if they could only have one source of news. Nationally at about that time, 58% named TV and 19%, newspapers. Among *The New York Times* readers, 19% chose TV and 52%, newspapers.

One indicator of the link between editorial content and reader acceptance might be the number of awards for excellence that are presented to newspapers and their staff members by the Pulitzer juries, Sigma Delta Chi, and the

Donohue, & P. J. Tichenor, "Community Structure and Media Use," *Journalism Quarterly*, Vol. 55, No. 3, Autumn 1978, pp. 445–455.

Overseas Press Club. A compilation shows that 17 major papers (of over 100,000 circulation) winning three or more awards between 1963 and 1972 increased their circulation by 18%. Those 28 newspapers winning one or two awards held even in circulation, whereas the 81 large papers that won no awards dropped 16% in circulation during that period. Thus, it would appear that in the practice of journalism, virtue carries more than its own reward.

As we reflect on the evidence reviewed in this chapter about why people read the newspaper and how they approach it, move through it, feel about it, and use it in their daily lives, it is the similarities rather than the differences that may be most striking. General expectations about newspapers and general patterns of usage are clearly apparent, even though individual newspapers vary as much as they do in the loyalty they generate and the positions they hold in their own communities. To find out why this is so we must look at what's in the paper and how it varies from place to place.

6
WHAT'S IN
THE PAPER?

American newspapers vary enormously in size, just as they do in circulation and advertising volume. In Chapter 2, we saw how the amount of news space available to the reader reflects the amount of advertising the newspaper carries. This in turn, generally reflects the size of its circulation, to the degree that larger papers are located in larger markets with a larger base of potential advertisers. In 1979, papers of over 100,000 circulation averaged two and a half times as many pages of editorial matter on a weekday as those with circulations under 10,000.

We have already noted, in Chapter 2, that editorial matter occupies over half the space in smaller papers and only a third in larger ones (according to the 1986 Inland Daily Press Association member survey). Our national study of newspaper editors also found that the news hole ranged between 49% in papers under 25,000 to 37% in papers over 10,000 (1977a).

The total character of the package of news and advertising reading matter that the publisher puts into the reader's hands must be considered both in terms of its actual size and in terms of how the space is distributed. Big papers are fatter than smaller papers because they carry more advertising, which gives them a bigger news hole. But this means that their news hole is less as a *percentage of total* pages. As we see in Chapter 8, staff-written copy and feature material represent more of the content of larger papers than of smaller ones.

Newspapers in competitive markets are under pressure to keep up with the competition in serving their readers. Thus, the paper that ranks second (or below) in advertising pages cannot maintain the same ratio of news to advertising as the number one paper. It usually runs less editorial matter, to be sure, but this represents a higher proportion of the total pages it prints. And even in cities where the morning and evening papers are owned by the same publisher, or produced by an agency arrangement, the amount of advertising each carries may in no way directly relate to the comparative size. The reason for this is that advertising rates are usually set to encourage the use of both papers in combination. Thus, the editors of the weaker paper may have nearly as much news hole to work with as the editors of the stronger one, even though they have far fewer readers.

In 1986, the 46 large-and medium-sized morning newspapers measured by Media Records had an average news hole of 34 pages per issue, or 38% of their total space. For 32 evening papers measured that year, the average paper carried 30 news pages per issue, or 39%. For 47 Sunday papers, the average was 100, or 28%. However, these averages masked substantial differences. Among morning papers, the range was from 26% for the *Los Angeles Times* to 54% for the *Boston Herald.* Among evening papers, it went from 24% for *The Record* (Bergen County, New Jersey) to 58% for the *New York Post.*

Advertising occupies most of the space in a typical paper, but there is editorial matter on most pages. (See Table 5.13 in Chapter 5). Table 6.1, drawn from our 1987 survey, shows the distribution of a cross-section of pages in a probability sampling of newspapers in the hands of a national sample of readers.

Although nearly half (49%) of all newspapers carry only one or two

TABLE 6.1
Dominant Types of Content on Newspaper Pages, 1987

National/International news	17%
Sports	14
Local/State/Regional news	12
Business/Financial	10
Entertainment/Celebrities/Movies	6
Editorial opinion/Analysis	4
Comics	3
TV/Radio	3
Food	2
Health/Science	2
Fashion/Lifestyles/Society/Home	2
Advice columns	2
Weather	1
News summaries	1
Calendar of local events	1
Other editorial matter	4
Advertising	14

physically separate or identifiable sections, these represent only 18% of the newspapers in readers' hands (1987a). The typical weekday edition in the hands of a reader has four separate parts. Two out of five small weekday newspapers of under 10,000 circulation are produced in a single section, and the number of physically separate sections that a newspaper runs tends to increase with circulation and physical bulk. Papers with circulations over 25,000 typically have four sections on weekdays. Those of 10,000 to 25,000 run two. In the case of papers of 100,000 and over, nearly half (46%) have five or more sections on a typical day. Eighty percent carry a daily section on sports, 43% on lifestyle, 31% on business and finance, and 34% on entertainment.[1] On Sundays, the papers of over 100,000 run 11 sections; those of 50,000 to 100,000, 7; those 25,000 to 50,000, 5; those between 10,000 and 25,000 run 5; and those under 10,000 run 3.

The nature of the reading process naturally changes when papers are sectionalized. They can be shared and read simultaneously by different family members, and individual sections of specialized content may receive more intense attention than if the same material were incorporated in an undifferentiated newspaper. Or they may be discarded after a glance at the front page that designates their special purpose. Apart from the main news section, papers with two-thirds of the circulation run a second news section daily. Nine out of 10 have a sports section. A majority run a food section and a leisure or entertainment section once a week (Table 6.2).

On Sunday, the separate sections most commonly run (apart from the news) are the sports and comics, with three out of four papers also running a physically separate or labeled lifestyle section and the same proportion a TV section or magazine. Table 6.3 shows how many newspapers run identifiable or physically separate sections.

When circulation is taken into account, virtually all Sunday papers distributed have sports, comics, and a magazine as well as main news sections; nearly 9 out of 10 have a TV section or magazine and a business section; about 4 out of 5 have a separate lifestyle or women's section, an editorial or news analysis section, and an entertainment section. Although only 36% of the papers have a travel section, they account for 70% of the circulation. Nearly two-thirds of the comics sections (weighted by circulation) have over 20 individual features.

The typical paper circulated has between 20 and 29 different strips in its comics section. Although only 19% of the papers produce their own locally edited Sunday or weekend magazine, these have 35% of the circulation. This compares with 56% for *Parade* and 22% for *USA Weekend*, the two nationally distributed magazines. A number of papers carry more than one.

---

[1] All but 7% of the papers carry an identifiable sports section at least once a week; 83% carry a food section; 79%, an entertainment section; 82%, a business and finance section; and 71%, a lifestyle or women's section.

TABLE 6.2
Identifiable Sections Carried At Least Once a Week and Every Day, 1987a

	At least once a week		Every day	
	% of newspapers	% of circulation	% of newspapers	% of circulation
Main news	85	95	85	95
Second or local news	49	68	45	64
Sports	84	93	80	90
Food (separate)	61	83	2	3
Home (separate)	12	15	2	2
Food & home (combined)	7	3	2	1
Entertainment	63	79	34	47
Business, finance	57	82	31	60
Lifestyle, women	58	71	43	57
TV section	42	25	14	14
Fashion	19	31	5	5
Science	7	17	1	1
Travel	5	6	1	2

TABLE 6.3
Physically Separate Sections Appearing Every Sunday/Weekend, 1987a

	% of newspapers	% of circulation
Main news	93	98
Second or local news	58	75
Book review	26	46
Business, finance	67	86
Comics	95	94
Editorials or news analysis	67	81
Entertainment	58	78
Fashion	17	23
Food	16	17
Home	21	35
Lifestyle, women	76	84
Magazine	71	93
Real estate (with editorial content)	34	56
Sports	90	98
TV section or magazine	75	88
Travel	36	70

In 1979, about half the Sunday papers carried classified advertising sections devoted to real estate and to employment, in each case generally with accompanying editorial matter. (This was not recorded in 1983 and 1987.)

COVERAGE OF SPECIAL INTERESTS

The newspaper's ability to compete with television news may be said to depend in good measure on the efficiency of the reading process that permits useful information to be extracted from a complex information environment with maximum speed. The newspaper's unique appeal is that it tells too much—far more than any one reader wants to know. Thus, he is able to follow his own unique reading patterns to match what is offered to his own special interests.

Newspapers' characteristically large editorial staffing permits them to do interpretive, investigative, in-depth reporting, and to generate fresh and exclusive stories that comparatively few TV stations have the capacity to do or the time to present. In 1986, the typical TV station had a news staff of 17 including the newscasters.[2] A TV station generally has quite a number of daily newspaper markets in its coverage area. The median newspaper published (with its circulation of about 12,900), has a news staff of 19 (according to a 1978 survey of the Associated Press Managing Editors), but of course this number is multiplied in the case of the large metropolitan paper in the hands of a typical reader. *The New York Times*, not a typical paper, has a news staff of about a thousand. Are newspapers exploiting the potential advantage they have over television in their ability to cover the varied and segmented interests of their heterogenous audiences?

What specific areas of editorial content and features are covered by the press on a regular continuing basis? In a 1987 study of this subject, replies were received from 987 daily newspapers, representing 79% of circulation. (Similar surveys were conducted in 1967, 1974, 1979, and 1983.)

Altogether, 58 categories of content were examined in the 1987 survey. Fifteen of them appear at least once a week in a majority of U.S. dailies, and 32 are carried by at least a quarter. The typical paper carries about 36 standing features. Twenty-four features are carried at least once weekly in the majority of all newspapers in readers' hands. Not surprisingly, larger papers, with their larger news holes, cover more subjects than small ones do—except for school news, society items, farm and ranch news, and religion items that fit the small paper's intimate nature (Table 6.4).

Certain subjects are covered at least once a week on weekdays by virtually

---

[2]This comes from a study conducted for the Radio–Television News Directors Association by Vernon A. Stone of the University of Missouri.

TABLE 6.4
Average Number[a] of Daily Columns or Features Carried Once a Week
or More Often, by circulation size, 1987a

	Average number
Total newspapers	35.9
Circulation 100,000 & over	54.5
Circulation 50,000–100,000	47.0
Circulation 25,000–50,000	42.1
Circulation 10,000–25,000	34.6
Circulation under 10,000	28.8

[a]Out of 58 listed types of features or columns.

every major paper: weather, sports, comics, horoscopes, crossword puzzles, and obituaries (Table 6.5). A number of other categories are covered by *almost* all larger papers (over 50,000 circulation) and by a majority of the smaller ones.

On every weekday, papers with at least 70% of total circulation run crossword puzzles, comics, coverage of both spectator and participant sports, a TV log, a weather map, an astrology column, games and puzzles, columns of personal advice (like "Dear Abby"), a bridge column, and business and financial news, including security quotations. Over half carry daily a health feature or column, the movie timetable, sewing patterns, society features, a theater column, and TV reviews (Table 6.6).

Between 1967 and 1987 there was a remarkable drop in the proportion of papers that offer, at least once a week, coverage of specialized reader interests. There were declines, and in some cases sharp declines (when circulation is taken into account), in the proportion of papers offering coverage at least once a week of such staple subjects as fashion, recipes, beauty, home repair, child care, gardening, and science. Of 49 categories of special interest measured in at least three of these surveys, 39 showed a decline in the number of papers that carried them.

The only significant upward change was in the number of papers carrying horoscopes. But there were significant downtrends in the number of papers covering on a regular basis the other subjects already mentioned, as well as college news, etiquette, and the radio log.

Many editors apparently find it easy to cut the items that rank at the bottom of the list in terms of the percentage of people who read them. But an item or feature that gets the attention of only a small percentage of the readers may involve them intensely, while bland material that is noted by all may be of concern to none.

The coverage of special interests in Sunday newspapers runs closely parallel to the weekday pattern. At least three out of four Sunday papers carry weekly features on astrology, business, crossword puzzles, spectator and

TABLE 6.5
Percentage of Dailies Carrying Features At Least Once a Week, 1967–1987[a]

Feature	1967	1974	1979	1983	1987
Advice on personal finance	–	–	42	38	37
Astrology, horoscope	–	75	78	84	85
Automotive	18	18	18	13	16
Beauty	45	36	36	23	15
Best food buys	–	–	50	50	55
Boating	25	16	–	–	–
Books	49	38	33	25	26
Bridge	60	62	57	55	57
Business, financial	77	78	66	67	69
Career advice	–	–	15	11	10
Child care	36	22	17	11	10
College	30	33	16	10	8
Computers (personal)	–	–	–	7	9
Consumers (action line)	–	–	28	21	18
Crossword puzzle	–	–	–	–	95
Diet, nutrition	–	–	–	44	43
Environment, ecology	–	–	16	9	7
Etiquette	31	22	13	12	16
Farm & ranch	53	43	40	34	34
Fashion, men	18	20	26	16	15
Fashion, teenage	25	28	27	16	14
Fashion, women	57	47	41	26	23
Games & puzzles	–	81	75	78	–
Gardening	53	47	43	37	30
Health & medical	68	71	66	63	55
Home furnishing, decorating	39	35	28	18	17
Homebuilding, repair	47	37	29	22	16
Household hints	–	–	–	43	35
Motion pictures	61	60	–	–	–
Movie reviews	–	–	46	46	49
Movie timetable	–	–	50	48	49
Music, records, tapes (CDs)	–	–	37	31	33
Outdoors: camping, hunting	64	60	47	44	39
"People"	–	–	–	50	47
Personal advice	76	82	74	71	68
Pets	18	21	14	14	14
Photography	17	13	9	6	4
Physical fitness	–	–	–	–	13
Radio	32	22	–	–	–
Radio log	43	29	22	16	13
Real estate	–	–	–	16	15
Recipes	81	78	78	74	71
Religion	–	–	58	48	49

TABLE 6.5 (*continued*)

Feature	1967	1974	1979	1983	1987
Restaurants	–	–	–	28	34
Retirement, social security	–	–	33	23	23
School news	73	66	61	52	55
Science, technology	34	24	14	9	11
Security, commodity tables	67	66	56	48	46
Sewing patterns	62	57	50	44	31
Society, social news	93	95	85	80	77
Sports	95	99	–	–	–
Sports, participant	–	–	86	78	81
Sports, spectator	–	–	92	88	89
Stamps, coins	–	–	8	6	3
Television	73	80	–	–	–
Theater	56	56	54	41	44
Travel & resort	23	22	19	11	8
TV log	91	91	85	87	83
TV reviews	–	–	61	51	47
Videotape reviews	–	–	–	–	15
Weather	94	98	–	–	–
Weather map	–	–	63	65	67
Wine	–	–	15	14	14
Youth, teenage	61	45	24	24	19
N (Total papers responding)	(1,182)	(1,335)	(1,575)	(1,310)	(987)

*a*Percentages are not strictly comparable. Figures for 1967, 1983, and 1987 were weighted to compensate for a below-average response rate from small circulation newspapers, whereas 1974 and 1979 figures are based on *responding* newspapers only. The decreases shown since 1967 in this table and commented upon in the text would actually be greater than indicated if the nonresponding (and smaller) newspapers had been included in 1974 and 1979.

participant sports, and the television log (Table 6.7). At least half also cover personal advice, society news, books, bridge, television reviews, and the weather map.

The pattern of decline in the regular use of specialized features was not as pronounced in Sunday or weekend papers, which were measured in 1974 and afterward. Still, of 47 features measured in three or more surveys, 38 showed a drop, and only one (etiquette) returned to its earlier level. Surprisingly, in this period of concern with the reading habits of young people, a number of papers dropped regular features devoted to teenagers and to school and college news.

Many newspapers publish special-interest sections on an ad hoc or occasional basis to tie in with commemorative events, sporting victories, or seasonal interests, like hunting, new cars, or fall fashion. Not a few of these sections are developed with the direct interest of developing new business for

TABLE 6.6
Percentage of Dailies Carrying Features Every Weekday, 1967–1987

Feature	% of Newspapers					% of Circulation
	1967	1974	1979	1983	1987	1987
Advice on personal finance	–	–	26	15	13	19
Astrology, horoscope	–	73	77	83	84	92
Automotive	1	2	3	2	4	5
Beauty	14	8	14	7	5	5
Best food buys	–	–	3	2	1	1
Boating	1	1	–	–	–	–
Books	2	2	3	2	3	7
Bridge	52	57	54	53	55	77
Business, financial	56	54	45	40	43	78
Career advice	–	–	3	2	2	2
Child care	13	4	4	2	2	4
College	7	9	6	3	3	2
Computers (personal)	–	–	–	1	1	2
Consumers (action line)	–	–	13	10	10	21
Crossword puzzle	–	–	–	–	94	97
Diet, nutrition	–	–	–	6	6	5
Environment, ecology	–	–	5	2	2	4
Etiquette	14	8	6	6	7	8
Farm & ranch	4	6	7	5	4	6
Fashion, men	1	1	5	2	3	2
Fashion, teenage	1	1	6	3	3	3
Fashion, women	15	6	12	6	7	6
Games & puzzles	–	76	71	75	–	–
Gardening	1	1	3	3	1	1
Health & medical	50	52	51	43	31	31
Home furnishing, decorating	2	1	3	2	2	2
Homebuilding, repair	1	1	2	1	–	–
Household hints	–	–	–	27	22	21
Motion pictures	27	32	–	–	–	–
Movie reviews	–	–	15	13	12	29
Movie timetable	–	–	39	34	34	52
Music, records, tapes (CDs)	–	–	6	3	3	8
"Op Ed" page	–	–	–	–	49	71
Outdoors: camping, hunting, etc.	9	8	7	6	4	7
"People"	–	–	–	42	40	62
Personal advice	69	77	72	68	66	80
Pets	2	2	2	3	2	3
Photography	1	3	2	2	1	1
Physical fitness	–	–	–	–	2	4
Radio	21	16	–	–	–	–
Radio log	37	23	17	12	8	26

TABLE 6.6 (continued)

Feature	% of Newspapers					% of Circulation
	1967	1974	1979	1983	1987	1987
Real estate	–	–	–	2	2	3
Recipes	15	9	13	8	6	4
Religion	–	–	6	4	3	2
Restaurants	–	–	–	4	5	5
Retirement, social security	–	–	8	4	3	3
School news	15	17	33	25	25	20
Science, technology	6	4	7	2	2	5
Security, commodity tables	62	60	52	44	40	67
Sewing patterns	38	33	37	35	26	31
Society, social news	86	88	76	69	63	50
Sports	91	98	–	–	–	–
Sports, participant	–	–	81	73	75	68
Sports, spectator	–	–	91	85	88	93
Stamps, coins	–	–	1	1	1	2
Television	55	60	–	–	–	–
Theater	29	34	36	24	19	37
Travel & resort	1	1	2	1	1	2
TV log	75	74	69	67	66	87
TV reviews	–	–	39	32	29	61
Videotape reviews	–	–	–	–	2	2
Weather	93	98	–	–	–	–
Weather map	–	–	62	64	66	88
Wine	–	–	–	–	–	–
Youth, teenage	9	10	10	7	7	7
Other	–	–	–	–	2	2

the advertising department. But many have the primary purpose of building readership, and they can be expensive productions.

An important development during the 1970s was the emergence of the special-interest section as a regular weekly feature of both Sunday and weekday papers, approaching specialized reader interests in a nontraditional way, in an effort to make the paper more attractive to people for whom the conventional news was uninviting. Many larger papers added zoned editions covering news of local areas.

CHANGING CONTENT AND APPEARANCE

The American press had a very different look in 1989 than it did a decade earlier. On July 1, 1984, most American newspapers moved to a standard

TABLE 6.7
Percentage of Papers Carrying Features Every Sunday, 1974–1987

Feature	1974	1979	1983	1987
Advice on personal finance	–	44	39	43
Astrology, horoscope	81	85	89	86
Automotive	16	21	9	19
Beauty	31	32	17	15
Best food buys	–	14	14	13
Books	61	61	50	52
Bridge	64	62	56	61
Business, financial	76	78	73	79
Career advice	–	19	10	12
Chess	14	14	–	–
Child care	15	12	6	10
College	22	16	10	7
Computers (personal)	–	–	4	12
Consumers (action line)	–	31	22	15
Crossword puzzle	–	–	–	94
Diet, nutrition	–	–	19	17
Environment, ecology	–	14	6	7
Etiquette	22	13	11	20
Farm & ranch	27	28	22	20
Fashion, men	12	17	9	7
Fashion, teenage	16	16	8	8
Fashion, women	39	34	19	20
Games & puzzles	84	79	85	–
Gardening	57	47	33	27
Health & medical	57	62	50	36
Home building, repair	41	45	26	25
Home furnishings, decorating	33	36	19	19
Household hints	–	–	37	30
Movie reviews	–	52	44	42
Movie timetable	–	59	52	46
Music, records, tapes (CDs)	–	48	34	33
Outdoors: camping, etc.	–	54	45	44
"People"	–	–	59	48
Personal advice	80	76	71	67
Pets	24	26	19	17
Photography	18	20	11	12
Physical fitness	–	–	–	9
Radio log	33	31	19	20
Real estate	–	–	31	37
Recipes	–	38	33	25
Religion	–	43	38	40
Restaurants	–	–	20	22
Retirement, social security	–	32	19	16

TABLE 6.7 (*continued*)

Feature	1974	1979	1983	1987
School news	43	38	40	35
Science, technology	16	15	9	10
Security, commodity tables	56	55	46	47
Sewing patterns	55	55	42	33
Society, social news	96	88	84	71
Sports	98	–	–	–
Sports, participant	89	89	81	81
Sports, spectator	98	96	92	90
Stamps, coins	–	29	18	19
Theater	65	64	48	45
Travel & resort	43	50	41	47
TV log	90	91	89	82
TV reviews	–	64	55	56
Videotape reviews	–	–	–	13
Weather	97	–	–	–
Weather map	–	–	75	73
Wine	–	–	8	6
Youth, teenage	33	22	23	12

6-column, 13-inch wide page designed to facilitate the placement of advertising. (Tabloid papers adopted a compatible format.) The trend toward six columns and narrower page widths was already apparent in our 1979e survey, and the changes have accelerated since then, with 43% of the papers in 1983 reporting modifications in column widths, 25% in the number of columns, 38% in page size. In those same four years, 36% redesigned the masthead, 35% increased their use of photography, 30% changed typefaces, and 23% went to a modular layout. The proportions were even higher among the larger papers. The use of modular layouts was spurred as newspapers moved to adopt computerized page-makeup systems to replace pasteup, which had only recently, in turn, replaced the metal makeup procedures that had been in use for a century.

Again, in our 1987a study, 69% of the papers (with 82% of the circulation) reported "substantial changes" in content since 1983. Fifty-three percent of the papers increased business coverage; 45%, sports; and 35% increased the ratio of local and state news to national and international news. (This was four times as common as the reverse.) Eighteen percent reported more emphasis on features, and 10% reported more emphasis on hard news, accelerating the shift in emphasis reported in earlier years. Thirteen percent of the papers (with 36% of the circulation) said they had zoned for better neighborhood coverage.

Eighty-two percent of the papers (representing 91% of the circulation) reported substantial changes in graphics or layout. Sixty-one percent reported more use of ROP color; 60%, changes in format to correspond to the new standards;. 28% (with 52% of the circulation) said they were using more graphics; 43% had changed the masthead; 37%, the typeface; and 36% were using photographs more often (Table 6.8).

The so-called sectional revolution is most brilliantly exemplified by the efforts of such journalistic leaders as the *Chicago Tribune, Los Angeles Times, Washington Post,* and *The New York Times.* Their sections package utilitarian information of the kind formerly regarded as the province of specialized magazines. These sections have emerged as part of a wider process of editorial experimentation and innovation stimulated by new production technology (more flexible formatting, greater use of color). In at least several successful cases, these sections have brought in enough new advertising to make possible an enlargement of the total number of pages of editorial matter. But the main effect has been to change the overall balance of news and features in those papers.

The old sociological concept of *lifestyle,* first adopted by the advertising business during the brief heyday of motivation research in the 1950s, has had

TABLE 6.8
"Substantial" Changes in Editorial Content, Graphics, or Layout, 1983–87

	% of papers	% of Circulation
Changes in editorial content	69	82
Increased business coverage	53	70
Increased sports coverage	45	55
Changed ratio of local, state to national, international coverage		
Increased local/state	35	30
Increased national/international	8	9
Added special lifestyle sections	24	36
Changed ratio of features to hard news		
Increased features	18	18
Increased hard news	10	12
Zoned for (more) neighborhood, suburban coverage	13	36
Changes in graphics or layout	82	91
More use of ROP color	61	91
Changed to SAU (Standard Advertising Unit) page and column specs	60	65
Changed masthead	43	48
Changed typeface	37	40
Increased use of computer graphics	28	52
Went to modular layout on front page	22	23
Other	11	14

continued currency in the field of magazine sales promotion. Its adoption within the newspaper business represented a marketing *tour de force*.

In its original usage, lifestyle describes a subtle complex of designations (including social class, ethnic origins, area of residence, position in the life cycle, and so on) that corresponds to a distinctive set of tastes and patterns of consuming goods, services, and leisure time. But in the new argot of newspaper marketing, the term has been applied not to distinguish the numerous slivers of a complex metropolitan society but rather to encompass their presumably common preoccupation with self-improvement. In times past, editors might have assumed that the normal news content of the paper fulfilled the function of providing the citizens of a community with a common agenda and that it was the task of magazines to define and sustain the differences of values and interests that make them individuals. In many cases, "lifestyle" may be little more than a euphemism for the old "Women's" pages, retitled to placate feminist sensitivities.

COLOR

The coming of *USA Today* in 1982 had an extraordinary catalytic effect on the American press. Although many editors objected to its optimistic tone, bland editorial posture, and miniaturized articles, they borrowed ideas extensively from its excellent graphics: weather maps, diagrams, and charts. *USA Today's* principal effect, however, originated in its high color quality standards. These were controlled at the headquarters in Arlington, Virginia, but carried out in the pressrooms of different newspapers across what Allen Neuharth, the founder, liked to call "the USA." The improvements were immediately manifested in the regular local products of these newspapers and were widely emulated by others. Inspired by its success with *USA Today*, the Gannett Company launched the Four Color Network, which represented 270 papers with a combined weekday circulation of 23 million, all of which met rigorous quality criteria. Spurred by a strong joint effort of the Newspaper Advertising Bureau and the American Newspaper Publishers Association, newspapers increased their investment and training to improve their color capabilities. Even the grey *New York Times* made plans to introduce ROP color into its Sunday editions.

By 1987, 82% of all papers (with 88% of the circulation) were printed daily in full process color. In total, 94% (with 95% of circulation) offered spot color, using additional color ink besides the basic black. Apart from its advertising applications, spot color was used by most papers for editorial purposes, usually in headlines and line art (1987a).

One important reason why newspapers rushed to upgrade their ROP color was the steady move of certain categories of advertising from ROP into inserts, which (as already mentioned) were highly vulnerable to competition from direct mail. Retailers had gone into inserts from a variety of motives, but good color reproduction was an important one of them. National food advertisers relied increasingly on coupon promotions in their battles for brand share of market; their coupon ads printed in brilliant color on heavy glossy stock produced a higher rate of return (4.0%) than their ads in the black and white pages (2.2%). Quite apart from its value to advertisers, color was understood to be an attraction to readership. In an experiment in Tampa, Media General's John Mauro found that a color picture on the front page sold more copies than the identical black and white picture in an adjacent vending rack.

That readers want more color in their newspapers was shown in a 1986 study conducted for us by Market Facts. Younger readers showed particular eagerness for color and set higher standards for it. Those people who perceived their papers as giving them more color also rated them higher in printing quality. But the kinds of pages on which readers most want color are not the same as the pages they look at most regularly.

A Bruskin study of 1,006 adults in 1987 asked people about their reading of 12 types of newspaper content. The average reader "usually looked" at 5.8 types. Asked which kinds of pages or subjects were wanted in color, the average reader named 4.5. Again, the preference for color was greatest among younger people. In fact, among women under 35, four out of five said they wanted color on the fashion pages, three out of five wanted it on the food pages, and over half wanted it on the comics, home, travel, and entertainment pages. Overall, among men and women of all ages, the comics were the only content that was both usually looked at by as many as half the readers and also wanted in color by half. Well-read sections like the editorial pages, TV, and business pages evoked relatively little demand for color, and only 43% said they wanted color on the front page. Only a fourth of the readers said they now see color in their papers at least half the time, and those who see it most often rated it most favorably. Those who rated their own paper's color as poor were also more likely to describe the paper as "old-fashioned."

MAGAZINE AND OTHER PRINT COMPETITION

The drop in newspapers' regular coverage of special interests is especially noteworthy in contrast to what has happened in the same years to their principal print competitors. Consumer magazines became increasingly specialized after the advent of television and the subsequent demise of the four mass circulation publications: *Collier's, The Saturday Evening Post, Look,* and

Life.[3] (Between 1970 and 1987, the number of consumer magazines measured by the Audit Bureau of Circulations grew by 64%, from 303 to 496, and their aggregate circulation grew by 37% to a total of 336 million per average issue.)

In contrast to newspapers, magazines in general tend to have a highly youthful reader profile, and this is particularly true of specialized interest magazines. Special-interest weeklies range downward in size from *TV Guide*, with a weekly circulation of 17 million, to influential journals of opinion like the *National Review* and the *New Republic*. Specialized publications like *Sports Illustrated* and *Business Week* cover areas of content that newspapers traditionally have included.[4]

The newsweeklies, which in 1987 had an aggregate circulation of 10,112,000, are even more directly competitive with newspapers in their content and function. Their editorial authority and sophistication, their access to a variety of news sources, their use of original reporting, their ability to summarize, synthesize, interpret, and package information all make them especially attractive to the better-educated part of the population with its cosmopolitan orientation. Their circulation increased by 67% between 1960 and 1970, but only by 7% between 1970 and 1980, and by 8% between 1980 and 1987.

For an average issue week in 1988, the unduplicated audience for the newsweeklies accounted for 25% of adult men and 20% of all women. Readership of the newsweeklies is highly concentrated. Of those whose education did not go beyond grammar school, only 7% read an average issue of *Time*, but the proportion was 23% among college graduates. A similar disparity exists for the other news magazines.

People who read more than the average tend to do so through every available means. Frequent readers of daily newspapers read more weekly newspapers, more books, and more magazines. They are especially more likely to be readers of news magazines, even though the average age of a frequent newspaper reader is considerably older. Young adults aged 18 to 34 account for 40% of the adult population and 36% of the adult newspaper readers. But they account for 45% of the readers of *Time*. Young adults, as we have already noted, are not only better educated, but also more oriented to a broader arena than that of the community in which they live.

---

[3]The latter three were all eventually revived (*Look* only briefly) at circulation levels a fraction of those these titles had in their heyday.

[4]Since magazines increasingly reflect individual interests, magazine preferences may provide a clue to newspaper readers' concerns. A 1979 survey by R. H. Bruskin Associates asked, "If you could subscribe to only one magazine, devoted in full to just a single subject, what would that subject be?" Twenty-three percent of the men said sports and 17% said news, with the other replies widely scattered. However, men under 25 showed twice as much interest in sports as men over 50, but only half the interest in news. Among women, cooking was mentioned by 14%, news by 12%, decorating by 12%, and movies and TV by 7%.

At the same time that newspapers encounter stronger competition for the attention of more sophisticated readers, they also face new competition at the low end of the social scale. Flamboyant big-city papers that appealed mainly to a working-class constituency have been most vulnerable to TV competition. A number of them have departed the scene in New York, Chicago, Boston, Washington, and elsewhere. The general press, with its middle-class orientation, has not met the needs that were served by the sensational journalism of another era, with its emphasis on gossip, scandal, horror, and mystery. Into the breach came the fast-growing national feature weeklies that bought prime positions at the supermarket checkout counter and quickly developed enormous readership: the *National Enquirer*, with 4,383,000 circulation; *The Star*, with 3,770,000; *People*, with 3,311,000. These publications also draw disproportionate numbers of young readers, self-evidently from a different social stratum than the news magazines.

The late 1960s saw the burgeoning of the underground press, centered in the vicinity of university campuses rocked by student revolts. These publications gave expression to the youth culture of the era, with an intensely antiestablishmentarian outlook and an aggressive display of vocabulary that had never surfaced in family newspapers.

As the radical youth movement receded with the end of the Vietnam war, the underground press began to ebb, and many papers disappeared altogether. The survivors lost much of their strongly political cast, and their language returned to that of the mainstream as their readers matured and they became prosperous business enterprises. Many of them carried millions of dollars' worth of advertising, and their leftist politics were tempered accordingly. (Rupert Murdoch sold New York's *Village Voice* for $55 million in 1986.)

In the 1980s, a new wave of publications emerged, also aimed at young readers, mostly through free distribution, and with a strong orientation to entertainment and leisure activities. A number of them went in for enterprising reportage on local subjects with political overtones, digging into stories that the daily press underplayed or ignored. By 1988, there were 54 weeklies in the Association of Alternative Newspapers, including such editorially notable titles as the Chicago *Reader*, the Boston *Phoenix*, and the Phoenix *New Times*. In the aggregate, they claimed a circulation of three million. Seven had circulations of more than 100,000.

City magazines represent another important new competitive force, offering utilitarian local information and in some cases outstanding investigative reporting of local issues. By 1988, there were over 30 major city magazines with an aggregate circulation of 2,300,000. They included giants like *New York*, with a circulation of 427,000, and *Chicago*, with a circulation of 204,000.

The rise of these publications compensated to some degree for the reduced numbers of competing metropolitan papers. Their success suggested also that there was a significant constituency for local information of a kind that newspapers were apparently not providing.

THE CONTENT OF THE NEWS

The specific content of the news varies continuously, and the mix of subjects, locales, and personalities is constantly changing. However, in spite of the changes described in this chapter, there is a certain stability, in the aggregate, in the selection and balancing of content in the American press.

In 1987, 17% of all newspaper pages were dominated by national and international news, 14% by sports, 12% by local, state, and regional news, 10% by business and financial news, 6% by entertainment, celebrity, and movie items, and 4% by editorials and opinion features. Five percent of the pages were dominated by items on fashion, food, homemaking, society news, or other elements of interest to women (Table 6.1).

The 1977 study included a much more detailed analysis of content. It was based on current issues of three hundred different newspapers that were carried by interviewers during the period from March 14 to 22. (Nine-tenths of the interviewing was concentrated in that week.) These papers represented a sample of what was available to readers in relation to their actual circulation. This means that metropolitan papers received their appropriate weight relative to smaller ones. All the articles of 75 agate lines (5 ½ inches) or over on the front page and nine other selected pages were studied. Altogether, 109,331 editorial items were classified among over 80 categories of content. A similar procedure had been followed in 1971.[5] The smallest papers ran about 80 items of 75 lines and over each day. The larger papers had an average of 210.

Did the briefer items and filler material cover a different range of subjects than the items of 75 lines or over to which the questioning was limited? To check this out, 20 newspapers included in the 1977 survey were examined. On each of the 200 measured pages, there were 2.7 stories of less than 5½ column inches, as well as the 3.6 longer stories that normally would have been included in the sample. The smaller items disproportionately represented minor local news items of a general nature, crime news involving adults, reports of accidents and disasters, and obituaries. These four catego-

---

[5]The same coding system was used both in 1971 and 1977. (Three categories not separately identified in 1971 were coded in 1977: news in brief, energy problems, and editorial cartoons.) To avoid coding any given item more than once, a variety of reference points were set up. For example, when a city council denied the request of a business for a zoning variance, this item was classified as "business news (state and local political or government)."

ries accounted for 46% of the smaller items, but for only 18% of the larger items. In fact, 88% of the smaller stories, compared with 65% of the longer ones, could be coded within 16 content categories. It appears that small news items are those that editors regard as having comparatively limited interest, which explains why their size is restricted.

The average daily newspaper covers a tremendous range of subject matter. About two-thirds of the news and editorial items might be labeled of general interest, but no specific topic within this broad category accounts for as much as 10% of the newspaper's total content.

The bulk of the nonadvertising items carried by the American press represents news items and other articles, as distinct from editorials, columns, listings, and features that occur each day in a predictable format (1971). Soft news, together with hard news of current events, interpretive and utilitarian articles, and feature stories (as distinct from features), accounts for 71% of all content (Table 6.9). Although this analysis refers to the number of items of 75 lines or more, not to the amount of space given to a particular category, the two measures are generally related. (Listings, of course, include financial and sports tabulations that occupy a disproportionate number of column inches.)

It is a comparatively simple matter to classify the content of a newspaper, or any other printed matter, in terms of the topics with which it deals. It is far more difficult to dig into the deeper symbolic meaning and connotations of what is printed. The style of writing (its sparseness or embellishment), the length of articles, the treatment of individual personalities and abstractions, the ratio of narrative to interpretation, the accompaniment of photographs or graphics, the presence of editorial color—all these may have far more effect on the reader's response than the specifics of where the news originates or its ostensible subject matter. (The typical newspaper devotes 10–20% of its weekday news hole to photographs and other illustrations [1979a].)

As the public's average educational level continues to rise, the problems of editorial judgment become more complex. A product that is geared to the lowest common denominator becomes more remote from the vocabulary and interests of precisely those better-educated readers for whom reporters enjoy

TABLE 6.9
Composition of Daily Newspaper Nonadvertising Content, 1971

	% of Items
News and information	70.9
Editorials	3.5
Columns	11.9
Listings[a]	7.9
Other features[b]	5.8

[a]"Listings" denotes stock quotations, radio–TV programs, ship sailings, etc.
[b]"Other features" includes puzzles, horoscopes, comics, etc.

writing and for whom editors like to edit. Does this, then, create a danger that the daily newspaper, traditionally the mass medium par excellence, will become an elite medium with a restricted appeal?

Newspaper researcher John Mauro applied a standard reading comprehensibility scale to one issue of a metropolitan newspaper and found that the average wire service story was written at the third-year college level, while the average locally written story was at a second-year college level.

Considering this, it is worth noting that in a national survey of women readers, asked to appraise the writing style of the newspaper they know best, 83% described it as "about right for me" (1979b). And in our 1978 study of children, it will be recalled that few of those who looked at a newspaper considered it too difficult for them. Readers respond not merely to the words, but to the manner in which these words are laid out: the size, character and number of illustrations, the type face and size of the headlines, the sheer number of elements competing for attention on the page. The combination of all these attributes composes a newspaper's individual character, as much as or more than its mix of topics and features or its editorial posture. Yet these more subtle descriptors evade the kind of tough definitions required to classify newspaper content or reader response to it on a large scale.[6]

From the standpoint of the reader, what really counts is whether a story is lively or dull, routine or surprising, related or remote from his own self-interest or his familiar surroundings, and capable of mobilizing his feelings, either by its intrinsic scenario or by its presentation of character and setting.

Our studies classified articles insofar as possible in terms of the categories commonly used by editors to describe newspaper content. Do these accord with the way readers look at it? To shed light on this, 40 diverse newspaper articles were shown to a sampling of 300 readers in four metropolitan areas and were sorted in terms of which ones went together (1979e). The labels that readers ascribed to the categories they had themselves set up generally accorded with those conventionally used by journalists. Four out of five created a "sports" category; three out of five, a category for "editorials" or commentary; half set up one for international news; half had one for "entertainment" news; and half had a business or financial category. But only two out of five used "national" news and two out of five used "local" news as definable categories. This merely reflected a broader ambiguity. For the kinds of items that fill most of the space in American newspapers, a majority of readers classified them under a variety of personally defined labels. Thus, the

---

[6]This does not mean that approaches cannot be made to this delicate research problem. Stone, Schweitzer, and Weaver examined a sample of jointly owned morning/evening papers in 100 cities and concluded that "modern design was among the first life preservers that metro papers grasped when their circulation began sinking in the early 1970's." Gerald C. Stone, John C. Schweitzer, & David H. Weaver, "Adoption of Modern Newspaper Design," *Journalism Quarterly*, Vol. 55, No. 4, Winter 1978, p. 761.

study reinforces the supposition that writing style, the treatment of personalities, and the idiosyncrasies of subject matter may predominate in determining how readers regard the specific elements of the paper.

THE CHANGING NEWS MENU

The content of the news is different from day to day, and even major events continue to be referred to in the media for only a comparatively brief span of time after they occur. Public familiarity with an event does not grow steadily over time; it waxes and wanes. The less important an event is, the more likely it is that people who know of it have gotten the news by word of mouth rather than directly from the media.[7]

The news each week necessarily includes many prominent items that are easily forgotten. For example, just before our 1977 survey, in the week of March 14, a group of Hanafi Black Muslims had terrorized Washington, taking hostages and killing one person. The booking of the suspects and the follow-through on the story continued in the week of the study. In the same week, Zaire was attacked by rebel forces aided by Angola. Prime Minister Indira Gandhi was defeated in the Indian elections. A Spanish airliner was hijacked. In the United States, President Carter proposed a new tax bill, visited the UN, and made a speech at a town meeting in Clinton, Massachusetts. Senator Barry Goldwater was accused of having links to organized crime in Arizona. There was a ban on saccharin, a drought in California, the late flurries of a severe winter in the Northern states. Needless to say, the news in each community was made up of innumerable local stories that often overshadowed everything else.

In addition to the large national cross-section of the press on which our 1977 study was based, 14 morning and evening newspapers were examined intensively to see how consistently they treated the events of the same week. Local news stories produce a huge variation both in what is printed and with what emphasis. Of 316 newspaper items that exceeded 5½ column inches, 56% were unique to a single paper; 25% of all the front-page news items were unique to only one front page.

This variation is all the more remarkable in that more and more newspapers are relying on a single primary wire service for their nonlocal news. (In 1979, 18% subscribed both to Associated Press and United Press International, compared with 25% ten years earlier. During the 1980s UPI experienced growing financial difficulties and lost a great many subscribers after it was sold by Scripps-Howard. At the same time, an increasing number of

---

[7]G. Ray Funkhouser, "A General Mathematical Model of Information Diffusion," Institute for Communication Research, Stanford University, September, 1968, pp. 74–75.

newspapers were buying the secondary services of *The New York Times*, *Washington Post*, *Los Angeles Times*, Knight-Ridder, and other organizations that specialized in background and interpretative reporting rather than comprehensive worldwide coverage of spot news.)

To what extent does the balance of content reflect the singularities of the time period measured? In 1971, the nation was still absorbed in the Vietnam war; in May, 1982, the Falklands war was raging. The detailed content analysis of individual items that we did in 1971 and 1977 was simplified in 1982, and the comparison is shown in Table 6.10. (There was no analysis of individual items in 1987.)

Although the specific content of the news was very different in the survey week in March 1977 and the two weeks in June, 1971, there were generally close similarities in the content of newspapers for those two periods. (Table 6.11 gives a more detailed breakdown of the types of news measured in those two surveys.) The Vietnam war and other war news accounted for 7% of the item count in 1971, but only 1.5% in 1977. U.S. government and other domestic news represented in 1977 half the proportion it did in 1971. Crime news went up from 4% to 7% of the total. Womens' interest items became a somewhat greater proportion. But by and large, the essential stability of the mix is more impressive than the differences. There would, after all, be variations between any two parallel samples of newspaper content taken at the same time. Beyond that, the ordinary day-to-day and week-to-week changes in the news could account for a considerable part of the differences that emerge when 1971 is compared with 1977 or with 1982.[8]

It is not easy to demarcate news and features, hard and soft news, information, and entertainment; we have more to say about this in another chapter. But the method of classification used in our studies indicates that hard news—timely reports of specific events—occupies the major part of the editorial menu for the items analyzed in all three surveys.

The increased emphasis on local news reported in our surveys of newspaper managements was also manifested when we analyzed the trends in actual content. Items (over 5 inches) of national and international news represented a larger share of the total in 1971 (17%) than local items (13%),

---

[8]A sample of 206 daily newspapers, analyzed by the Urban Research Corporation, reveals substantial variations between one year and the next in the proportion of urban affairs content devoted to specific subjects. For instance, comparing the summer quarters of 1973 and 1974, Morris Janowitz finds that education went from 14.6% of the total of 17.5%, and that under this heading space devoted to desegregation and to women increased 2 times. In the same period, "law and order" declined from 11.5% of the total to 9.9%, with a five-fold increase in coverage of community activity and a four-fold increase in stories on gun control. Morris Janowitz, "Content Analysis and the Study of Sociopolitical Change" (unpublished paper presented before the American Association for Public Opinion Research,1975.)

TABLE 6.10
Editorial Content of Sampled Pages, 1971–1982

	1971	1977	1982
Total items (of 5 column inches or more)	100.0%	100.0%	100.0%
Economic news, actions & policies	9.4%	9.2%	11.6%
Environment, resources, population, energy	1.5	2.2	1.6
Government actions (U.S. & foreign)	14.3	12.6	7.1
Wars, rebellions, defense activity	6.8	1.4	4.2
Crime	3.7	6.9	5.9
Professional sports	13.4	13.1	11.3
Other sports			4.2
Editorials, unsigned[a]	NA	NA	2.1
Editorial cartoons	NA	0.9	1.3
Other editorial page content[b]	1.6	2.2	4.1
Education, child care	3.1	2.9	4.0
Cultural events, arts, reviews	2.4	2.2	2.6
Other amusements[c]	12.5	12.9	14.2
Personal advice columns	2.9	1.6	1.6
Other general interest[d]	11.0	10.4	15.4
Health, welfare, social issues	5.4	4.7	3.8
General local news[e]	6.9	6.9	NA
News summaries, briefs, index	NA	2.2	1.4
All other content[f]	5.1	7.7	3.6
International news items	10.2%	6.3%	6.0%
National news items	6.9	3.5	4.8
State & local news items	12.7	12.4	14.0

[a]In 1971 and 1977, unsigned editorials were classified by content (i.e., education, government actions, etc.).

[b]Includes letters to the editor and political columns that may not appear on the editorial page.

[c]Includes comics, puzzles, horoscopes, radio & TV listings.

[d]Includes food, home, society, obituaries, & gossip columns.

[e]In 1982, general local news items were classified by content (economic news, other sports, etc.).

[f]Includes science, inventions, disasters, religion, etc.

but by 1977, the balance had shifted (10% to 12%) and in 1982 it stood at 11% to 14% (Table 6.12). The Vietnam war and its consequences in Washington may explain why the balance was tilted toward a worldwide perspective in the early part of this period, but editorial judgment seems to have sustained a shift to local coverage. In 1982, news of U.S. or foreign government actions accounted for only half the percentage of items that it did in 1971. Economic news showed an increase between 1977 and 1982 as inflation progressed.

TABLE 6.11
Editorial Content of Sampled Pages, 1971 vs. 1977

	1971	1977
General interest	66.8%	66.6%
Local and state news	12.7	12.4
General local news	7.3	7.3
Local and state government	5.4	5.1
International news	10.2	6.3
Wars, rebellions	7.2	1.5
International, diplomatic	3.0	4.8
U.S. government, domestic	6.9	3.5
Other general interest	37.0	44.4
Crime	3.9	7.3
Education, school news	3.3	3.1
Cultural events, reviews	2.6	2.4
Public health, welfare	2.4	2.8
News in brief	—	2.4
Accidents, disasters, natural phenomena	2.4	1.9
Social problems, protest	2.1	1.6
Obituaries	2.1	1.2
Labor, wages	2.1	1.6
Environment	1.6	1.7
General nonlocal human interest	1.2	2.7
Energy problems	—	0.7
Racial news, minorities (peaceful)	1.2	0.6
Weather	1.1	1.7
Science, invention	1.0	0.7
Travel	1.0	1.0
Taxes	1.0	0.9
Religion	0.6	0.6
Comics[a]	2.6	2.8
Editorial cartoons	—	1.0
Puzzles, horoscopes	2.4	2.9
TV/Radio logs	1.2	1.1
Entertainers, Hollywood	0.9	1.0
Letters to the editor	0.6	0.7
Men's interest	21.1	21.2
Sports	14.2	13.9
Business, finance	6.9	7.3
Women's interest	5.4	3.3
Fashion, society	3.9	2.0
Food, home, garden	1.5	1.3
Columns		
Advice	3.1	1.7
Political	1.1	1.6
Humor	0.8	0.4
Gossip	0.3	0.2
Other items not classified elsewhere	1.4	5.0
Grand Total	100	100

[a]Number of comics in 1977 survey adjusted to compensate for coding differences between 1971 and 1977. In the 1977 survey, each comic was coded as a single item to permit coding of specific strips. In the 1971 survey, a block of several adjacent comics was coded as a single item.

TABLE 6.12
Distribution of Editorial Content, 1982

	% of all items	Items 5 column inches or more		
		Median size in inches	% weighted by size	% of items under 5 inches
Total items	100.0	13.2	100.0	100.0
Economic news, actions & policies	11.6	14.2	12.7	13.8
Environment, resources, population, energy	1.6	13.8	1.7	1.5
Government actions (U.S. & foreign)	7.1	13.5	7.2	7.5
Wars, rebellions, defense activity	4.2	16.1	5.1	3.5
Crime	5.9	12.0	5.3	6.9
Professional sports	11.3	15.0	12.7	9.0
Other sports	4.2	13.5	4.3	4.4
Editorials, unsigned	2.1	14.4	2.3	1.5
Editorial cartoons	1.3	14.9	1.5	0.7
Other editorial page content	4.1	21.4	6.6	3.1
Education, child care	4.0	14.1	4.2	5.6
Cultural events, arts, reviews	2.6	16.5	3.2	2.9
Other amusements	14.2	6.6	7.0	10.9
Personal advice columns	1.6	17.0	2.0	1.2
Other general interest	15.4	13.5	15.5	18.3
Health, welfare, social issues	3.8	14.2	4.1	3.5
News summaries, briefs, index	1.4	11.5	1.2	1.5
All other content	3.6	12.6	3.4	4.2
International news items	6.0%	15.2	6.8%	5.6%
National news items	4.8	14.2	5.1	4.0
State & local news items	14.0	14.2	14.9	17.4

Features like comics, puzzles, horoscopes, food, home, and society columns grew from 24% of all measured items in 1972 to 30% in 1982, again confirming what newspapers told us in our surveys of content.

Since our analysis was limited to items of at least 5 inches, the median article was 13.2 inches in length. Somewhat surprisingly, the length of a typical item appears to depend on its specific character, rather than on the general subject heading under which it falls. Personal advice columns (at 17 inches), cultural items (16.5 inches), and war dispatches (16.1 inches) ran above average in size, and miscellaneous amusement items like comic strips and puzzles (6.6 inches) were unusually small, but other categories were close to the median.

The items under 5 inches in size, measured in a special analysis of 144 newspapers, turned out to be distributed across the range of subject matter

TABLE 6.13
Percentage of Editorial Items by Type and Location in Paper, 1982

	Total items	Front page	First interior spread	Second interior spread	Third interior spread	Last interior spread
International	6	23	9	6	4	2
National	5	11	7	5	4	2
State & local	14	21	14	12	13	12
General interest	15	10	18	17	13	11
Amusements	14	1	9	12	17	28
Professional sports	11	1	2	9	18	19
Other	35	33	41	39	31	26
Total	100	100	100	100	100	100

very much like the larger items. As we found in our 1977 study, they were somewhat more likely to deal with local news, miscellany, economic news, crime, and human interest.

Front-page items were predominantly real or hard news, whereas features tended to be concentrated in the center and back parts of the paper (Table 6.13). On the front page, 23% of the items were of international news and 11% were national news, though these topics represented only 6% and 5%, respectively, of all the items in the paper. (The balance of front-page news might have been different had the survey been done in a different period than May, 1982, when the Falklands war made dramatic headlines day after day.) Local news, which accounted for 14% of all the items, made up 21% of the elements on the front page. As a matter of fact, local news items were fairly evenly spread through all parts of the paper and accounted for 12% of those on the last measured spread, where only 4% of the items were national or international.

In 1977, the total of 21% oriented to men (sports and business) contrasted with 3% devoted to the traditional women's interests: food, home, garden, fashion, and society news.[9] One reason for this, already mentioned, is that sports and business pages customarily incorporate large amounts of tabular material that has no counterpart on the homemaking or society pages (e.g., stock market lists, box scores and batting averages, etc.). Still, the discrepancy is too great to be explained entirely on this basis. But it is nonetheless pertinent to ask whether material of interest to women readers is as prominent in the news columns as it is in the advertising, and whether so-called

---

[9]A comparable analysis was not made in 1982, but economic and sports news accounted for 27% of the items, whereas miscellaneous general interest (which included food, home, and society) items amounted to 15%. This was a less egregious imbalance, to be sure, reflecting the erosion of the traditional gender-defined barriers.

women's news properly reflects the preoccupations of the working women who are now 67% of those of working age.

VARIATIONS IN CONTENT

There is little variation in the mix of content by day of the week, Monday through Friday (1971). The only significant exception is that on Wednesdays and Thursdays (one of which is traditionally the "best food day" in almost every newspaper) there are more pages devoted solely to advertising, much of it from supermarkets. The question of which day, Wednesday or Thursday, is best for food advertising depends on local supermarket shopping hours, which often reflect the comparative proportions of salaried and wage employees in a community. Sixty-eight percent of newspapers (with 63% of circulation) list Wednesday as food day; 14% (with 25% of circulation) list Thursday. Food-related editorial matter and national coupon advertising customarily add to the bulk of newspapers on "best food day."

Smaller papers place more emphasis on local news and less on national and international news (1982).[10] A detailed analysis (1971) shows that they run fewer articles on business, the entertainment industry, and crime, and more horoscopes, puzzles, advice columns, and women's features (fashion, society, food, home). But when one considers the difference in the size of these papers and in the resources with which the editors work, the resemblances are far more striking than the differences in the mix of content. Apart from differences in the percentage of items devoted to particular types of subject matter, it should be remembered that the big circulation newspapers publish a larger *number* of items on most topics because they have more space available.

The most striking difference between small and large newspapers is in the business and finance category. On the average, papers with more than 250,000 circulation carried nearly five times as many items of this type in 1971 as did those with 50,000 or less. This helps explain why for newspapers of 50,000 circulation or less, the ratio of men's to women's items was about three to one, whereas among newspapers of more than 250,000 circulation (which publish more listings and tables on both the business and sports pages), the ratio was almost eight to one.

Bigger papers not only contain more information by virtue of their sheer bulk, but a higher proportion of their editorial content is made up of hard news. Table 6.14 shows that the smallest papers devote much more of their

---

[10]The detailed analysis of 1971 content by circulation size, region, and time of publication was not repeated in the subsequent major surveys, but there is no reason to assume that the findings would be very different.

TABLE 6.14
Composition of Editorial Items on Opened Pages, by Size of Paper, 1982[a]

	Number of pages			
	24 or less	25–40	41–60	61 +
Hard news categories	20.8%	22.3%	28.0%	32.4%
International news	4.7	5.0	5.9	11.1
National news	4.0	3.6	5.9	7.0
State & local news	12.1	13.7	16.2	14.3
Editorial, opinion pages (total)	6.7	6.5	7.7	9.3
Sports (total)	16.8	20.5	11.1	7.5
General interest (total)	42.3	37.4	37.0	33.0
All other	13.4	13.3	16.2	17.8

[a]*Base*: Editorial items of 5 or more inches on opened pages in newspapers read by qualified "yesterday" readers.

limited space to sports and general interest features. Over all, American newspapers devote a considerably larger proportion of items to local and state news than they do to international and national news. However, the biggest papers tend to contain comparatively more international and national items, while the opposite situation is found among smaller papers. News from the State Capital, or from other towns in the State, represents a substantial flow of information over the State Wires of the AP and UPI, but it represents a very small percentage of all published stories and shows considerable variation in importance, state by state.

If we look at the actual *number* of stories printed, the typical big-circulation paper runs three national and international news items for every one run by the average smaller paper. (This should be kept in mind when we note in Chapter 9 that readers in smaller towns show less interest in the national and world scene. Does this reflect what their newspapers offer to them, or do the papers merely reflect the readers' interest?)

Minor differences among papers in different geographic regions turn out to be a reflection of minor differences between smaller and larger papers, which are differently represented in the various regions.

As a carry-over of an earlier period in American journalism, it is often assumed that afternoon papers are breezier and more flamboyant than those published in the morning. This may still be true in individual instances, but not as a generalization. Among major city newspapers, editorial matter represents virtually the same share of total space for morning (40% in 1986) and for evening papers (42%). Moreover, morning and afternoon newspapers allocate their content rather similarly to various types of subject matter. (As we see in Chapter 9, this content receives exactly the same kind of reader attention.) In 15 out of 36 content categories measured in 1971, the variation between morning and evening dailies was one-tenth of one percentage point or less. Differences in the way that space is distributed primarily reflect the differences in newspaper size rather than the time of publication. I have made the point that morning papers tend to be larger and evening papers are published mostly in smaller towns. In the 1971 study, *all* of the papers with less than 5,000 circulation whose content was analyzed were evening publications, but among the dailies with more than 500,000 circulation, 73% were morning papers. In 1987, of all dailies under 5,000, 80% were p.m.; of those over 500,000, 80% were a.m.

Our studies have looked at what's in the newspaper from the standpoint of subject matter, without regard for the idiosyncrasies of style or makeup that give newspapers their individuality of character. These stylistic differences may be very important to readers, but (quite apart from the difficulty of determining how to define and measure them on a large scale) it is hard to believe that they can be disassociated from the specific topics to which editorial technique is applied. and the evidence shows that these topics are generally similar among papers of different kinds.

The overall consistency of newspaper content suggests that there is a general acceptance, both by the public and by newspaper managements, of certain principles as to what constitutes news, as the major component of the newspaper. But there can be no discussion of the nature of news without taking into account the transformation of news values by newspapers' principal competitor.

7
NEWS,
THE NEWSPAPER,
AND TELEVISION

The content and appearance of American newspapers have undergone many subtle changes in the four decades of television's growth and dominance of leisure time. Undoubtedly, many such changes would have been introduced even if television were not present, shaping the public's perception of news personalities and events, providing an alternative perspective on the news to that of the daily press.

In addition to the newscasts that compete directly with newspaper headlines, television provides live coverage of the news as it happens, discussions of the meaning of news—sometimes newsworthy in themselves, and documentary reviews and interpretations of specific news subjects. Yet the newspapers of today, despite their contemporary subject matter and design, are not radically different from those of earlier generations. The continuity in editorial outlook helps explain the high degree of uniformity that I have just described in Chapter 6. To understand it, we must go back to the very essence of news itself.

News, it is said, is what news media choose to report within the limits of space or time they devote to this purpose. Every news organization works within a functional framework that reflects its economics of production. The fact that the news is packaged in a familiar and predictable format creates the comfortable feeling that confident forces are in control; it reduces anxiety about its content.

Consumers of news routinely make allowances for the exigencies of format. The newspapers that reported the assassination of Lincoln had headlines of identical size over advertisements in the adjacent front page columns. And even the newspapers of our own day reported with equal prominence the news of a tornado and news of a spaceship landing on Mars.

The formal structure and style of news media impose a sense of order and priority that is inevitably converted by the public into attributions of importance or unimportance for different items. Feature, background, and staff-generated stories that may have been sitting around for days or weeks may be perceived by the public as fresh and important news when they are positioned appropriately. This positioning is in part determined by the competition for time or space in the news budget of a particular day; in part it is determined by the recency of a story's delivery, even though it may be timeless in content. Editors working under pressure tend to select from the top of the pile in the in-box.

The positioning and prominence of a news story, the extent to which it is covered in depth, are not merely a reflection of its inherent importance, but a function of what other stories are breaking that day. The same story that may be the lead news item on one day may be crowded into the back of the paper on another. As we have seen, the amount of editorial space available in any given issue varies to a considerable degree with the amount of advertising. This is very different on some days than on others and even different at different seasons of the year. (This variation is also reflected in different ratios of hard news to feature content within the editorial space.)

There are but small variations in format relative to the great variations in the day's news. The day has long since passed when headlines sold significant numbers of papers, and many papers use the same size type to headline the trivial and the portentous.

TV newscaster David Brinkley illuminates a critical difference between TV's spot news emphasis and newspapers' ability to provide background when he complains: "There are many days when there is so little real news that we have a hard time finding anything to lead the program with that is not embartassing to use as a lead. On those same days, the [New York] *Times* . . . will come out with sixty pages, and it looks like a paper fat with news. But when you get down to it, it's not."

Another consideration is the extent of the news organization's own investment of energy and expense in the generation of a particular news story. (Local news costs 90% more to produce than wire news.[1]) When a reporter or camera crew have covered an assignment and produced copy or film, there is a powerful inclination to use it in preference to canned material

---

[1]Ben Bagdikian, *The Information Machines* (New York: Harper & Row, 1971), p. 128.

of one kind or another, even when a disinterested observer might rate it at lesser importance.

On dull days, the news media must convert nonnews into news to meet an allotment of space or time, because the advertisers who support them expect their own messages to be balanced by content of more general interest. For newspapers and newscasts to develop regular audiences they must satisfy the public's demand for something to pass the time, quite apart from the meaning of what has happened on any given day. Adherence to the format of publication or programming is necessary to sustain the audience's reading or viewing habits, on which the commercial prosperity of a medium depends. But the resulting uniformity in the volume of output can easily add to the difficulties that face public and newspeople alike in determining which items reported as news are real contributions to the chronicle of current history and which ones are merely accidental accompaniments to the main show.

THE NATURE OF NEWS

News undergoes redefinition with every succeeding generation. In the era of televised news, this reassessment has taken place rapidly but without general awareness. If a man bites a dog, it is generally known today that that is not news. It would be considered a contrived act of publicity, a media event, of which it would be *infra dig* to take notice.

What type of information do we call "news"? Is it a report of events that are literally new? "No," answered Ecclesiastes, "there is nothing new under the sun." That statement holds in the sense that familiar human foibles, emotions, and interactions resurface in every society and in every epoch. But the perennial dramas are reenacted in different disguises and contexts, so that the news is something more than the repetition of those ancient universal myths that tell of the common human experience.

When people are asked what "news" means, their replies mirror the conventional definitions that journalists use: "Everyday goings on in the world," "current events . . . that which has happened that affects our lives," "wars, accidents, speeches, weather," "something in the city that's current," "important things that happen during the day," "disasters, tragedies, bad happenings," "facts of everyday life that affect you," "what's rotten in the world today" (1979e).

Does the freshness, novelty, or immediacy of the event itself make it news? No, what matters is not the timing of the event, but the word of it. The report of the American Declaration of Independence was big news in England when it arrived there by slow boat many weeks after July 4, 1776. The Pentagon Papers made big news when *The New York Times* published them years after they had been written.

Does this mean that news reports something noteworthy that the public had previously not known? What is true of the public at large is not necessarily true of any individual. We may say, "It's news to me," when we learn of something long after it has already appeared in the press and if we have happened to overlook it. Yet the news can hardly be defined as something of significance unknown to a given individual, because this might cover most of human knowledge.

Very often what appears to be news is actually the haphazard or accidental revelation of a continuing condition that may be highly familiar to specialists, residents of a particular area, or others in the know. Most people are probably unfamiliar with the exact details of the occurrences that led up to the Whiskey Rebellion. We would hardly consider them news if they were reported in tomorrow's newspaper. On the other hand, if documents should be discovered tomorrow that cast fresh light on this obscure subject, that would be news. Public ignorance rather than individual ignorance determines what is news and what is not, and news media periodically run stories that are already familiar to insiders but strike others as news.

Nor is the news simply "what happened," a report of events. It may be a new explanation or interpretation of already familiar events or a concatenation of known but isolated events into a single narrative that shows previously unknown relationships.

Robert Park observed that, "History is often quite as interesting as news. But the events history records have ceased to be important because there is nothing one can do about them. On the other hand, when there is nothing to be done about the events recorded in the newspapers, they have ceased to be news."[2]

This seems in retrospect to be a questionable criterion. Much of the daily flow of news encompasses unique and nonrecurring stories about which no one can do anything, and almost all of it reports events over which the overwhelming majority of the audience feels no sense of control or influence whatsoever. Could not precisely this feeling of remoteness from what is reported account for the public's massive ignorance of happenings, places, and personalities that are the subject of news reports to which it is repeatedly exposed?

The news encompasses useful current information that is not necessarily *generally* important but is of considerable importance for some people. Stock and commodity quotations, baseball scores, movie timetables, and the prices of merchandise offered for sale might not be considered news in the traditional sense, but they represent information that is for at least some members of the news audience both fresh and meaningful. Unlike newspapers, televi-

---

[2]Robert E. Park, "Introduction." In Helen MacGill Hughes, *News and the Human Interest Story*, Chicago: University of Chicago Press, 1940. (Westport, Conn.: Greenwood Press, 1968.)

sion news cannot report such useful minutiae, which are tedious to anyone not seeking them.

NEWSPAPER JOURNALISM–TV JOURNALISM

In considering the nature of print and broadcast news, it is essential to distinguish between events and developments. Most wire service stories, all radio newscasts (except for the backgrounders and interpretive reports heard on the handful of all-news stations), and much of TV newscasting deal with events. That is, they report on specific occurrences that have just taken place and that the reader or listener is expected to be able to position in relation to his acquaintance with what has happened earlier. An event may be isolated or it may represent part of a continuing story. Needless to say, it is part of the newswriter's function, where appropriate, to show that events are not necessarily idiosyncratic. A traffic accident can be treated as a nonrecurring and unique event or it may be related to a series of other accidents at the same location or involving drunken driving or a particular make of car; in short, it may be transformed into a confirmation of a development.

In the reporting of news, time and space are always at a premium, and the speed with which stories are processed, as well as the limited number of column inches or broadcast minutes that can be devoted to any one item, act to discourage the elaboration of reports on incidents that make it possible to interpret them as part of a developing pattern. Live television news reporting, precisely because it is presented as a literal depiction of reality and accepted as such by viewers who do not see it as the focused viewpoint of a particular camera under the control of a particular director, almost inevitably deals with the news as events; when it attempts to bind events together in the form of commentary, then it is reduced to showing reporters reading words that they have written out ahead of time. The spontaneous comments of a brilliant television journalist or the interplay of experts engaged in a panel discussion may be enlightening, stimulating, informative, and above all entertaining, but they are simply not a substitute for the researched, considered, digested, and edited analysis of news developments that one expects to find in print. This is simply because the symbols of the written language permit abstraction, synthesis, and rapid marshaling of much disparate information for the record with an efficiency that has no counterpart for broadcast messages that flow in time.

Daily newspaper reportage is unique in its ability to combine depth and complexity of analysis in a context of urgent timeliness, with all that this implies in the intensity and immediacy of the message. Newspaper articles carry additional impact from the fact that "everyone" reads the same story on the same day, so they are assumed to be part of the common pool of current information and concern. A well-prepared piece of investigative reporting can pack enormous amounts of information into a limited amount of space, so that the readers rapidly absorb a whole dramatic experience that would be attenuated on TV.

NEWS, INTERPRETATION, INVESTIGATION

"News is sin and sin is news," said Mr. Dooley. The pattern of news coverage long established in the American press provides for reporters' beats at predictable points of origin for news—including police stations and courts where conflict, crime, violence, and the most sordid aspects of urban life are grist for the mill. Critics of the media have suggested that a different news balance might well be created if the same routine effort were made to cover those social institutions that reflect the more positive aspects of society, like schools and research laboratories. The balance would be more wholesome, to be sure, but would the audience stay with it?

And yet, another related source of criticism suggests that the emphasis on spot news leaves more fundamental subjects uncovered. "The real news isn't in distinct, bizarre events. The real news is what happens twenty-four hours a day all day long everywhere. This is the news we don't read about in the daily papers because the people who control those papers don't want us to know about it and do everything they can to distract our attention from it."[3]

Routine newsbeats can be equated with complacency, conservatism, and timidity of news coverage. Jack Newfield of the *Village Voice* writes passionately:

> Objectivity can be defined as the way the mass media reported the history of the Vietnam War before the Pentagon Papers; the way the racism in the North was covered before Watts; the way auto safety was covered before Ralph Nader . . . Objectivity is printing a dozen stories about minor welfare frauds but not a word about the Mylai massacre until Seymour Hersh [whose investigative reporting uncovered it]. Objectivity is not shouting "liar" in a crowded country.[4]

Honoré de Balzac writes in *Lost Illusions*, "Journalism is an inferno, a bottomless pit of iniquity, falsehood, and treachery; one can only pass through it and emerge from it unsullied if one is shielded as Dante was by the

---

[3]Marty Glass, "What's News," *Dock of the Bay*, Vol. 1, No. 3, August 18, 1969, p. 4 (Quoted by Robert J. Glessing, *The Underground Press in America*, Bloomington: Indiana Univesrity Press, 1970, p. 109).

[4]Jack Newfield, "Is There a New Journalism?" *Columbia Journalism Review*, July/August, 1972, p. 47.

divine laurels of Virgil."[5] The American tradition of reporting the news has been to disembody it from the possible biases and values of the reporter. But if these values can be effectively disengaged in the reporting of spot news, it is hard to see how they can be disassociated from the background article or interpretive essay.

The historical emphasis on objectivity in American journalism has always meant a deemphasis on the colorful personal style of writing that other journalistic traditions have fostered. There is rarely in the American press a positive emphasis on good writing for its own sake or on the expression of a peculiarly personal (and often myopic) vision of the kind that has flourished in the European and Latin-American press. In each of the provincial newspapers of Latin America, it is customary to find one or more daily columns that the authors fill with whatever trivia come to mind—reports on conversations with friends, observations of street life, reminiscences, comments on articles or films. The style is that of a letter to an intimate friend, with no concessions to the demands of the mass audience. The reader is indeed addressed as the "gentle reader" of the early Victorians. This tradition of personalized, miscellaneous commentary survives to a degree in U.S. weekly papers (especially in the alternative press), but it has largely disappeared from daily journalism where a columnist usually has a clearly assigned area in which he is expected to pundit.

An interpretation of events that relates them to each other and thus transforms them into developments is not conceivable except as an exercise of judgment. This means that there is often a very thin line indeed between the stance of an individual writer's interpretative commentary on the news and that of the editorial column that reflects the paper's considered institutional opinion. Commentary involves a point of view, and to express a considered point of view at length and for the record is the peculiar property of the written word. Thus, the decline of the actively competitive daily press carries serious consequences in all the realms of civic interest and culture in which independent criticism is essential to preserve standards and sanity. The real function of editorials and critical commentaries is not to carry the public along with whatever argument is being upheld, but rather to provoke discussion, to create issues where there were formerly none.

The investigative reporter—the relentless critic of follies hitherto unrecognized, the self-appointed defender of the public interest—can flourish only in an atmosphere in which the issues are laid out for all to see and in which those with an opposite viewpoint can freely enter the same arena. On any local scene, a climate of controversy requires that there be several organs, each

---

[5]Another Balzacian *billet-doux*: "Si la presse n'existait pas, il ne faudrait pas l'inventer." (If the press did not exist, it would not be necessary to invent it.) But of course he made this crack in a periodical, the *Revue Parisienne*, in 1840).

reflective of a distinctive viewpoint. Rebuttals in the form of letters to the editor or of different columnists appearing side by side and espousing diametrically opposed politics simply do not permit the same coherent advocacy of causes that can be manifest in a publication that carries a particular, and consistent, point of view.[6]

Newspapers have the vital function of supplying independent criticism and thus of stimulating public debate on matters that would not independently be taken up by individuals or groups as matters of direct concern. Independent investigations of civic corruption, commentaries on the aesthetics or properties of proposed civic and private construction schemes, revelations of unrecognized civic problems—all these have been the traditional concerns of newspapers and all transcend the direct reporting of news events. To conduct penetrating and fearless journalistic inquiry is by no means inconsistent with the canons of objectivity. Such inquiry demands not merely the technical capacity to search and report; it requires passion. It is possible for a news medium to report the news objectively and still to promote active public discussion by creating new issues in its very selection of what to report.

NEWS AND HUMAN INTEREST

News encompasses not only those stories that are inherently important because of their implications for the general welfare, but those of human interest, which are dramatic and involving, either because they deal in the universals of human experiences and emotions or because of their bizarre and curious character.

A good many newspapers have adopted a formula of summarizing the news, particularly on national and international affairs, on the assumption that many readers are already aware of it from the newscasts and that many of the others simply don't care enough about it to struggle through a complete report. The effect is to emphasize individual items reduced to bulletin form and disassociated from their context and implications and to deemphasize human interest stories that, partaking of the character of fiction, must be

---

[6]National magazines once had such a strong inner consistency of character and editorial viewpoint and provided on the national scene some of the same opportunities for debate and for choices in reader identification that could occur in local competitive daily newspapers. But *Liberty, Collier's*, the *Saturday Evening Post, Look*, and *Life* departed one by one. To be sure, there are still a myriad magazines expressing their own unique philosophies, but what distinguished the magazines that have perished is that they all had vast audiences, and generally broadly assorted audiences, which means that their messages fell within the same arena of open public debate. Until we see the era of many competing national daily newspapers, we are unlikely to see a recreation of this climate of open and universal access to the same subjects of discussion in print.

spun out at length. Newspapers have traditionally sought to uncover stories that are beyond the normal investigative capacity of the very much smaller news staffs of other media.

A great human interest piece may be run at any time; it need not be tied to any particular date. But it gains impact when it appears in the crowded, dense, living atmosphere of a newspaper.

Anecdotes of human interest become infused into the news to the degree that there are not more important things for reporters to write about or for editors to publish. The reports of a war are generally reports of objectives taken or positions lost, interspersed with reports of battle losses ("the body count" in the argot of the Vietnam war). Rarely, and often only by chance, are the stories infused with the human touch. Incidents of human interest are commonplace in wartime, but they enter reportage in the mass media only in the occasional story that a reporter happens to hear about or observe and happens to write up and happens to get published on a day when there is not more important news to report of actual strategic changes in the battlefield. This accidental character of the news has its counterparts in everyday life.

Park points out that real-life human interest stories reported in the news are hardly distinguishable from fictional stories in which a writer's imagination recreates and reorders reality to mobilize the reader's attention and enrich his understanding of the human condition. For Park,

> Time and place are the essence of news, and this is precisely the difference—to use the language of the newsroom—between a news story and a fiction story. Another way of stating the matter is this: News has to do with events in a real world and gets whatever importance it has from that fact. Fiction and art, generally, are symbolic in character and concerned with incidents in an ideal world beyond time and space. For that reason, fiction and art have no importance in the sense in which that term applies to the news . . . Events, if they are to have for the reader the character of news, must be not merely interesting but important. Importance seems, however, to be a quality like hot and cold; that is, relative to time and space.[7]

But time and space are subject to constant redefinition as a result of new technology in communications and transportation. Thus, editors worry about the newsworthiness of items already reported a few hours earlier on radio or television. The traditional parochialism of judgments regarding newsworthiness is diminishing because of increased population mobility and the corresponding growth in the public's exposure to national rather than local news media—that is, to TV network news and the news magazines in contrast to newspapers and local newscasts. Thus, what is of human interest in the news is likely to touch universal concerns rather than to be a matter of geographic propinquity.

---

[7]Park, op. cit.

NEWS AS THE UNEXPECTED

It is the unexpected that makes news most exciting and dramatic, just as it is the unexpected that captures our attention in fiction. The news being made today that will most fascinate us when we read or hear it is the news that we could not possibly anticipate. This by no means suggests that such events are unplanned (Pearl Harbor, after all, took quite a bit of planning), but it implies that their timing and character must have been kept secret not only from the public but from the news media as well.

Events that are both unanticipated and important occur infrequently, however. The bulk of the straight news reports that come our way occur either on a fixed schedule (election days, press conferences, ground-breaking ceremonies, and the like) or in relation to an established reportorial beat (the police blotter, the United Nations, the motion picture industry) in which personalities and situations are covered as a matter of course. There is always a certain amount of uncertainty in the handling of such conventional assignments, but there is also much that is predictable, and the real surprises are rare. Much hard news, in fact, follows continuing stories that merely inch along from day to day but that must be followed because of their inherent significance. The public regarded news of the Vietnam war as important but also considered it a bore because of the absence of major military engagements.

The flow of news as it emerges through the 24 hours of the day from a wire service ticker is very different from the news in its packaged form as we read it in the paper or hear it on the air. Much of what comes over the wire consists of updates, amplifications, and corrections of what has come before, so that there is an almost imperceptible sense of change through time as the same bulletins are endlessly repeated. Anyone who follows a 24-hour-a-day radio station for a period of hours can quickly develop the illusion that nothing new ever happens at all. But characteristically, the news audience takes bites of the news only at occasional intervals, and in distinctive and familiar formats. And news value, it is generally understood, reflects not merely what is new and what is pertinent, but what arouses the attention of the audience.

NEWS AS DRAMA

As with an ongoing fictional drama, a continuing news story, being incomplete, is more likely to arouse our propensity for role playing, our imagination, and our emotions than a news report of a completed event. The story whose outcome is in doubt is the one that impels us to seize the latest word; once our interest is engaged, we cannot get enough of the news through every source that might add, however little, to what we already know. Watergate had some of this flavor, and so does an occasional important trial. Battles and wars have this character when our future depends on them, and our concern is higher when the enemy is at the gates than when he is 10,000 miles away.

But much of the news deals with nonrecurring events and not with those that are still happening. To create audience identification, a news story must be on a human scale; it must deal with individuals. Casualty figures arouse few emotions when they appear as statistics without names and faces. A report of 9,000 dead in an earthquake in West Irian (Indonesia) was given 5 inches in The New York Times. A dispatch from the scene would get more public attention and more space from editors or producers if it came from an eyewitness observer who reported specific instances of heroism as well as suffering.

It would be foolish to argue that more than a fraction of the stories that a newspaper carries on a typical day are infused with drama. And yet the reader can always turn to the paper with the expectation, hope, or dread that the drama will be there. It is precisely the newspaper's evanescent daily character that evokes this expectation of the unexpected. Only rarely can less frequently published periodicals evoke the same kind of response. A magazine article typically represents an account that stands on its own. It is complete, while a news story is almost always to be continued. This does not mean that magazine articles cannot be as engrossing, as informative, and as satisfying to the reader as anything in the daily press. But they cannot be as timely, except when an enterprising magazine editor commissions a piece that is inherently newsworthy. One can curl up cozily with a magazine, certain of being entertained; the newspaper must be approached warily.

The news, as I showed in Chapter 6, remains the main element of the newspaper. But in its expanding feature content, the daily press increasingly partakes of the character of the magazine—nonthreatening and easy to take. Embedded in a tissue of gourmet recipes, instructions on furniture repair, and counsel on premarital sex, the breaking (and unsettling) news is swathed in reassurances (not however to the degree that reports of mayhem, havoc, and iniquity on the TV news are comfortingly interspersed with commercials for denture cleaners and muffler repair services).

Park's insistence that news must be both interesting and important sets a standard that can be met by comparatively few events on any given day. However, those stories that combine these attributes are the most compelling and memorable; they can not only arouse the public's emotions but change its mind. For this to happen may require a conviction that what is being learned—good news or bad—has a direct bearing on the individual, that it relates to one's own life. Thus, there is a threat to one's own personal security in any local crime report where the setting is familiar and the victim a subject of empathy. The more we are told, if the telling is skillful, the more familiar the setting will appear to be and the better we will seem to know the characters involved.

I have tried to suggest in this section that there are critical dimensions to newspaper content that do not readily lend themselves to the kind of content analysis presented in Chapter 6. And yet, these qualitative dimensions may be precisely the ones that govern the readers' response, to which we turn later. The contemporary reader's response to the newspaper cannot be separated from exposure to the news on television.

TV AS A COMPETITOR

In the history of mass communication, technical changes have always had great cultural consequences. Every new medium, once past the early developmental stage that follows its invention, has disturbed the existing equilibrium of communications and has brought about a new balance of leisure time, information flow, aesthetic experience and popular symbolism. How has the growth of television, and of its news functions, affected the oldest instrument of modern mass communication, the daily newspaper?

Television occupied a substantial segment of each day as it came to maturity, but by 1960 it was present in 9 out of every 10 households and viewing patterns had stabilized. Including weekends, the average American adult watches slightly over three hours of television a day. Although this figure has fluctuated from year to year during the 1970s and 1980s, it has not followed a significant upward or downward trend. Sets have been on for more hours (though use dropped slightly in 1987), but there are fewer viewers per set—23% fewer in prime time in the late 1980s than there were in the early 1960s.

It seems convenient to think of the public's available time and attention as a pie that the media carve up (so that the share taken by one is denied to the others); but this is an erroneous metaphor. The evidence suggests that each medium makes its own unique demands on the time and attention of the public. In fact, the media compete for time only up to a point. To some extent (as in reading and listening), they actually overlap in time. In the age of automation, the supply of time seems far less exhaustible than it appeared a few years ago. Most important, the distinctive functions of each of the media for the common audience make them far less incompatible than they are often thought to be.

The news media complement each other in a number of ways:

1. To some degree, they convey the same information to different people.
2. They display different aspects of the identical information to different people.

3. They also display different aspects of the identical information to the same people.

4. Finally, they arouse and reinforce interests that other media help to satisfy. (Television has stimulated interest in spectator sports, but this only increases the readership of newspaper sports pages.)

THE GROWTH OF TV NEWS

Of course, the presence of television news in all its aspects has dramatically changed the communications environment in which newspapers operate. So, for that matter, did radio news and the movie newsreel, before TV.

Newspaper editors remain perplexed by the problem of adapting their own product to meet the competition of television. As I showed in Chapter 5, on an ordinary day, the editor must expect that the paper's leading headlines are already familiar to some readers from radio or TV newscasts; yet a large part of the paper's readership has not been exposed to the broadcast news, and the editor must satisfy them without boring the others.

News programming has been a regular part of television for well over a quarter-century. During television's growth period, a variety of surveys showed a continuing growth in the public's expressed confidence in television as a news source.[8] This cannot be explained only on the basis of what has happened to television news during this period. As we have already noted, the same years have seen tremendous social change.

During this period, the amount of television news time has been steadily growing, and the audience has grown proportionately. With the coming of the Cable News Network and the Cable Headline News, viewers were served around the clock. The very fact that news programs are on at the same time night after night means that they develop an habitual viewing pattern, with viewers drawn regularly to the particular programs whose news teams they find most agreeable as personalities. The viewers' relationship to the newscaster, as to any other show business star, is an emotional attachment that exists independently of whether or not they watch that newscaster on a particular day.

A 1978 Bruskin survey found that 45% of the public said that if they have a choice, they would "rather watch a TV news program than an entertainment program which is broadcast at the same time." Be that as it may, much of the exposure to TV news is casual in nature. An analysis of "audience flow" measured by broadcast ratings services shows that for every 100 television households that tune in to one of the early evening network newscasts once

---

[8]Most widely reported were the studies made by The Roper Organization, Inc. for the Television Information Office, which are discussed later.

or more over a four-week period, 60 will tune only to a single broadcast, and only 12 will be tuned in to more than four out of every five. Viewer loyalty to local newscasts is even less than for network shows.

Like every other type of TV programming, news draws audiences in ratio to the amount and positioning of the time it receives on the the the air. In recent years, on both local stations and the networks, news has been getting bigger and better time spots. News programs contribute 40%–50% of the profit of most TV stations.[9]

In 1962, each of the networks was offering a quarter-hour of news a day. A year later, they had gone up to a half hour. And by 1966, CBS and NBC were each up to an hour and a half a day. ABC followed in 1969. In 1987, 60% of 622 network affiliates surveyed by the Television Information Office broadcast half an hour of local early evening news, and the remainder (an increasing percentage) broadcast an hour or more. Network news was predominantly carried at 6:30 p.m. in the Eastern Time Zone and an hour earlier in the Midwest. Thirty-three percent of the local network newscasts were on for a half hour following the network news, 26% for a half hour following, 19% both for a half hour before and for another half hour afterward, and 14% for a full hour before. Altogether, in all parts of the day, the average station was airing at least an hour of network news and well over two hours of local news each weekday. That does not mean the same proportions of exposure to general as compared to local news, because the local newscasts include a certain amount of national and international material fed by the networks or supplied by independent services.

THE CONTENT OF TV NEWS

What is actually in the TV news? The three evening network newscasts closely resemble each other in format, according to an analysis by the Tyndall Report, produced by ADT Research of New York. For the period between October 1987 and March 1988, all three networks averaged 16 items per half hour newscast. Of these, five or six were text reports read by the newscaster, in some cases with a background graphic. Six or seven items consisted of edited videotape with a recorded voice-over by a correspondent. (Of these taped news reports, just under half originated in the United States outside of Washington, 3 in 10 from the nation's capital, and 1 in 4 from abroad.) The remaining items included videotapes with a live voice-over, interviews, live coverage, and commentaries.

Of the 21 minutes in the average broadcast, 17 were devoted to prere-

---

[9]This estimate is by a securities analyst, Dennis Liebowitz, of Donaldson Lufkin and Jenrette (*Broadcasting*, October 5, 1987, p. 61).

corded taped reportage, and the remainder were split between straight narration of copy and miscellaneous items. The leading story averaged 5 or 6 minutes in length; the top five stories took 13 minutes altogether.

A similar analysis made from Vanderbilt University data in 1977 found that the typical network news program then carried more items–21–in more time–27 minutes. (Presumably there were fewer commercials rounding off the half hour.) It therefore appears that television has been reducing the number of news stories to which a viewer is exposed each day, changing the perspective from which this handful of major events can be viewed against the vast panorama of happenings that might be reported and that, in fact, many newspapers do report.

In 1987, the Tyndall Report shows that U.S. foreign affairs activities accounted for 23% of network news items and time, while international news not involving the United States took another 15%. (By way of comparison, in 1987 foreign news accounted for only 6% of the items in the American press, though it represented a substantial percentage of nonlocal, nonfeature material.) Domestic politics and government stories represented 23% of the television news items and 26% of the time. Other domestic stories were the subject of the largest proportion of items (38%) and time (37%). Of the domestic nonpolitical items (in which a few stories fell into more than one category), 28% concerned the economy. Accidents and disasters represented 21%; crime, 20%; health and medicine, 13%; sports, 10%; and the arts and entertainment, 7%.

In October, 1987, the month in which our newspaper survey was made, the impending 1988 election race accounted for only 4% of television network news time, but U.S. government activities accounted for 22% and nonpolitical domestic stories for 43%. Nearly half of this domestic news (47%) was devoted to the stock market and related financial economic developments. (The weekday paper in the hands of the typical reader carried about 14 times as many items of editorial content.)[10]

I said in Chapter 6 that on any day newspapers exhibit great variety in their selection and play of the news, in part because editors make different judgments, in part because local stories forced changes in the treatment and emphasis given to wire service and other nonlocal copy. By contrast, as national media, the three networks show considerable agreement in their

---

[10]This disparity is less imposing when only news items are counted and when the full array of offerings for all TV stations is considered. A study by Keith Shelton for the weeks of November 1–15, 1976 in Dallas found that of the 301 local stories carried on the three TV stations' locally produced news shows, the morning *Dallas News* carried 69 and the evening *Times Herald* 58. Of these stories, 241 were only carried by a single station. But in the same period, the two newspapers ran 882 local stories, of which 127 were not on TV. Many of the stories were of course continuing or follow-ups. (Keith Shelton, "Timeliness in the News: Television vs. Newspapers," *Journalism Quarterly*, Vol. 55, No. 2, Summer 1978, pp. 348–350.)

news coverage. The fact that all three use the two major wire services for the breaking news obviously facilitates this similarity. Of the 16 stories each network carried on a particular day's newscast, 7 were carried by the other two also, 10 were carried by one other program, and 6 were unique to that network. But these exclusive stories occupied nearly half the total air time, while the major stories that all three carried occupied 8½ out of the 21 minutes.

A closer comparison of how network television and newspapers handle the same day's news was made during the seven March days of our 1977 survey.[11] Morning and evening network news programs were monitored so that their content could be compared with that of the press.[12] On the 42 broadcasts analyzed, 534 different news items were counted.[13] One hundred fourteen appeared once; 33, twice; and 50, three or more times. Since many stories were continued over the course of several days, the actual number of individual stories was about 200. In fact, 50 major stories that were covered on three or more days accounted for 67% of all the items measured.

The most dramatic stories were not necessarily the ones that continued for days. The most frequently used story was the rebel invasion of Zaire, which accounted for 28 broadcast news items in the seven days. Twenty-four items dealt with a U.S. delegation in Vietnam to investigate the fate of soldiers missing in action. Another 24 dealt with the Indian election campaign and the defeat of Indira Gandhi.

Local TV news had not been monitored. Thus, to compare TV network news with what is in the newspaper, local and state news items in the press were excluded from our analysis, as well as such subjects as sports and fashions, which the two media handle in a different way (Table 7.1).

Even so, a full third of newspaper items covered miscellaneous categories, many of them local in content, and business news was much more important in newspapers than in TV. Crime represented an identical proportion (one sixth) in network news and in newspapers. Newspapers gave somewhat less play than TV to U.S. government and political news. International subjects showed the greatest discrepancy. They accounted for nearly half of the

---

[11]By coincidence, Eric Levin had been examining TV network evening news for the preceding week. He attributes some of the differences in network coverage of major stories to the fact that some stories were cut out at the last minute. (Eric Levin, "How The Networks Decide What is News," *TV Guide,* July 2, 1977; and Eric Levin, "On Wednesday the Hanafis Struck," *TV Guide,* July 9, 1977.)

[12]On the morning programs, the news on NBC and ABC is embedded in a two-hour long entertainment feature format, and the hour-long program on CBS repeats news items. For this reason, any particular item that occurred in the course of these programs was counted only once for each network.

[13]This count is incomplete. A check of program transcripts indicates that perhaps one-fifth of the shorter items occurring late in the news broadcast may have been missed by the monitors. These were largely brief mentions that TV newsmen call "tell" stories.

TABLE 7.1
Major Categories of News Stories on TV Network News Programs and
in the Press, March 14–22, 1977

Story category	TV news programs		Newspapers[a]
International news		45.6%	16.1%
Wars, rebellions, arms control	12.2		4.0
Diplomatic, foreign events	33.4		12.1
Domestic government, politics		13.5	8.8
Other general interest		40.9	75.1
Crime	15.8		15.7
Public health, welfare	7.4		6.2
Entertainers, celebrities	3.6		2.3
Business, finance	4.4		12.6
Accidents, disasters	2.8		4.6
All other items	6.9[b]		33.7
		100.0%	100.0%
Total No. Items		(362)	(41,771)

[a]Local and state news items are excluded.
[b]No content category contained more than 2% of all items.

network TV news program items and for only one sixth of the newspaper
items.

The 16 leading stories on television were also among the stories most often
covered by the 14 newspapers that were individually analyzed. Their 13
top-ranking stories were also major news items on network TV. But of 63
major stories in newspapers, 35 were not covered by network television. And
24 out of the 52 major TV news stories did not show up as major stories in the
press on the measured days (though they may have appeared on other days.)

But even when the same stories are covered, the treatment they receive
can be quite different. On major stories, television may supply a direct visual
sense of vicarious participation that newspapers can not match, while newspapers have the capacity to reveal the same events in all their complexity
from multiple perspectives. And on many stories that the television newscaster must dismiss with a brief bulletin, newspapers can present a full report.

THE TV NEWS AUDIENCE

In 1987, 68% of the public reported watching television news in the course of
a typical day. Half watched two or more news programs (including the
variety-type of morning news and interview show on the networks). The
average news-watcher reported 58 minutes a day, with 45% watching over an
hour. (The amount of actual news watched during this time is, of course, only
a part of the total.)

Young people of 18 to 24 consumed less news on television, as they do in newspapers (Table 7.2). Only half (52%) watched any TV news, 25% watched more than an hour, and the average time was 41 minutes. The fact that fewer young people are regular newspaper readers really reflects their lower level of interest in the news itself. It is hard to blame that on TV. (The 18 to 24-year-old group listened to radio news in the same proportion as the general public—46% "yesterday." But this is because they are above-average radio listeners, and news bulletins periodically interrupt their musical pleasures.)

With the growing strength of cable, a diminishing part of the total news viewing was of locally originated programming in 1987, compared to 1982. An analysis of the specific programs reportedly watched indicates that 60% saw only network and cable news; 23% only local news shows; while 17% watched both kinds. (In 1982, 43% watched network and cable news only; 33%, local news only; and 24%, both.)

Are the viewers of television news a different breed than newspaper readers? Not at all. As we saw in Chapter 3, frequent newspaper readers watch more TV news.

In 1987, over half of the 68% who watched any TV news on the preceding day had watched at more than one time. There were no tendencies for people of any age or income group to cluster in either type of news program, network or local. Nearly four out of five news viewers (78%) had tuned in deliberately, though. Twenty-three percent had merely been watching a preceding program on the same channel, and the remainder could not say how they had come to tune in.

In 1977, those who had watched TV news on the previous evening were asked if there was "any other news program on at the same time that you could have watched instead," and 58% said that another news program was available. Sixty-five percent of these people had been watching a local news show. Forty-three percent of them explained their choice by referring to the viewing situation, the fact that they were already tuned to a particular

TABLE 7.2
Percentage Who Watched TV News "Yesterday" and
Time Spent Watching, by Age, 1987

	% who watched any	Average minutes viewers spent
18–24	52	41
25–29	63	45
30–34	58	57
35–44	68	54
45–54	67	55
55–64	73	65
65+	84	78

channel from the previous show or tuning in to the next one: 25% mentioned the style of presentation; 23%, the quality of the content; and 26% gave general reasons.

Among those who had been watching a network news program, and had chosen it over one on another channel, fewer (33%) explained that they were tuned to the channel, but more (38%) referred to the newscaster; 21%, to the quality of news content; and 26% gave general reasons.

It is apparent that for both local and network programs, a substantial number of viewers acknowledged that inertia is a major reason for tuning in and that the professional handling of the news (as distinct from the allure of the newscaster's personality) was not, consciously at least, a significant factor.

To what extent are newspapers read for the full information that TV news items are unable to cover in depth? The 1977 survey asked, "Some people feel that generally you can find out all you want to know about big news stories from TV news programs. Others generally want the additional details that newspapers give you on a big story. Which best describes the way you feel?" One-third said they got enough detail from TV; two-thirds preferred the additional details from the newspaper. In 1982, 30% said that television news programs told them as much as they wanted to know about those big stories and a 53% majority said they wanted the additional detail they could get from newspaper reports. But by 1987 the balance had shifted; 42% said they were satisfied with what they got from TV, 26% wanted the additional information from the newspaper, and 25% (compared with 16% five years earlier) volunteered the comment that they wanted both. The feeling that TV news provides enough detail was greater among women (46%) than men (38%), and among those who did not graduate from high school (48%), compared with college graduates (33%). Only 23% of the frequent readers said TV gave them all they wanted to know about the big stories, compared to a majority among the infrequent readers (57%) and nonreaders (71%).

THE ISSUE OF CREDIBILITY

Since the early days of the press, it has been generally understood that journalists play an active role in politics; their very presence changes the events on which they report. Especially in the era of the Vietnam war and Watergate, the activist function of "The Media" became a matter of commentary, debate, and opprobrium. The Nixon Administration, before its downfall, launched a many-sided attack on its media enemies, led by the infamous Spiro T. Agnew's denunciation of the "nattering nabobs of negativism." To what extent did the public share these critical views?

Newspaper editors' anxiety over the public's attitudes toward the media was triggered by a 1979 survey by the Yankelovich Organization for the

Public Agenda Foundation.[14] In the context of the survey, a concern for fairness and "equal time" appeared to extend from the regulated broadcasters to print journalism as well. Fifty-nine percent of the public believed that major third parties should get as much coverage as Republicans and Democrats, both on television and in newspapers; 29% disagreed. Eighty-two percent approved a law requiring newspapers to give major party candidates equal coverage. Seventy-three percent favored laws requiring newspapers to give equal space to both sides of a controversial policy, and 63% favored laws requiring newspapers to cover major third parties. The survey report concluded that "people make little distinction between what is expected from televison and from major newspapers. In the public's mind, the same standards apply to both."

Substantial minorities were also found in favor of laws that would severely limit freedom of information. For example, 26% favored prohibition of newspaper articles that embarrass the President, the government, or the country. Twenty-four percent would prohibit newspaper articles that are biased or that "unfairly criticize" a prominent person. Forty-two percent thought the President ought to be able to close down a paper that prints stories he feels are biased and inaccurate.[15]

Concerned by these warnings, the American Society of Newspaper Editors commissioned a study by MORI (Minnesota Opinion Research, Inc.) in 1985, which also concluded that "one-fifth of all adults deeply distrust their news media" and "three-fourths of all adults have some problem with the credibility of the media."[16]

---

[14]John Immerwahr, Gene Johnson, & John Doble, *The Speaker and the Listener: A Public Perspective on Freedom of Expression* (New York: Public Agenda Foundation, 1980).

[15]In 1984, a study by Clark, Martire, and Bartolemeo found the proportion had decreased to 25%. Although in 1979 the Public Agenda Foundation found 76% of the public agreeing that "newspapers pay too much attention to bad news and not enough to the good things," the 1984 survey found 66% who agreed. Clark, Martire, and Bartolemeo also found only 38% agreeing that "newspapers are usually fair" and 50% disagreeing. But in the case of television, the proportions were 29% and 63%. Similarly, 41% agreed and 48% disagreed with the statement that "newspaper stories are usually accurate." For television, the proportions were similar—43% and 48%.

[16]MORI Research, Inc., *Newspaper Credibility: Building Reader Trust*, The American Society of Newspaper Editors, 1985. This study was done among a nationwide telephone sample of 1,600 adults, of whom 1,002 completed a second interview. Strong minorities were suspicious of media integrity. Thirty-nine percent agreed that "people who advertise in the news media often get favored treatment in news coverage," and 39% agreed that "the news media often are manipulated by powerful people." About 3 in 10 said that the news media usually try to cover up their mistakes, but 7 in 10 said they usually try to correct them.

Half agreed (51%) and only one-fourth disagreed (24%) that "the news media give more coverage to stories that support their own point of view than to those that don't." Half (47%) disagreed and a third (34%) agreed with the statement that "if a newspaper endorses a candidate in an editorial, the news coverage will still be fair to all candidates." Only 52% felt that the

The survey found that strong majorities of the public favored suppressing certain kinds of news: the name of a CIA spy whose life may be in danger, a photograph of a woman escaping half naked after being held hostage, secret documents dealing with national security, poll results before the election is over. Although a majority felt that investigative reporting is very important, there was substantial disapproval for many of the devices that investigative reporters often use (not identifying themselves as reporters, recording conversations secretly, paying for information, quoting unidentified sources). Forty-two percent agreed that "sometimes there's too much freedom of the press."

Four out of five agreed that most news reporters "are just concerned about getting a good story, and they don't worry much about hurting people." Over half agreed that the press looks out for "ordinary people", but nearly half (46%) agreed that "the press looks out mainly for rich and powerful people."

Still, majorities generally felt that newspapers give "just about the right" amount of coverage to each of 21 different groups. And majorities rated their own daily newspaper as patriotic, concerned about the community's well-being, moral, fair, and trustworthy. Only 22% said the paper is concerned mainly about making profits, compared with 42% who said it is concerned mainly about the public interest.

Majorities also gave positive ratings to the daily newspaper they were most familiar with on reliability and the quality of reporting. A majority (54%) said that if they have a problem, complaint, or something they want to discuss with a newspaper, they know whom to contact there. Two out of three were aware of corrections columns in their paper, and a third knew that their paper had an ombudsman or readers' representative.[17]

A series of Gallup surveys conducted for Times-Mirror in 1985, 1986, and 1987 came up with a more positive interpretation of rather similar findings.[18]

---

editorial page is "more opinionated" than the rest of the paper, and 38% agreed that when a reporter's byline is on a story, the reporter is entitled to put his or her opinion in it (41% disagreed). Misunderstanding the nature of journalism, 87% agreed with the statement that "news reports should stick to facts rather than containing a lot of interpretation."

[17]A reanalysis of the data from this study found very little difference between "yesterday" readers and nonreaders in the credibility attributed to newspapers. However, people for whom newspapers were the first choice for local news also rated them higher in credibility. Tony Rimmer and David Weaver, "Different Questions, Different Answers? Media Use and Media Credibility," *Journalism Quarterly*, Vol. 64, No. 1 (Spring 1987), pp. 28–44.

[18]The Gallup Organization, *The People and the Press*, Times-Mirror, 1986. The 1985 survey echoed the Public Agenda findings. Less than half the public knew that the First Amendment or Bill of Rights provides for freedom of the press. When asked, "What does freedom of the press mean to you?" 61% chose the answer "that the public has a right to hear all points of view," and only 23% "that the press can cover and report what it chooses." Substantial minorities also felt that the government should ensure equal access for candidates in newspapers (38%) or should require all sides to receive news coverage in controversial issues (42%).

The public overwhelmingly believed news organizations to be highly professional and to care about the quality of their work.[19] However, only one
person in three agreed that news organizations "deal fairly with all sides" of
political and social issues; slightly over half disagreed.

Large majorities agreed that news organizations are "often influenced" by
such bodies as the federal government, business corporations, advertisers,
labor unions, Republicans and Democrats. When people were asked why
news organizations sometimes don't do such a good job, the number one
reason (named by 23%) was the need for attracting a big audience. Twenty-
one percent referred to pressure from special interests.

Three-fifths of the public said the media pay too much attention to bad
news, and 36% said that they do not. More people felt that news media "try
to cover up mistakes" (55%) than said the media are willing to admit them
(34%). Seventy-three percent said the media invade people's privacy.

A majority was inclined to agree that the press gave too much attention to
terrorism, but two out of three people also agreed that this coverage helped
the public interest. If the press sometimes fails to cover terrorist events well,
the major reason given is the competition among news organizations.

What was missing in both the ASNE/MORI and Gallup surveys was a
benchmark. Although the interpretations of the two studies appeared contradictory on the surface, in fact, the findings were highly congruous. Both
revealed that public opinion about the media is very complex and that there
is an ignorant, suspicious, and hostile minority as well as a group of skeptics
and concerned critics. But it is likely that this mix of attitudes toward the
press has long existed and that the presence of television has not changed the
majority's support of free expression.

HOW THE PUBLIC COMPARES TV NEWS AND NEWSPAPERS

How people actually use the news media is inseparable from the question of
how they regard them. Only 23% of the public in the 1985 ASNE/MORI
study expressed "a great deal of confidence" in the people running the press
(meaning news media in general), and 24% expressed "hardly any confidence." Asked specifically about newspapers, the proportions were 26% and
16%; for television, the response was less favorable: 21% and 29%.[20]

---

[19]Television was somewhat more likely to be described as invading people's privacy and less to
be "watching out for your interests."

[20]Similarly, about 3 in 10 thought that their newspaper sensationalizes, and the same number
said it doesn't. The proportion who said television sensationalizes was twice as large as those who
did not agree. But the public gave higher marks to television journalists. The honesty and ethical
standards of newspaper editors were rated high by 27% and low by 9%. Reporters were ranked

At about the same time, when Gallup's respondents were asked to rate 20 news media, the local daily newspaper received a rating at virtually the level of *Newsweek*, the most highly rated medium. Both local and "nationally influential newspapers" received high ratings comparable to those given to national TV news and radio news and to the news magazines—all substantially more favorable than those given to Congress, Ronald Reagan, the military, or business corporations.

Public attitudes toward network TV news and toward the "daily newspaper you are most familiar with" were virtually identical, with about one person in four very favorable and a majority mostly favorable.[21]

A well-publicized series of studies conducted for the Television Information Office by the Roper Organization, Inc. has tracked public attitudes toward television and newspapers since 1959. In that year, 57% said they usually got most of their news "about what's going on in the world today" from newspapers, while 51% named television, and 34%, radio. (Over half the respondents named more than one source, suggesting that the question was not altogether a realistic one.) By 1963, television and newspapers were about evenly ranked, and in 1967, television had swung ahead. In 1986, it was named by 66%; 36% named newspapers, and 14%, radio. (These figures include 16% who named more than one source.)[22]

The Roper surveys have also shown a change in the relative credibility of newspapers and television, as measured by a question on which of the four major media people would be most inclined to believe if they got "conflicting or different reports of the same news story." In 1959, 32% said newspapers and 29%, television. By 1968 television had assumed a lead of over two to one, and in 1986 it was preferred by 55%; newspapers, by 21%.

It is worth noting that the rating of newspapers in these studies

---

high by 18% and low by 18%. For TV news anchors, the rating of honesty was 40% high and 8% low; for television reporters, 28% high and 11% low. (The high ratings ranged from 53% for the clergy to 3% for used car salesmen.) Forty-eight percent said that newspaper reporters were well trained; 57% gave the same rating to TV news reporters.

[21] An indication of the volatility of public ratings of the news media was indicated by the changes between July and December, 1986, after a series of terrorist incidents. The "very favorable" rating for newspapers fell from 28% to 19%; for network TV news, from 30% to 19%.

[22] Reviewing the findings from 15 different studies, John Robinson concludes that newspaper use correlates with gains in information, whereas television acts as an information leveler for the less educated. Based on television interviews with a national cross-section of 544 adults in 1983 (as well as comparable studies in Washington, D.C., and in England), Robinson and Mark Levy found that only 62% of the public, on average, said they had read or heard about 31 major events or people in one week's news. Of 12 major stories, only 4 were correctly identified by a majority of the public. These comprehension scores were lower for the people who were most dependent on TV as their main news source. Television news exposure did not contribute to understanding the news as much as exposure to newspapers and other media, and so, "television news should not be considered the public's main source of news." (John P. Robinson & Mark R. Levy, *The Main Source: Learning from Television News* [Beverly Hills: Sage, 1986].)

remained rather stable during the 1970s, the period in which circulation-to-household ratios fell most. Between 1971 and 1978 the proportions who described their local television stations as excellent grew while ratings of schools and local government remained at about the same levels.

To what extent does the expressed preference for TV news (as measured by the opinion polls) reflect the psychological impact of major televised events (the political conventions, the Watergate hearings, the Middle East war) rather than of the routine reporting on newscasts? To check this out, we conducted 100 telephone interviews in five cities in December, 1973, using the standard questions asked by the Roper surveys. Those who said they got "most of their news" from TV were asked whether they had in mind background programs, regular news programs, live coverage, or interviews and debates. Seven out of ten said it was, indeed, the regular newscasts that they had in mind. And six out of ten said they were thinking primarily of local news. (Of those who said "most of their news" came from newspapers, local news was mentioned by seven out of ten.)

Further corroboration of the dramatic change in public attitudes toward the individual media came from a series of studies initiated at Columbia University and continued by the Bureau of Social Science Research. Among people with a grade school education, 48% in 1960 said newspapers gave the most complete news coverage and 26% named television. By 1980, newspapers were named by 22%, TV by 59%.[23]

Other surveys, not all conducted by disinterested parties, affirm the primacy of television in the public's mind. In 1985, a Bruskin Survey for the Television Bureau of Advertising found that TV outranked newspapers as "most authoritative" by 57% to 20%, "most believable" by 46% to 24%, "most exciting" by 81% to 3%, and "most influential" by 80% to 9%. A poll of 4,006 Canadians conducted by Environics in 1986 found that two out of three relied most on television, and less than one in five on newspapers, as the media source for international and national news. For the local news, 39% named television; 32%, newspapers; and 22%, radio. A 1987 survey of 1,012 U.S. adults done for *Parents Magazine* by Kane, Parsons, and Associates found 56% naming TV as the main source of news; 28%, newspapers, and 11%, radio.

The ASNE/MORI survey in 1985 found that if people got conflicting or different reports for the same news story, about half would choose the television version; 25%, newspapers; 14%, magazines; and 9%, radio. About

---

[23]For the high school educated, newspapers went from 62% to 29%, TV from 18% to 55%. And for the college educated, newspapers fell from 69% to 41%, and television rose from 10% to 42%. (In this group, magazines rose from 1% to 10% in these 20 years.) See Robert T. Bower, *Television and the Public*, (New York: Holt, Rinehart & Winston, 1973) and Robert T. Bower, *The Changing Television Audience in America* (New York: Columbia University Press, 1985). The fieldwork for the surveys was also done by the Roper Organization.

half the public had, in fact, heard conflicting reports of the same story from different news sources. Three out of four (73%) had seen daily newspaper coverage of a news event or issue of which they had personal knowledge, and 6 in 10 gave the paper high ratings for both fairness and accuracy on those stories. Only about half had seen television news that covered events they personally knew of, and the ratings were equally high. If they had to choose one source for national and international news, 72% named television and 18% named newspapers; 57% picked TV and 33% chose newspapers for state news; and 50% chose television to 36% for newspapers on local news. (Among newspaper readers, newspapers came out ahead.) Even among the newspaper readers interviewed, 44% said they would prefer reading news and information in a newspaper or magazine if they had only one way of getting news and information, while 56% said they would rather get it on television or radio. Still, more people chose newspapers over television when asked which local news medium they would trust the most to help them understand a situation in their local area that was hard to understand or was controversial.

Opinion surveys that compare newspapers with television tap the feelings of strong dependence that most Americans now have toward the medium that is their most common leisure-time diversion. But these positive feelings about television and its news programming are not necessarily parallelled by a preference for television over newspapers in specific instances of news reporting.

The way in which people distinguish among the functions of the different news media is suggested by the answers to questions asked in an early survey (1971b). For "news you are very much interested in," 50% of the public said they were "most likely to find out all there is about it" from newspapers and 46% from TV. For "very complicated" news, 36% would turn to newspapers and 19% to television. And for "news that you yourself are very much interested in but hardly any other people would be interested in," 25% mention newspapers and 11% said television, but 34% said they would go to the library!

When asked in 1987 which they relied on most to keep up with a list of eight different topics, newspapers were named overwhelmingly for news of local events and by a small plurality for fashion and lifestyles, but majorities (in some cases by only a narrow margin) favored television on the other points.

When people were asked about the most important problem facing the country and then about their main information sources on that problem, newspapers were named as the one most relied-upon source by 49% of newspaper readers; 28% named TV (1979e).

The 1987 Gallup study found that for information on national affairs, 56% of the public rely most on television; 28% on daily newspapers; and 9%

on radio.[24] Those who rely on newspapers were better educated, more involved in politics, more likely to vote, and less likely to hold highly intolerant views or to be highly religious or politically alienated. Since preference for newspapers was so closely linked to education, it was also related to partisan orientation, with more Republicans relying on newspapers and more Democrats leaning toward television.

General media preferences are revealing, especially when tracked through time, but we can get a better sense of the public's perceptions the closer we come to specific cases. In our 1966 study, short, one-sentence summaries were prepared of 120 stories, taken in equal numbers from television, newspapers, magazines, and radio.[25] For each summary statement, the public was asked what was "the best way" to find out about it. Newspapers were considered the best way to find out for 59% of the statements studied; television, 29%; magazines, 8%; and radio, 4%. To look at it in another way, for the average item, newspapers were named as "the best way" by 37%, TV by 26%, radio by 14%, and magazines by 7%. Newspapers' preeminence derives from the great breadth and variety of material they cover. On the handful of top interest stories, television was ahead.

On no subject was there complete consensus that a certain medium was "the best way to find out." As I note in Chapter 9, there are no items that get universal agreement as to their interest or lack of interest. The highest choice for newspapers was 64% on an item about a local zoning board. The highest for TV was 54% on an item about bombings in Vietnam.

When we look beyond the average interest scores for different subjects and examine the individual items under each of these headings, it is apparent that there are great variations from one specific story to the next. Here are some

---

[24]The Gallup Organization, *The People, Press, and Politics,* Times-Mirror, *1987.*

[25]In this study, interviewers around the United States followed a predesignated random plan, surveying not only ads and commercials (which were analyzed separately), but also the editorial and programming content of particular publications and broadcasting stations, exclusive of entertainment. They culled a thousand messages in the form of one-sentence distillations of what originally had been rather complex communications, colored in texture and style by the characteristics of the medium in which they originally appeared.

Reducing an article or announcement from its printed or spoken form to a sentence on a 3" × 5" file card obviously did violence to the full flavor of the original presentation. Yet, the intention was precisely to reduce all the statements to a point at which the message might just as easily fit into one medium as into another. Layman's language was used rather than the language of editors or program producers to see what filtered through at the end of the line to the typical reader, listener, or viewer.

In the field survey itself, 120 news and information messages were used along with an equal number of advertisements and commercials, similarly digested. These 240 items were picked from the thousand to yield equal numbers of editorial and advertising items from each medium, and at the same time to cover the full array of subject matter. There was no way for respondents to identify the original source. In each interview, a person was asked about 12 randomly selected items of general information and 12 advertising messages.

examples: Under the heading of foreign politics, newspapers were named as the best way to find out about the following items: "the leader of the German government is having political difficulties"; "a charge has been made that the U.S. is shipping large quantities of liquor to troops in Vietnam"; "many of China's top scientists and engineers hold degrees from American universities."

Television came up strong on these messages: "tension is rising in Red China because of the activities of the Red Guard"; "the Defense Department reported the shooting down of two more jets in North Vietnam"; "U.S. military leaders in Vietnam believe that intensive bombings may have stopped a major enemy attack"; "Russia casts its 104th veto in the United Nations."

On domestic news, newspapers won out for such items as "a nationally known politician has been sentenced and fined for contempt of court," and "an aging state senator has been reported to be critically ill." But curiously, a somewhat similar but bigger story, "a world leader is going to have a series of operations," was linked with TV more often than with newspapers (no doubt, because the public associates this kind of personality story with video illustration).

Television came up big on stories of fire, snowstorms, tornadoes, and explosions—all vivid in pictorial form. "The Secretary of Defense will confer with the President at his ranch home" immediately suggests the film clip of a man entering a long black limousine. But the message "a bandit gets a 20-year sentence for a $2,000 robbery of a finance company" is associated with newspapers, because it requires explanation.

Television scored well on foreign and national politics, disasters, space, and science. The stories on which television ranked high were not merely those with a highly charged emotional content. On the high-interest item, "the weather tomorrow will be clear and cool," 53% regarded TV the best way to find out; 29%, radio; and only 13%, newspapers. Obviously, radio represents the most accessible way of getting up-to-the minute weather information. Why should television represent the best way to find out about the weather? It must be the personality of the weathercasters who make this mundane subject come to life.

Radio made a strong showing on the local bulletins that require a minimum of elaboration—"an auto accident at a nearby grade school," "a two-hour delay in highway traffic as a result of a restaurant fire," "students given a holiday because of a threatening phone call." These are simple stories in which the headlines essentially tell all—except to the reader or listener who is personally involved.

Newspapers were most often named as the best way to find out about subjects farther down the scale of general interest—community affairs, local personalities, and crime. Newspapers showed strongly on such items as plans to install traffic signals at a major intersection, the development of a new vaccine, the reduction of rates by a local utility, "a local girl will spend a year in Vietnam," a story that "a local youth was the lone survivor of a North Korean ambush." All of these are stories that require background and interpretation of the kind that the public instinctively expects from the newspaper.

Of the top-scoring 10 stories measured in the study, four dealt with the Vietnam war. The preference for television on big war news is not just a matter of newsreel imagery. For example, a high-rated item was "the Defense Department reported the shooting down of two more jets over North Vietnam." One hardly expects to see the events described on the TV screen, but one does expect perhaps to hear them in the context of film clips that convey the real and bitter flavor of the war itself.

Does TV's more cosmopolitan news emphasis make it the particular choice of people who have a less parochial outlook? Apparently not. The people who described themselves as more interested in national and international news showed no different balance of preference for newspapers over television or radio than those who were more interested in local news.

Even if newspapers are primarily identified with local news in the public mind, this should hardly challenge their capacity to deal effectively with important subjects. Consciously or unconsciously, newspaper editors may recognize that the public turns to television for the stories of war, politics, and disaster and to the newspapers for the human interest stories, the background items, and the details on events of local or specialized interest. The findings of the 1966 study may reflect the fact that by that time many editors *already* pursued a policy of concentrating on local happenings, playing down national and world news items of greater reader interest and disassociating the big news from the newspaper.

THE EVENING NEWS AND THE EVENING NEWSPAPER

If people who actively seek news get it from both newspapers and television, it is reasonable to conclude that the habit of television news viewing cannot be blamed for the attrition of readership levels during the 1970s. Still, a study conducted in 1974 for the Associated Press Managing Editors found that two-thirds of the editors of metropolitan evening papers considered TV news to be a strong competitor.[26] And certainly conventional wisdom assigns to television at least some of the responsibility for the problems of afternoon dailies.

In spite of the plausible theory that holds TV responsible for evening

---

[26]*Editor & Publisher*, December 14, 1974.

newspaper losses, TV news ratings were actually 9% higher in competitive markets where evening papers gained circulation between 1960 and 1973 than where they failed to gain or actually disappeared. In the noncompetitive markets, the reverse is true; ratings were 11% lower where evening papers were gaining. This is probably to be explained by differences in the character of the markets in each case.

Since the competitive newspaper markets were bigger, they also had more TV news competition, which means that the network newscasts had a somewhat smaller share of viewing compared to the local news programs. The overall size of the TV news audience was identical in markets where newspaper ownerships competed and in those where they did not.

The network newscasts had identical ratings where evening papers had been gaining and where they had been losing. And in the large competitive markets where the evening papers had their biggest problems, local TV news audiences were actually smaller in those places where circulation had been going down than in those where it had been rising. (Incidentally, TV news ratings were not significantly different in markets where *morning* papers had gained circulation and where they had lost.)

A second analysis of similar data confirms that both for local and network news programs, ratings were actually higher in markets where afternoon papers had their best circulation gains between 1970 and 1976 than where circulation dropped most. In 92 markets where ratings of the network evening newscasts were analyzed, metropolitan afternoon newspaper circulation declined least where news viewing showed the greatest increase and dropped most where the news ratings also showed a loss.

Unquestionably, television has changed the public's experience of the news and its personalities. But to summarize, local variations in the amount of TV news viewing do not meaningfully explain circulation losses for specific papers, evening *or* morning. The problems of big-city afternoon papers cannot be blamed on TV competition.

TV IN THE 1978 NEW YORK NEWSPAPER STRIKE

There is yet one other piece of evidence to cite. When for some reason newspapers are unavailable, it can only be expected that people would turn to broadcast news to fill the information gap. Certainly, broadcast newspeople in New York City accepted this as a responsibility in public statements made during the 1978 newspaper strike. To what extent did the public turn to TV newscasts as a substitute for three major metropolitan newspapers that normally serve millons of readers each day?

Before answering this question, it must be mentioned that during the 13 weeks of the strike, New York was not totally without daily papers. A variety

TABLE 7.3
Percentage Change in Total Evening News Viewing on Three Network-Owned
New York TV Stations, 1978 vs. 1977

	Network news 7:00–7:30 p.m.	Early local news 6:00–7:00 p.m.	Late local news 11:00–11:30 p.m.
Prestrike	−11%	−9%	−10%
Three papers out	−14	−8	−9
Times, News out	−12	−8	−3
Poststrike	−12	−4	+9

of substitutes sprang up, and among them they reached an aggregate claimed circulation of about one million. This compares with the March 31 Audit Bureau total of 3,325,000 for the *Daily News*, *The New York Times*, and the afternoon *New York Post*. Papers based in other parts of the New York area continued to publish, though most of them kept their print run at prestrike levels. Before the strike, the three metropolitan dailies accounted for 60% of total weekday circulation int he Consolidated New York Statistical Area. That area, incidentally, includes 91% of the households in the market as the television industry defines it for purposes of audience measurement, the Designated Market Area for the New York stations. What all this means is that any effects of the newspaper strike would not be apparent in the TV news-viewing patterns of a substantial minority of the homes in the area. However, since those effects would be felt by a majority, they should be traceable, though much less dramatically than if *all* newspapers in the metropolitan region had ceased publication.

Table 7.3 shows changes in television household viewing levels in the New York TV market as measured by A. C. Nielsen's local Metered Market service. It compares the differences between 1978 and 1977 audiences on the three network-owned stations that then accounted for about 82% of the total evening news viewing in New York during the prestrike, strike, and post-strike weeks.[27]

Audiences for both the network and local news were lower than during the previous year in the period that all three papers were out, to approximately the same degree that was true for the prestrike period. After the *New York Post* resumed publication, the network and early evening local newscasts

---

[27]For reasons extraneous to the newspaper strike, news-viewing levels in the prestrike period were lower than they had been in the identical weeks of the preceding year. (This variation may have been due to differences in the weather, in the overall mix of programming and activity on independent stations, the timing of major sports telecasts, etc.) In any case, the appropriate benchmark against which to assess what happened during the weeks of the strike is to compare them with the comparable weeks in 1977, rather than just with the preceding time period. (Viewing levels, especially in the early evening, are affected by the varying length of daylight, as well as by summer vacation schedules.)

still had fewer viewers than in 1977, and the late evening local newscasts moved closer to the previous year's levels. In the three weeks after *The New York Times* and the *Daily News* came back, network news viewing was still at the same level, lower than in 1977, although the early evening news had edged up, and the late evening news was actually higher than in the equivalent weeks of the preceding year.

At the very least, one must conclude that in the absence of the major newspapers, the public did *not* turn in massive numbers to TV news as a substitute. It could be inferred, to the contrary, that the unavailability of the newspapers may have desensitized normal interests, especially in local news. When first the *New York Post* and then the other papers resumed publication, some people may have been reminded of local news subjects. Somewhat more of them came back to the local TV news after the metropolitan dailies were back and began once again to stimulate their interest.

The changes in television news viewing that occur in the absence of regular newspapers are a reminder that the consumption of information responds to what is available as well as to what is needed. I have emphasized in this chapter the quantum effects that television has had on the definition of news, as this is perceived both by journalists and by the general public. But I have also tried to suggest that even in the absence of television (if one could imagine such a thing), the meaning of news is continually being reassessed by the professionals who collect, sift, and disseminate it. What editors consider newsworthy is what they print, and as we have just seen, the indications are that when people see things printed, they assume that they are worth knowing about.

8
NEWSPAPER EDITORS AND THEIR READERS

In the August 3, 1752 issue of the *New York Gazette*, the editor, James Parker, "earnestly entreats all those who are angry at him for printing things they don't like, calmly to consider the following particulars:"

> Being continually employed in serving all Parties, Printers naturally acquire a vast Unconcernedness as to right or wrong Opinions contain'd in what they print . . . If they sometimes print vicious or Silly Things, not worth reading, it may not be, because they approve of such Things themselves, but because people are so viciously and corruptly educated, that good things are not encouraged. Thus I have known a large Edition of the story of an old Woman drowned at Ratcliff Highway sell here to good profit, whilst a Piece recommending Piety and Religion never sold at all.

Today's newspaper editor still faces the same dilemma. On the one hand he is a moral agent, voicing the aspirations of his society, turning his lantern into its dark corners. But he is also an artisan, out to earn an innocuous dollar, and often finding that he can best do so by satisfying the public's meanest appetites. His peculiar art is to balance these two requirements: to say what he wants to say and to sell it "to good profit" as well. In arriving at this compromise, the editor is continually testing the limits of the reader's attention to what *he* knows to be important.

It is the moral underpinning, the ideals of editorial integrity, that distinguish journalism from mere printing. But mass media are profitable, which is to say they survive, when they give advertisers what they want, and as we saw in Chapter 2, advertisers want saturation coverage of their markets, however *they* define them.

THE EDITORIAL DILEMMA

How do editors reconcile their professional mission with the need to attract the largest possible audiences they can? Critics of the press are fond of suggesting that advice to the lovelorn and Hollywood gossip be replaced by more book reviews and art columns. This type of criticism and the rebuttal to it are not unique to the press at all but have their counterparts in the criticism of all mass media. Take an editor who cuts out a background story on the political lineup in Ecuador and substitutes a feature article about a cat caught in a drainpipe. His problem is no different than that of the TV executive who must choose between a Western and a program on the modern dance for a prime spot in the evening. In either case, the personal taste of the decision maker is set aside in favor of professional judgment. James Gordon Bennett, the editor-publisher of the *New York Herald*, was once asked if he preferred it as a newspaper. He replied, "I do not but the public do — I make a newspaper for the public, not for myself."[1]

The quarrel of the critics is really with the criterion that the public must be pleased. And since the editor or producer shapes or confirms popular taste at the same time as he follows it, he is always uncomfortably uncertain as to whether he is hatching a chicken or laying an egg.

A specialized medium can win a huge audience and resounding success from a national constituency that still represents only a sliver of the mass public. Newspapers, operating within a restricted geographical area, cannot survive (as they did in the 19th century) by limiting their appeal to a narrow segment.

Editors' efforts to uplift their readers' tastes can sometimes be frustrating. Charles Reich's "The Greening of America" was serialized in seven install-ments by the *Louisville Times* in 1971 after 10 days of heavy promotion that included five full-page ads. Only 14% of the readers of the paper reported afterwards that they had read any of the installments, and only 1% said they had read them all. The others said they "hadn't seen" them or were too busy; only 11% said they were not interested.

There are alternate ways of interpreting this. The same book was origi-nally serialized in the *New Yorker*, whose average issue readership represents about 1% of the adult population, not all of whom read every article. So the newspaper's publication of this book brought it before vastly greater numbers of readers, at least in Louisville. It was an unfamiliar addition to a familiar (and anticipated) assortment of content. When Elvis Presley died, the Louis-ville editors rushed to press with a special memorial picture section that sold

---

[1]Carl Sandburg, *Abraham Lincoln: The War Years*. Vol. 2 (New York: Harcourt Brace, 1939), p. 585.

out rapidly and was reprinted on a large scale. Was Reich a failure and Presley a success?

As expressed in James Parker's lament, editors have always sought to meet, and even to anticipate, readers' changing expectations. At the same time, it is in the nature of their calling to seek to mold readers' values. In producing a daily newspaper, these sometimes contradictory goals can be approached not in terms of any grand design, but rather as the outcome of innumerable specific decisions on how to handle individual items of content. A typical metropolitan newspaper receives and processes each day about 10 times as many words as it eventually prints. This means that the assignment of stories, as well as the selection, reduction, synthesis, placement, and assemblage of stories, take place at great speed on the basis of assumptions, intuitions, and experiences that are virtually impossible to articulate or formalize into a theoretical framework.

A catch phrase among editors in the late 1970s was, "Give the readers what they want." What they want, presumably, is what they report to interviewers in surveys designed to elicit their opinions on the various elements of the newspaper and on anything else that might be relevant (such as the interests now satisfied by other media). In Chapter 9, I examine the evidence that such surveys yield. But the fact that people say they read or want to read certain kinds of material does not, or should not, mean that editors will automatically give it to them.

As the British Broadcasting Corporation's Robert Silvey has argued most persuasively, "giving the public what it wants" is a meaningless phrase which, if replaced by what it comes to mean in practice, namely, "giving the majority of the public what they seem most disposed to consume," does not *sound* so attractive and is not likely to be preferred to "giving various segments of the public what they most need."[2]

Since the perception of readers' attitudes represents one horn of the dilemma, we should first consider how editors define their own professional objectives and how they reconcile these with the mundane requirements of the business they are in. We can next consider how their perception accords with what we have learned from the standpoint of the readers themselves.

WHAT EDITORS WANT; WHAT EDITORS DO

Information on this subject comes from our survey of working editors (1977a).[3] Staff-written copy fills a higher proportion of the content of larger

---

[2]R. J. E. Silvey, "Giving the Public What It Wants," *Contemporary Review*, May, 1961.

[3]A total of 746 questionnaires were returned in this mail survey, representing 56% of about 1,300 sent to actively employed members of the American Society of Newspaper Editors and the Associated Press Managing Editors (after screening for dual membership). Fifty-six percent of the

TABLE 8.1
Percentage Staff-Written Copy, by Circulation Size, 1977a

	Actual	Ideal
100,000+	58	61
50,000–100,000	52	57
25,000–50,000	46	53
Under 25,000	49	57

TABLE 8.2
Percentage Features, by Circulation Size, 1977a

	Actual	Ideal
100,000+	33	34
50,000–100,000	29	32
25,000–50,000	27	30
Under 25,000	23	28

newspapers that can draw on greater resources. In fact, the big-city editors don't show much of a gap, on the average, between the percentage of staff-written copy they actually run and the proportion they would ideally like (about three-fifths of the total). The small-town editors are somewhat inclined to sense that they fall short of their own ideal and to take the big-city paper as their model in this respect (Table 8.1).

There are similar differences between editors of large and small papers when we consider the proportion of editorial content devoted to feature material, however each editor individually defines that. Editors of big papers carry a higher percentage of feature material than those on small papers, and they generally feel they are at the ideal ratio right now. Editors of smaller papers would like to run somewhat more feature material than they do (Table 8.2).

Will newspapers increase their circulation mainly by changing their

---

returns were from editors and executive editors and 37% were from managing editors; the remainder were associate editors or held other titles. This represents a good cross-section of the two editorial organizations. There were about the same proportions of bigger papers (over 50,000 circulation) represented by those who answered (42%) and those who did not (43%), suggesting that the replies came from all sectors of the two organizations. The memberships of ASNE and APME overrepresent the larger papers. Seven percent of all the dailies, with 49% of *all* circulation, are over 100,000. But 24% of the replies came from these big-city editors. At the other extreme, the small papers of less than 25,000 represent 70% of the newspapers, 21% of the circulation, and 32% of the replies. The editors of the larger papers were split evenly between morning and afternoon publications, while, corresponding to the realities, most of the smaller papers represented come out in the afternoon.

TABLE 8.3
How Editors Think Newspapers Will Increase Circulation, 1977a

	Circulation up	Circulation down
Mainly by changing content	40%	24%
Mainly by improving the way they promote, sell, and deliver	39	57
Both	21	19
	100%	100%
N	(458)	(81)

content or by improving the way that they promote, sell, and deliver? The answers editors give depend very much on how well their own papers are doing. Editors of papers whose circulation went up in 1976 split evenly between those who think the solution is primarily editorial and those who say it is primarily a matter of distribution. However, those editors whose papers lost circulation in 1976 vote overwhelmingly to put the onus on the circulation department (Table 8.3).

A request for specific suggestions turned up rather *unspecific* responses (Table 8.4). The big-city editors offered the fewest proposals on content (perhaps simply because they were most impatient with the questioning procedure). The thought mentioned most often is to "tailor" the content to reader interest, a marketing strategy but not a concrete solution. Next (a low second) come references to writing or editorial quality. These turned out to be of comparatively greater concern to editors of smaller papers. It is worth noting that only a small proportion of editors regard changes in the appearance of their papers as a way to improve their reader appeal.

Are newspapers that do an outstanding professional editorial job also likely to be the most successful in building circulation? The editors' answers apparently depend in part on how well they are doing themselves. Of those whose papers gained circulation in 1976, 70% agree that "good papers are successful in building circulation," while 26% think "there is no clear rela-

TABLE 8.4
How to Increase Circulation: Content, 1977a

	Over 100,000	50,000– 100,000	Under 50,000
Tailor content to reader interests	34%	55%	43%
Improve writing, editorial quality	15	18	25
Local information	13	11	16
Color, graphics, layout	5	11	14
Personalize, human interest	8	13	10
Entertain, less depressing news	11	9	8

TABLE 8.5
How Editors Rank Attributes of Editorial Quality, 1977a

All editors	Over 250,000	Under 25,000
1. Accuracy	1	1
2. Impartiality in reporting	2	2
3. Investigative enterprise	3	3
4. Specialized staff skills	4	5
5. Individuality of character	5	7
6. Civic-mindedness	7	4
7. Literary style	6	6

tionship between quality and success," and 2% agree that "papers that I admire professionally are actually least successful." Among those whose circulation went down, only 56% agree that "good papers are successful," and 42% see "no clear relationship."

DEFINING "QUALITY"

If editorial quality leads to circulation success, as a majority of editors think, the definition of quality is of more than passing importance. A 1987 study of 525 editors of smaller newspapers by Jeanne Abbott found that they considered the best papers to be those that informed readers thoroughly about local issues, had a high ratio of staff-produced copy, covered a majority of local events, reported honestly, and used photos and graphics effectively.

The editors in our 1977 study were asked to rank seven attributes that might be associated with quality. The top three were ranked in the sequence shown in Table 8.5. Editors on all kinds of papers, big and small, competitive and noncompetitive, agreed on the first three: accuracy,[4] impartiality in reporting, and investigative enterprise.

The next four attributes of editorial quality were rated somewhat differently by editors on papers of different sizes. Among the editors of the biggest dailies with circulations of over a quarter of a million, fourth place is given to specialized staff skills, fifth is individuality of character, and sixth is literary style. Civic-mindedness is last on the list, perhaps because metropolitan editors might assume it to be a necessary by-product of accuracy and investigativeness.

---

[4]Accuracy may appear to be a self-evident value, but it is not all that easily achieved. Fred C. Berry, Jr. questioned 371 people mentioned in 270 local news stories reported in two California newspapers. By their reports, 20% of the articles had names misspelled and 45% contained errors. "A Study of Accuracy in Local News Stories of Three Dailies," *Journalism Quarterly*, Vol. 44, No. 3, Autumn 1967, pp. 482–490.

Editors of the smallest papers give these four attributes quite a different ranking. Civic-mindedness is number four, then specialized staff skills and literary style. Individuality of character is less important to a small daily that reflects its whole community than to a big competitive paper that has to make its own special mark.

All these attributes, like motherhood and the flag, are beyond discussion.[5] Editors commonly use subjective criteria like these when they look at their own papers or at others. But although such values are important in judging editorial awards, they cannot very well be used on a large scale to relate editorial excellence to trends in circulation, advertising, profitability, or other worldly criteria of success. To establish such relationships requires yardsticks that can be readily determined or actually measured.

The editors were given 23 such attributes to rate on a scale of $+3$ to -3. These 23 criteria were by no means an exhaustive list, and a number of editors suggested additional ones. Their suggestions did not fall into any pattern that indicated that something critical had been left out of the original selection. The other points they raised include: the proportion of editorials on local subjects, the ratio of "people" stories to total content, the presence of a "people" column, a detailed weather report, a front page photo, a local editorial cartoon, a "where-to-go" calendar, texts of statements and speeches.

One thoughtful critique was written on the back of a questionnaire:

> If I were judging a paper from the outside, I'd look first at the obvious: looks, typos, general pattern of seeming to cover the kinds of things all good newspapers cover. Once past that hurdle, I'd look for writing style, variety, well-told [local] stories . . . and selection variety, judgment and editing of wire and syndicate stuff. And finally—and perhaps most important of all—I'd look for something in that newspaper every day that would, could, and should be a topic of conversation over the back fence or on the commuter train for every possible group of readers of the paper.

COMPARING QUALITY AND READER INTEREST

These may well be the kinds of criteria that editors instinctively use as they look at other papers. But they simply do not lend themselves to any systematic effort to differentiate newspapers in the aggregate.

---

[5]A modified version of these attributes was taken to a cross-section of working journalists questioned by Judee Burgoon, Michael Burgoon, and Charles Atkin in a 1982 study commissioned by ASNE. These included 489 in eight cities who filled out questionnaires and another 187 who were personally interviewed. In ranking the attributes of quality in a news story, accuracy again came first, then depth, impartiality, investigative enterprise, literary style, and sophistication of treatment. (Judee K. Burgoon, Michael Burgoon and Charles Atkin, *The World of the Working Journalist*, New York: Newspaper Readership Project, 1982.)

As shown in the first column of Table 8.6, here are the attributes of quality that editors put at the top of the list, when their ratings are averaged and ranked:

1. First, a high ratio of staff-written copy to wire service and feature service copy.

2. Second, the total amount of nonadvertising or editorial content in the paper. This, like the preceding indicator, reflects a paper's circulation size, so in effect editors seem to feel that bigger papers are likely to be better.

TABLE 8.6
Editors' Ratings of Editorial Quality and Reader Interest, 1977a
(In aggregate rank order)

	Editorial quality	Reader interest
High ratio of staff-written copy to wire service and feature service copy	1	7
Total amount of nonadvertising content	2	11
High ratio of news interpretations and backgrounders to spot news reports	3	12
Number of letters to the editor per issue	4	3.5
Diversity of political columnists	5	13
High "readability" on Flesch or similar scoring systems	6	8
High ratio of illustrations to text	7	5
High ratio of nonadvertising content to advertising	8	14
High ratio of news to features	9	15
Number of staff-by-lined features	10	17
High ratio of sports news and features to total news content	11	2
Presence of a news summary	12	3.5
Presence of an "action line" column	13	1
Number of editorials per issue	14	20
Number of wire services carried	15	21
High ratio of cultural news, reviews, and features to total news content	16	16
High ratio of homemaking news features to total news content (not "best food day")	17	10
High ratio of business news and features to total news content	18	18
Number of political columnists	19	19
Number of comic strips	20	6
Length (opposed to brevity) of average front-page news story (including jump)	21	22
Presence of an astrology column	22	9
High ratio of state, national, and world news to local news	23	23

3. Third is a high ratio of news interpretation and backgrounders to spot news reports.

4. Fourth is the number of letters to the editor.

5. Fifth, the *diversity* of political columnists. This is worth noting, because the *number* of political columnists is rated as having virtually no relation to quality at all.

6. Sixth is a high "readability" score on a Flesch or similar test of reading ease.

7. Seventh is a high ratio of illustrations to text.

8. Eighth is a high *ratio* of news, or nonadvertising, content to advertising. Paradoxically, this contradicts the high value placed on the absolute size of the news hole, which generally goes up as the amount of advertising goes up, but not in exact proportion.

9. Ninth is the number of staff-by-lined features.

As already noted, most editors feel that editorial excellence is rewarded by success in circulation. Does that mean that the traits that make a newspaper good are also considered to make it popular? The answer is given in the second column of Table 8.6, which shows the rank order of editors' ratings of the same 23 items from the standpoint of reader interest. (The actual rating scores, which range from positive to negative, are not shown in this table).

The three attributes that are ranked most highly on success with readers are *not* high on the list of attributes of quality. First is the presence of an action-line column; next, a high ratio of sports news and features to total news content, and third, the presence of a news summary. However, the next four attributes rated high for reader interest also come up strongly rated on editorial quality: the number of letters to the editor, a high ratio of illustrations to text, a high ratio of staff-written copy, and a high "readability" score.

Consider the attributes that are rated much higher on reader interest than on editorial quality. The biggest gap between the two ratings is for the number of comic strips. An astrology column gets a slight negative on quality without being much of a plus for reader interest. The interest ascribed to an action line and to a large sports section has already been noted. Their quality scores are positive, but there is still quite a gap between these and the assumed interest levels. Also rated higher on interest than on quality are the presence of a news summary and a high ratio of homemaking news and features to total news content.

On the opposite side of the equation, there are a number of points that editors rate higher for themselves than for the reader. The number of wire services carried is considered moderately indicative of editorial quality but of absolutely no interest to the reader.

Readers were also assumed to be indifferent to a number of attributes that editors link to quality: a high proportion of staff-written copy, a high proportion of news interpretation, a diversity of political columnists, the total amount of editorial (nonadvertising) content, a high ratio of news to features, and the number of editorials per issue.

One attribute turned out to be unrelated either to quality or to reader interest, and that was the length (as opposed to brevity) of the average front-page news story (including the jump). This suggests that there is a standoff in the continuing debate over whether newspapers overwhelm or underwhelm readers with the number of stories they array before them and the number they cover in depth.

Another way of examining the same data is suggested by Table 8.7, which compares the ratings that *individual* editors give to each of the 23 attributes, for quality and reader interest. A substantial proportion, ranging from 27% to 58%, rated the items identically by both yardsticks. Those attributes that are generally considered to be much higher in reader interest than as indicators of quality tend to be entertaining rather than informational in character.

In filling out the questionnaire, one editor wrote in a comment that he would answer it differently if he were running a bigger paper. But in fact, it turns out that there is virtually total agreement between editors of small and big papers on the comparative ratios of quality to reader interest scores for all of the attributes.

In both big and small towns, there was fairly high agreement among editors of both competitive and noncompetitive papers. This was also true for the rankings of the seven subjective attributes: accuracy, impartiality, and the like. That does not mean that the actual scores are always identical. For example, the presence of a news summary is rated higher on quality by editors of smaller papers but higher on interest by editors of larger ones. The same is true on the number of letters to the editor, on the readability score, and on the number of comic strips. But such differences in judgment appear minor relative to the substantial differences in the conditions under which small-town and metropolitan editors operate.

EDITORIAL CONSENSUS

This examination of editors' opinions suggests a number of conclusions:

1. Editing appears to be a profession whose members really have common values. There is a surprising degree of consensus as to what makes a newspaper good and what makes it attractive. For executive editors and managing editors, on big papers and on small ones, the variety of

TABLE 8.7
Individual Editors' Ratings on Editorial Quality and Reader Interest, 1977a

Ratings on editorial quality higher	Higher rating on editorial quality %	Higher rating on reader interest %	Same rating on both %
Number of wire services carried	58	9	33
High ratio of staff-written copy to wire service and feature service copy	52	6	42
High ratio of news interpretation and backgrounders to spot news reports	49	11	42
Diversity of political columnists	47	10	43
Total amount of nonadvertising content	47	11	42
Number of staff-by-lined features	46	9	45
High ratio of news to features	45	16	39
High ratio of nonadvertising content to advertising	40	20	40
Length (as opposed to brevity) of average front page news story	40	22	38
Number of editorials per issue	38	10	52
High ratio of business news and features to total news content	33	15	52
High ratio of cultural news, reviews, and features to total news content	32	20	48
High ratio of state, national, and world news to local news	30	27	43
High "readability" on Flesch or similar scoring systems	28	19	53
Number of political columnists	26	16	58
Ratings on reader interest higher			
Number of comic strips	2	70	28
Presence of an astrology column	3	70	27
Presence of an "action line" column	3	60	37
High ratio of sports news and features to total news content	8	49	43
Presence of news summary	10	45	45
High ratio of homemaking news and features to total news content	11	45	44
High ratio of illustrations to text	15	35	50
Number of letters to the editor per issue	20	28	52

opinion *within* each group is greater than the differences *between* groups.

2. Editors define quality in a newspaper, above all, as dedication to the truth: accuracy and fairness in reporting.

3. Editors of small papers have to run them differently, but they would run them like big ones if they could.

4. Editors seem to have a high degree of confidence in their readers. What they think is good in a newspaper is in most cases not too wildly different from what they think readers like. They must sugarcoat each day's bitter pill of news, but they do not seem torn by any great inner conflict about the need to do this. When they rate quality, there are few strong negative votes, even for features like comics and astrology columns that they consider to be moderately interesting to readers. What is surprising is that such established utilitarian features as business, culture, and homemaking do not rate strongly either on quality *or* reader interest.

5. Editors think that an attractive paper also creates reader interest. They associate reader interest with participation (through letters and an actionline). They connect it to a strong sports section and to the kind of packaging that a news summary typifies. Amazingly, they don't consider the total size of the news hole to be of any interest to readers one way or the other.

An important objective of this study was to find out whether editors whose papers were losing circulation were using different standards of editorial judgment than the majority whose circulations had been going up. In fact, there is very little difference both on quality and on interest scores.

TABLE 8.8
Characteristics of Newspapers Gaining and Losing Circulation,
as Reported by Editors, 1977a

Size category	Average news hole	Staff-written copy	Features
Over 100,000			
Circulation up	36%	58%	33%
Circulation down	39	56	32
50,000–100,000			
Circulation up	42	50	30
Circulation down	42	57	27
Under 50,000			
Circulation up	46	48	25
Circulation down	46	45	25

That does not mean that there are not important but subtle differences in the *style* of these two groups of papers, differences that sensitive editorial antennae might detect. But these differences are not of the kind that can be pointed out as guidelines to fame and fortune.

Moreover, the actual editorial practices of the papers that are failing to gain circulation are in three important respects objectively identical with those of their more successful contemporaries in the same circulation-size bracket. (The proportion who report gains is 67% among papers of over 100,000 and 77% for those of under 25,000.) Table 8.8 shows that within each circulation-size group, gainers and losers are almost identical in the size of their news hole relative to advertising, the proportion of their editorial matter that is staff-written, and the proportion that is feature material rather than news.

If the editors showing losses are using the same kinds of editorial standards as the rest and are producing rather similar papers on the whole, this provides some confirmation for their feeling that their losses are for the most part due to external conditions, to problems of selling and promotion, and not to matters of content.

9
WHAT DO
READERS READ?

The investigation of reading patterns and interests has become a major preoccupation of newspaper editors precisely as a response to changes in those patterns and interests. Such changes, as we have seen, are widely believed to be reflected in the reduced frequency of reading. So we must address ourselves to a related series of questions: What do people remember in the news? To what degree can they actually remember what they have looked at in the paper? How does their reading reflect their interests? How can their interests be defined? How do their expectations of the newspaper reflect their interests?

WHAT NEWS IS MOST MEMORABLE?

The news represents a vast array of evolving and often interpenetrating stories that unfold simultaneously through a number of different media sources. This must often make it impossible for an individual to know precisely where or when a story first surfaced to his attention.[1] Editors of

---

[1]To illustrate the point that most news items represent developments in continuing stories, a content analysis by Herbert Gans of personalities appearing in network TV news stories in 1967 found that 71% were known people who had already figured in the news; in the national news magazines Gans examined in 1975, the proportion was 85%. Only between 10% and 21% of the

newspapers and of broadcast news programs are constantly trying to create orderly arrangements and priorities out of the chaotic mass of words and pictures they receive. How does the public perception of the news differ from the judgments and intentions of the news professionals?

As I stressed in Chapter 7, the salience of one kind of news at a particular moment diminishes the importance of another kind of news. Moreover, the top stories may be local on one day and national or world news on the next. This is documented by a weekly sampling of people in 10 cities, conducted by the Response Analysis Corporation between October, 1975 and July, 1976. They asked two locally oriented questions: "Can you give me an idea of what things are going on in and around [the city] these days?" and "Are there any things happening in [city] that bother you and that you should like to see something done about?" Mentions of local political topics ranged from 5% to 47% in different weeks, while mentions of national politics (in relation to immediate concerns) ranged from 0 to 33%. When one topic got more mentions, the other got less.

We saw earlier, in Chapter 6, that the day-by-day coverage of one week's news seems to result in a mixed bag of stories reported by the press with, however, rather consistent attention to a handful of major events. At the same time, as we described in Chapter 7, television network news concentrated rather heavily and even more consistently on the big running stories.

However, the variety and character of events will produce at different times a kind of public awareness that is sharply focused or broadly diffused. For example, no single news event was mentioned by more than 5% of the public in 1977 when they were asked, "To the best of your recollection, what was the biggest thing in the news you found out about yesterday or today?" Eighty-three percent gave some answer: 5% mentioned President Carter's speech to the United Nations, and 4%, his visit to Massachusetts, with a grand total of 14% remembering some activity of the President's. But other major stories were mentioned by only a small fraction: 4% referred to the Hanafi Muslims, 3% each to Goldwater and the Spanish hijacking, 2% to Mrs. Gandhi, 1% to the attack in Zaire, and 3% to the plane crash in the Canary Islands, which had occurred a week earlier.

The most striking feature of the response is the public's disproportionate sensitivity to unpleasant stories that actually represent only a small fraction of those that fill the media.

What people consider big news covers a different gamut of content than what either newspapers or television network news programs treat in detail. Table 9.1 compares the kinds of stories the public remembers with the distribution of newspaper content. Crime, accidents, and the weather ac-

---

stories dealt with unknowns whose activities were reported for the first time. Herbert J. Gans, *Deciding What's News: A Study of CBS Evening News, Newsweek & Time* (New York: Pantheon Books, 1979).

TABLE 9.1
News Remembered and News Published, 1977

	"Biggest thing in the news"	News items published
Local and state politics/government	4%	15%
Other local news	12	11
National politics/government	22	12
International	6	8
Crime	26	11
Accidents/fires/disasters	13	4
Sports	6	21
Weather	6	2
All other general content	12	17
	107%[a]	100%
	(100% = all who mention biggest story)	(All news items, excluding feature content)

[a]Some respondents gave more than one answer.

count for a disparately large proportion of comments, while local political news and sports items account for an especially small ratio of comment to coverage. The differences certainly cannot be explained by the impact of network television news, with its very heavy emphasis on overseas stories that account for only 6% of the public's mentions. It would appear that what people perceive as memorable news reflects their idiosyncratic personal interests and needs. This is borne out by the fact that there are only minor variations in the events mentioned by different age, educational, and income groups, and by the fact that frequent newspaper readers do not differ from others.

At the time of our May, 1982, survey, the Falklands war was far and away the biggest running news story, mentioned by 50% of the respondents. A variety of domestic stories were mentioned by 20%, though only 3% of these were local stories other than crime. But 29% could think of no big story in the news "yesterday."

Although a number of major and even dramatic news stories were being widely covered during the October weeks when the 1987 study was under way, the public distributed its selections widely when asked to name one of particular interest that had been in the news within the past few days. The controversy over the nomination of Judge Robert Bork to the Supreme Court was named by 17%. The ordeal of a little girl, Jessica McClure, who fell into a well, was mentioned by the same number (11%) as the growing involvement of American naval vessels in the Persian Gulf war between Iran and Iraq. Ten percent referred to an earthquake and other major disasters; 8% brought up a crime news story; 7%, the continuing slide of the stock market (which culminated in the crash of October 19, at the end of the interviewing period). Six percent referred to the baseball playoffs and the World Series and 5% to the players' strike that had temporarily crippled the National Football League. Only 3% brought up a local news item, apart from a few recorded as crime news.

Curiously enough, considering the public's growing dependence on television news for the stories it considers the big news of the day, the proportion able to mention any outstanding story has shown a steady decrease, from 83% in 1977 to 71% in 1982 and 65% in 1987. This can hardly be ascribed to a decline in the number of major stories, though it may reflect a growing insensitivity to the unpleasant and vivid imagery that fills the tube in reports on problems to which no solution is in sight.

News evokes interest and involvement to the degree that it is emotionally arousing. The evocation of human feelings may be inherent in the dramatic character of an event itself, but it is also dependent on the way its story is depicted. Audience response may be largely due to narrative style, imagery of language or visual montage, the individuation of the participants, the length and prominence of the story. These elements are inseparable from the communications properties of the various media.

But in any medium, the grimmer side of the news is quite memorable. Seven out of 10 people in 1977 could think of some news story that had been personally upsetting to them in the past few months. Of these, 49% were crime stories. In fact, 16% of all the responses referred to the ordeal of the hostages taken by the Hanafi Muslims. Fourteen percent mentioned accidents, fires, or other disasters. So a small proportion of items accounts for a high proportion of the unpleasant feelings aroused by the news. Altogether, 22% had no emotional reaction to the news at all. At least they could think of no story that either made them upset or feel good: 8% could think only of a good news story; 29%, only of a story that upset them. The remaining 42% could think of both kinds of news. Women were more likely to mention something that upset them, and men were more likely to remember news that made them feel good. In another survey (1979e), two-thirds (65%) of the readers mentioned something in the paper that they found unpleasant; 28% referred to crime news.

Critics of the news media have long complained that they overemphasize disaster and that the traditional reporters' beats—police headquarters and the criminal courts—convey a distorted picture of the peaceful and positive aspects of society. It has been suggested that a properly written news lead might begin, "While 4,000 students of Central High School went diligently about their studies today, one of their number assassinated the principal." In the same vein, the columnist Art Buchwald chided TV for showing the on-field violence of a scrappy football game between Ohio State and Purdue "rather than the peaceful scenes on the sidelines."

Herbert A. Otto, research director of the Stone Foundation, has deplored the emphasis on bad news in the media and suggested that it should be balanced with good news. "The widely prevalent concept of what constitutes news is a narrow, destructive concept—a sick concept, destructive to society as a whole. The news format in all our media in in general inimical or opposed to the development of human potential.[2]

In rebuttal, Roger Tatarian, former editor of UPI, insists that "society as a whole often benefits precisely because the media have reported disaster or violence with such insistence and such detail that public opinion has been led to demand and get overdue reforms." He recalls that when Cleopatra denounces the messenger who brought the bad news of Antony's marriage to Octavia, the man replies, "Gracious Madam, I that do bring the news made not the match."

But the "good news" theory has strong adherents. A significant development in television local news has been the "happy talk" program, which features not merely "the brighter side," but gratuitous one-line jokes and sarcastic commentaries.[3] It has frequently been suggested that newspapers, too, should emphasize the cheerful aspects of news.

Only one reader in four acknowledged in 1982 that the newspaper "prints too much bad news"; infrequent readers were only slightly more likely to say so, though other evidence suggests that many of them are turned off by the complexities and unpleasant aspects of news itself.

Stories of crime, violence, and disaster are, of course, not the only unpleasant news that people remember. Items related to national politics and government were next most frequently mentioned (24% of the total in 1977). Characteristically, these represented administrative or Congressional actions of which people disapproved. Stories of local politics and government accounted for only 6% of the mentions. Another 10% dealt with the international arena, and 8% with the cost of living.

Not surprisingly, somewhat more of the people over 65 were unable to think of any items, upsetting or otherwise. Women mentioned crime stories more often than men. Blacks referred to accidents, fires and disasters, and national political events more often than Whites. Better-educated people, with their more sophisticated view of what constitutes bad news, thought more often of foreign and national political items and were less likely to mention crime and accident news.

Although 70% could think of upsetting news, only half the respondents could recall a news item in the last few months that made them feel good.

---

[2]Speech to the Center of American Living, 1968.

[3]In New York City, WABC-TV's "Eyewitness News" became a success with a "good news" format that stressed the bright and light side of the day's events. Thus, when a 12-year-old boy died of a disease that speeded up the normal aging process eight times, the "newsman" joked, "At that rate, he must have been frustrated by the time he was two and a half." (Quoted by Richard Townley in *TV Guide*, June 5, 1971.)

News of national politics and government accounted for 57% of the items mentioned. In fact, news about President Carter accounted for 36%. As with bad news, local stories were a minor category, mentioned by only 5%. By contrast, 12% mentioned improvements in the weather and 13% brought up a human interest story.

The same story carries different meaning to different people. President Carter's election was good news for some people and bad news for others.

And evolving stories may change their emotional color from day to day, as in the course of battle in wartime. Items that make people feel good, like a tax rebate proposal, may actually represent transient responses to a continuing story that eventually turns into bad news. (The tax rebate idea was scrapped.) Similarly, the Hanafi Muslim story, which many people found upsetting, eventually became good news when the hostages were released.

Naturally, the kind of news—good and bad—that people find memorable occurs in different proportions from day to day. This is reflected in the results of any survey taken at a particular point in time, as is the prevailing state of the public's morale.

One might suppose that people who find the news upsetting are more likely to avoid exposure to it. In fact, emotional response to the news has no bearing on frequency of newspaper readership. Frequent newspaper readers and infrequent readers were no different in their ability to recall either good new or bad news.

THE SOURCES OF MEMORABLE NEWS

Where do people *first* find out about the specific news stories that they best remember? For each of the major stories mentioned in 1987, television outranked newspapers as the "main source," although a substantial percentage of people named more than one medium (including radio, magazines, and word of mouth), as Table 9.2 shows. When the respondents were asked to narrow their reply to the one main source, television's lead became even more pronounced. On average, for all the stories mentioned, television was called the main source by 57%, newspapers by 25%. Even among college graduates, newspapers (with 61%) came close behind TV (with 69%) as a main source for the most interesting news stories.

Television is more important for the kinds of people who depend on it most: those with less education, older people, and Blacks. Newspapers are more important for better-educated people and those of higher income. Although newspapers are less well read by young people, mentions of them as the initial source of news do not vary very much by age. However, young people more often cite word of mouth as their first source.

Although there were no startling differences between frequent and infre-

TABLE 9.2
Top News Stories and Main Sources on Each, 1987

	% naming story	Main sources				One main source			
		TV	News-paper	Radio	Word of mouth	TV	News-paper	Radio	Word of mouth
Bork nomination	17%	78%	52%	22%	2%	63%	24%	10%	–
Jessica McClure	11	76	30	37	4	59	17	20	1%
Persian Gulf	11	78	49	23	3	61	25	10	–
Earthquake,disasters	10	75	36	30	21	57	20	13	6
Crime news	8	71	55	16	7	48	37	6	5
Stock market	7	80	54	32	12	56	25	11	3
Baseball playoffs, series	6	79	53	30	9	60	24	13	1
NFL strike	5								

quent readers in their listing of specific news events of particular interest to them, infrequent readers were more likely to mention television as the main source of news on those events. But in every segment of the day, frequent newspaper readers were more likely to have watched news on television than were the infrequent readers. For example, in the preceding evening, 68% of the frequent readers had watched TV news and only 52% of the infrequent readers. So although television gets a greater expression of comparative preference from the less regular readers, it cannot be described as a powerful substitute drawing them away from the press.

People link the media to different kinds of news. Their notions of how they first actually got a news story are colored by their sense of which medium works best or most appropriate for that kind of news.

Consider those who remembered a major disaster—a plane crash, an earthquake. Over half who mentioned this kind of a story in 1977 said they first found out about it on television. TV is often associated with big news stories in the area of foreign affairs and with national, political, and government news, especially those items dealing with the President. It is also associated with news that involves strong visual imagery: accidents, fires, major sports events.

Forty percent who thought the weather was a big story—and it was in the winter of 1977—mentioned radio. Newspapers were named first on complex stories with substantial detail that requires explanation and background. For example, 43% who mentioned inflation referred to the newspaper as their first source. And newspapers came up tops, necessarily, for the news that hit people where they lived: 38% of those who mentioned newspapers mentioned some miscellaneous news item that reflected specialized interests.

Of course, every particular category of news, like crime, covers a multitude of different stories. Consider three that were fresh at the time of the 1977 study. All might be loosely categorized under the heading of crime news, but each involved a very distinctive response. The plane hijacking was a fast-breaking story that did not lend itself to large amounts of detail or to film-clip illustration. Fresh developments were occurring continually, creating an atmosphere of great suspense. Of those who called this story the biggest news, 41% said they found out about it first on the radio. The Hanafi escapade in Washington was associated first with television by 59% of those who considered it the main new story. Television had the ability to provide films taken at the scenes of action, interviews with the released hostages, and, eventually, close-up shots of the kidnappers themselves. The Goldwater allegations involved complex charges that required extensive explanation and background. So, it is logical that 42% said they first learned the story from the newspaper.

Whatever the biggest story was considered to be, 45% of the public got their news of it from another source later in the same day as well as from the first news source mentioned. As an additional source, 39% mentioned newspapers; 30%, TV news; and 16% radio. Better-educated and higher-income people were more likely to mention newspapers as a collateral news source.

As we just saw, the biggest current news story named in our 1982 study (by half the public) was the war in the Falklands. Despite the paucity of TV coverage and the censorship of news on the British side, television gained from the fast-breaking character of the Falklands story and was named as the prime source by 57%. Whatever news story was mentioned, television was named by 51%, newspapers by 27%, as the first news source on that story. The most important problem facing the country, in the eyes of two out of three people in 1982, was the economy. (Only one in eight said it was the danger of nuclear war or disaster.) When it came to the problem they identified as the most important one, television was named as the information source relied on most by 45%; newspapers, by 30%. (Newspapers led TV among college graduates by 42% to 30%.)

It is important to remember that the realities of information flow may be quite different than how the public perceives them. Television today has an edge over newspapers when it comes to specific, high-impact stories, probably because of the sense it gives the audience of seeing for itself the personalities and places in the news. Four out of five people in 1982 agreed that "seeing the news on TV makes it easier to understand what's happening." But, as noted earlier, a clear majority consistently say they do not get enough news from TV and want the added details from newspapers on the big stories. The two news media actually complement one another in people's perceptions and in the way they use them.

WHAT DO READERS READ?

The news stories that people remember are only a fraction of those they have read or heard. For many years, the most common method of determining what people read or don't read in a periodical has been the recognition or noting technique, which uses interviews with people who identify themselves as already having read the particular issue being measured. The interviewer takes the reader back through the publication page by page and, pointing to each article or advertisement, asks whether he looked at or read it during the original reading. This method (which is conducted with minor variations by a number of research firms) has been widely used to assess the performance of advertisements, and it has also been used by editors to evaluate various elements of content. Sometimes the method is embellished by asking how much of the item the reader looked at, differentiating those who "read most" of it from those who merely remembered having noted it.

This technique has the advantage of avoiding the kind of generalized reactions that people give to broad categories of content, like "movie reviews," or "stories about local politicians." Its disadvantages relate to the fragility and selectivity of the memory processes.

Recognition scores are larger when large amounts of space are used for the ad or article in question. The scores vary tremendously for different types of newspaper content, both articles and advertising. However, what people remember seeing represents a highly selective and only partial report on what they have actually seen.

"Recognition" reflects the predispositions that individual readers bring to what they are looking at. Men are more likely to note (or remember seeing previously) content that is addressed to men, and women remember content addressed to women.

This means that the reader approaches the content of a publication much as he might a Rorschach test; he projects his personal interests into what is in front of him. This processing of what is looked at occurs instantaneously. What is registered and perceived is only what is potentially meaningful; the rest is seen by the eye and rejected by the brain; it is simply ignored.

No two readers look at the newspaper in an identical fashion. To illustrate this point interviews were conducted in 1964 on the same issue of the *Newark Evening News* with nine women of similar age and social background in one suburban community. In spite of the homogeneity of the group, their sequence of reading and their attention to different articles and ads assumed highly individual patterns. One woman remembered reading about 20 ads but only 16 articles, while one of her neighbors read 33 ads and 108 articles.

The front page carried 16 stories, a main headline, two large photographs, and one smaller one. Only one story, involving the murder of a local grocer, received the attention of all nine readers. Three readers failed to note the main headline about a revolution in Brazil, and only four read the article that followed. None of them noted a major story on local politics, while six of them read a small item on the weather at the bottom of the page.

Of the seven front-page stories that were each read by at least five of the nine women, five dealt with death or disaster. As one woman remarked, "We all have a morbid curiosity." The only reader of an item headlined "Stock Trend is Irregular" was also the lone widow in the group, who said she was living on her investments.

The same kind of personal selectivity was manifest within the paper itself. One reader who had read a double-page food ad observed that the advertiser was her favorite store. She claimed not to have seen another double-page ad for a different supermarket and explained that "I don't shop there so I didn't look at that ad."

Attention caught by a headline may be arrested as the reader moves into the article: "That 'Mix Match'? I thought from that title it would be about matrimony or matching up a couple, but when I saw it wasn't, I just stopped reading right there."

Similarly, another reader commented: "Well, the word 'recitals' just gets me. My daughter, when she was little, had them every year, and I grew to hate that word. Do you think that's why I didn't see this?"

Other comments further illustrate this selective process: "I never read that column. It just doesn't interest me." "I always read this column [of obituaries] through and through . . . The other week I went to three funerals in three days. If I hadn't read this column I might never have known." "I never bother reading the sports pages." "I'm always interested in Rockefeller, especially since his recent marriage. It's funny how one's eyes are trained to spot things of interest."

In short, newspaper content may be looked at and still not win attention.

In an experiment conducted in Des Moines,[4] five matched samples of subscribers received five different versions of the newspapers. In four of them, blank spaces substituted for ads. The reported opening of two facing pages was at approximately the same level among women readers for a general news and feature page (on the right) and a page of material directed to women (on the left). Among men readers, reported opening of the general news page was at almost the same level (9 out of 10 readers) as for women readers. However, only three men in five reported opening the women's page, although it was physically impossible not to have opened and scanned it in order to see the facing page. In other words, the others had looked at it only long enough to screen it out of awareness. As different elements of the page were left out, the other elements were perceived differently by the readers. Each blank space resulted in a page that was different in its meaning and appeal.

When content of a particular kind is lumped together and is identifiable as a section, this may add to the visibility of its individual components. A 1965 experiment by the Milwaukee *Journal*, using two matched sets of newspapers and readers, found that ads for health-related products and services got higher attention levels when they were grouped together along with health-related editorial matter than when the identical elements were spread out through the paper. However, this kind of grouping may reduce the casual readership of items by people who quickly pass over an entire aggregation of content because they perceive it as uninteresting or irrelevant (young people skipping the obituary page, businessmen discarding the food section).

The lesson of these experiments is that the way a newspaper is made up, the juxtaposition of different elements of content, in some measure governs the kind of attention these elements receive from different kinds of readers. In

---

[4]Leo Bogart & B. Stuart Tolley, "The Impact of Blank Space: An Experiment in Advertising Readership," *Journal of Advertising Research*, Vol. 4, No. 2, June 1964, p. 21ff. There were approximately 1,800 respondents in this study.

this respect, the news and advertising seem to have comparable connotations.

FINDING WHAT'S RELEVANT

In the newspaper reading process, individual items are experienced as part of a visual environment that includes other items, both advertising and editorial. The complexity of this environment is obviously far greater in the case of the newspaper spread, with its substantial space and its heterogeneous content mix, than for other forms of reading matter. We have examined the reading process in a series of studies that focus on advertisements, but with lessons that apply to editorial matter as well.[5]

Response to individual items varies widely, not only with their idiosyncratic substance and style, but also with the degree of congruence between their orientation and the characteristics of the reader. In its simplest form, this point can be demonstrated when readers are separated by sex and advertisements are grouped into those appealing primarily to men or to women.

For example, noting scores for 2,628 weekday newspaper ads run between 1972 and 1979 indicate that ads for products oriented to women are recognized by women at a level 60% higher than by men, while those for male-oriented products score 77% higher among men than among women.

These differences are dramatized when we look at specific kinds of ads. Overall averages of noting scores cannot be compared, because different kinds of newspaper advertisers characteristically use different size units, and the size of the ad has long been known to affect the level of recognition. If we limit the analysis to local ads of comparable half-page size, it is apparent that, both for men and for women, there are wide variations in the average scores for different kinds of advertisers.

Is it reasonable to assume that the creative people designing ads for tire stores are more talented than those making restaurant ads or that those working for apparel stores do a better job than those designing floor-covering ads? No. We correctly interpret these findings to mean that some things that are advertised are inherently more engaging to more people than others and that the creative execution therefore has to work within different limits. Similarly, we can infer that certain types of editorial subject matter hold inherently greater interest for more people than others do. The style with which a particular reporter or writer addresses a subject may be fascinating

---

[5]These studies are discussed at greater length in Leo Bogart & B. Stuart Tolley, "The Search for Information in Newspaper Advertising," *Journal of Advertising Research*, Vol. 28, No. 2, April/May 1988, pp. 9–19.

and ingenious or may be pedestrian and tedious, but there are still limits as to what an unimaginative writer can do to repel readers from an exciting story or what a brilliant writer can do to attract them to a dull one.

It has long been understood that the reader's feelings about the advertised product or brand are reflected in a willingness to recognize an ad, even when it could not previously have been seen. Moreover, the disparity between noting levels and reader reports of page opening indicate that many ads that might well have been seen are quickly forgotten and never recognized.

This limitation led us to seek an alternative procedure for assessing advertising performance. This method was first used in 27 studies of daily newspapers between 1978 and 1981. A second series of 18 studies was conducted between 1984 and 1986.

Just as in the analysis of noting scores, interest in an ad goes hand in hand with propensity to purchase what is advertised. The interest aroused by the average ad is three times higher (74%) among those who were defined as prospects (those who said they were likely to buy what was advertised within the next year) than among nonprospects (23%). (This analysis was based on nearly 90,000 instances in which prospect status and interest could be related for an individual ad and respondent.)

We examined the interest scores for ads in 70 different product or store classifications and found that the variations in interest from category to category were just as great among nonprospects as among prospects. Interest in advertisements seems to be governed in large measure by the inherent appeal of the product, quite apart from the question of whether or not one defines oneself as a prospect. This would seem to reinforce the inference made from our analysis of recognition scores: The substance of what the reader confronts in any particular newspaper item defines the potential within which style and treatment can make a difference. And yet, there were substantial differences in interest scores among ads selling the same thing, just as there might be great differences in response to two different reports of the same news event.

The habitual reader is accustomed to finding certain items in particular locations—the weather map, the help-wanted ads, a favorite columnist or comic strip. Yet the specific content of even these anticipated elements is largely unpredictable, and the content of the remainder, news and advertising, altogether so.

Observation of readers offers a convenient starting point for an understanding of this process. We videotaped four men reading their usual newspapers (which they had not previously looked at that day) and immediately afterward interviewed them about what they had read and why. They read their papers in a manner long verified from large-scale surveys: They either checked out the first page or first turned to certain pages within the paper. They leafed through the sections to look at each section's first page.

They glanced at the summary of the news on the second page. They started through the sections, reading as they went, skipping some pages, pausing on others. They followed stories that jumped to pages further back in a section or in another section. They leafed back to the beginning of a section or of the paper. On occasion, they spent several minutes or even longer reading an article, then glanced at the ads on the page. Sometimes they checked back through a section, leafing quickly, sometimes re-reading parts of the articles they had looked at before. When they were finished, they put down either the section or the entire paper.

What was apparent in each case was the concentration devoted to reading. As each respondent finished, he easily described the articles he looked at, the ads, the steps he went through, and why he used that particular pattern of going through the paper. Only rarely was there any need to go back to the videotape to ask about a particular sequence. All four readers remembered quite vividly what they read and in what sequence, and they had ready answers to explain why. Several mentioned saving what they liked most for last when they could spend more time with it.

Each one also had an implicit list of editorial and advertising topics to avoid (e.g., stories of the maltreatment of children). All four avoided ads for some products they never use. These readers did not open the pages likely to contain those topics to be avoided. When they came upon these topics on pages they had opened, they quickly skipped by. They were looking for some things, they were trying to avoid other things, and they knew they would not be able to read everything in order to find what they wanted.

In effect then, reading the paper is an organized search to which a limited amount of time and effort is allocated. To use that time efficiently, the readers used two kinds of procedures: (a) a pattern of looking through the paper and (b) a way of looking at the material on a page. To extract meaning out of large amounts of printed material in a very short period of time, the reader must scan—absorbing a limited amount of information from a few visual fixations spread out from the top of a page to the bottom. Those few fixations are sufficient to cover a large area. The reader must be able to shift easily from scanning to a more leisurely or careful reading.

Our observations of the reading process made it clear that reading the paper requires a high degree of concentration, represents a purposeful search for information that might prove interesting or useful, and follows a highly unique pattern that is never duplicated between one reader and the next.

VISUAL SEARCH AND MENTAL AROUSAL

These conclusions were corroborated when we examined the videotapes of 10 women reading the same day's issue (June 26, 1985) of the Danbury (CT)

News-Times. All of the subjects were regular readers of that newspaper who had agreed to postpone their reading that day until we gave them a copy.[6]

Through electrodes taped to the head, a second-by-second EEG (electroencephalograph) record, synchronized with time recordings on the videotape, permitted the measurement of mental energy or arousal in both brain hemispheres. There were striking differences in the brain wave patterns of different individuals looking at the same content.

What about the intensity of the reading process? We compared average levels of arousal for periods of time when the video record indicated that a subject was skimming or looking at content and when she was actually reading an item. Our initial hypothesis was that brain activity accelerates when attention is concentrated, as it is in reading rather than skimming or when it is engaged by a subject of interest. But the data seem to question whether, for most people, a sharp distinction can really be drawn between reading and scanning. The mental processing shown by the brain-wave records is similar or identical for these two activities, even though readers draw a subjective difference between them. The implication seems to be that the process of search, of attributing meaning, of sifting, rejecting, or reserving for a higher level of attentiveness seems to involve, for most readers, every bit as much mental energy as the process of reading itself!

What goes on in the brain represents the processing of the visual signals received through the mechanisms of the eye. To understand these better, we turned to a newly developed camera that tracks eye movements in relation to the visual field.[7]

As in the brain-wave analysis, we wanted our eye camera records to concentrate on a homogeneous sample: 12 women readers of a single day's issue of *The Boston Globe.*

Examination of the videotaped record shows that the characteristic

---

[6]This study was supervised at Neurocommunications Laboratories by Sidney Weinstein, in consultation with Herbert Krugman. Each subject was videotaped for a half hour from two angles, one of which provided an image that permitted us to code the quadrant of the page at which she was looking at any given moment. (Five independent judgments found virtually no disagreements on these attributions.) At the conclusion of the videotaped reading session, each subject was interviewed with the same sequence of questions used in the Ad Performance studies. Michael Macht was the Bureau's project director for this study.

[7]The camera, originally developed by Applied Science Laboratories for aerospace research, uses a lightweight helmet—actually a bicycle rider's plastic helmet—on which a camera is mounted, and the video image is transmitted through an optical fiber. Unlike the eye camera we had used in our earlier experiments, the subject is able to move her head and body freely and can read the paper as she normally would. Years earlier we had run a similar experiment using an eye camera called the Optiscan. The actual photographic record of what 15 women focused on when they looked at a sequence of tabloid-sized newspaper pages was compared with what they later remembered having noted in a standard recognition interview. (See Leo Bogart, "How Do People Read Newspapers?" *Media/Scope,* January 1961, pp. 53ff.)

pattern is to move around, first in broad sweeps that encompass whatever stands out either because of its physical characteristics (size or contrast) or because of its content salience, and then to move back in for short fixations. The same reader never follows the identical pattern on different pages that follow different configurations of shapes and subject matter. And as Figure 9.1 shows, no two readers look at the same material in the same way.

How accurately do readers remember what they look at? We can compare the actual eye-movement records with recall obtained in interviews conducted immediately after reading. Aggregating all the page-opening reports, 89% were accurate.

The individual item is certainly a lot easier to forget than the spread or page, which provides more cues to the memory. For all the ads sampled for our analysis, 52% were directly focused on, but 7% were claimed as seen.

We defined "looking at" an ad if the eye-camera record showed at least one direct fixation, that is if the eye's focus stopped upon it at least once. Although it is possible to see an item without actually fixating on it, to read something it is necessary to look at it repeatedly. We counted an item as read

FIGURE 9.1 Two readers look at the same page: Eye movement track as recorded by the eye camera, showing fixation points.

if the reader's gaze made at least four separate stops on it. Ads larger than half a page received more fixations and more multiple fixations than smaller ads.

The eye-camera record verifies that prospects for what is advertised remember ads better and are more interested in them. (Among prospects, 38% read the ads, and only 8% did not focus on them directly. For nonprospects, 14% read and 23% did not focus on them.) People not only remember reading more advertising that interests them or for products they are inclined to buy; they actually do read more of those ads.

But what the eye camera reveals and what interviews cannot is that prospects actually focus on or look at more of those ads once they have opened the page. To understand why this is so, we must refer to the fundamentals of visual perception. When our eyes are open to the world, everything we look at is always being checked out automatically against memory and experience, which is what allows us to attribute meaning to it. Within the visual span of about 120 degrees—which extends ever farther if we include peripheral vision—we are continually widening and narrowing the area of concentration. Attention is instantly and constantly shifting; without any conscious thought, we are always selecting what we want to focus on. Looking and not looking are matters of degree, not sharply defined categories.[8]

When we look at a newspaper at normal reading distance, the area of concentration has a diameter about 2 inches wide, but we are actively processing what we see within a diameter of 10 or 12 inches. It is from the edges of this wider gaze that we pick up the cues that automatically tell us to shift the eye's direction. This is why the eye travels on to the items that engage us and not to the ones that do not. In the case of advertising, consumption interests and propensities govern the direction of attention. But analogous processes operate to attract the reader's eye to those editorial elements that are relevant and meaningful.

This selective process is much more important in reading the newspaper than in confronting other forms of print, because of the sheer complexity and variety of stimuli that are presented to the reader's eye when he opens a typical double-page spread. The spread may be open just long enough to determine that there is nothing to hold him there, so that he rapidly turns the page. Even so, the searching and screening process has taken place.

THE PROBABILITY OF READING SOMETHING

The limitations and inaccuracies of readership scores are self-evident. However, laboratory techniques and instruments (like the eye camera) are not

---

[8]R. J. Christman, *Sensory Experience* (New York: Harper & Row, 1979).

applicable to any large-scale sampling of reading activity under normal conditions. There is no practical substitute for the old-fashioned method of talking to people directly and accepting their memories.

In our 1963 and 1971 studies, readership was defined in terms of a scale of probabilities. People who had read a newspaper were asked a series of questions that gave an indication of the likelihood that they had actually seen each individual item. The lowest likelihood that an item had really been seen was assigned to those readers who had no recollection of having opened the spread (of two facing pages) on which it appeared. The highest likelihood was ascribed to those who said they had opened the spread, read the item, also had read one or more adjacent items of editorial matter or advertising, and even said that they were actually looking for the particular item. At neither extreme of the scale could there be absolute certainty that the reader's report was accurate. But this represented the best possible assurance of accuracy under the conditions of a field interview.

There is a disadvantage to this method that also applies to the recognition technique. Both obscure the fact that people perceive the newspaper as a totality; their overall response to it is in a sense independent of their readership or response for individual items. As they turn the pages of the paper, readers perceive them as a whole. The news and the adjacent advertising, the high and lesser interest material, all form part of a pattern.

An individual may read purposefully in a conscious search for particular items, or readership may take a more random pattern, with the eye darting back and forth to settle on items of interest and then returning to other items that have been passed by. The same item may be looked at a number of times, since readers often pick up the paper on a number of different occasions. But each time an item is looked at it may be perceived in a different context and with different thoughts in mind.

Thus, general attitudes toward the newspaper emerge in reports of reading specific items. When people are asked general questions about their reading interests, the responses reflect the habits and value judgments they have accumulated over a lifetime of reading. This makes the results quite different from the answers to specific questions about what they remember reading in a particular issue on a particular day. The more general kind of attitude is tapped when people are asked whether they are more interested in news or in features, in national or in local events. Answers to such questions cannot be taken literally. However, they do get at predispositions which are, in a sense, more predictive of actual reading activity than inquiries about the individual items of a specific issue of a given paper.

WHAT DO READERS WANT IN THE PAPER?

Most people appear to think of the newspaper as having universal appeal, though it is seen as tilted toward the older and better educated and, very slightly, toward men. (We have already seen that the paper does actually have much more male-oriented material.) However, the perception of the paper most often read as being unbalanced in its coverage is not consistently greater among those who might be considered disadvantaged, as Table 9.3 shows (1982). More women than men think the paper is of equal interest to both sexes, and the college educated are more likely to detect imbalance in their favor than those with less education. (However, Blacks are slightly more likely than Whites [36%–29%] to say that the newspaper has more in it for the better educated.) In general, readers seem to be able to ignore the content that is aimed at someone else and do not resent its presence.

We have seen that the reader's progress through the paper is a search, partly purposive and partly random, for anything that warrants attention because of its utility, informativeness, relevance, curiosity, or amusement. I have emphasized the difficulty of distinguishing the reader's predispositions from the recollections of what was looked at. A number of approaches have been used in the effort to differentiate both the overall levels of attention aroused by different types of newspaper content and also the characteristic responses of different kinds of people. The commonly used procedure of asking people what they looked at or read has limitations, as we have seen, but it has the merit of great specificity. When people are asked more general questions, they may correctly reveal their underlying attitudes, but these are not always directly expressed in the attention they give to actual and specific items.

The reader appears to approach the newspaper as an integrated but highly heterogeneous package. The very heterogeneity he expects may be the major attraction for him. To require him to express a preference for one kind of content or another may do violence to the complexity of his responses. Yet it is often useful to ask survey respondents to make such artificial choices, simply in order to compare those that different kinds of people make.

TABLE 9.3
"Is there more in the paper for (one group) or about the same amount for both?" 1982

	Men	Women
More for men	16%	10%
More for women	6	5
	Under 35	35+
More for younger	6	4
More for older	39	34
	Some college	Others
More for better educated	44	21
More for less educated	8	5

NEWS OR FEATURES?

As we saw in Chapter 5, newspapers have met the competitive entertainment challenge of TV with some striking innovations in appearance and content. Still, most people expect and want *news* from their newspapers. Newspapers always have been and probably always will be a mixture of information and entertainment, but as we have seen, the proportions are changing. Our studies have addressed the subject in two ways—by asking people what they enjoy and also asking them what they consider essential.

A strong preference for news was voiced in 1961 when people were asked which they looked forward more to reading, the news items or the regular features (Table 9.4). That preference has been maintained over the years, but the proportions have somewhat changed. The growing orientation to features corresponds to the changing mix of content described in Chapter 6.

The leaning toward news (68%) over features (28%) was identical among every-day and less frequent readers in 1961, and it showed little variability in different size communities. In 1982, 59% of the public looked forward more to the news items, while 40% said they looked forward more to "regular features, such as columnists, editorials, comics, reviews of movies and books, and other features." By 1987, the proportion was 46% for news and 40% for features.

The preference for news over features does not differ greatly among readers of different size papers, though readers of large papers are most likely to volunteer the comment that they want both (1987). There is a striking difference between men and women: Men overwhelmingly (54%) said they look forward more to news, while 46% of women leaned to the features. College graduates showed a much higher preference for news (71%), compared to those who did not finish high school (55%). The preference for news over features held up in every age group (Table 9.5).

We approached the question of reader preference in a different way in 1977, in 1982, and again in 1987 (with half our sample), asking people how

TABLE 9.4
Percentage Who Look Forward to News and Features

	1961	1982	1987
Much more to news	40	27	22
Somewhat more	28	32	24
Somewhat more to regular features	15	24	22
Much more	13	16	18
No preference, no answer	4	1	13
	100	100	100

TABLE 9.5
Looking Forward to News and Features, by Age, 1987

	More to news		More to features	
	Much	Somewhat	Somewhat	Much
18–24[a]	14%	30%	34%	7%
25–29	15	20	35	16
30–34	22	31	21	16
35–44	23	29	17	20
45–54	27	18	21	18
55–64	24	14	21	26
Over 65	29	23	13	21
All readers	22	24	22	18

[a]Total number of respondents in each age group = 100% (including no preference).

they would choose between a paper that was all news and one that just gave a news summary and consisted mostly of entertaining features. In 1977, 59% said they would prefer an all-news paper, and 39% preferred the entertainment package. (The remainder made no choice.) In 1982, when faced with a direct choice, 49% said they personally preferred a paper that is mostly news; and 30%, one that is mostly features; 26% volunteered the reply that they want both. And in 1987, 50% chose news; 21%, features; and 22% volunteered that they wanted a balance.

Infrequent readers were no more likely to say they look forward to features (41%) than frequent readers (40%). But faced with that forced choice, 58% of the frequent readers prefer the mostly news paper, compared with 40% of the less frequent readers.

Among people 18 to 24, a forced choice produced only a minority who wanted the all-news option. Forty-nine percent would choose a paper that was mostly features over one that was all news (25%).

Much earlier research done for individual newspapers had already documented this strong orientation of young people to entertainment and their resistance to the (often unpleasant) news of the day. Much of the editorial experimentation of the 1970s was aimed at attracting this generation, and a variety of feature sections were added by many metropolitan newspapers that gave them more and more the character of magazines. But it was not clear that this new emphasis had the unanimous approval of the great majority of established readers.

Although, as just noted, half of the adults under 30 said in 1977 that they preferred features to news, this attitude is not borne out by what they told us of their specific reading behavior. Their level of interest in the average feature or entertainment item was actually 27% less than that of people over 30, as we see shortly.

INVENTING A PERSONAL NEWSPAPER

The examples just presented suggest that when people look at specific articles, they do not automatically assign them to the conventional categories used by editors or by students of the press. The writing style, level of abstraction, personalization, drama, human interest, or evocativeness of a story may have far more to do with reader response than its classification as local or national, as news or feature. Yet in practice, these criteria are not easily codified, although the conventional subject areas are generally understood both by editors and by the public.

In 1977, respondents were asked how much space they would give to each of 34 listed subjects for "a paper tailor-made to your own interests": a lot of space, some space, a little space, or no space.

Such a question requires each reader to make his own assumptions about the kinds of articles that would fit under each heading and the way in which they would be written. Thus, different people would be visualizing each of the general categories in terms of a different array of individual topics and items. But while this makes the results artificial and abstract, they can be compared for different sectors of the public. Moreover, when people are required to state their reading interests in general terms, they are confronted with essentially the same criteria of choice that editors use when they try to satisfy a great variety of public interests, needs, and tastes.

The major categories of general news were deliberately omitted from the list of 34 subjects in order to concentrate on those more specialized interests over which editors have more individual control than they do over the day's flow of unpredictable events.

For 13 of the 34 topics, more than half of the public said that they would give at least some space or a lot of space (Table 9.6). For the 7 highest ranking topics, two-thirds would give a lot of space or some space.

What is most striking is the comparatively small proportion of people who would dispense with any one of these 34 categories of news or feature information. This is true even though, by the ground rules, they were answering only in terms of a paper designed to meet their personal interests. Most people want a newspaper to cover a vast array of subjects, including those of comparatively little direct value to them, just on the chance that from time to time they might have a use for that kind of information.

During a time of growing inflation, "best food buys" was given more space than any other item, followed by health, nutrition, and medical advice. Consumer news, a related category of service information, came up fourth, just behind human-interest stories on people in the news.

The highest proportions who were willing to do away with a category altogether named horoscopes, crossword puzzles, mysterious events and psychic predictions.

TABLE 9.6
Percentage of Respondents Who Would Give "A Lot of Space" and "Some Space"
to Selected Subjects, by Sex, 1977

	Total	Male	Female
Best food buys	78	72	84
Health, nutrition, medical advice	75	68	82
Human-interest stories on people in the news	75	71	78
Consumer news	73	73	73
Articles on the environment	72	71	73
Editorials	70	69	72
Stories on political figures or public officials	67	69	66
Sports news	59	72	47
Home maintenance and repair	58	58	57
School news	56	51	61
Letters to the editor	54	53	54
Advice on personal finance	54	53	56
Free-time activities (hobbies, etc.)	53	53	54
Religion	49	43	56
Stories on sports or show business people	49	56	44
Home furnishing and decoration	49	41	56
TV reviews and schedules	49	48	51
Book reviews	44	37	50
Obituaries, death notices	43	34	50
Travel	41	42	41
Comics	41	44	38
Recipes	38	22	52
Hunting and fishing	38	52	26
Women's fashions	37	24	50
Personal advice (Dear Abby, etc.)	36	27	44
Music, records	34	32	36
Movie reviews	33	32	33
Pets, stories about animals	33	30	36
Weddings and engagements	30	23	37
Beauty tips	28	16	39
Mysterious events, psychic predictions, etc.	28	28	29
Men's fashions	27	29	26
Crossword puzzles	23	19	26
Astrology, horoscopes	22	16	27
Average percentage for 34 subjects	*47.5*	*44.9*	*50.1*
N (100%)[a]	(3,048)	(1,525)	(1,523)

[a]Statistical adjustments brought the weighted base to 147,184.

Sixty-five percent would give at least a little space to 30 or more of the 34 subjects, and only 5% would give space to 19 or fewer. Frequent readers want space on more subjects than infrequent readers. Still, Blacks opt for more topics than Whites, even though fewer of them are frequent readers. Fewer people over 55 would give space to a great many topics (suggesting a constriction of interests in later life).

When the two sexes are compared, certain predictable differences emerge, but the similarities on most subjects are remarkable. Women turn out to want space devoted to somewhat more subjects than men. To put it another way, slightly more women (50%) then men (45%) would give some space or a lot of space to the average subject (Table 9.6). Women are more ready to assign space to traditionally feminine subjects and to entertainment: best food buys, health and nutrition, human interest, religion, home furnishing and decorating, book reviews, obituaries, women's fashions, personal advice, beauty tips, crossword puzzles, and horoscopes. Men assign greater weight to stories on sports or show business people, to sports news, comics, hunting and fishing. Men and women show comparable interest in men's fashions; this has long been apparent from their similar response to men's-wear advertising.

The different age groups rank the 34 subjects in somewhat different priority, but on the whole their preferences have the same general shape (Table 9.7). Young people of 18 to 24 include fewer individuals with home-making responsibilities, so they demand less in the way of best food buys and recipes. They are less attracted by religious news than older readers and predictably want more frivolity in the form of sports, stories about entertainers and sports figures, music and records, movies, psychic predictions, horoscopes, and fashions for men. They show high interest in health and the environment.

The differences among age groups are in fact relatively small and contrast with very substantial differences when content preferences are compared by levels of education (Table 9.8). The average subject gets at least some space from college graduates (44%), from people who have not gone beyond high school (49%), from high school graduates (48%), and from people with some college (51%). The reason for this is that the college graduates want markedly less space for horoscopes, men's and women's fashions, psychic predictions, beauty tips, weddings and engagements, pet stories, personal advice, hunting and fishing, recipes, obituaries, TV reviews, stories on sports or show business people, religion, school news, home maintenance and repair. But they do want more generally on serious subjects: consumer news, articles on the environment, editorials, stories on political figures and public officials, personal finance, hobbies, book reviews.

The point has been made that younger people today have had more years of education than older ones. Thus, when we look at their responses either by age or by education, one may be influencing the other. The solution is to look

TABLE 9.7
Percentage of Respondents Who Would Give "A Lot of Space" and "Some Space"
to Selected Subjects, by Age, 1977

	18–24	25–34	35–54	55+
Best food buys	71	79	82	80
Health, nutrition, medical advice	76	75	74	75
Human-interest stories on people in the news	77	74	75	74
Consumer news	77	77	77	64
Articles on the environment	77	78	74	60
Editorials	67	68	72	74
Stories on political figures or public officials	68	67	69	67
Sports news	69	56	61	53
Home maintenance and repair	54	56	62	59
School news	56	53	62	52
Letters to the editor	52	51	56	55
Advice on personal finance	59	57	58	47
Free-time activities (hobbies, etc.)	53	53	54	53
Religion	38	40	53	60
Stories on sports or show business people	55	43	51	48
Home furnishing and decorating	45	48	53	47
TV reviews and schedules	48	40	49	57
Book reviews	45	46	46	39
Obituaries, death notices	35	32	41	57
Travel	38	39	42	43
Comics	44	39	42	39
Recipes	27	34	41	44
Hunting and fishing	38	35	33	37
Women's fashions	35	32	40	42
Personal advice (Dear Abby, etc.)	34	26	34	46
Music, records	46	34	33	28
Movie reviews	43	34	33	22
Pets, stories about animals	30	30	31	40
Weddings and engagements	31	24	29	35
Beauty tips	27	25	32	27
Mysterious events, psychic predictions, etc.	37	28	27	23
Men's fashions	31	26	29	23
Crossword puzzles	23	18	24	24
Astrology, horoscopes	26	16	24	23
Average percentage for 34 subjects (weighted)	*48.0*	*45.1*	*48.9*	*47.6*
N (100%)	(503)	(693)	(929)	(923)

TABLE 9.8
Percentage of Respondents Who Would Give "A Lot of Space" and "Some Space"
to Selected Subjects, by Education, 1977

	Some high school or less	High school graduate	Some College	College graduate
Best food buys	78	81	79	74
Health, nutrition, medical advice	74	77	77	72
Human-interest stories on people in the news	71	77	80	73
Consumer news	65	72	80	85
Articles on the environment	60	63	82	81
Editorials	62	71	78	79
Stories on political figures or public officials	61	65	76	76
Sports news	57	61	60	59
Home maintenance and repair	62	60	56	51
School news	57	59	54	47
Letters to the editor	51	55	55	56
Advice on personal finance	49	54	51	61
Free-time activities (hobbies, etc.)	50	56	52	59
Religion	58	51	46	34
Stories on sports or show business people	54	51	48	39
Home furnishing and decorating	49	52	48	41
TV reviews and schedules	60	48	43	39
Book reviews	34	39	55	63
Obituaries, death notices	53	44	35	27
Travel	39	42	43	43
Comics	43	41	39	38
Recipes	45	39	32	27
Hunting and fishing	44	41	31	29
Women's fashions	43	39	34	28
Personal advice (Dear Abby, etc.)	46	37	29	21
Music, records	37	33	35	30
Movie reviews	34	32	30	33
Pets, stories about animals	43	33	28	21
Weddings and engagements	37	32	25	19
Beauty tips	31	32	24	17
Mysterious events, psychic predictions, etc.	31	29	30	17
Men's fashions	31	30	22	21
Crossword puzzles	25	23	20	20
Astrology, horoscopes	31	24	15	9
Average percentage for 34 subjects (weighted)	*49.0*	*48.3*	*50.7*	*43.8*
N (100%)	(1,050)	(1,021)	(546)	(420)

TABLE 9.9
Percentage of Respondents Who Would Give "A Lot of Space" and "Some Space" to Selected Subjects, by Race, 1977

	White	Black
Best food buys	78	79
Health, nutrition, medical advice	75	78
Human-interest stories on people in the news	75	71
Consumer news	74	67
Articles on the environment	72	69
Editorials	71	65
Stories on political figures or public officials	67	70
Sports news	59	64
Home maintenance and repair	58	60
School news	54	68
Letters to the editor	54	55
Advice on personal finance	54	59
Free-time activities (hobbies, etc.)	54	47
Religion	48	65
Stories on sports or show business people	48	62
Home furnishing and decorating	48	53
TV reviews and schedules	49	55
Book reviews	44	43
Obituaries, death notices	43	43
Travel	42	40
Comics	41	37
Recipes	36	50
Hunting and fishing	38	39
Women's fashions	35	58
Personal advice (Dear Abby, etc.)	35	39
Music, records	33	45
Movie reviews	31	43
Pets, stories about animals	33	35
Weddings and engagements	30	34
Beauty tips	26	44
Mysterious events, psychic predictions, etc.	27	38
Men's fashions	25	46
Crossword puzzles	22	30
Astrology, horoscopes	21	33
Average percentage for 34 subjects (weighted)	*47.1*	*52.5*
N (100%)	(2,347)	(701)

at age and education in relation to each other. Although space allocations to music, records, and movie reviews are primarily influenced by age rather than by education, education turns out to be of prime importance in most other respects. This means that generational differences have less to do with what readers want in a newspaper than the socioeconomic and cultural differences reflected in educational attainment.

These social class influences are also mirrored in the differences between Blacks and Whites. Blacks want more space for religious news, stories on sports or show business people, recipes, women's fashions, music and records, movie reviews, beauty tips, psychic predictions, crossword puzzles, men's fashions, and horoscopes. They are less keen on free-time activities and hobbies (Table 9.9). Here again, for most categories, the differences are small.

There are other differences worth noting: Not surprisingly, hunting and fishing turn out to be more popular in small towns than in large ones. And as might be expected, small-town residents are more likely to express interest in obituaries, weddings, and engagements. They show less interest in fashions, music, and movies. But the differences are not very large and are outweighed by the commonality of interests among people with diverse styles of life.

DOES SPACE ALLOCATION MATCH READERS' PREFERENCE?

How do the public's interests, as reflected in their answers to this question, jibe with what newspapers put before them? For 28 of the 34 subject areas, it was possible to obtain or estimate the number of individual news or feature items in the sample of newspaper content. These were adjusted so that the public's allocation of "a lot of space" or "some space" could be compared with the actual distribution of items under the same headings (Table 9.10). (It must be remembered that the real distribution of space is not identical with the distribution of items, since our analysis includes only items of 75 lines and over, and these are not necessarily of comparable length in the various categories.)

The resulting computations suggest that readers want more of certain kinds of content than they presently get: "best food buys," health, nutrition, and medical advice, consumer news, articles on the environment, home maintenance and repair, letters to the editor, religion, home furnishing and decorating, travel, recipes, women's fashions.

At the same time, certain other items occur more frequently in the newspaper than appears warranted by public demand: human interest stories, sports news, school news, stories on sports or show business people, comics, hunting and fishing, crossword puzzles, and astrology.

This comparison of the public's preferences against newspapers' actual

TABLE 9.10
Percentage of Newspaper Space Devoted to 34 Subjects, and
"Ideal" Space in a Personal Newspaper, 1977

	Actual/ Estimated %	"Ideal" %[a]
Best food buys	1.5	5.8
Health, nutrition, medical advice	3.5	5.6
Human-interest stories on people in the news	6.5	5.6
Consumer news	1.6	5.5
Articles on the environment	4.0	5.4
Sports news	13.3	4.4
Home maintenance and repair	0.5	4.3
School news	7.4	4.2
Letters to the editor	1.7	4.0
Advice on personal finance	2.4	4.0
Religion	1.3	3.7
Stories on sports or show business people	13.5	3.7
Home furnishing and decorating	0.4	3.7
TV reviews and schedules	2.5	3.7
Book reviews	0.9	3.3
Obituaries, death notices	2.8	3.2
Travel	2.3	3.1
Comics	6.6	3.1
Recipes	0.7	2.8
Hunting and fishing	8.6	2.8
Women's fashions	0.8	2.8
Personal advice	1.6	2.7
Music, records	2.4	2.5
Movie reviews	2.3	2.5
Weddings and engagements	3.5	2.2
Men's fashions	0.6	2.0
Crossword puzzles	3.5	1.7
Astrology, horoscopes	3.3	1.6
Total of listed items	100.0	100.0

[a]The proportion of adults who would give a lot of space or some space to each subject has been redistributed against the grand total for the 34 listed subjects.

allocation of space follows a similar analysis made of the 1971 survey, which obtained reports of readership on a cross-section of editorial items. In that case also, the purpose was to see whether or not a particular category of content developed reader interest in proportion to the amount of space that editors give it.

On this basis, the subjects that attract readership to a disproportionately greater degree than would be indicated by their presence in the paper are: the weather, accidents and disasters, letters to the editor, human-interest stories from the wire services or syndicates, crime, fashion and society, obituaries, and advice columns. The categories that generate disproportionately low levels of readership relative to their presence are puzzles and horoscopes, political columns, and TV and radio logs.

The discrepancy between these conclusions and those based on the 1977 study partly reflects the differences beween the categories of content covered in each case. (The "personal newspaper," after all, did not include such important items as weather, crime, and accidents.) But the discrepancy also demonstrates the difficulty of improving on editorial judgments through the application of formulas.

CAN CHANGE IN CONTENT ATTRACT INFREQUENT READERS?

The real objective for any study of what kind of articles people claim to like or look at is, of course, to rearrange the assortment of content to make it more attractive both to the faithful readers and to those whose loyalty has yet to be won.

Frequent readers (the 66% of the public who reported reading the news-paper on at least four out of five weekdays in 1977) may be compared with the less frequent readers. (This latter group includes both the occasional readers and also the 8% who have not read a daily paper in the last five weekdays, nor a Sunday paper on the last four Sundays.) The percentage who would give at least some space to the average subject is virtually the same for infrequent and frequent readers (46% against 48%).

Frequent readers are more likely to mention consumer news, editorials, articles on the environment, and stories on political figures and public officials, letters to the editors, hobbies, book reviews, and personal advice columns. Infrequent readers are somewhat more likely to mention music and records, movie reviews, and animal stories, psychic predictions, and horo-scopes.

But the differences are small compared with the overall similarity of the two lists. In effect, an ideal newspaper constructed to meet the specifications of infrequent readers would differ only in minor matters of emphasis from the paper that frequent readers want.

This point is corroborated by an exercise conducted among 39 editors in 1979. They were individually asked to redistribute the present allocations of space for a typical newspaper among the 34 categories. The results for each rearrangement were then computer-weighted to project the level of public satisfaction it would produce, based on the findings of the national survey. The purpose was to see what alternative uses of space might attract new readers with minimum sacrifice of the present readers. But none of the proposed rearrangements produced the same level of overall satisfaction as the present space formula.

READER INVOLVEMENT

Every newspaper editor is engaged in a continual effort to engage and involve his readers, but how is that involvement to be defined? The reader can express his opinions as to what he likes or doesn't like in the paper, but when he does so in general terms, it is difficult for the editor to draw conclusions that apply directly to the actual stories that the staff must handle each day. We have already described what specific items readers report they read and noted that these reports have some limitations. In two of our studies we approach the subject of reader involvement from a different angle.

Our 1966 study (already described in Chapter 7) dealt in the specifics of which the news is actually composed rather than in the generalities that surveys have often used to compare media. People were asked to rate their interest in each of the 240 items covered in this study from "a great deal" to "none at all," and also to tell "the best way" to find out about it. The phrase, "the best way," was used because prior research had shown that the "quickest" way, the "most complete" way, the "most interesting" way, the "most accurate" way, or any other specific adjective automatically gave an advantage to one medium over the others.

The items that originated as radio news received the highest interest scores; next, those from television; next, newspapers; and last, magazines. A high proportion of magazine stories represents feature material of no pressing immediacy. By contrast, since the typical radio newscast can handle only a handful of stories, a higher proportion of radio bulletins deal with big news. This does not mean that radio bulletins arouse higher interest in practice than news in the other media. It means that radio deals largely with a restricted range of stories from the top of the interest scale.

Men and women have the same level of overall interest in what the mass media are telling them, and young people display no less interest than their elders. There was a very high degree of agreement between men and women in the interest scores of the individual items. However, there was less agreement between adults and teenagers.

Not surprisingly, teenagers showed far higher interest in stories that dealt directly with their age group: "70 cars expected to compete in the auto races," "a local radio personality to play at a gathering of young people." They liked a story about the pantssuit for women, another about the filming of a James Bond movie, and one on two local girls in a sewing contest in Paris. Also, it's no surprise that they gave lower rankings than adults to stories that dealt with the facts of business and civic life: a consumer protest against high supermarket prices, developments in a strike against a major corporation.

For adults, the news and feature items of highest interest were not necessarily those of major significance. For example, high-interest scores went to the weather and to a nearby accident. However, the low-ranking items tended to be those of objectively small importance, even though they may have had human interest value and (as complete stories rather than one-sentence synopses) been quite entertaining to the reader.

The highest interest scores for any subject in 1966 went to stories related to health. Next came items dealing with space, and with accidents and disasters. News of the Vietnam war and other articles about world and national politics also scored high.

There is almost no category of news item that does not have a great deal of interest to at least some people, but the reverse is also true. Even those stories which are of great interest to a large proportion of the public have little or no interest for a substantial minority. And in the case of items that score in the middle range of interest, there is often a remarkable division of opinion, with about the same proportions of people rating them of great interest and of no interest. For example, here are three statements that aroused great interest from a minority of the public, compared with other items with the same average scores: "a school for brain-damaged children uses special teaching techniques"; "a new plant for manufacturing defense products will open near here"; "students were given a holiday because of a threatening phone call."

A weather report was of mild interest to almost everybody, but of intense interest to very few, while at the same overall level, news of a reduction in electric rates was of intense interest to a larger group but encountered a fair number of people who have almost no interest in it.

The death in action of a local soldier was of strong interest to a minority but left another substantial group relatively apathetic, whereas news about a tornado, with the same average level of interest, found comparatively few who felt any intense involvement.

Of course, what the average person perceives as the gist of a summarized item may or may not be what the original communicator intended. A statement which on the surface appears to be of low interest may rise to a high level of interest when embodied in words or pictures. Moreover, interest in a real story reflects the play or exposure it gets in context. A dull program will get many viewers when it is aired in prime time; a dull article, many readers when it is played as first lead. Research tells us what people *are* interested in rather than what they *might be* interested in. But interests and tastes are acquired through familiarity, and people are familiar with what editors and program producers choose to give them. A majority will always reject at first glance offerings that they will later adopt enthusiastically.

MEASURING INTEREST AND IMPORTANCE

The findings just reported shed light on how the public responds to subjects in the news, but a summary of a specific story still represents a level of abstraction that is several steps removed from the story itself perceived—and responded to—in context. In the 1977 study, a fresh approach was taken to the measurement of interest and an additional dimension of reader involvement was added, following the lead of Robert Park—that of importance.

One limitation of the recognition method is that it is confined to people who were already readers of the paper. This suits the purposes of advertisers interested in comparing the levels of attention given to different ads. But from the perspective of an editor, one of the main objectives of readership research might be to compare the reading interests of those who are currently readers and of others who are not, and whom he wishes to attract.

In the 1977 study, the people interviewed were not asked (as they had been in 1971) what items they remembered having seen or read; instead, they were asked to rate that material regardless of whether or not they had read the particular issue of the local paper and, indeed, whether or not they were newspaper readers.

Each interviewer carried copies of the preceding day's issues of the three newspapers with the largest local circulations. If the respondent usually read one of the three, he was interviewed on that paper. If not, he was asked which of the three papers he would be most likely to read. Thus, 73% of the interviews were carried out on papers selected by the respondents, whether or not they had read the particular issue. The remaining 27% were selected at random when the respondent was unable to express a preference.

Every respondent was taken through the first page and nine other randomly selected pages (excluding pages completely devoted to classified advertising). Each news and advertising item of 75 lines (5 column inches) or longer on the sampled pages was rated twice by the respondent. First he was asked, "When we look at a newspaper, we usually find some things more interesting than others. Now I'm going to show you some pages from yesterday's paper, and I would like to know whether you personally find the news stories and ads on that page very interesting, somewhat interesting, or not at all interesting. You don't have to read every word, but enough to decide whether you personally find each article or ad interesting." (When someone did not answer or could not provide an answer for a particular item, this itself was coded as a response, but in the analysis of the results, these reactions were lumped with those of people who said the particular item had no interest or importance for them.) After the respondent had rated every item on each page in terms of interest, he was asked to go back and rate every news and feature article as follows: "Now I would like you to consider just the articles and not the ads with something completely different in mind. I'd like you to tell me which articles have information that is really important for you yourself to know about, regardless of how interesting they are."

Naturally, readers had a wide range of reactions to the individual items classified under a particular category of content. Moreover, the adjectives "interesting" and "important" are only two of the many that can be applied to media content. They were selected as key dimensions in this analysis because they seemed to correspond both with the public's reading experience and with its expectations of the newspaper. They also reflected the compulsion of editors to make their papers appealing to the largest possible number of readers and their professional desire to be useful and informative at the same time.

The meaning of "interest" has been explored in studies of advertising as well as of editorial content. In one experiment (1987c), conducted in Middlesex, Massachusetts, half of a sample of readers who were asked the usual questions about interest in ads were also asked what made the particular advertisements interesting. The answers reflected the whole range of associations that people had with the purchase and use of the product, as well as the inherent appeal of the ads themselves. Similarly, we may infer that interest in news items reflects both the nature of the subject and the way it is handled by a writer and editor.

With all the variety of subjects that a newspaper must cover, many of them of a specialized nature, it is somewhat unexpected that a majority have at least some interest to the average person, whether or not he is actually a reader. In 1977, 25% of all items were classed "very interesting" by the average person, 30% as having some interest, 34% as having no interest, and for 11% no answer was given.

The broader the interest in a particular kind of content, the more intense that interest is also likely to be. That is, we can consider what proportion of stories in a particular content category are rated as being either somewhat or very interesting. To evaluate the intensity of interest we can consider what proportion the very interested represent of all those who consider an item to be of at least some interest. The two go together.

The average item was ranked somewhat lower in importance than it was in interest (Table 9.11). Eighteen percent were rated as very important to the respondent personally, 26% as having some importance, and 34% as having no importance at all. Twenty-two percent were not rated on importance.

Interest and importance tend to be related, but by no means perfectly. (There was a .61 Spearman rank-order correlation between the two measures.) Of the items that were rated very interesting, 61% were also rated very important. Of items rated somewhat interesting, 61% were also rated as somewhat important. Of those rated as not at all interesting, 75% were rated not at all important. Similarly, 85% of the items that were not rated on interest were also not rated in importance.[9]

---

[9]Some of this may reflect a respondent's resistance to this part of the interview; more likely it mainly reflects apathy toward particular elements of newspaper content or toward the newspaper as such. Infrequent readers were most likely to refrain from answering.

TABLE 9.11
Daily Newspaper Content and Reader Ratings of Content, 1977

	Total number of items (%)[a]	Reader ratings of average item	
		% very interested	% very important
General interest	66.6	28	20
Local and state news	12.4	21	17
General local news	7.3	19	13
State & local government	5.1	25	22
International news	6.3	29	24
Wars, rebellions	1.5	33	26
International, diplomatic	4.8	28	24
U.S. government,. domestic	3.5	33	29
Other general interest	44.4	29	20
Crime	7.3	33	23
Education, school news	3.1	23	19
Cultural events, reviews	2.4	15	10
Public health, welfare	2.8	35	33
News in brief	2.4	32	23
Accidents, disasters, natural phenomena	1.9	39	26
Social problems, protest	1.6	36	29
Obituaries	1.2	26	21
Labor, wages	1.6	29	26
Environment	1.7	35	32
General nonlocal human interest	2.7	22	13
Energy problems	0.7	40	38
Racial news, minorities (peaceful)	0.6	28	22
Weather	1.7	37	27
Science, invention	0.7	32	22
Travel	1.0	25	20
Taxes	0.9	37	34
Religion	0.6	18	15
Comics	2.8	19	6
Editorial cartoons	1.0	24	14
Puzzles, horoscopes	2.9	16	7
TV/Radio logs	1.1	26	16
Entertainers, Hollywood	1.0	16	8
Letters to the editor	0.7	37	27
Men's interest	21.2	16	12
Sports	13.9	14	9
Business, finance	7.3	21	20
Women's interest	3.3	18	9
Fashion, society	2.0	15	3
Food, home, garden	1.3	23	17
Columns			
Advice	1.7	28	19

TABLE 9.11 (continued)

	Total number of items (%)[a]	Reader ratings of average item	
		% very interested	% very important
Political	1.6	31	24
Humor	0.4	23	14
Gossip	0.2	19	13
Other items not classified elsewhere	5.0		
Grand total	100.0		

[a]Covers items of 75 lines or greater. The categories shown combine a larger number of classifications which were coded.

I have commented earlier on the difficulties of interpreting the meaning of conventional readership or noting scores that represent what readers remember seeing but that also reflect their predispositions and interests. For this reason, the 1977 interest scores have been compared with the reported readership of items in the same content categories in 1971. (Since the earlier study was based on people who had read the paper on the preceding day, the results were compared with those for frequent readers in 1977.) There is a rank-order correlation of .59 between the readership scores and ratings of the same material as very interesting. This can be taken to mean that the two sets of measures are strongly related, but there were certain discrepancies. Political columns and the weather were rated higher for interest in 1977 than for readership in 1971. The interest scores were lower for personal advice columns, obituaries, comics, religion, fashion, and wedding and birth announcements. But overall, an article in which people express interest is likely to be the kind of article they say they read.

No category of newspaper content is of interest to everyone; every category of content is of at least some interest to a substantial minority.

Although an individual respondent may consider a particular item more important than interesting, there is no category of content that readers in the aggregate consider to have greater importance than interest.

It is to be expected that the elements of the paper intended to entertain the reader should receive lower ratings for importance than for interest. What might not be anticipated is that the interest ratings for these entertainment items are lower than those for straight news items.

The weather is not only an interesting subject to the public, it is also considered quite important. But articles dealing with amusements and culture, comics and puzzles turn out to be positioned low in interest as well as in importance.

TABLE 9.12
Percentage with at Least Some Interest in Editorial Items, by Sex, 1977

	Male	Female
Local and state news	56	56
General local news	51	55
Local and state government	63	58
International news	65	64
Wars, rebellions	66	65
International, diplomatic	65	64
U.S. government, domestic	68	67
Other general interest		
Crime	68	67
Education, school news	56	54
Cultural events, reviews	46	50
Public health, welfare	66	73
News in brief	64	65
Accidents, disasters	75	74
Social problems, protest	66	72
Obituaries	50	59
Labor, wages	65	67
Environment	72	67
Energy problems	77	71
Racial news, minorities	64	65
Weather	69	70
Science, invention	65	66
Travel	61	58
Taxes	71	68
Religion	49	59
Comics	49	42
Editorial cartoons	49	47
Puzzles, horoscopes	40	45
T.V./Radio logs	63	63
Entertainers, Hollywood	51	61
Letters to the editor	66	70
Advice columns	53	69
Political columns	66	62
Men's interest	52	32
Sports	52	27
Business, finance	52	45
Women's interest	35	59
Fashion, society	30	52
Food, home, garden	42	69
Other items not classified elsewhere	51	52

On really serious issues, importance and interest come more closely together than they do on most subjects. Consumer safety was number one in interest and tied with energy as first in importance. News related to the military aroused a high level of attention. Items of international news were considered both more important and more interesting if the U.S. government was directly involved.

Overall, there are not very large differences among various types of news categories in the interest and importance scores assigned to the average item. The range was from 75% for social welfare to 45% for international crime in the proportion with at least some interest. The proportion who attributed at least some importance ran from 72% for welfare to 40% for miscellaneous human-interest stories. These results seem to suggest that the range of interest and importance attributed to individual items within many single categories is often greater than the differences in response to the various kinds of news as such.[10]

The percentage "very interested" ranged from at least 4 out of 10 people for the average item under the headings of consumer safety, energy, social welfare, juvenile crime, and accidents down to a level of about 1 in 7 in the case of fashion, cultural events, sports (when both men and women are counted), wedding announcements, and puzzles.

The public's interest in science appears to have been on the increase between 1971 and 1977. Of the various kinds of content, 47% got a higher level of readership than items under the heading of science and inventions in 1971. In 1977, only 27% ranked higher in reader interest.

Certain kinds of news can occur either in a local setting, elsewhere in the nation, or abroad. Although the individual event undoubtedly determines the public's reactions, some general conclusions do emerge. For example, news of business and of labor and wages was definitely more appealing when it dealt with the local business scene. However, crime stories got similar average interest whether they occurred locally or elsewhere in the nation, but less interest if they took place abroad. News involving social problems or welfare aroused similar interest whether it involved local government, the federal government, or no government actions at all. News of travel and transportation got the same level of response regardless of where it occurred. Human-interest stories that occurred outside of the local area were rated very low in importance and fairly low in interest. (These included the wire service "brights" that editors often use as filler material.)

In 1979, approximately 13% of all American newspapers (with a third of total circulation) were running a daily action-line or "hot-line" column with reporters assigned to investigate readers' grievances and complaints against

---

[10]The corresponding rank-order correlation between 1971 readership and 1977 ratings of "very important" is .52.

the powers that be in their communities. Although, as mentioned in Chapter 8, editors believe that action lines are high in reader interest, too few were picked up in our sampling of items to permit a separate analysis.

We commented in Chapter 6 that despite the differences in size between morning and evening newspapers, their mix of editorial content is remarkably similar. The number of readers per copy and reading time are almost identical. Their readership patterns also turn out to be virtually identical. In the evening papers, 25% of all items were read in 1971 by the average reader, which is not a statistically significant difference from the 24% of the items read in morning papers.

This similarity is especially interesting since we know that morning papers tend to have larger circulations, to be found in larger cities, and to have a greater number of pages. This distinction in overall character rather than in the time of publication explains the differences that do occur. Content favored by morning-paper readers includes news of the federal government, obituaries, weather, science, and invention, taxes, food–home–garden, and gossip columns. Evening papers got higher readership for accidents and disasters, environment, nonlocal human interest, letters to the editor, sports, business, and political columns.

Although the morning papers (being larger) contain a somewhat higher percentage of men's interest items, reported readership for both sports and business was higher in the evening papers. In the area of women's interest, fashion and society items were more widely read in the evening papers, but food, home, and garden content received more attention in the morning papers.

HOW INTERESTS DIFFER

We saw in Chapter 6 that newspapers publish far more articles in the categories of interest to men than in those generally oriented to women. Still, the overall levels of both interest and importance for the average item turn out to be identical for men and women (Table 9.12), just as readership scores for men (25%) and women (24%) were identical in the 1971 study for the average item. But the averages mask variations for various kinds of content.

It comes as no shock to find that men and women show interest in different subjects, just as they report different levels of noting (1971). We have already seen this reflected in their replies to the question on the personal newspaper. But when the totality of content is considered, ratings of both interest and importance are similar for men and women. Even in the case of items that are clearly oriented toward one sex or the other, there are no cases where virtually everyone of one sex is interested in all the news of a particular category or where none of the other sex are interested in it at all.

For all articles in the traditional women's categories of fashion, food, and society news, the average item arouses at least some interest from 58% of the women and 34% of the men. It is considered to have at least some importance by 45% of the women and 29% of the men. Although women show more interest than men in local school news, all other news related to schools, education, and child rearing is of equal interest to men and to women. Women are more strongly oriented to advice columns, obituaries, society news and announcements, somewhat more interested in news related to social problems and social welfare, and a shade more interested in letters to the editor. They are, of course, less interested in the business news, and in labor and wages, but they are not as far from men in their response to these categories as might be supposed. And they are much more interested in food, home, and garden features than they are in fashion.

The average sports item is of at least some interest to 52% of the men and to 27% of the women. This, like much of the data, can be read in a number of ways. The aggregate score makes sports appear to rank lower in interest than it is often considered to be. It is evident that sports subjects arouse the attention of a substantial minority of women, just as food, fashion, and society news are viewed with interest by a fair number of men. It must be remembered, too, that coded under the heading of sports are a great many items that have limited appeal even to sports buffs: reports on high school track events, softball tournaments, and lacrosse championship playoffs. A reader may be highly interested in the popular sport of the season and be uninterested in a great many other sports items that newspapers routinely cover.

Younger people rate the average item higher in interest than older ones. 18- to 24-year-olds reflect above-average interest in news about jobs and wages, consumer safety, and science. They also are strong on subjects that might be put under the general heading of diversion and entertainment: cultural events and reviews, news of entertainers and Hollywood, fashion, sports, puzzles, comics, horoscopes. They show low interest in obituaries (Table 9.13).

The higher the level of educational attainment, the greater the level of interest in the average newspaper story. Better-educated people are more likely to rate the typical item as very important. This jibes with the recurrent research finding that people of higher education are generally interested in a greater variety of subjects. They are more curious, they talk about more things; they absorb information more rapidly and hunt for more of it.

Better-educated people are particularly responsive to international news, news of U.S. government actions, news of local and state politics, local government news involving civil rights and minorities or transportation, news of education and business, news of government actions related to

TABLE 9.13
Percentage with at Least Some Interest in Editorial Items, by Age, 1977

	18–24	25–29	30–34	35–44	45–54	55+
Local and state news	55	56	60	57	57	54
General local news	51	51	57	53	57	52
Local and state government	60	63	64	63	58	58
International news	65	67	67	66	65	63
Wars, rebellions	66	71	68	69	61	62
International, displomatic	65	66	67	65	66	63
U.S. government, domestic	68	67	71	67	68	67
Other general interest						
Crime	71	70	66	70	65	64
Education, school news	57	58	65	57	55	48
Cultural events, reviews	59	50	47	42	49	42
Public health, welfare	71	72	72	65	78	67
News in brief	65	70	70	63	65	61
Accidents, disasters	77	72	79	74	76	73
Social problems, protest	64	70	70	75	67	64
Obituaries	45	42	51	61	58	63
Labor, wages	70	59	65	68	66	58
Environment	66	70	74	74	79	61
Energy problems	73	78	68	81	78	72
Racial news, minorities	63	61	74	61	72	58
Weather	70	74	75	68	67	68
Science, invention	74	77	60	58	60	66
Travel	53	60	66	60	64	60
Taxes	63	74	78	67	79	65
Religion	57[a]	68[a]	68[a]	54[a]	46[a]	46
Comics	56	48	47	50	46	34
Editorial cartoons	56	60	47	47	53	35
Puzzles, horoscopes	49	43	41	42	44	37
T.V./Radio logs	66	67	61	59	66	61
Entertainers, Hollywood	68	52	62	56	54	50
Letters to the editor	69	61[a]	60[a]	76	59	72
Advice columns	58	56	66	64	64	60
Political columns	66	62	64	64	68	59
Men's interest	47	43	40	43	43	37
Sports	48	39	35	40	37	32
Business, finance	44	51	51	51	55	48
Women's interest	53	50	51	45	54	42
Fashions, society	50	48	39	37	49	34
Food, home, garden	58	43	67	57	60	55
Other items not classified elsewhere	52	55	52	53	50	49

[a]Bases less than 100.

TABLE 9.14
Percentage with at Least Some Interest in Editorial Items, by Education, 1977

	Not high school graduate	High school graduate	Some college or more
Local and state news	51	55	62
General local news	49	53	58
Local and state government	54	58	67
International news	55	62	75
Wars, rebellions	55	63	75
International, diplomatic	55	62	75
U.S. government, domestic	61	67	74
Other general interest			
Crime	65	67	70
Education, school news	50	53	62
Cultural events, reviews	38	46	58
Public health, welfare	61	71	76
News in brief	58	66	70
Accidents, disasters	72	77	75
Social problems, protest	59	68	77
Obituaries	58	59	46
Labor, wages	58	59	72
Environment	62	68	76
Energy problems	68	72	80
Racial news, minorities	61	63	68
Weather	65	70	74
Science, invention	55	70	73
Travel	53	57	67
Taxes	62	72	74
Religion	50	52	62
Comics	38	46	53
Editorial cartoons	42	46	55
Puzzles, horoscopes	37	44	44
T.V./Radio logs	59	67	64
Entertainers, Hollywood	51	55	62
Letters to the editor	62	65	76
Advice columns	58	63	63
Political columns	55	60	74
Men's interest	38	40	45
Sports	36	38	40
Business, finance	43	44	57
Women's Interest	44	47	52
Fashion, society	38	43	45
Food, home, garden	54	54	63
Other items not classified elsewhere	47	50	57

energy and business, and news of travel and cultural events (Table 9.14). They also show more interest in science, political columns, social problems, and crime in national government and politics. Because more of them are younger, they are less interested in obituaries.

Blacks rate more editorial items as both interesting and important than do Whites, perhaps reflecting a more acquiescent style of responding to interviewers' queries. This helps explain why they show above-average interest in some low-interest subjects: items dealing with local news on jobs and wages, news of disarmament, farm news, travel news.

They also show more affinity for: sports, school news, religion, show business people, home furnishings, TV schedules and reviews, recipes, women's fashions, music, records, movie reviews, beauty tips, psychic predictions, men's fashions, crossword puzzles, and astrology.

Whites are evenly balanced in their interest in national or world news and in local news. Blacks, on the other hand, have a preference of over two to one for local news (1966), and the difference persists at every age level. They are less likely to express "a great deal of interest" in political news and editorial cartoons and more likely to express strong interest in sports, personal advice columns, religion, and farm news (1977). Table 9.15 compares Whites and Non-Whites (mostly Black) by the less stringent criterion of "at least some interest."

Whites have much more interest in consumer news (1977). (This reflects a common research finding that the people that most need information are least likely to go out after it and use it.) Whites, with their higher average income level, have more interest in hobbies. They show an orientation to political subjects and find more interest in editorials.

Still these differences should not obscure the most important conclusion of our comparison: For a very large array of newspaper items dealing with food, health, nutrition, human interest, environment, "people" stories about politicians (as opposed to news stories), features on home maintenance, letters to the editor, book reviews, obituaries, travel, comics, hunting and fishing, pets, weddings—there is no significant difference in the interests of Blacks and Whites. There is also no difference between Blacks and Whites in their choice between a paper that is straight news and a paper that is mostly made up of entertaining features (1977).

MODIFYING THE MIX OF CONTENT

A persistent challenge to anyone concerned with increasing the frequency of readership is the possibility of modifying the mix of content to meet the needs of people who are not now reading the paper on a regular basis.

In keeping with what we have already determined from our analysis of the

TABLE 9.15
Percentage with at Least Some Interest in Editorial Items, by Race, 1977

	White	Non-White
Local and state news	56	62
General local news	53	60
Local and state government	60	65
International news	64	65
Wars, rebellions	65	72
International, diplomatic	64	64
U.S. government, domestic	67	68
Other general interest		
Crime	67	73
Education, school news	53	73
Cultural events, reviews	49	46
Public health, welfare	69	77
News in brief	65	64
Accidents, disaster	75	76
Social problems, protest	69	76
Obituaries	54	53
Labor, wages	67	70
Environment	69	69
Energy problems	74	82
Racial news, minorities	64	72
Weather	69	81
Science, invention	66	63
Travel	59	70
Taxes	68	79
Religion	53	69
Comics	45	50
Editorial cartoons	48	50
Puzzles horoscopes	42	42
T.V./Radio logs	63	68
Entertainers, Hollywood	55	59
Letters to the editor	62	65
Advice columns	61	64
Political columns	64	61
Men's interest	41	44
Sports	37	45
Business, finance	49	42
Women's interest	47	51
Fashion, society	41	45
Food, home, garden	50	58
Other items not classified elsewhere	51	54

personal newspaper, the infrequent readers greatly resemble the frequent readers in their levels of interest in specific kinds of subject matter (1977). For many kinds of content there is no difference at all. There is no type of content that is *much* more appealing to infrequent readers than to frequent ones. Infrequent readers are slightly more interested in food, religion, school news, science, health, TV logs, war and disarmament talks. They are less interested in welfare, labor and wages, race, travel, comics, letters, political columns, taxes, and cultural news.

Do people who prefer the particular newspaper on which they were interviewed differ in their reading interests from those who have no preference? As a matter of fact, they do: 25% of them rated the average item as "very interesting," while among the indifferent the rating was 21%. However, the importance ratings were virtually identical. But the differences in interest levels are merely an expression of differences in reading frequency between the two groups. Of those with a preference for a particular newspaper, 84% were frequent readers; among the remainder the proportion was only 20%. Frequent readers ascribe the same levels of interest and importance to items in the papers they prefer and to items in papers for which they have no preference. Among infrequent readers, interest levels are slightly higher for items in the preferred papers.

Among people over 35, both frequent and infrequent readers prefer an all-news paper to one consisting mostly of features. The frequent readers in this age group are distinguished by a very strong preference for the kind of detail on major stories that newspapers offer and that television does not. The nonreaders would prefer a feature paper.

Age does make a real difference in the interests of people who read the paper infrequently or not at all. Those under 35 are disinterested in politics and current events. They are more interested in music, records, and consumer subjects. The older group shows more interest in home maintenance and repairs, home furnishings, fashion, religion, weddings and engagements, hunting and fishing, and TV program logs.

These findings suggest that there is no single magic prescription for an editor who is trying to win over people to more regular reading habits. The very elements of content that he might strengthen to attract the younger people who read lightly, or who don't read, might make his paper seem less inviting to the older people he is anxious to convert.

Unfortunately, there are no historical trend data to show whether newspaper reading interests in the United States have undergone a change during the period that audience levels dipped. However, two comparable studies made in 1962 and 1975 for the Canadian Daily Newspaper Publishers Association suggest that they have. Readership of classified ads went up, and there was no significant change in the reported reading of front-page news, entertainment, business and editorial pages, or of retail ads. But there were drops in the reading of comics and of the radio–television columns; somewhat fewer men readers reported reading the sports; and fewer women readers, the women's pages. In every case, the dip was more pronounced among younger people than among older ones. This was especially true of the one category of content where the initial level of interest was lowest (among those measured) and the drop most severe: the news of births, marriages, and deaths—precisely the kind of highly localized information that was once the backbone of the newspaper's traditional community function.

DO EDITORS KNOW THEIR READERS?

How do editors' assessments of reader interests jibe with the actual findings of the national survey which was being conducted at the same time (1977)?

Editors' judgments are, by definition, impeccable when it comes to evaluating quality in journalism. Who else, after all, can set standards of excellence? But how accurately do editors perceive readers' *interests*? Even to ask this question invites editorial mistrust, for it suggests that the judgments that go into the creation of the living newspaper can be second-guessed by readers reacting to out-of-context questions in an interview. Several studies have indeed shown a discrepancy between editors' and readers' ratings of the same subjects. In conjunction with our 1966 study, managing editors were asked to rank the public's probable response to the same 120 news items, presented in summary form, that the public had already rated. They scored 11% better than chance.

Ralph Martin, Garrett O'Keefe, and Oguz Nayman got 65 editors of daily newspapers in Wisconsin to evaluate newspaper treatment of a story involving campus demonstrations at the University of Wisconsin in 1969.[11] They then compared their evaluations with those of over one thousand Wisconsin newspaper readers. They found that readers did not clearly perceive the newspapers' stand on a particular news event and that there was little agreement between editors and their readers. Moreover, "editors think they agree more with their readers than they indeed do."

Further evidence of the misperception by editors of the public's news interests comes from a 1977 Harris survey, in which 162 leading editors and journalists were questioned, along with a cross-section of the public, about 14 different types of news. Among the public, 74% said they were very interested in local news, but 88% of the newspeople described the public as very interested, an overstatement of the order of one-fifth. Interest in sports news

---

[11]Ralph K. Martin, Garrett J. O'Keefe, & Oguz B. Nayman, "Opinion Agreement and Accuracy Between Editors and Their Readers," *Journalism Quarterly*, Vol. 49, No. 3, Autumn 1972, pp. 460–468.

was heavily overestimated, probably because editors had only men readers in mind. And interest in entertainment and cultural news, and in fashion news, was also overestimated. But for all the other listed types of news, the professional newspeople substantially underestimated the levels of public interest, partly because they were far more selective in their judgments. In particular, they attributed far less interest than the public showed on state, national, government and political, and international news. (To illustrate, 41% of the public said they were very interested in international news; only 5% of the editors correctly perceived this interest.)

Newspaper editors have given a mixed review to one of USA *Today*'s basic premises—that a generation reared with television news prefers its information in many short takes rather than in lengthy reportage. Although this is a hard subject to tackle in abstract terms, we asked our 1987 national cross-section of readers whether they would prefer their newspaper's available space to be used for in-depth coverage of the main news stories or for a greater number of short items. The edge went to in-depth coverage: 46% against 39% for more short items, while 15% could not make a choice. Among frequent readers, the preference for in-depth coverage was not very different, 49% to 41%.

This relates to yet another point of controversy among editors—the handling of "jump" stories, continued from the front page of the paper or of a section to the inside. Here, the evidence is clear: Three out of four readers (73%) say that if they are reading an article they turn to the page on which it is continued and keep on reading it. Another 16% stay on the first page and read the jump when they come to it. Only 6% report that they usually do not read the rest.

Do readers classify newspaper editorial content as journalists do, or do they use different criteria? To find out, we selected 40 items and had readers sort them into separate piles if they considered the content as similar; they were then asked to code a smaller set of items in terms of a limited number of conventional categories (1979e). The first list of items included movie listings, TV logs, a comic strip, an editorial cartoon, letters to the editor, advice, medical and political columns, and a wide range of news items (including local news specific to each city). The average reader divided these items into about 10 piles but created a total of 80 different labels for them. "Sports" was assigned as a label by 85%, "international news" by 55%, "entertainment" by 53%, "business and finance" by 47%. Only a minority of readers assigned an assortment of other descriptions.

When 19 editors from the same four cities were given the identical task, they came up with about the same number of categories. In general, they gave similar descriptions, although they also added several that reflected their professional orientation, like "breaking," "hard," "soft," and "advance" news.

A local sports story was coded under "sports" by 83% of the readers and

95% of the editors, but other items aroused a high degree of ambiguity. For example, a report on hearings into the cause of a jet air crash was described as "general news" by 21% of the readers, as "national" by 19%, as "local" by 12%, and under the heading of "accidents and disasters" by 12%, but a third used 14 other categories. The editors were much more focused: Two out of five called it "national"; a third, "hard;" and one in six labeled it "spot" news.

A second part of the same exercise involved a coding game, which used only 10 news stories and eight predesignated categories: international, national, local, crime, accidents and disasters, business and finance, sports and "none of the above." On 6 of the 10 items there was virtual unanimity both among editors and readers. There was disagreement on a local human interest story, an article about the atmosphere of Venus, one about a local theft, and the previously mentioned story about the jet crash hearings. Apparently some events defy easy categorization and arouse different responses from readers who bring different perspectives and expectations to bear on them or who respond to different cues within the context of a complex story. Certain kinds of items, like crime or sports, may be local, national, or even international in scope.

WHAT READERS REMEMBER READING

The articles and ads that people recognize a day after they have read the paper are, as I have pointed out, only a selection of the ones they actually looked at in their initial reading. Yet readers' reports reflect their inclinations, and the comparison of their responses to different types of content is revealing.

In our 1982 national survey, we reverted to the use of the recognition method to measure "yesterday" readership of all items of 5 or more inches on 10 selected pages (the front and back pages and four interior spreads randomly selected) among readers who reported opening them. People who had not read a paper "yesterday" (but who were newspaper readers) were taken through 10 pages of the paper they ordinarily read and asked about their interest in each item over 5 inches. The average item received a higher score for interest (44%) than for readership (35%), but the general pattern of the results for the various kinds of content turns out to be similar on both measures.

There is, however, a discrepancy between what readers report when they are asked about specific articles and what they respond to a more general question on what they "usually" read. For instance, international news items get higher average readership among women (37%) than local news (29%), even though women rank local news higher both by the criterion of "usual" readership and in answer to a question about what they care about most.

The average item on opened pages was read by approximately the same percentage of readers on morning (35%) and afternoon (33%) papers, even though morning papers were more likely to be thicker metropolitan publications. (The tendency for thicker papers to get higher readership for items on opened pages holds up across seven major kinds of content and is especially marked in the case of sports news.)

Larger items over 20 column inches in size were more likely to be read in every content category than smaller items, except that comic strips, though small in size, got high readership. Illustrated articles (42%) and solo illustrations (42%) did better than items of straight text (31%). Articles on right-hand pages (34%) and left-hand pages (32%) did almost equally well, corroborating the results of recognition studies of many thousands of newspaper ads.

For technical reasons, it was not possible in 1982 to break out readership for every minor category of content that had been identified separately in 1977 and 1971. However, when the major categories are compared, as in Table 9.16, the range of readership levels is roughly two to one, with highs of 51% for the average news summary and 48% for the typical item of crime news and a low of 22% for the average story on amateur sports. This variation is far less than what we get in response to more general and subjective questions.

Hard news stories receive higher scores than features, other than personal advice, which is by far the best read thing in the paper among women. International news scores higher (40%) than national (36%) and local news (31%). Among people who did not read the paper "yesterday," we also find international and national news higher in interest than local items, but there is no clear advantage for hard news over features.

The detailed analysis of 80,000 specific items documents the diversity of readers' interests and reading habits. Different kinds of readers respond to different kinds of content, but every kind of content finds at least some readers in every population segment. Some young adults read obituaries and some older people read rock concert reviews.

The better educated tend to report reading slightly more items in most categories, but the variations among different types of readers are less striking than they would be if it were possible to make more detailed subdivisions of the content (Table 9.17). The average item of international news, for example, is read by the same proportion of those at the highest and lowest income levels, but different kinds of international stories might attract readers more selectively along social class lines.

Among nonreaders, the proportion "very" or "somewhat interested" in the items under each content heading shows the same kinds of variations for each sex as does the readership reported by readers who opened the page (Table 9.16). Except for the markedly different response to sports by men and

TABLE 9.16
Reported Readership and Interest in Different Types of Editorial Items, by Sex, 1982

	% of readers reading average item on opened pages			% of nonreaders "very" or "somewhat" interested		
	Total	Males	Females	Total	Males	Females
Average for all editorial items	35	35	34	44	46	42
Economic news, actions & policies	31	34	28	44	46	41
Environment, resources, population, energy	36	37	35	50	61	44
Government actions (U.S. & foreign)	30	32	28	43	40	45
War, rebellions, defense activity	44	48	40	57	55	59
Crime	48	48	47	58	56	60
Professional sports	30	39	20	29	50	14
Other sports	22	27	17	35	49	23
Editorials, unsigned	27	32	22	50	47	53
Editorial cartoons	36	44	29	47	46	47
Other editorial page content[a]	31	34	29	47	46	47
Education, child care	33	31	35	45	43	46
Cultural events, arts, reviews	29	25	32	43	42	44
Other amusements[b]	36	31	40	44	39	47
Personal advice columns	47	34	57	56	47	66
Other general interests[c]	36	32	40	44	39	47
Health, welfare, social issues	40	38	42	61	59	62
News summaries, briefs, index	51	51	51	45	44	46
All other content[6]	40	39	41	63	53	69
International news items	40	44	37	53	52	54
National news items	36	37	35	51	51	50
State & local news items	31	33	29	41	44	39

[a]Includes letters to the editor and political columns that may or may not appear on the editorial page itself.

[b]Includes comics, puzzles, horoscopes, TV & radio listings.

[c]Includes food, home society, obituaries, and gossip columns.

[d]All other content not classified elsewhere (science, inventions, religion, etc.).

women, the variations are remarkably small, suggesting that the character of the individual item is what counts rather than the general category into which it can most easily be fit.

Among readers, attention levels are much higher for illustrations (photos) or for stories accompanied by illustrations than they are for straight text. Cartoons, comics, and graphics fall in between. Among nonreaders, the interest pattern is similar. Reading and interest scores are both about the same for editorial items on right and left pages. Stories arouse slightly more

TABLE 9.17

Percentage of Editorial Items Read on Opened Pages, by Reader Characteristics, 1982

	Average: All items	International	National	State, local	Editorial page	Total sports	Amusements	Other general interest
Total adults	35	40	36	31	31	27	35	36
By age:								
18–24 years	28	32	28	22	29	24	25	29
25–34 years	36	39	32	32	30	31	41	39
35–44 years	36	38	38	32	28	32	32	41
45–64 years	37	45	38	34	33	29	35	37
65+	35	41	41	31	32	21	37	35
By education:								
College graduate	38	47	42	36	57	28	35	40
1–3 years college	34	42	37	24	34	27	32	37
High school graduate	34	33	33	31	28	30	36	36
Some high school or less	32	42	33	29	27	22	32	32
By household income:								
$35,000 +	35	40	38	33	34	23	36	37
$15,000–$34,999	34	42	32	28	30	36	28	36
$25,000–$24,999	36	44	33	32	29	37	26	39
Under $15,000	34	40	36	30	31	23	39	41
By census region:								
Northeast	38	42	42	35	38	27	36	42
North Central	31	37	23	26	24	25	34	32
South	34	40	36	33	31	26	33	35
West	37	44	33	28	33	31	39	38
By locality type:								
Central city	39	41	38	35	29	20	37	41
Suburban	37	42	40	31	33	26	38	40
Nonmetropolitan	28	34	28	27	28	19	28	30

reader attention and interest when they appear on pages that consist over half of advertising than on pages on which text predominates.

Front-page stories get much better readership than the average item, as well as higher interest among nonreaders. Stories on the back pages of the paper or of separate sections get slightly more reading or interest than does the average item. But apart from that, reading levels vary remarkably little as we move from the front to the back of the paper.

Similarly, readership and interest are appreciably higher for larger articles (many of which include illustrations), but items of different sizes below 18 column inches show virtually no difference. This supports our conclusion that people going through the paper engage in a systematic search for what is relevant to them and will read it or judge it as interesting or not, regardless of size.

WHAT IS USUALLY READ?

Responses to specific items provide a more authentic picture of reading patterns than do answers to more general questions, yet specific items run only once, while general categories of content are perennial and evoke the continuing predispositions to read or not read that editors must confront. In 1987, we presented readers with a shuffled set of 30 cards, each naming "a different kind of news, feature, or advertising item appearing in most daily newspapers." Readers were asked to set aside the ones they do not usually read and then to pick the three they most like to read.

For men, as Table 9.18 shows, the news categories—and even several types of advertising—surpassed the features. For women, supermarket and apparel ads surpassed the average category of news, and features were close behind.[12]

Local news ranked number one. Frequent readers mentioned an average of 18.1 out of 30 choices shown in Table 9.19; infrequent readers mentioned fewer, 15.2. The infrequent readers were actually more likely to say they usually read movie ads and help wanted ads, and they were just as responsive as frequent readers to real estate classified ads, clothing ads, supermarket ads, movie reviews, crossword puzzles, and fashion and lifestyle features. But they were substantially less likely to say they usually read other types of content, particularly hard news and political commentary. The inescapable conclusion is that they read papers less often because they are less attracted by most

---

[12]This echoes a finding of our 1982 study. Of the readers who reported opening to the page on which an ad appeared, 16% said they saw or read it, but the proportion ranged from 12% of the ads of less than a quarter page to 44% of the ads of a page or larger. Ads on pages that were more than half advertising were better read than those on pages where editorial content predominated. This did not merely reflect the greater attention paid to larger ads, because the relationship held up even when ads of half a page or more were excluded from the analysis.

TABLE 9.18
Kinds of Items and Advertising Usually Read,[a] 1987

	Adults	Men	Women
Average (mean):			
13 kinds of news items	62%	77%	59%
Average (mean):			
12 kinds of features	49	43	55
Supermarket ads	58	40	73
Store ads for clothing	57	40	73
Movie ads	50	47	53
Help wanted classified	43	42	44
Real estate classified	31	34	28

[a]Q: "Each of these cards contains a different kind of news, feature, or advertising item appearing in most daily newspapers. Please look through them and put to one side the kinds of things you don't usually read or look at. Now, from the cards you have left, please pick out the three that are the kinds of things in the paper you most like to read."

of the editorial content. Yet every type of that content is still usually read by a substantial proportion of these less frequent readers.

When asked which three things in the paper they most like to read, local community news ranks high with both frequent and infrequent readers. The infrequent are predictably less likely to single out international news and news about local politics and show a stronger interest in advertisements.

The widest assortment of content is usually read by men (Table 9.20) and by people of better education (Table 9.21) — which means also by more Whites than Blacks (Table 9.22). The age differences shown in Table 9.23 are somewhat predictable, with older people more likely to read obituaries and young ones comics, movie reviews, and help wanted ads. What is more surprising, however, is that younger newspaper readers say they usually read most of the gamut of newspaper content. Though they are less avid readers of national and world news and of features with a political aspect (editorials, opinion columns, and polls), most of them dip into the full range of what newspapers offer — that is, once they have defined themselves as newspaper readers.

HOW IMPORTANT IS LOCAL NEWS?

In his novel, The Genius, Theodore Dreiser (a former newspaper man) describes a midwestern town of "somewhere near ten thousand" a century ago. On the public square were the county courthouse and four newspapers. "These two morning and two evening newspapers made the population fairly aware of the fact that life was full of issues, local and national, and that there

TABLE 9.19
Kinds of Items Usually Read or Looked At and Most Liked, by Frequent and Infrequent
Readers, 1987

	Usually read or look at			Most like to read		
	Total	Frequent readers	Infrequent readers	Total	Frequent readers	Infrequent readers
News about local community	84%	90%	75%	30%	32%	27%
International/World news	75	83	64	25	28	20
News briefs/summaries	74	84	62	15	16	13
News about President/Congress	72	81	59	9	10	8
Local government/politics	69	78	57	14	16	10
Economy	68	74	59	9	10	8
Celebrity/Famous	65	70	60	7	6	9
TV program listings	60	62	58	8	6	11
Advice columns	59	65	49	16	16	16
Comics/Funnies	58	60	54	17	17	17
Supermarket ads	58	58	57	12	9	16
Calendar/Local events	57	61	51	5	3	8
Store ads/Clothes	57	59	55	6	4	9
Editorials/Editorial opinion	55	67	39	8	10	5
Letters to editor	55	66	39	7	8	5
Food pages	54	59	47	9	8	10
Local sports	53	58	44	15	15	14
In-depth investigative	53	61	42	6	6	6
Public opinion polls	52	62	37	2	3	2
Professional sports	51	57	44	23	23	25
Obituaries	50	58	39	9	11	7
Movie reviews	48	49	47	4	3	5
Fashion/Lifestyle	47	49	44	7	5	8
Business/Financial	46	55	34	10	13	7
Political opinion	45	55	31	2	2	1
Help wanted classified	43	40	47	8	5	12
Movie ads	40	48	53	6	3	9
Real estate classified	31	31	30	3	2	5
Book reviews	27	31	21	1	1	2
Crossword puzzle	26	26	25	5	6	3

were many interesting and varied things to do." Dreiser goes on to describe the

> dingy office of the so-called editor, or managing editor, or city editor—for all three were the same person . . . It took him from eight in the morning until two in the afternoon to gather what local news there was and either write it or edit it. He seemed to have a number of correspondents who sent him weekly

TABLE 9.20
Kinds of Items Usually Read, By Sex, 1987

Feature	Total	Male	Female
News about local community	84%	84%	83%
International/World news	75	79	71
News briefs/summaries	74	77	72
News about President/Congress	72	79	66
Local government/politics	69	74	65
Economy	68	73	62
Celebrity/Famous	65	56	74
TV program listings	60	58	62
Advice columns	59	43	73
Comics/Funnies	58	60	56
Supermarket ads	58	40	73
Calendar/Local events	57	52	61
Store ads/Clothes	57	40	73
Editorials/Editorial opinion	55	53	58
Letters to editor	55	51	58
Food pages	54	35	72
Local sports	53	63	43
In-depth investigative	53	52	54
Public opinion polls	52	54	50
Professional sports	51	72	32
Movie ads	50	47	53
Obituaries	50	43	57
Movie reviews	48	48	54
Fashion/Lifestyle	47	26	67
Business/Financial	46	57	36
Political opinion	45	48	41
Help wanted classified	43	42	44
Real estate classified	31	34	28
Book reviews	27	21	32
Crossword puzzle	26	22	29

batches of news from surrounding points. The Associated Press furnished him with a few minor items by telegraph, and there was a "patent insides," two pages of fiction, household hints, medicine ads, and what not, which saved him considerable time and stress. Most of the news that came to him received short shrift in the matter of editing. "In Chicago we used to give a lot of attention to this sort of thing," [he] was wont to declare to anyone who was near, "but you can't do it down here. The readers really don't expect it. They're looking for local items. I always look after the local items pretty sharp."

Journalists still distinguish between the local stories that are generated in the paper's own newsroom and the dispatches that come in over the wire

TABLE 9.21
Kinds of Items Usually Read, By Education, 1987

Feature	Total	Not high school graduate	High school graduate	Some college	College graduate
News about local community	84%	80%	83%	86%	85%
International/World news	75	67	72	76	86
News briefs/summaries	74	70	73	78	78
News about President/Congress	72	64	66	74	86
Local government/politics	69	62	65	72	79
Economy	68	63	65	66	77
Celebrity/Famous	65	61	65	70	66
TV program listings	60	63	62	59	55
Advice columns	59	56	60	61	55
Comics/Funnies	58	56	57	61	57
Supermarket ads	58	69	62	52	45
Calendar/Local events	57	52	53	60	63
Store ads/Clothes	57	60	59	55	55
Editorials/Editorial opinion	55	43	54	56	67
Letters to editor	55	47	54	52	66
Food pages	54	65	56	51	44
Local sports	53	49	54	52	55
In-depth investigative	53	41	52	54	65
Public opinion polls	52	40	46	57	69
Professional sports	51	46	49	53	59
Movie ads	50	39	49	57	54
Obituaries	50	56	54	43	44
Movie reviews	48	36	47	53	57
Fashion/Lifestyle	47	41	48	50	48
Business/Financial	46	32	43	48	63
Political opinion	45	35	43	42	61
Help wanted classified	43	44	46	42	40
Real estate classified	31	29	32	29	32
Book reviews	27	16	24	28	40
Crossword puzzle	26	28	25	26	23

from farther afield. What is a meaningful distinction for those who produce a newspaper may not be perceived in the same way by readers.

For a daily of 8,000 circulation in a rural area, local news *is* community news; it deals with personalities, people, and situations to which almost any reader can relate directly. Not everything that happens locally has the same news value, of course, but it all fits into the mosaic of common everyday experience.

In a huge metropolitan region, events that make news are those that meet

TABLE 9.22
Kinds of Items Usually Read, By Race, 1987

Feature	Total	White	Black
News about local community	84%	85%	72%
International/World news	75	76	67
News briefs/summaries	74	76	64
News about President/Congress	72	74	64
Local government/politics	69	70	65
Economy	68	68	66
Celebrity/Famous	65	66	63
TV program listings	60	59	69
Advice columns	59	60	53
Comics/Funnies	58	59	48
Supermarket ads	58	56	71
Calendar/Local events	57	58	50
Store ads/Clothes	57	56	65
Editorials/Editorial opinion	55	58	47
Letters to editor	55	58	42
Food pages	54	54	55
Local sports	53	51	60
In-depth investigative	53	55	45
Public opinion polls	52	54	49
Professional sports	51	50	54
Movie ads	50	49	55
Obituaries	50	53	42
Movie reviews	48	44	52
Fashion/Lifestyle	47	47	51
Business/Financial	46	47	42
Political opinion	45	46	44
Help wanted classified	43	41	57
Real estate classified	31	30	38
Book reviews	27	28	22
Crossword puzzle	26	25	31

general criteria of interest and importance. Apart from public figures, the protagonists of stories are not known personally to the readers.

A majority of the American public reads metropolitan papers, but a majority of the papers published falls somewhere between the extremes of size. Their editors must therefore distinguish between what is inherently newsworthy for most of their readers (either because of its areawide impact or dramatic character) and what hits home to those readers who live in the specific neighborhood where the event takes place or who share some common attribute with those involved. Both kinds of stories are local news; both can generate widely varying levels of interest.

TABLE 9.23
Kinds of Items Usually Read, By Age, 1987

Feature	Total	18–34	35–54	55+
News about local community	84%	79%	88%	85%
International/World news	75	68	80	78
News briefs/summaries	74	69	80	74
News about President/Congress	72	62	76	80
Local government/politics	69	57	76	76
Economy	68	61	74	69
Celebrity/Famous	65	66	68	62
TV program listings	60	61	58	62
Advice columns	59	56	58	63
Comics/Funnies	58	64	53	55
Supermarket ads	58	53	56	66
Calendar/Local events	57	53	60	57
Store ads/Clothes	57	60	58	53
Editorials/Editorial opinion	55	40	60	70
Letters to editor	55	43	57	68
Food pages	54	44	57	63
Local sports	53	53	54	50
In-depth investigative	53	48	60	51
Public opinion polls	52	43	57	57
Professional sports	51	52	52	50
Movie ads	50	69	48	27
Obituaries	50	34	52	69
Movie reviews	48	61	48	31
Fashion/Lifestyle	47	51	48	42
Business/Financial	46	35	54	51
Political opinion	45	33	48	56
Help wanted classified	43	54	45	27
Real estate classified	31	30	34	28
Book reviews	27	21	33	27
Crossword puzzle	26	24	24	30

The distinction between what is local and what is not is increasingly hard to make. If a Marine from the newspaper's area is injured in a foreign trouble spot, is that local or international news? Similarly, the line between national and international news is increasingly blurry. Is the debate over U.S. policy in Central America national or international? Readers respond to stories in terms of their relevance, importance, or human interest, regardless of their dateline.

A person who is absorbed in the political and civic affairs of his own community might be thought to show a more realistic involvement with life's problems than one who seeks out accounts of earthquakes on distant continents or of the lovelife of European royalty. Yet normally we assume the reverse: Parochial concerns seem far less appropriate to the realistic demands of our complex society that does an interest in the broader affairs of the nation and the world. It seems reasonable to assume, moreover, that an interest in the wider world hinges on a capacity for abstraction and on the imagination necessary to emphathize with remote figures in an unfamiliar environment. Accounts of local news events, even in the impersonal metropolis, have points of reference to the reader's own experience. The reader who seeks out the news of his own immediate world must be thought of as more literal-minded and as taking comfort in the security of familiar scenes and protagonists. Correspondingly, as he reads he resists any involvement with the threatening forces that impinge on his little world from the great and troublesome world outside.

Few people would claim to be exclusively interested or totally uninterested in the events of one sphere or the other. But forced to choose between local and world news, the American public divided rather evenly in 1961: 45% reported a greater interest in the national or international scene, 52% in what is happening in their own city or town. However, there was a sharp difference between men and women. Men showed a greater preference for national and international news, women for news of local events. Interest in local news was greatest among older people, whose roots in the community go deep, and least among young people in their 20s who have the greatest feelings of personal mobility.

Among both men and women, interest in national and international events increases with education and income. The better-educated person, more cosmopolitan in outlook and least attached to television entertainment, continues to rely on newspapers for his daily orientation to the changing world around him.

Common sense tells us that urbanity is an urban phenomenon, and the evidence bears this out. In cities of half a million and over and in suburbs, less than half those interviewed expressed more interest in local news, whereas in communities of under 2,500, nearly two out of three preferred it.

By the time of our 1982 study, a majority of the general public, and three-fourths of the college graduates, were more interested in international and national news than in the news of their own city or town. Not surprisingly, local news is of greatest interest in rural areas and of least interest in large metropolitan areas.[13] And within metropolitan areas, in-

---

[13]As we saw earlier, the balance of content is different in papers of different sizes. The biggest papers carry 27% more national/international than local news, small papers 28% less, but hard news (international, national, and state/local items) accounts for only 21% of all the items in the small papers and 32% in the big ones.

terest in local news is less among suburban readers than it is among central-city residents. It is of most concern to the people who have lived longest in a community. But it is not the exact obverse of interest in the world scene. Interest in local news is highest among people in their 30s and 40s. It is higher among women than among men. It is higher among people in the middle income range than among those at either extreme. It is not related to the level of education, but it is somewhat greater among frequent newspaper readers.

Readers who say they are more interested in national and international news "usually read" those categories of content more than those who are interested in local news (1982). But they "usually read" news items about the local community to the same extent as the locally oriented, and they actually read news of local government and politics more. They are, in short, the most news-hungry people around.[14]

In addition to the 84% who said in 1987 that they usually read news about the local community, 69% read the news about local politics or government; 57% read the calendar or schedule of local events; 50%, the obituaries; and 53%, sports news about local schools, colleges, or clubs (Table 9.19).

Although a high proportion said they usually read the calendar of local events, only 3% said it is one of the things they care about most. Taking men and women together, 15% care most about local schools and college sports news, while 23% care most about news of professional sports. Fourteen percent said they care most about news about local politics or government; 9% care most about obituaries. Thus, the *intensity* of appeal of these locally originated types of coverage can vary substantially among those who scan them regularly. Although virtually everybody reads some kind of local news, and it is considered an important element of the paper, different kinds of readers respond to different kinds of specific local stories.

Recent decades have undoubtedly reshaped the concern of most Americans with the broader events of the nation and the world. This would follow logically from the steady movement into metropolitan areas, the rising levels of education, and the impact of network television news coverage.

In 1966, more people (57%) said they were interested in local news than in national and international news (45%), with the preference greater in small towns than in big ones. But this general orientation in attitude was not borne out by the responses given in 1977 to specific items of local news and of national and international news. Compared to local items, the same proportion of international items were rated both "very interesting" and "very

---

[14]A 1984 study by Clark, Martire, and Bartolomeo found that 19% of the readers were most interested in news of their own town or city, 15% in the region or area, and 13% in the state. This total of 47% contrasted with the 33% who said they were most interested in national news and 18% most interested in international news, for a total of 51%.

important," but the ratings for national items were a fourth higher. Among those 18 to 29, the average international item was rated 17% higher and the average national news item 49% higher.[15]

Women questioned in 1974 about the kinds of news they usually read mentioned news of their local community first, then national news, news of the whole metropolitan area, world news, and news of downtown. The margins of differences were not great, since most women reported usually reading news on all these subjects. But it is worth noting that when people express an interest in local news, they are not always necessarily thinking of the conventional reporting of "downtown" events that have historically been the metropolitan newspaper's stock in trade. Naturally, city dwellers tended to mention the city more often; suburbanites, the neighborhood. News of the city was far more important to residents of Kansas City; in Los Angeles it was neck and neck with news of the neighborhood—illustrating the great differences between living patterns in these two metropolitan areas.

Local news covers a variety of subjects. Of all the stories classified under this heading in 1982, 23% dealt with the actions of local governmental authorities, 22% were crime stories, 21% were school news, 11% dealt with accidents, and 7% were traditional "society news"—births, marriages, engagements, "chicken dinners." When we break local news into its components, these draw quite a range of responses from the public.

Responses to specific news stories are more pertinent than the answers readers give to general questions about their reading habits. Compared with the typical item of state or local news, national news stories in 1982 scored 11% higher in reported readership and international news stories scored 29% higher. Is this because international stories are more often played up on the front page or toward the front of the paper? They are, but that is not the explanation. No matter where they appear in the paper, the readership of world news is markedly ahead of local stories. And the advantage holds for stories of every size, though international stories tend to run longer. (Among people who had *not* read "yesterday's" paper, interest in the typical international story also ran 29% ahead of interest in local news items.)

It is clear that readers are interested in the news from around the world. Television network news has made international settings and personalities increasingly familiar to the American public. Still, a 1983 Harris survey found that only one American in four knew that the United States was supporting the government rather than the rebels in El Salvador.

The metropolitan newspaper editor must always assume that his hetero-

---

[15]This is corroborated by a study of the reading habits of young people in Virginia, West Virginia, and Michigan, which also concluded that world and international news are comparatively more interesting to them than strictly local news. John C. Schweitzer, *Readership Habits of the Young*, Bloomington, Indiana, July, 1976.

geneous, constantly changing readership is largely unfamiliar with many of the personalities on whom he reports. The small-town editor can assume otherwise, as in the (complete) item, "Mrs. Millard Lang is just about as she has been for a while."

As markets expanded their geographic boundaries, many newspapers dropped the city names from their mastheads, broadening their scope but making their identity somewhat ambiguous. As a result, there are today many dailies scattered across the country carrying generic names like The *News*, The *Tribune*, or The *Journal*. As in the past, markets become what newspapers cover.

Since local news is increasingly hard to define, readers in our 1987 survey were asked to indicate from a list of four definitions which ones applied and also which one fit best. As Table 9.24 shows, almost all of them accepted both news of the city or metropolitan area and news of their neighborhood as applicable, but news of the city was considered the best fit.

THE CHANGING IMPORTANCE OF LOCAL NEWS

The detailed reporting of local news in all its variety, complexity, and minutiae demands the kind of staffing and space that newspapers are uniquely equipped to provide and that is their best guarantee of continuing success in the face of television news competition.

A key editorial tenet appears to be that a good paper reflects the work and effort of its own staff and is produced for its own community with a minimum of canned or boilerplate material. This gives rise to the further assumption that a good paper will carry a large proportion of local news, since that is the kind of copy that a newspaper's own staff is likely to generate. As we have noted, editors rank emphasis on local news high in reader interest as well. Few individual newspapers can afford the luxury of a Washington bureau, and only a handful have foreign correspondents. The ascendant power of television network news has led many editors to concentrate on local coverage, where the newspaper's preeminence is rarely challenged.

According to the editors, about half of the copy in their papers is

TABLE 9.24
How Readers Define Local News, Which Areas Fit the Definition? 1987

	Fits	*One best fit*
News about my neighborhood	92%	19%
Happenings in (name of central city)	91	45
News about this region	73	30
Events in this state	34	7

staff-written, somewhat less than the ideal proportion. Of the straight news items measured in the national survey, about three out of five were local in content and the remainder were general.

As already noted, between 1977 and 1987 most papers changed the proportions of local and state news to national and international news in the direction of greater emphasis on local news. Proportionately fewer of the papers of over 100,000 circulation shifted the balance of their news content in the direction of local material, but more of them boosted features at the expense of news. The shift from coverage of national and world news was especially marked in the case of smaller papers with under 25,000 daily circulation. Two-thirds of those who reported any substantial editorial change in 1979 reported an increased emphasis on local news.

Still, as we have shown, the average item of local news has fewer readers (in 1982) and slightly fewer people who say they are interested in it or very interested in it (in 1977) than the average item of general (national or international) news. This runs counter to what most editors believe and to what many of them appear to have practiced. There may be a number of explanations:

1. One might be that TV news has steadily intensified public interest in the major national and international issues and news personalities. They are vivid, familiar, and meaningful to the average person in a way that was not true in the past.

2. In today's mobile society, people are more cosmopolitan and less parochial in orientation. They feel less rooted in their local communities and more closely connected to others with similar occupational or avocational interests in other parts of the country.

3. As I stressed in Chapter 1, fewer of the metropolitan newspaper's readers live within the political jurisdiction that is a major source of its news. Local news is far more segmented than it used to be, and any particular event is likely to affect far fewer people.

As I noted earlier in this chapter, the memorability of local events as big news, upsetting news, or good news is extremely low relative to the amount of space they occupy in the press and relative to the more dramatic stories that are likely to be occurring in the wider world at any given time.

Editors correctly perceive the public's concern with the big news story that "hits them where they live," in contrast to events that seem remote and impersonal. But many local news stories come under the heading of minutiae. A high proportion of local news items are actually sublocal in that they deal with events and people with whom the vast majority of readers can not identify. Even with regional editions, it is harder than ever for a metropolitan newspaper to give the kind of detailed coverage of neighborhood events, politics, and personalities that community weeklies cover as a matter of course.

It should not be necessary to point out that in talking about local and other kinds of news we are drawing an unrealistic and arbitrary distinction. Of course, readers expect to be given *both*, just as they expect their newspaper to entertain as well as to inform them.

NEWS AND ENTERTAINMENT

The subject matter of the news is an infinitely more complicated business than it used to be. There are over twice as many sovereign countries in the world as there were in 1950. American government—federal, state, and local—has a budget in constant dollars over six times as big as it was then, and its structure is vastly more complex, with more different specialized agencies all generating news. This means that vastly more news is being made in the area of public affairs—internationally, nationally, regionally, locally. Increasingly, more of it is of specialized interest and requires complex background information to make it understandable. Government news involves a volatile cast of easily forgettable characters. Yet tedious as much of the news sometimes appears to be, it is, not surprisingly, the preoccupation of editors.

Editors have always wanted to meet the latest possible deadlines that their production and circulation departments could give them, to present the very latest news. Broadcast news bulletins have eliminated the newspaper extra. In today's tangled traffic, the logistics of timely distribution are tougher than ever. The net effect may be to put more editorial emphasis on feature material as well as on news interpretation, both of which can be prepared at a more deliberate pace. The preference for features is strongest among younger people, whom newspapers are especially eager to attract as readers.

As we have seen, some entertainment features are larded into the newspaper because they are presumed to be high in reader interest, even though many editors appear to believe their papers would be better without them.

Greater use of features may also reflect newspaper editors' response to the challenge of television news. Television news on the local level makes considerable use of "soft" and feature material that can be filmed in advance. This comes off better as on-air entertainment than a talking head reeling off bulletins on fresh-breaking stories that remain unillustrated. It may well be that this has had an effect on the press. Whatever the reason, the non-news content of newspapers has recently had more visibility, as we saw in Chapter 6.

It was noted in Chapter 8 that about three-tenths of the average news hole represents features, according to what the editors report, and that they generally feel this proportion is right. (The definition of "features," was left to the editors' own judgment. Many features, such as political columns, undoubtedly are serious and informative in character, while many news items, such as those purveying personality gossip, are intended to be read for fun. Still it does not seem unreasonable to identify features with entertainment.) Feature or entertainment material also represents about one-eight of the items measured in the 1977 national survey.[16] But it is hard to square the findings of that survey with the prevailing editorial assumption that entertaining features enjoy greater interest than most straight news items.

The first relevant finding is that a majority (59%) of the public would choose a paper entirely devoted to news rather than one which just provided a news summary and consisted mostly of entertaining features. This response might be dismissed as merely an expression of a socially acceptable attitude, yet it tells us that people want and expect a newspaper to cover subjects that, individually, they would not normally read about.[17] At one time, *The New York Times* promoted circulation with the slogan, "You don't have to read it all, but it's nice to know it's all there." The survey findings suggest that this corresponds to a very genuine public sentiment.

Similarly, it will be recalled that when we ask people to construct their "personal newspaper," the formula they typically concoct for themselves gives considerable weight to informational material (like health and medical news) and rather little to pure amusements (like comics or puzzles).

But if the question just mentioned relate to the ideal notion of what a newspaper *should* be, the expressions of interest in individual items or articles provide a dispassionate measurement of public response to newspaper content as it actually is. (The classification of these items by subject matter took place during the processing of the survey results and was invisible to the respondents.) It is worth reiterating our findings:

Except for TV and radio program logs,[18] personal advice columns, and travel articles, entertainment features all score below average in reader

---

[16]The proportions are not identical because editors in many cases may have had in mind feature articles pertaining to news subjects. For example, a personality profile on a baseball player might be considered a feature story, but would have been classified under "sports news" in our national study.

[17]This point is also supported by the disparity between the newspaper articles people rate as "interesting" and those they rate as "important." For example, half of those who find the average sports item "very interesting" also rate it as "not very important."

[18]For years, some publishers, unwilling to give comfort to the competition, refused to run radio—and later television—program listings. Today, virtually all recognize that television is a major subject of interest and of news. A 1987 Roper Survey conducted for United Media found that 68% of adults refer to their local newspaper for information for what to watch on television. Forty percent say they regularly read both daily TV logs and weekend sections. Nineteen percent use only the weekend sections; and 9%, only the daily listings. Thirty-eight percent use *TV Guide*; 24%, the guides distributed by local cable companies.

interest. (Even when the more popular types of material just mentioned are combined with humor and gossip columns, comics, puzzles and horoscopes, cultural and show business stories and reviews, the typical item is rated "very interesting" by 31%.) Again, it must be remembered that the minorities who follow a favorite comic strip, a chess column, or concert notices may be intensely devoted to these features. Editors cannot deal with them lightly.

Editors indicate that they run entertainment features for business rather than professional reasons: to build audience rather than to enhance editorial quality. Yet much of what they run for this purpose turns out to be something less than ideally successful to achieve this objective.

Is this conclusion valid? The national survey findings can be questioned on the grounds that people distort their real feelings when they are interviewed, that they disguise their true interest in trivia, and that they *claim* to be interested in the subjects they *ought* to be interested in as good citizens. Indeed, as we have noted, they do tend to rate articles as interesting if they consider them important. But it is hard to sustain the argument that it is prestigious to admit interest in crime stories (which rate high) and déclassé to acknowledge interest in cultural reviews and events (which rate low).

When research findings contradict expert wisdom or prevailing assumptions, this does not necessarily mean that the experts are wrong; the trouble may lie with the research. This type of inconsistency is nonetheless useful to establish, because it pinpoints areas of controversy for further discussion and inevitably, for further research.

10
MARKETING
AND JOURNALISM

The history of mass media reflects the tension between two conflicting impulses, one to conserve and reinforce existing values and tastes, the other to innovate and thereby to undermine the prevailing conventions. Satisfying current demand is commercially safe in the short run, but it is vulnerable to attrition from the sea-change in values and tastes inevitably brought about both by media competition and by changes in society itself. Moreover, it has never been in the nature of those who create media content to rest comfortably with the formulas of the moment; since their work is in the realm of ideas, they cannot avoid innovation and the unpopular.

I have tried throughout this book to stress the point that the cultural and political functions of newspapers are interdependent with their economic function and thus with their ability to sustain themselves as profitable enterprises. The risk a newspaper takes when it alters its content is the risk of losing readers, whose number is the generally accepted yardstick of its commercial success.

And yet historically, the circulation of a publication—the number of copies distributed—has not been considered a proper measure of its political, cultural, or social impact. In Chapter 3, I commented that with the rise of broadcasting this tangible measure (circulation) was suddenly countered by an intangible: having a radio or television set tuned to a particular program within one's range of hearing or sight. Competition for advertising forced the print media into the realm of using surveys to measure the intangible experience of exposure—audiences and readership rather than printing and physical distribution.

As measurement moved toward the intangible, there has been a widening of the gap between the standard of achievement accepted by the people who regard media seriously as a form of communication, expression, information, and persuasion and the yardsticks used by the people who are concerned with the hard necessities of survival for media as business institutions. Today, most of our knowledge of the media is embodied in very repetitive, expensively collected aggregations of survey statistics that only superficially reflect the realities of communication. These measurements are rarely questioned. Because of the regularity of their appearance, they coincide with the kinds of measurement to which businessmen are accustomed—the balance sheet; records of merchandise purchased, sold, or shipped; payroll reports; and all the other figures that are the very stuff of business cost accounting.

The audience data that come from the media correspond to the business executive's production and sales statistics. Since he thinks of them as being equally real, he regards these numbers on audience size as accurate indications of the effect that he, as a business executive, is actually achieving when he uses media to advertise in. Except at a great expense and after an enormous lapse of time—he has no real way of judging whether or not his advertising is having an effect.

Advertisers like to feel that they differentiate audiences by their characteristics, but in actual practice the criterion of success is audience size, and the complex reality of communication is reduced to bits and pieces that advertisers call "impressions" or "exposure opportunities." Sheer numbers are no indication of the intensity of communications experience that takes place as the result of the audience's exposure to the medium. Yet definable units of measurement are precisely what is required by the businessman's system, of which mass media are a part.

The result of all this is that the media no longer tend to be planned, programmed, edited, and produced for the sake of the communications experience that originally motivated their content. In their origins, the mass media represent the impetus to say something—to get an idea out, to get a message across, to have people listen, react, respond. Today, the media are governed by different principles.

Former RCA Chairman David Sarnoff once defined the public interest as what the public was interested in. CBS's former vice-chairman, Frank Stanton, has given a similar definition: "A program in which a large part of the audience is interested is by that very fact . . . in the public interest."

In the newspaper business, the same philosophy has many powerful adherents. One is Dean Singleton, who built a remarkable publishing empire in the 1980s and who says:

> We do not feel an obligation to print what we think readers ought to know, but what they want to read . . . Some people think a newspaper is a hallowed institution. A newspaper is a product, like a candy bar. You have to package it to make it attractive to the reader. You have to put in the ingredients they want. You have to market it properly.[1]

On another occasion, Singleton observed, "The newspaper of tomorrow is going to have to give readers what they want and not what they need. Who are we to say what they need?"[2]

Undoubtedly, a great many editors would, knowing that "wants" reflect the diet to which consumers are accustomed because someone has fed it to them.

Criticism of the standard of commercial acceptability that prevails in most media usually starts from the premise that an alternative (and better) standard exists than the one imposed by media publishers and broadcasters. However, this position is not invulnera l to the argumbnt that the media operator merely serves the public taste in the interests of "cultural democracy."

Listen to Charles L. Gould, then publisher of the *San Francisco Examiner*, take issue with William Rivers, professor of journalism at Stanford University, who had testified earlier in 1969 Senate hearings on the Newspaper Preservation Act.

> He sneered at the New York *Mirror* as a tawdry newspaper. Does he not then sneer at the 900,000 readers[3] of that paper, many of them from minority groups, who are neither emotionally, psychologically, or educationally on his wave length? . . . By what labored logic can he presume to establish himself as an authority to measure the quality of a newspaper? Do you believe that a newspaper should be judged by professors, by advertisers, or by the public? . . . If all newspapers were tailored to the image and ideas of Professor Rivers, would they not all be tailored to the image of *The New York Times? The New York Times* has always, according to its demographic studies, appealed to families and individuals at the top of the economic and social ladder. Its appeal to those less privileged has been admittedly low. Would these so-called experts deny the right of our less fortunate citizens to newspapers of their liking? Is there not and should there not be encouragement for newspapers with a broader range of appeal than those aimed primarily at the intellectual?

Almost every newspaper editor and publisher today must grapple with this question.

---

[1]Quoted in David Sachsman & Warren Sloat, *The Press and the Suburbs: The Daily Newspapers of New Jersey* (New Brunswick: Center for Policy Research, Rutgers University, 1987), p. 123.

[2]Quoted in *Editor & Publisher*, October 3, 1987.

[3]Gould mistook circulation for readership. The *Mirror* had at least two million readers each day.

CAN THE READERSHIP TREND BE REVERSED?

Are American newspapers locked into an inexorable downward trend in readership formed by great social forces totally beyond their control? If this were so, it would have to be part of a worldwide phenomenon, for many of the same changes in living patterns and personal values are occurring elsewhere, and the effects of electronic media competition are universal. But per capita consumption of newspapers varies widely in countries where the press is privately owned, and the rate and direction of change also show great differences.

Between 1964 and 1984, the ratio of newspaper circulation to total population fell in 11 of 20 Western countries (and Japan) for which comparable data are available, but it rose in the other 9 (Table 10.1). The countries with the lowest living standards, Portugal and Spain, appear on the down side, but they are also among those—like Italy—that showed great economic progress in these two decades. During this period, the penetration of TV grew everywhere, but at very different rates. The growth in the number of television receivers per thousand people ranged from 49% in Sweden (where TV was already well established by the early 1960s) to over 8,000% in

TABLE 10.1
Comparative Circulation/1000 Population, 1964–1984

	1964	1984	% change
Australia	348	296	−15
Austria	248	365	+47
Belgium	285	223	−22
Canada	223	220	−1
Denmark	344	359	+4
Federal Republic of Germany	323	350	+8
France	248	212	−13
Iceland	434	469	+8
Ireland	244	186	−24
Italy	101	96	−5
Japan	439	562	+28
Netherlands	284	310	+9
New Zealand	399	325	−19
Norway	387	501	+29
Portugal	66	49	−26
Spain	153	80	−48
Sweden	505	521	+3
Switzerland	365	392	+7
United Kingdom	523	414	−21
United States	314	268	−16

Source: U.S. Statistical Abstracts

Portugal (where it had barely been introduced). But the median growth was actually greater (192%) in the countries where newspaper penetration went up than in those where it went down (144%). And there was no overall relationship (a rank-order correlation of +.09) between the TV penetration growth and newspaper penetration change.

Though the number of receivers per capita and the number of channels available varied both then and now from country to country, total time spent viewing television in TV homes is remarkably similar. It does not readily explain the differences in circulation trends between England and Germany or between Belgium and Holland. In Japan, where television viewing time is equivalent to that in the United States, daily newspaper circulation is larger, in a country with less than half as many people. This is partly explained by the small size of the Japanese papers and the fact that subscribers to the great national dailies get both a morning and a (totally different) evening edition. But the high level of readership also reflects the high value that the culture gives to information and the strongly cohesive character of this homogeneous society.

An explanation of differences in the circulation penetration levels and trends must be sought case by case by examining the social structure and media system of each country. Whatever the variety of explanations one might come up with, there are no grounds for concluding that the press is everywhere in a period of general and inevitable decline. And that gives good reason for American newspaper managements to be both optimistic and determined to reverse the steady decline in readership levels.

THE "ORGANIZATION OF VICTORY"

Comparable newspapers are regarded by their readers in remarkably different ways, as I showed in Chapter 5. High or low regard is reflected in reactions to *all* the newspaper's ingredients. Subtle distinctions of style, treatment, or physical appearance may be much more significant to readers than the conventional subject matter categories of content analysis used in our national surveys. Readers seem to look at and react to newspapers as a whole rather than in terms of their component parts. They respond to the total package of what a paper represents, rather than to the individual bits and pieces.

The public's perception of what a newspaper is and what it stands for is inseparable from the self-image of those who produce it. This self-image is apt to be reflected throughout, in the paper's preoccupations, its writing style, its political stance. And the people who write for newspapers do not always have a clear view of the paper's readers or of its mission. A study by Cecilie Gaziano and Kristin McGrath of MORI concludes that the press may be losing credibility because a significant minority of journalists are isolated from both their readers and news sources.[4] In a study for the ASNE,[5] Michael Burgoon, Judee Burgoon, and Charles Atkin found that working journalists tended to underestimate the amount of time the public spends with newspapers and the intensity of reading but overestimated the amount of time spent with TV news. They exaggerated the public's interest in features and gave inadequate credit to the interest in hard news. Three out of four disagreed with the idea that "most readers prefer to read a few in-depth stories than a number of shorter items." Significant disaffected minorities (ranging between a quarter and two-fifths) disagreed with optimistic statements and agreed with negative statements about the outlook for newspapers. Both editors and reporters indicated that their own news priorities were different from those of the paper.

It would be difficult to argue that the characteristics of individual newspapers, and their guiding editorial philosophies, have no bearing on their success with readers in the marketplace. But the effects of editorial content are extremely difficult to sort out from all the social forces that bear on the newspaper reading habit.

Many publishers and editors have been convinced that somehow or other their losses in audience stemmed from a failure to keep up with the changing needs and values of their readers. Much soul-searching and beating of breasts follows from this proposition, as well as a considerable amount of editorial experimentation and innovation. Soul-searching and innovation are always all to the good. But the really critical steps required to reestablish the position of newspapers as a universal mass medium involve distribution and not content. Here is the evidence:

1. In the period that circulation has stagnated, or even dropped, public esteem for the press has been stable or rising relative to other institutions.

2. Differences in response to different elements of newspaper content by regular newspaper readers, occasional readers, and nonreaders are comparatively minor. If we were to invent an ideal newspaper to suit the interests of the people who are not reading one today, it would not be too different from the ones now being published; at the very least, it would fall well within the existing range of variety.

3. As we saw in Chapter 8, editors whose papers were gaining circulation and those who had failed to gain showed no visible differences either in their philosophies or in their editorial practices.

---

[4]Cecilie Gaziano & Kristin McGrath, "Newspaper Credibility and Relationships of Newspaper Journalists to Communities," *Journalism Quarterly*, Summer/August 1987, Vol. 64, Nos. 2/3, pp. 317–328, 345.

[5]Judee K. Burgoon, Michael Burgoon, & Charles K. Atkin, "The World of the Working Journalist," ASNE/Newspaper Readership Project, September 1982.

4. The content of the newspapers that people buy at newsstands or from vending racks is identical with the content of the papers that are delivered by a home subscription. Yet the percentage of Americans who read an individually purchased copy is less than it was in 1970. Single-copy sales are concentrated in the major cities, where competition has been most intense and social conditions have generally deteriorated. The inescapable conclusion is that the problems of distribution infinitely outweigh the deficiencies of content as explanations of the drop in readership.

American newspapers show great variability in their editorial formulas and styles. Partly these reflect differences in the nature of the local populations they serve. Partly they reflect the character, objectives, and principles of the owners and editors. It is apparent that editors can exercise considerable leeway in improving both the excellence and the popularity of their papers. As they ponder such possible changes, they must be aware of yet another research conclusion: Readers appear to have certain expectations of a newspaper that go beyond their own immediate and personal reading interests and needs. They expect a newspaper to cover content that they themselves might not read or even approve of. They recognize that newspapers are a community institution, and they want it to serve interests other than their own.

Some years ago, Nobel prize winner Herbert Simon coined a new term that has found its place in modern econometric theory: to "satisfice." To satisfice is to establish the optimum common denominator of acceptability that allows an institution to meet the competing and conflicting needs of many masters. In effect, newspaper editors do just this. They produce something less than the best product they can, but one that the minimum number of people will turn away from. The danger of the marketing approach is that it makes this kind of compromise explicit. If the editor has to worry in advance over how many people will read an article, he may decide not to run it at all. He becomes a follower of public taste when he should be shaping it.

Editors have a wide range of options in handling content, if only because the activity of newspaper reading is profoundly influenced by pricing, delivery service, promotion, and civic conditions over which they have no control. Operating within this latitude of choice, editors may do better to exercise their own professional standards, to go where they believe it wisest and best to go rather than to accept the dictates of what surveys represent to be the reader's wants.

And yet, they should ever keep in mind Hugh Chisholm's observation in his article on "Newspapers" in the authoritative 11th edition of the *Encyclopedia Brittanica*:

> The great journalist is he who makes the paper with which he is connected a success; and in days of competition the elements necessary for obtaining and

keeping a hold on the public are so diverse and the factors bearing on the financial success, the business side of the paper, are so many, that the organization of victory frequently depends on other considerations than those of its intrinsic literary excellence or sagacity of opinion, even if it cannot be wholly independent of these.

EDITORS AND RESEARCH

American newspapers have maintained journalistic integrity by separating the news from the business function. The professional ethos of journalism, however vaguely defined this may be, rests on the principle of independence from commercial constraints.

Still, the constraints are always present, since editors work within a budget of manpower determined by the newspaper's profitability and of space determined by advertising volume. Editors generally retain the power to decide how to deploy their manpower and fill the space. This is precisely the point at which the marketing perspective is apt to intervene, with its fundamental premise that a successful newspaper is one designed to meet consumer desires rather than one that meets the editor's perception of the public's needs. And it is in the business office, with its concern about circulation and advertising revenues, that the marketing perspective arises, thus appearing to pose a new threat to editorial prerogatives.

Is it any wonder that editors have been warned to "Beware the market thinkers"?[6] Market thinkers are those who abandon the traditional task of telling readers what they need to know in favor of the new philosophy of giving them what they want, or claim to want. What they claim to want is, of course, what they say in reader surveys, which have been on the scene since George Gallup started them at the *Des Moines Register* in 1932.

It is no longer uncommon to refer to the newspaper as a product to be marketed, though "product" is an objectionable term for journalists. The ascendancy of the much publicized "program doctors" in local television news has left many newspaper editors concerned about how research might be used to dictate editorial changes.[7] At the 1978 convention of the American

---

[6]William Hornby, "Beware the Market Thinkers," *Quill*, January, 1976, p. 14.

[7]Research has been used to shape local TV news programs exactly as it has been used for many years to evaluate entertainment programming content. The personality of the newscaster is a key determinant of what makes a TV news program attractive, just as the personality of the performers is a primary ingredient in determining the attractiveness of any entertainment show. Research has been used to get newscasters to modify their speech, form of delivery, dress, haircuts, and makeup. It can also lead to decisions on hiring and firing. It has been used to put newscasters in uniform, to change the sets on which they perform, and to set the number and length of items they use, with and without illustration. Research has suggested an emphasis on

Society of Newspaper Editors, hollow laughter greeted one speaker who suggested to his colleagues that they might be replaced by computers. His attempt at facetiousness masked a genuine anxiety. After all, computer runs were at the time (though no longer) routinely used at one newspaper to demonstrate the comparative yield in readership produced per pound of newsprint devoted to one subject rather than another.

Some editors criticized our 1977a survey of their opinions as "invalid," apparently with the apprehension that what they rated as indicative of editorial quality could be quoted back to them as a "true" measure of quality.

Yet in spite of this suspicion, there has never been a time when research was as widely used in the newspaper business as it is at present. And it appears to have won a high degree of acceptance from many editors. Naturally, the first papers to call in the researchers have been the big ones, especially those that have failed to make circulation gains.

A majority of editors on papers of over 50,000 circulation and a third of those in the 25,000–50,000 bracket reported in 1977 that they had used an outside research firm to survey their readers within the past two years; the proportion went up to four out of five on papers of over 100,000. Even on dailies of less than 25,000, 13% had done reader surveys (1977a).[8]

What is the value of this outside research? Only 6% of the editors found it "not particularly useful," while 37% found it "very useful," and 57% described it as "somewhat useful."

The principal utility of this considerable volume of research may well be that it gives editors a better understanding of who their readers are. But in the process of coming to use research, there is always the danger of overenthusiasm and overexpectation.[9]

The premier value that American editors place on truth and accuracy in reporting reflects a principle that is instilled in every undergraduate journalism course. The insistence that reporters get the facts straight goes back to an era before the camera and the tape recorder were available to provide an

---

happy news, on action film clips of fires and crime scenes. All this has often made broadcast news professionals think of researchers as adversaries.

[8]Confirmation of the editors' reports came from 402 circulation managers question in 1979c. On papers of 100,000 and over, 92% said that a readership survey of some kind had been conducted in the past three year. On papers of 50,000–100,000, the proportion was 73%, and for those of 25,000–50,000, it was 55%. Even among the small papers of under 25,000, 46% of those replying were doing research. (This last figure probably overstates the actual use of research by smaller papers, since those replying tended to overrepresent the larger papers in this group.)

[9]Seventeen news research projects were ranked by 278 ASNE members and 91 members of the Newspaper Research Council. Both groups gave highest priority to "why people stop reading and subscribing to the newspaper," a well-worn subject of research. Only 24% of the editors and 41% of the researchers gave the highest priority to "reader interest in various types of newspaper content and sections." Thirty-seven percent of the editors, but only 22% of the researchers, gave high priority to "what readers mean when they say they want more local news."

independent record of events. The prime resource of journalism in its firsthand coverage of the news is the accurate quotation from a newsmaker, eyewitness, or authoritative commentator, freshly taken down in the reporter's notebook.

Regrettably, the concern with getting the words right can lead to a confusion between authenticity and truth. This is nowhere better seen than in those stories where the journalist's task is to describe the public mood or temper. In the absence of proper samplings of opinion, it is traditional and common practice—even in otherwise sophisticated news organizations—for a reporter to talk to anywhere between a handful and a score of conveniently accessible informants. The resulting assessment of "what people are thinking" is then supported by quoting those to whom the reporter has talked. The occasional reporter who concocts suitable quotations would be heartily condemned by colleagues, and yet they might be guilty of far more sinister distortion of the realities in their own stories because of their unsystematic choice of respondents.

Good reporters are, of course, responsive to what people are saying about the issues of the day, and they may have remarkable insight into the changing wishes and anxieties of a population. But political sensitivity and insight are no substitutes for proper investigation of public opinion; they are a supplement to it. Periodically, professional practitioners of public opinion research inveigh against this type of journalistic impressionism, especially when it deals with sensitive public issues. In defense against the indignation of the pollsters, the journalist can point to the indisputable fact that his evidence, though flimsy, is authentic. He has merely reported what someone has actually said. The question of whether the sentiment is widely held can be considered irrelevant, just like the question of whether it is well founded.

Not surprisingly, the same confusion sometimes arises when journalists deal with the public's assessment of their own handiwork. They are predisposed to ascribe credibility to utterances that are presented firsthand in preference to those that are multiplied, digested, and spewed forth in the form of abstract statistics. And thus many of them have been beguiled by those commercial vendors of research whose stock in trade is to collect quotations rather than evidence.

Conventional research reports require their users to conjecture about their implications. Editors often prefer reports that brook no ambiguity, that state unequivocally what they should and should not do, and that do so in the most "authentic" way possible, in the words of the readers themselves.

It is fantasy to believe that a newspaper can be designed and packaged like a bar of soap or a can of dogfood or even like a television news program. Its symbolic texture is too complex for that; its elements are too rich.

Not many publishers would arrive at their advertising rates by polling their customers. Not many editors would arrive at their editorial policies by polling their readers. There are similar dangers in tailoring content and format by poll results. A fundamental principle in consumer product testing is that people like what they are used to. Moreover, when they are confronted with concrete and specific choices, they do not always react the way they say they will. The wise researcher understands these pitfalls.

In consumer research it is well understood that people cannot imagine what has not yet been invented; they can only comment on what is right or wrong with what they know and make choices among specific alternatives that are presented to them. They cannot ordinarily dream up the ideal alternatives themselves. And there is never any guarantee that they will really accept in practice what they say they want in theory. This is an important limitation to the marketing approach.

Marketers are great at identifying potential markets; they are pretty good at understanding consumer motivations; they are competent at testing proposed alternatives; but they are not exceptionally skilled at coming up with creative solutions. If they were, and in the newspaper business, they would be editors and not marketers.

SOME UNSOLICITED ADVICE

Advice is cheap, and in recent years newspaper editors and publishers have received much of it, some cheap indeed. Advice is more likely to make sense when it is specific and when it is based on data. Since the evidence cited throughout this book reflects national generalizations, I can draw lessons from it, only with hesitation. But here are some of the things that I would be thinking about if I were running a newspaper.

With a growing, maturing, better-educated population, newspapers' potential is due for a vast expansion. The American press has never been more prosperous or more essential to the political health of the nation. Newspaper managements have invested heavily in new plants and technology essential for their future growth in a competitive environment. A comparable investment is necessary to assure the future of newspapers' principal resource: their circulation and readership. This requires measures to advance the efficiency of newspapers' distribution system by further professionalizing circulation personnel and upgrading their status within the organization and also by improving the mechanics and systems through which papers are sold, paid for, and physically handled and through which subscribers' demands and complaints are handled.

Such improvements cost money. So does any increase in promotional activity. Television and radio stations build their audiences not only through a constant parade of promo commercials that tell the viewer or listener what's coming up later, but also by buying promotional ads in newspaper entertainment sections. The $200 million that they spent in newspapers in 1988 bought more space than the same newspapers devoted to house ads in their own columns to tout their features and writers and to encourage their readers to read more and more often.

It is probably easier for most publishers to understand why an increased investment should be required in distribution and promotion than to accept the idea that they will earn more profit by enlarging the budget of the editorial department. It takes money to enlarge the news hole, to add editorial color and graphics, to hire better staff, to cover more stories, do more investigative reports, bring in more specialists, and buy more wire services. Few editors are *not* asking for these things, and few publishers do not face similar demands and pressures from other quarters, especially from owners or stockholders weighing the return from their newspaper investments against other alternatives. It takes courage to visualize the ultimate payout when the immediate prospect is for nothing more than new expense.

Those great newspapers that have improved their editorial content most strikingly in recent years have done so at considerable cost, and although the verdict is not in, in all cases, the results appear to be well justified through increased acceptance both by readers and by advertisers.

SEGMENTING THE MARKET

Some of the most critical editorial needs on many newspapers can be tackled only in association with noneditorial activities. This is especially true as newspaper managements look at significant segments of their potential audience.

1. Metropolitan newspapers must set as a very high priority the task of gaining more Black and Hispanic readers. To accomplish this necessarily requires more than the addition of a Black columnist or expanded editorial coverage of Black neighborhoods and interests. It requires special efforts in the circulation department, in promotion, and above all, in personnel recruitment. The latter is a formidable challenge to an industry that until only a few years ago was generally lily white. Both affirmative action pressures from government agencies and moral convictions have impelled many newspapers forward in this area, but self-interest should provide the most powerful motive. Who can accept the notion that cities whose majorities are minorities can be served adequately by newspapers produced by staffs that are nearly all White or that such newspapers can attract wide readership within the cities themselves?

2. A somewhat parallel set of statements might be made about women, whose rapidly changing outlook and expanded reading interests have con-

fronted editors with serious and fascinating new questions. We have already reviewed these in Chapter 3: The Pill changed sexual mores. Equalization of educational achievement brought a new appetite for careers; inflation increased pressures to pursue them. All this has transformed not only the women who are employed and those who are not, but also the men in American society. As a result, many newspapers have abandoned the traditional woman's page or section in favor of new sections or features that deal with food, home decoration, and other domestic activities as subjects of common interest to both sexes. (The counterpart of this has been the demasculinization of business and sports pages, with more emphasis in the former on articles that translate economic issues into terms of their effect on the ordinary consumer or wage earner and in the latter on participant sports and outdoor activities that many women share with men.)

Most women think newspapers are of equal interest to both sexes. They don't seem to have noticed that newspapers run six or seven times as much editorial matter dealing with sports and business as in the traditional "women's" subjects. As we have seen in Chapter 9, no subject that newspapers treat is of exclusive interest to just one sex.

Work is the norm today, and a whole generation of American housewives now feel cheated of this crucial life experience. As newspapers move to desegregate more of their content sexually, and as they increasingly meet the new career interests and somewhat distinctive homemaking interests of working women, they face the new problem of avoiding alienation of the nonemployed women. These include not only the one out of three who are of working age, but also the 16.5 million women over 65, many of whom have never had an outside job. For newspapers to handle their needs intelligently obviously requires greater representation of women in editorial management. The movement to achieve this goal is well under way, but still has a long way to go. (In 1987, women represented 7% of the membership of the American Society of Newspaper Editors and 13% of the "directing editorships"listed in the *Editor and Publisher* Yearbook.)

3. A third and even more significant target for the newspaper industry's attention is the 30% of the adult American population under 30, all of whom have been born since the presence of television became virtually universal.

We have seen that the downward trends in newspaper readership are marked among younger people, including adolescents reared by parents who are themselves largely part of the TV generation. It is essential for newspapers to reverse these trends if they wish to remain a mass medium a generation hence.

There is, moreover, another reason why it is important to newspapers that the reading habit be established early in life. As we saw in Chapter 4, among youngsters, reading the paper goes with understanding and support for freedom of the press. As we look at their opinions, their knowledge of public affairs, and their media habits, it is apparent that the future of democratic institutions is linked to the continuing vitality of newspaper reading. As children mature, their interest in the news, and their understanding of democracy, undergo a natural development that is greatly facilitated when the newspaper is on the scene, either in the home or in the school. This adds to the importance of the Newspaper in Education. Too many children today are growing up in households in which newspapers are no longer staple fare for the parents and no longer a daily presence. This means that the newspaper industry must more than ever turn to the schools, as well as to the family, to familiarize children with its output.

When newspaper managements worry about how to attract more young readers, there are two cautionary notes they must keep in mind. First, they must remember that children, adolescents, and young adults are just as heterogeneous as any other age groups and that even within the most sharply defined age segment there may be important subgenerational differences that show up in media choices and cultural tastes. Just as the flower children emerged from among the earnest crewcut types of the Eisenhower era, so the long-haired rebels of the early 1970s gave way to a new, more introverted, and more individualistic generation. When middle-aged editors and publishers try for more youth appeal, they must beware lest they tailor their changes to the mood of a group that has already passed into history.

Newspapers have much to learn from the alternative press, but they can be wasting time and paper if they try to imitate it. Its readers are a minority. What young readers expect from specialized periodicals is a different slant and a different subject matter than they expect from the daily papers that most of them also read.

To attract young readers it is not enough to add a rock music column. Young people are more critical than older ones of newspapers' editorial posture and also of their editorial performance. Newspapers have the greatest chances of success with them if they perform very well their traditional functions of reporting and explaining the world in which they will be living and working.

A second caveat to remember is that when we talk about "today's young people" or "today's children," we must be very careful that we are not confusing what is unique to their generation with what is generally true of all young people or of all children.

We have seen that children are much more responsive to the parts of the paper that are fun than they are to the news. That is, of course, consistent with a recurrent finding in our adult readership surveys. Younger people are much more interested in features than older ones and correspondingly less in the news. I have stressed the notion that interest in the news grows as people assume more responsibilities, as they strike roots. Some newspapers are giving more space to features and less to news in an effort to attract younger readers.

To the degree they do this, they are taking note of a perennial difference between young and old and handling it like a brand new problem. Of all the media, comic books have the most youthful reader profile, but even children recognize that newspapers serve a different purpose. In an era when TV offers little more than the headlines, the traditional information function of newspapers should be more important, not less.

By the time they enter school, most children have learned to differentiate between make-believe and reality. The fantasy world continues to have attractions for all of us. But it is not the real world into which children must grow up and that newspapers must report.

Important as the school may be in inculcating familiarity with the newspaper, especially among Black children, we have seen that to a very large degree children experience newspapers and other media in the context of the family. Family participation is something that newspapers must try to generate and harness. There are not many newspaper features that parents can share with children—stories to read to them, games to play together. There also appears to be a real need for features that children will turn to on their own, without the parent's discretion. Some of the attempts made so far are impressive. In 1988, a syndicated "Mini-Page" addressed to youngsters was being distributed to 450 newspapers. Other attempts to produce child-oriented features and supplements have been unsuccessful.

Apart from new features that might attract children, editors may find it intriguing to consider the general content of the paper from the standpoint of the child who finds it at home every day. Some papers have repackaged their Sunday comics section in a comic book format.

There are excellent psychological reasons why children's books have always been printed in extra large type. Yet more and more comic strips (and crossword puzzles, too, for that matter) now appear to be printed for the same people who enjoy reading the Lord's Prayer engraved on the head of a pin. A generation ago the typical comic strip had four panels; today it has three, signaling the demise of the continuity story that pulled young (and adult readers) back to the paper day after day.

Newspapers have increasingly covered one of youngsters' major interests— the world of popular entertainment. But they have been less successful in meeting the strong interest of teenagers in jobs and careers.

Sports news continues to be very important to boys, but newspapers don't excite quite the equivalent level of interest for girls in their women's pages. There is a special challenge to food editors in attracting young readers, as we noted in Chapter 9.

Blacks, women, and the young are by no means the only sectors of the public whose values and interests are in process of change. Nineteenth century American newspapers served audiences segmented along social class or political lines. With diminished competition, all but a few papers today must seek to win acceptance from their entire communities, offering something to everyone. The editor's task is to balance the heterogeneous needs of many constituencies. A newspaper that contained only content of maximum general interest would probably be remarkably unsuccessful, for it would fail to meet the concerns of the assorted minorities who make up its readership. This premise may always have been correct, but it acquires special meaning in an era when the average half-hour TV newscast covers only 10% of the stories that the typical newspaper carries.

The content of the newspaper is like a mosaic, and the individual pieces are meaningless unless they are seen as part of a pattern. As we have seen, there is no type of content in which every item is either of universal interest or of no interest to any one.

And average levels of interest in a particular category of content can be deceptive. Consider, for example, the fact that the average item of sports news attracts at least some interest from only two readers in five. This last surprising result reflects the fact that the percentages are based on both men and women; this also accounts for the comparatively low readership of society news. A reader may be highly interested in the popular sport of the season and be uninterested in a great many other sports items that newspapers routinely cover.

Similarly, there is a wide range of interest among different kinds of local news and among different kinds of world and national news. Where interest in a particular kind of news falls below average, it is usually obvious that it has a limited constituency. Educational news is an example, But for that constituency of pupils, their parents, and teachers, the school news may be of vital concern, and an editor would be foolish to minimize its value.

The challenge to editors is that of satisfying the special requirements of innumerable splinter groups of readers, while at the same time retaining the newspaper's traditional function of voicing the common concerns and interests of the entire community.

Those common concerns, I have tried to suggest, tend to be in the traditional domain of the breaking news, rather than in the utilitarian or entertainment features that tend to have more segmented appeals. In the last 20 years, as I pointed out in Chapter 6, a substantial number of papers have been cutting back on the regular columns and news features that appeal to particular segments and slivers of the audience. In this same period, the magazines that appeal to such special interests have enjoyed phenomenal growth. The tendency to drop items may well be a by-product of the movement to package feature content in generalized sections with titles like "Living" or "Lifestyle."

Only 1% of the readers may be stamp collectors, but for that 1%, the stamp column may be the most important thing in the paper. And what they most want from the newspaper is today's news about stamps, not just the same feature material that they can read in a philately magazine. News is what brings most readers to the paper rather than to alternative sources of fun or fact, and editors who turn away from their traditional and fundamental jobs as journalists will be most vulnerable to competition from unexpected places.

The New York Times's publisher, Arthur Ochs Sulzberger, puts it elegantly:

> Lifestyle material does have its place in the newspaper. If we can help our readers live better, healthier, more interesting and more amusing lives—if we can even help them attain self-fulfillment—then so much the better. But the founders of this greatest experiment in democracy didn't graft the First Amendment onto the Constitution to guarantee our freedom to print uncensored recipes. Our job is the reporting of the great international, national and local issues—the news that must be the concern of citizens if they are to maintain a free society.[10]

This does not mean that there is not an important spot for fun and useful facts amidst the assortment of offerings that newspapers provide. We have seen that many people who have dropped out of regular newspaper reading are actually turned off by the news itself. No decent editor would respond to them, as many television newscasts have, by adopting a "happy news" format. But he must still cope with the fact that the problem is not limited to the dropouts. Many good readers—especially women—find the news upsetting more often than they find it pleasant. The heavier leavening of entertainment along with the news may be one more reason for the Sunday paper's continuing strength; another is its coverage of special interests.

Aside from the fun, newspapers must leave space for the routine—the miscellany and minutiae that increase the paper's value to the readers and that can always be found in a particular and predictable place.

Newspaper advertising is attractive to the extent that it is specific, practical, and informative. In fact, a lot of it includes routine information that a clever advertiser repeats over and over again each day (e.g., the store's location, phone number, transit stop, and opening hours) simply because it represents valuable reference material that people expect to find in the paper when they want it. Could not the same principle be applied to the editorial element of newspaper content? Transportation timetables, street repair and parking schedules, maps, utility rates, court calendars all represent the kinds of minutaie that may get intense scrutiny from a very small number of people each day, and yet one such item may be worth the cost of the paper to a reader.

---

[10]Address before the ANPA Research Institute Production Conference, 1979.

ATTRACTING THE MARGINAL READER

There does not appear to be confirmation of the thesis that a growing proportion of the population has been weaned away from reading to a dependence on television imagery. There is no real foundation for the alarmist view that "the cancer of illiteracy" is spreading, though the problem of reading skill is a real one and the absence of motivation is even more serious.

There are very few people, about one in seven, it turns out, who do not pick up a newspaper at least occasionally. The newspaper industry's problem is one of increasing reading frequency among the people who are not regular daily readers rather than one of converting the small minority who don't read at all. This suggests more emphasis on the continuing suspenseful stories and features that pull the reader from one issue to the next. Increasing the frequency and regularity of readership does not simply require that publishers produce newspapers that people perceive as valuable, attractive, and even as compelling; it also requires that newspapers be made conveniently available when people want them at a price they are willing to pay.

The steady growth of advertising inserts has subtly changed the environment for news; it has had and can have profound effects on newspaper operations and economics. Historically, publishers have been in the information business first and the distribution business second. Now, some of them may not be too sure where the priority lies.

Dropout readers are turned off by the news, not by the newspaper. Only one in six of those who say they have reduced their reading frequency are reacting critically to changes newspapers have introduced. In general, they are far less aware of newspapers' content than are people with established reading patterns. Apparently their attention has waned even before they dropped out. "No time to read" expresses an attitude, not an explanation. People who don't want to be reminded of the world's woes are poor readers to begin with and may say they cut back when they've never read much at all.

Newspapers must strive to strengthen the personal links with the reader. They can sponsor community activities and events that get the crowds out and show their power. They should build the public identities of their news staffs with by-lines and pictures. They may go so far as to put them out on the lecture platform and on TV. Newspapers need to evoke reader participation. People should be able to write letters, not just to "the editor," but to a particular specialized editor.

Style and presentation technique may be more important than subject matter to motivate the infrequent readers. Though their interests are not very different from those of the people who read the paper every day, they may be responsive to different ways of telling the same story. For example, the publications that turn young people on are characterized by colorful, breezy, anecdotal, and often highly personalized writing style. Newspapers should cultivate good writing, interpretive writing, writing that evokes empathy and human interest. All this needs breathing space at a time when there is a premium on brevity to cut newsprint consumption. The argument against long stories is an argument against visual fatigue—not against narrative or exposition. Format devices can facilitate communication: sidebars, graphics, subheads.

MEETING THE NEWS COMPETITION

Television news is complementary to newspaper news, not a substitute for it. Our research has confirmed something that editors have known for a generation: The breaking news is no longer as important in making up the newspaper as it used to be before the days of radio and television bulletins. But morning and afternoon papers are read at various times throughout the day, at the reader's convenience. Timeliness has lost much of the significance it had in the day of the newsboy shouting, "Extra!"

Newspapers have a large, important, and exclusive audience that has not heard the news on radio and TV, and in any case, readers look to them for greater depth, detail, background, and interpretation. Editors cannot assume that their readers get all the national and international news they need on TV, because they don't and won't unless newspapers reduce their coverage to the level of their broadcast competitors. To copy them is to lessen people's dependence on newspapers as an authoritative source on what's going on in the world and to abdicate serious coverage of the news to the news weeklies. Remember that only 3 adults in 10 watch the network news on a typical evening.

Should newspapers try to be a print duplicate of the radio news, which excretes minute, standard-sized pellets of information on the hour? When everything is reduced to bulletins on the assumption that nobody cares, nobody *will* care, and then newspapers lose their real reason for being.

Newspapers win the attention of their readers when they generate news themselves, when they stir things up, when they go out and uncover fresh stories rather than expect them to turn up on the conventional beats.

Editors' labels on contents don't always match what readers see. They may be accustomed to thinking of stories in terms of traditional departments or assignments to whose origins or purposes readers may be oblivious. For many of them, with respect to at least some papers, there is only a murky distinction between news and opinion.

Editors should strive to articulate the real anxieties and concerns of their readers. Does the paper reflect what they talk about at home? Does it cover the "subterranean" news of the community? The big stories of social change may be reflected only fragmentarily as specific news items. To get at them requires something beyond routine reporting.

Editors might be well advised to look systematically at the other kinds of publications that people are reading in their towns, apart from their newspapers. There is obviously news in the city magazines, the neighborhood press, the suburban weeklies, the shoppers, the trade press, the union press, the alternative press that doesn't get into the daily papers at all.

Not all newspapers have moved quickly enough to adapt their content to the requirements of their readers in light of the tremendously rapid transformation in the structure of the society and the forms and values of the culture. Changes commensurate with this transformation must surely go beyond mere cosmetics. Yet editorial experimentation incurs the risk of turning off the majority who are comfortable with newspapers the way they are in the hope of attracting the minority who are not, some of whom might be unattractable under any circumstances. The case history of the *Saturday Evening Post* offers a grim reminder of the perils of tinkering with an established institution to meet the dictates of a marketing objective.

The most faithful newspaper readers have always been the most sophisticated and the most educated members of the community. Paradoxically, these are also the people who express the greatest amount of disagreement with the editorial policies of their hometown papers. Are newspapers, in their content and character, keeping up with the steady rise in the public's level of education? Can they become more sophisticated without alienating the mass audience? I believe they can. An expanding, maturing, better-educated population will have greater information needs than ever, and newspapers will remain an extremely efficient means of satisfying them. But their success will not come automatically.

GIVE READERS A CHOICE

The two-paper-a-day reader has been disappearing, in large part because of the attrition in the number of big city newspapers. But why should publishers reconcile themselves to this trend?

Yesterday's prime urban reader, who required a fresh metropolitan paper morning and evening, should have been even more inclined to need two papers when he moved out to the suburbs. Yet we have seen that the growth of suburban dailies has in no way compensated for the circulation losses of the metropolitan press. There are serious civic implications to the fact that so very few people today are routinely reading more than one set of editorials, one set of columnists, one set of judgments on the news.

The loss of any newspaper diminishes the civic sense that is the basis of civilized society. Reader excitement can best be sustained when there is simultaneous access to alternative rival sources, when newspapers take the kind of journalistic initiative that has shaken the nation in recent years, when they take strong and consistent editorial positions on the issues of the day.

The end of its newspaper competition therefore has tremendous consequences for the life of a city. The expansion of the suburban press cannot compensate or substitute for this loss.

With the best intentions in the world, it is difficult for a monopoly daily to avoid complacency and establishmentarianism. When these take over, there is a weakening of the newspaper's vital function as a voice of its urban region, as a watchdog on local government, as a gallant espouser of civic causes.

A competitive press permitted the expression of a broad range of ideas addressed to an intellectual elite but at the same time accessible to the mass of readers. Television is all mass, while magazines of ideas are confined to an elite. Neither medium can play the daily paper's special role.

In the dwindling competitive environment, editorial content and character can make the difference between success and failure. Certainly the newspapers in competitive cities tend to be more strongly differentiated in style, politics, and social class orientation than are those in markets where both a morning and an evening paper are published under the same ownership.

Can newspaper competition be revived? It takes enormous capital to start a metropolitan paper and to keep it running. The advent of desktop publishing technology makes it relatively easy and inexpensive to produce a new publication, but no one has yet successfully licked the problem of getting it efficiently distributed.

The challenge to editors who take their social obligations seriously is perhaps greatest precisely where the circulation and business fortunes of their newspapers are most secure—where theirs is the only daily newspaper voice in town and where their constituency is the entire community rather than a particular segment of class or taste. These are the situations that can lead to atrophy of editorial enterprise. Yet our inspection of newspapers of similar size in such cities shows an enormous variability in reader acceptance, as well as in the character and, yes, in the quality of the newspapers themselves. In part, these differences arise from the histories and nature of the papers' hometowns. But principally, they reflect the energies and the guiding spirits of their editors.

In at least some of the single-ownership markets, the morning and evening newspapers truly compete for readers in the city of origin. Two out of five (with half the circulation of this group) have separate editors. Of course, not all of these are really autonomous in their news operations and in their editorial policies. Can such autonomy exist unless both papers are maintained at reasonable parity in circulation and advertising? The answer to that last question represents a publisher's choice and an economic dilemma that may be insoluble in many middle-sized markets.

By the end of the 1980s, most publishers appeared to believe, regretfully, that the morning–evening combination was doomed. Advertisers have no interest in the duplicated audience. In most evening combinations, one of the papers is strong and profitable and the other is weak. Publishers have been accused of wanting things this way, maintaining a "corporal's guard" at the second newspaper only in order to keep potential competitors from moving into town.[11] This charge is hard to sustain, both because recent history shows few examples of successful new competitive entries into single-paper markets and because publishers generally feel a genuine affection for the weaker papers in their combinations, appreciate their history, and are anxious to see them prosper.

Publishers who are in the happy position of running both a morning and an evening paper in the same town should make them as different as they can. Competition between rival news staffs improves their output, gives readers a choice and an identity, adds to the newspaper's sense of excitement. Of course, this costs money. So did conversion to cold type and introducing computer terminals into the newsroom.

In 1988, American newspapers spent over $1.25 billion on new computer front-end systems, press and mailroom equipment, and other capital improvements of their existing plants. That impressive figure reflects their confidence in future growth. But they spent very little to investigate the basics of the product itself. All American industry invests 3.1% of its sales in Research and Development (R&D). The telecommunications industry invests 4.3%; information processing, 8.3%. If we consider all the money spent by industrywide organizations and by individual newspaper organizations for every form of R&D, including technical research, software development, and readership and market research, the grand total equals 0.2% of newspapers' gross sales as a business. Can newspapers do better than that? Can they afford not to?

MARKETING AND GROUP OWNERSHIP

The steady growth of publicly held, professionally managed newspaper groups and media conglomerates suggests that there will be mounting pressure on editors to adopt a marketing approach, to produce newspapers geared to public demand as interpreted from survey research. This brings new threats to the old tradition that made journalism a form of creative expres-

---

[11]Carl E. Lindstrom, *The Fading American Newspaper* (New York: Doubleday & Co., Inc., 1960).

sion, impelled by a concern with social values and with truth for its own sake. And it raises new questions as to whether and how editors can serve the public's interest as well as its interests.

The trend toward ownership concentration in the newspaper business directly parallels the prevailing pattern throughout most of the American economy. The growth of newspaper groups or chains has been viewed with alarm through nearly a century of American history. It received the most outraged attention in the heyday of Hearst, Pulitzer, and Scripps, when any foray by a publisher outside of his home territory was thought to threaten the independence of the press. The publisher was rooted in his own community, and a William Randolph Hearst, bestriding the continent, exuded a new kind of power that was regarded as particularly dangerous because it was not accountable to local interests and pressures.

Long gone are the days when press tycoons could dictate their editorials to run simultaneously around the country or require support of their political choices and opinions. By 1980, every major chain had given its local editors full autonomy, even on the endorsement of presidential candidates.

A tally by John Morton found that chains or groups in 1988 owned 76% of all U.S. daily newspapers, accounting for 83% of the circulation. However, of the 143 groups identified, 49 consisted of only two newspapers, usually small ones in nearby communities printed in the same plant. Nineteen groups numbered only three papers. Sixty-two of the groups had a total circulation of 50,000 or less. These are lumped with the mighty Gannett group, which had 88 dailies, with a total circulation of 5,944,055. Thomson Newspapers, with 120 newspapers, was the largest group, but ranked eighth in circulation (2,081,893). Knight-Ridder ranked second in circulation with 3,806,116 in 31 dailies; and Newhouse, with 26 papers, had 3,017,836 circulation daily.

And newspapers represent only one element in the agglomeration of media properties. Daily newspapers were quick to establish or acquire radio stations in their own communities when broadcasting first developed, and many later moved into television. Large newspaper organizations, and some not so large, have acquired or started magazine- and book-publishing subsidiaries. Conversely, broadcasting organizations (notably Capital Cities/ABC, Inc.) have become important newspaper owners.[12]

The history of American journalism is studded with examples of business organizations that acquired papers as investments or to advance the political purposes of the owners. What is new is the acquisition of newspapers by companies in other types of media activity. Some of these companies are, of course, highly diversified in fields that have nothing to do with communica-

---

[12]The acquisition of the Sunday magazine *Family Weekly* by CBS, Inc. in 1980 represented the first move by a network in this direction, but in 1986 this weekend magazine was sold to Gannett and renamed *USA Weekend*.

tions, and some newspaper companies, as they have grown and expanded, have themselves gone far afield in their new corporate interests.

The reduction in the number of independent newspapers has been accelerated by the pressure of inheritance taxes. A proprietor whose heirs place a higher value on capital than on continuing the family tradition, may be easily tempted to sell the paper in exchange for the stock of a larger company, which can be more readily sheltered, or partially disposed of, on the reckoning day.

Increasingly, more of the papers that are available for sale are owned by smaller chains that can be swallowed up by larger ones. As the larger chains themselves expand, their need for new capital leads them in the direction of public ownership through stock offerings. Accountability to shareholders inevitably changes management philosophy and style, even when the original family control is perpetuated by having two classes of stock. The New York Times Company, the Washington Post Company, Media General, Pulitzer, and McClatchy were organized from the start with two classes of stock. An attempt to take over control of Media General from the Bryan family led a number of other newspaper corporations to move in the same direction (Times-Mirror, Dow Jones, A. H. Belo, Affiliated Publications, and the E. W. Scripps Company).

Shareholders normally want the maximum appreciation of their investment rather than dedication to the pursuit of journalistic excellence or civic virtue. But even without the presence of these outside participants in ownership, the fact that an enterprise is diversified must force its management to adopt standard balance-sheet criteria in running its business. An individual who is merely running a newspaper can let pride, ambition, conscience, and loyalties counter the demands of his pocketbook. But one who is running three dailies, five weeklies, two television stations, and a handful of cable systems is bound to respond more as a businessman and less as a journalist.

In a symposium on Media Concentration, held in 1978, the Federal Trade Commission heard testimony that contrasted the current group ownership of dailies with nearly three-fourths of total circulation with the situation in 1960, when 109 groups, with 560 dailies, had under half (46%) of the circulation. But in one respect, the trend has been for less rather than more concentration. James N. Dertouzos, an economist, told the Commission that in 1946 the Hearst newspapers accounted for 10.4% of all daily circulation, compared with the 6% share in 1978 for Knight-Ridder, then the largest circulation chain. (In 1987, Gannett [including *USA Today*] had 9.6% of total weekday circulation.)

In his testimony before the Commission, a leading student of the press, Ben Bagdikian, cited the decline in the ratio of daily newspapers to urban communities. In 1890 there were 1,600 dailies and 1,348 urban places; in 1978 there were 1,760 papers and 7,000 urban places. "Many papers would insist that they try to cover all of the cities where they sell papers. But the fact is that they do not and cannot . . . A paper that covers 40 counties, in order to do minimal civic reporting, would have to cover over 1,000 governmental bodies. This is just a start of adequate community reporting and no paper comes even close."

This reasoning can be debated. The daily newspapers of 1890 were disproportionately concentrated in the larger markets of that era. An "urban place" in 1890 was a free-standing city or town; today's urban places, as I have stressed earlier, fade one into another in a suburban or interurban belt. Weekly papers by the thousands provide watchdog reporting on the innumerable agencies of local government which metropolitan dailies cannot cover.

But this is not the nub of Bagdikian's argument. He is alarmed by the growth of newspaper chains and cites the fact that the top 10 chains grew from 11% to 20% of all dailies in a 10-year period. He is apprehensive about the trend from family enterprise rooted in the community to publicly held companies whose managements are preoccupied with the stock market. He is concerned with the effects this has on newspaper quality and introduces as evidence on this point a study by Kristine Keller. She matched two groups of similar newspapers, 28 chain-owned and 28 independent, and measured their content for one day, January 18, 1978. The independently owned papers ran 16% more national news, 35% more international news and 25% more local and state news ("more of the most expensive kind of news, staff-written stories as opposed to syndicated news").

Bagdikian favors divestiture of chain-owned papers beyond a certain number, but he is "not optimistic that this will ever happen." He believes that the "basic solution" is to have newspapers mainly supported by subscribers rather than by advertisers. As I suggested in Chapter 2, this seems like an impractical alternative.

Group owners meet such criticism with the argument that the editors of their papers have access to far greater resources than are generally available under family ownership (like a Washington news bureau and specialized top-level counsel at corporate headquarters). They point out that their professional managements run more efficient operations, which make possible the recruitment of superior talent.

Lee Hills, the former chairman of Knight-Ridder Newspapers, points out that efficient business management of group-owned newspapers requires "financial controls through budgeting and profit planning" but that in news and editorial operations, "I do not see the need for the same controls . . . A newspaper must reflect its community and a newspaper inescapably has the proud and exciting responsibility of leading. It cannot lead or influence if someone from a distant headquarters calls the shots on news coverage and local editorial policy."

Editors of group-owned newspapers actually feel a somewhat greater sense of independence than their counterparts on individually owned papers. This conclusion emerges from a survey of 647 editors conducted in 1979 by Robert Stiff, editor of the (now-defunct) St. Petersburg *Independent*, for the American Society of Newspaper Editors. In general, the group editors show somewhat greater satisfaction with their budgets, staffs, and technological resources than the independent editors do. In fact, those editors whose papers had been acquired by groups overwhelmingly feel that their news coverage has improved as a result. Seventy-one percent of the independent editors say they check with the paper's owner in formulating editorial policy on controversial issues, but only 11% of the group editors say they check with headquarters. (Presumably, many of the remainder would, however, check with the publisher.) Only 39% of the group editors, compared with 71% of the independents, agreed that newspaper competition will be "stifled" if the growth of groups is not checked. The independent editors, however, consistently rate their papers higher by the criteria of professional performance: handling the news, serving the community, producing a "quality" newspaper. But all the opinions of editors must be taken with the cautionary word that it is as hard to generalize about group-owned papers as about independently owned ones.

An analysis of 114 newspapers by Stephen Lacy found that those in competitive markets (including those with joint operating agreements) carry more wire services and use more reporters to fill a given amount of space but do not allocate space very differently than those in noncompetitive situations.[13]

And a special analysis of results from the 1985 ASNE/MORI study showed no significant differences in the credibility scores given by readers of chain-owned and independent papers.

In 1988, 110 of 317 metropolitan areas had two or more dailies under separate ownership. There was some form of locally published daily competition in 76 of the 100 more populous areas. This compilation both overstates and underestimates the amount of competition that newspapers face. The presence of suburban dailies in markets dominated by single-ownership papers in the central city does not really represent competition throughout the whole area in the same sense as when there are rival ownerships of the

---

[13]Stephen Lacy, "The Effects of Intracity Competition on Daily Newspaper Content," *Journalism Quarterly*, Vol. 64 (Summer/Autumn, 1987), No. 2/3, pp. 281–290. Lacy also concluded that the amount of broadcast competition in a market did not appear to affect newspapers' newsroom staffing, the number of wire services they used, or the news hole. (Stephen Lacy, "Effect of Intermedia Competition on Daily Newspaper Content," *Journalism Quarterly*, Vol. 65, No. 1 [Spring 1988], pp. 95–99.)

metropolitan press. However, even a monopoly daily is likely to face vigorous competition for readership as well as advertising from out of town papers and from local weeklies, shoppers, underground papers, and city magazines – not to mention the competition it faces from broadcasting.

How much of the population actually has access each day to separately owned, locally produced daily papers competing directly for its attention? An analysis of 1987 circulation and population data shows that 23% of the people are in nonmetropolitan counties, where no such competition effectively exists. (There may be several small dailies in many such counties, each serving a separate town and its hinterland and competing for subscribers in the interstitial areas.) In the metropolitan areas, there is daily competition both in central-city counties with two or more newspaper ownerships and in suburban counties with one or more local papers (but in which the metropolitan papers are also circulated). Calculating from this basis, 46% of the U.S. population lives in counties where local daily newspapers directly compete, and 54% do not. The 1987 figures show a change in the balance since 1978, when 57% of the public had access to competitive local dailies. But the ubiquitous *USA Today* has injected a new alternative, and it is evident that there is a long way to go before competition disappears from the daily newspaper business. Moreover, the competition among newspapers may take on a new dimension as revolutionary changes occur on the mass media scene.

NEWSPAPERS IN THE NEW WORLD OF COMMUNICATION

As the 21st century edges closer, newspaper managements are more and more bemused by the prospect of new challenges from the growth of home communications technology. The most visible component has been the spread of cable television, which by 1989 reached over half of U.S. households.

On the advertising front, newspapers were beginning to meet competition from cable channels with the emergence of electronic classified ads for housing, cars, and jobs. "Audiotex" systems used the telephone to provide information updated to the minute for yellow-page telephone advertisers. The breakup of the telephone monopoly was accompanied by restrictions placed on the regional successor Bell operating companies to inhibit them from becoming providers of electronic data in competition with newspapers, but it seemed unlikely that these restrictions would remain in effect forever. Newspapers fought the threat of such powerful competition in the courts and by lobbying actions, but many went into electronic distribution on their own. On Long Island, *Newsday* dedicated a large and expensive staff effort to create a cable news channel; around the country, other papers leased channels or negotiated to find a place on independent cable systems. Many already owned systems of their own. At one point, 115 daily newspapers had some kind of cable or other electronic advertising or news operation going. The numbers fell sharply as it became apparent that for some time to come costs would greatly exceed revenues.

The capacity of cable systems for conversion to two-way transmission has been well demonstrated in a number of experimental situations. But the growth of cable television does not set the limit on the potential for new communications technology. The telephone system represents a virtually universal network capable of conversion to additional uses. Direct broadcast transmission to the home via satellite might provide a means of bypassing cable altogether.

Video recording and playback equipment using tapes and cassettes has already established a market, in spite of its substantial cost. The capacity to "freeze" frames on the picture tube of the home television set makes this equipment suitable for the transmission, storage, and display of text. This gives access not merely to the vast amount of fresh information being generated by news organizations each day, but to the entire content of the world's libraries. Daily packages of information could be transmitted easily in short bursts of data at off hours, periodically updated, and played back at convenience. An inexpensive hard copy printer could be activated by a pushbutton to keep a permanent record of anything that had more than passing interest.

By 1988, in the United States, wire service bulletins were being routinely transmitted on a continuing basis to cable households. UPI had launched Newsshare, providing its regular service to several thousand computer buffs. The Dow Jones news service was also accessible to a test panel. In Tama, Japan, a small facsimile newspaper had been routinely delivered for a test period to a sampling of experimental households. In the United Kingdom, the Post Office's Prestel system had assembled a vast body of information for retrieval at the convenience of participants. The B.B.C., Independent Television, and Reuters had all initiated services that gave subscribers access to news and financial data. The new world of home communications was a reality.

And what was to be the place of newspapers in this new world? For at least some observers, the advent of home communications meant, inevitably, a dwindling use of the traditional forms of print. Instant access could be provided not merely to the conventional package of information that editors had selected for their readers, but also to the much larger array of information that newspapers routinely discard for lack of space. The home viewer could, by the touch of a few keys at a video terminal, display all the wire service dispatches from the remote places in which he had a special interest, the views of every political commentator, the full details on even the most obscure sports event or financial transaction. To this convenience could be added the vast resources of an encyclopedic data base. If the viewer needed background information on any subject or personality in the news, the right touch of the keys would flash it on the screen. In 1988, IBM and Sears launched a videotex venture known as Prodigy to provide information services and a home-shopping capability.

With electronic transmission there is no concern for the escalating cost of paper, ink, and the energy required to power presses and carry papers to the reader. Since the newspaper's real stock in trade is its mastery of news and information, it has been argued that a shift from the printed page to the video screen could be an easy one. Newspaper managements have been urged to be the first to handle the transition to the new mode, by developing new ancillary services using electronic transmission systems at the same time that they continue to provide their familiar printed product. They have been warned that if they fail to take the necessary steps, either on-air broadcasters, cable operators, or new providers of information will move swiftly to fill the vacuum. A number of leading newspaper companies were persuaded by this line of reasoning and took steps to move in the indicated direction. In a notable one-year experiment, the AP and 11 newspapers, in association with a computer service company named CompuServe, made their combined news output available, for a fee, to anyone with a home computer terminal. (The price of the equipment was plunging, offering the promise of a mass market.)

Others have taken a more cautious view. Although the elements of a full home communications system exist in prototype, an enormous investment is required to put them into place and make them operative on a commercial basis. Is there a market to justify this investment? For the short run, it would be hard to demonstrate that there is, since the experimental systems operating prior to 1980 (like Warner Communications' "Qube") were heavily subsidized, and "Qube" went belly- up in 1986.

In Fort Worth, the *Star-Telegram* launched Startext in 1982, and it was still going six years later with 3,000 subscribers who got the newspaper's editorial text seven hours in advance and the classifieds a full day earlier. Other operations have been much less successful. Knight-Ridder invested a reported $65 million in Viewtron, a home videotex facility set up with 5,000 homes in Coral Gables and eventually another 15,000 nationally; it was abandoned after three years. Times-Mirror discontinued a similar Gateway system in California after a year; the Chicago *Sun-Times* sold its comparable venture, Keycom, which also was dropped. In a number of other cities, like San Francisco and Phoenix, newspapers launched public access videotex systems but abandoned them for lack of consumer support. In Canada, Infomart, a joint venture of two newspaper giants, Torstar and Southam, operated for several years before it, too, dropped its consumer service and concentrated on the corporate market. All of these abortive projects were designed to follow the classic European model of electronic publishing requiring mainframe computers and substantial investments. A variety of newer systems make it possible to operate videotex services at relatively modest cost.

What characterized all these experiments was that they were directed at the general consuming public and offered a wide range of information services—including such facilities as theater and airline reservations—as well as the newspaper's own news content. Although operated at a considerable loss, their subscriptions still cost a lot more than the public was willing to pay for information that was easily available in other forms. The videotex systems that have survived successfully, Dow Jones and Reuters, offer specialized financial and business data to business customers for whom the value is very great and the cost of minimal importance.

At some time in the 21st century, home communications will undoubtedly be as commonplace as today's telephones and television sets. The public will have ready access to a vast back file of video entertainment, as well as to current and filed information in the form of texts and still pictures. The system may be linked to equipment that provides the capacity for picture-phoning, for ordering merchandise, completing work tasks or school assignments, handling financial transactions and problem solving, and for security and fire detection.

Will this wonderful new system make the newspaper obsolete? I think not, though it will unquestionably have remarkable effects on newspaper content.

To begin with, it is hard to visualize a way of communicating as much information as there is in a metropolitan newspaper, with comparable economy, on a videoscreen. The essence of the home communication system is that it transmits information in customized form, on demand. This means that any user who is at all selective in what he wants, who responds to the array of information choices by wanting more and yet more of some and not of others, has to engage in a series of transactions. In reading the paper now he may choose not to go beyond a headline, but if he chooses to move on into the story he can do so very rapidly and efficiently.

Pressing keys and waiting for the computer to retrieve additional information takes time and inevitably costs money. The remarkable inertia which makes today's televiewers slow to switch channels might well be manifested in a reluctance to go actively looking for information, if each look involves a fresh expenditure of energy to press the right keys or to move a cursor across the screen.

There are certain classes of detailed information (stock market tables, film schedules, overseas weather reports, legal announcements) that are costly for newspapers to handle in print, and, as I have observed earlier, there is but thin public demand for the individual items though there may be a fairly good response for the aggregate. If such information were available on the videoscreen for a price, the demand might be great enough to eliminate the need for newspapers to print it in full.

Newspapers do contain a good deal of content that readers can anticipate, and for which they presumably might be ready to inquire through some other more flexible form of communication. But much, probably most of what is in the paper is not truly predictable. As I have suggested, part of the pleasure in reading the paper is the constant discovery of the unexpected on every page, in the advertising columns as well as in the news.

Few advertisers would want to depend exclusively on the trade of those shoppers who have a specific purchase definitely in mind. It will be convenient for the home viewer to call up all of today's sale specials on wing-tipped brown men's shoes size 10C in the price range of $60–75, and duly have the pictures and particulars fill the screen so he can order his choice. But every shoe merchant knows that many of the shoes he sells today will be to people who merely chanced to see his ad, and were not looking for it.

The enticement of the unexpected works no less powerfully in the editorial matter. And the secret of the whole thing lies in the speed with which the eye and the brain handle a complex profusion of symbols, simultaneously presented, and sort them all out. The tactility of the printed page, which we can set aside and come back to, which we can mark and clip, does not find a substitute in the videoscreen, even with its little hard-copy printing machine attached. There will always be improvements in the mechanical means of providing access to data, to information which is repetitive and self-contained. But though this represents a large component of newspapers' content, it is not their main reason for being.

Alexis de Tocqueville, that astute observer of Democracy in America, wrote in 1840 that

> nothing but a newspaper can drop the same thought into a thousand minds at the same moment. A newspaper is an adviser that does not require to be sought, but that comes of its own accord and talks to you briefly every day of the common weal, without distracting you from your private affairs. Newspapers therefore become more necessary in proportion as men become more equal and individualism more to be feared. To suppose that they only serve to protect freedom would be to diminish their importance: they maintain civilization . . . If there were no newspapers there would be no common activity.[14]

This assumes, of course, that the professional judgments of editors are being used to monitor and interpret events, so that the consumer of information is not left to his own devices, seated in front of a video display terminal with access to an inexhaustible data stream.

---

[14]Alexis de Tocqueville, *Democracy in America* (New York: Alfred A. Knopf, 1946, V. 2, p. 111).

There is a profound difference between reportage and journalism. An evolving communications technology is rapidly finding new ways to compete with the newspaper's function as a routine record of the day's events. But no technological change can ever challenge the newspaper's command of big ideas, its traditions of deep inquiry, sweeping synthesis, and inspired advocacy. Tomorrow's newspaper must be not merely a register, but a tribune, not merely a ledger, but a clarion.

MORE READING

Newspapers are a popular subject, and much of what is written about them fades into the larger literature on mass media and public opinion. Anyone who is seriously interested in keeping up with the matters touched on in this book should be reading the industry's trade weekly, *Editor and Publisher*, the principal scholarly journals of the field, *Journalism Quarterly* and *Journalism Monographs*, the *Newspaper Research Journal*, and the American Newspaper Publishers Association's *presstime*.

The *Columbia Journalism Review*, the *Washington Journalism Review*, *Nieman Reports*, and *Quill* frequently publish articles that shed light on the relationship between newspapers and their readers. In addition to the many books that deal with individual newspapers and their more colorful publishers and editors, here are a few with which the readers of *Press and public* might wish to become familiar.

Argyris, C. *Behind the front page*. San Francisco: Jossey-Bass, 1974. An intensive study of the inner workings of a newspaper's top management.

Bagdikian, B. H. *The information machines*. New York: Harper & Row, 1971. Summarizes an ambitious Rand Corporation study of the changing technology and economics of the press and broadcasting.

Bagdikian, B. H. *The media monopoly*. Boston: Beacon, 1983. Reviews with alarm the concentration of ownership in newspapers and other media.

Compaine, B. M. (editor). *Who owns the media? Concentration of ownership in the mass communications industry.* White Plains, NY: Knowledge Industry Publications, 1979. A review of the research literature on the subject.

Compaine, B. M. *The newspaper industry in the 1980's: An assessment of economics and technology.* White Plains, NY: Knowledge Industry Publications, 1980. Includes much useful reference material on industry trends.

Emery, E., & Emery, M. *The press and America: An interpretative history of the mass media.* Englewood Cliffs, NJ: Prentice-Hall, 1979. The most popular history of American journalism.

Ferguson, J. M. *The advertising rate structure in the daily newspaper industry.* Englewood Cliffs, NJ: Prentice-Hall, 1963. An econometric analysis of the mysteries of newspaper rates.

Fink, C. C. *Strategic newspaper management.* New York: Random House, 1988. An informed and comprehensive college text.

Fishman, M. *Manufacturing the news.* Austin: University of Texas Press, 1980. Analyzes how the demand for daily reports from every news beat affects the way news is generated and defined.

Ghiglione, L. (editor). *The buying and selling of American newspapers.* Indianapolis: R. J. Berg, 1984. A series of case histories of what happens when ownership changes.

Greenberg, B. S., & Dervin, B. *Use of the mass media by the urban poor.* New York: Praeger, 1970. For more on media usage by Blacks.

Hirt, P. S. *Newspaper presentations: A marketing approach.* Reston, VA: International Newspaper Promotion Association, 1979. Explains how newspapers sell themselves to advertisers and to the public.

Isaacs, N. E. *Untended gates: The mismanaged press.* New York: Columbia Press, 1986. A knowing and critical look at the media by a respected editor-publisher who headed the short-lived National News Council.

Johnstone, J. W. C., Slawski, E. J., & Bowman, W. W. *The news people.* Chicago: University of Illinois Press, 1976. A large-scale survey of the working press.

Krieghbaum, H. *Pressures on the press.* New York: Thomas Y. Crowell, 1972. Describes the forces that impinge on the management of news and suggests ways of narrowing "the credibility gap between media and their audiences."

Lee, A. M. *The daily newspaper in America: The evolution of a social instrument.* New York: MacMillan, 1947. A sweeping sociological examination of the medium as it existed in the pretelevision era.

Lichter, S. R., Rothman, S., & Lichter, L. S. *The media elite: America's new power brokers.* Bethesda, MD: Adler and Adler, 1986. A study of the characteristics and views of the country's most influential journalists.

McLuhan, M. *The Gutenberg galaxy: The making of typographic man.* Toronto: University of Toronto Press, 1962. Insights into the reading process as a form of communication.

Meyer, P. *Editors, publishers and newspaper ethics.* Washington: American

Society of Newspaper Editors, 1983. Reports on a fascinating survey of editing practices and dilemmas.

Meyer, P. *Ethical journalism*. New York: Longman, 1987. An expanded discussion of the same subject.

Rankin, W. P. *The practice of newspaper management*. New York: Praeger, 1986. An introductory text for journalism courses.

Roshco, B. *Newsmaking*. Chicago: University of Chicago Press, 1975. A reporter turned sociologist analyzes the decisions behind the news.

Schudson, M. *Discovering the news*. New York: Basic Books, 1978. An analysis of the origins of the doctrine of news objectivity.

Sigal, L. V. *Reporters and officials: The organization and politics of newsmaking*. Lexington, Mass.: D.C. Heath, 1973. Describes just what the subtitle says.

Smith, A. *Goodbye Gutenberg: The newspaper revolution of the 1980's*. New York/Oxford: Oxford University Press, 1980. Analyzes the effects of changing technology on the economics and communications functions of newspapers.

Sohn, A., Ogan, C., & Polich, J. *Newspaper leadership*. Englewood Cliffs, NJ: Prentice-Hall, 1986. A primer on newspaper management.

Sterling, C. H., & Haight, T. R. *The mass media: Aspen Institute guide to communication industry trends*. New York/London: Praeger, 1978. A massive compilation of data on all the media.

Stone, G. *Examining newspapers: What research reveals about America's newspapers*. Newbury Park, CA: Sage, 1987. Summarizes recent academic research on readership.

Thorn, J. with Pfeil, M. P. *Newspaper circulation: Marketing the news*. New York: Longman, 1988. First comprehensive text ever written on this important subject.

Tuchman, G. *Making news*. New York: The Free Press, 1978. A field study of the gatekeeping and newsmaking process.

Udell, J. G. (editor). *The economics of the American newspaper*. New York: Hastings House, 1978. A series of essays reviewing historical trends.

Weaver, D. H., & Wilhoit, G. C. *The American journalist: A portrait of U.S. news people and their work*. Bloomington: Indiana University Press, 1986. Report on a national survey of journalists.

INDEX

Date Due